THE ORAL HISTORY OF

THE ORAL HISTORY OF CHRISTIANITY

Eye Witness Accounts of the Dramatic Turning Points in the Story of the Church

Edited by Owen Collins

HarperCollins*Publishers*

HarperCollins*Religious*
Part of HarperCollins*Publishers*
77–85 Fulham Palace Road, London W6 8JB

First published in Great Britain
in 1998 by HarperCollins*Religious*

1 3 5 7 9 10 8 6 4 2

Compilation copyright © 1998 Owen Collins

Owen Collins asserts the moral right to be
identified as the compiler of this work

A catalogue record for this book is
available from the British Library

ISBN 0 00 628098 6

Printed and bound in Great Britain by
Caledonian International Book Manufacturing Ltd, Glasgow

CONDITIONS OF SALE
This book is sold subject to the condition that it
shall not, by way of trade or otherwise, be lent, re-sold,
hired out or otherwise circulated without the publisher's
prior consent in any form of binding or cover other
than that in which it is published and without a
similar condition including this condition being
imposed on the subsequent purchaser.

All rights reserved. No part of this publication may be
reproduced, stored in a retrieval system, or transmitted,
in any form or by any means, electronic, mechanical,
photocopying, recording or otherwise, without the prior
permission of the publishers.

Contents

Introduction xi

Part 1: The Bible

Moses: Before the Red Sea 3
Moses: After crossing the Red Sea 3
Moses: The Ten Commandments 4
Moses: The offer of life or death 6
David: I come to thee in the name of the Lord of hosts 7
Jesus Christ: The Sermon on the Mount 8
Jesus Christ: The parable of the Good Samaritan 15
Jesus Christ: The parable of the Prodigal Son 16
The apostle Peter: Ye shall receive the gift of the Holy Ghost 18
The apostle Paul: I saw in the way a light from heaven 20

Part 2: The First Century to the Fifth Century

Polycarp: Eighty and six years have I served him 25
Justin Martyr: This crucified Christ 27
Hippolytus: Whatsoever ... the Holy Scriptures do preach 29
Origen: The eternal generation of the Son 30
Athanasius: The Holy Scriptures and truth 31
Alban: I confess Jesus Christ 31
The First Council of Nicaea: We believe in one God 31
Cyril of Jerusalem: Great is the Baptism that lies before you 32
Cyril of Jerusalem: Of faith 36
Cyril of Jerusalem: The Creed of Jerusalem 38
Hilary: We need humble faith 39
Basil the Great: Render due praise to the Creator 42
Gregory of Nyssa: We needed a God put to death 45
Gregory of Nyssa: What have you to say about the Holy Ghost? 48
Gregory of Nyssa: The war of heresy surrounds us 53

Ambrose: There is nothing therefore for you to fear 57
John Chrysostom: Is there anyone who is a devout lover of God? 60
John Chrysostom: Rejoice in all things which befall us 62
John Chrysostom: Eulogy for the martyr Ignatius 69
Augustine: Renewal does not happen in one moment of conversion 72
Augustine: In fearing not to fear, and in not fearing to fear 73
Augustine: Our hearts are restless until they find their rest in Thee 75
Cyril of Alexandria: Repent and receive the heavenly gift 79
Cyril of Alexandria: The Son of God was begot of the very essence of the Father 83
Cyril of Alexandria: A Christmas homily 94
Nestorius: Neglect of the Holy Communion 97
Leo I: Partakers in Christ's resurrection life 98
Leo I: All share in the joy of Christmas 101
Ephraem the Syrian: How merciful is God 104

Part 3: The Sixth Century to the Fifteenth Century
The Rule of St Columba: Be single-minded in your imitation of Christ 111
Isaac the Syrian: A Christmas sermon 113
Isaac the Syrian: Be a herald of God's goodness 114
Methodius: The cross and the passion of Christ 116
Bernard of Clairvaux: If you love Christ tenderly 120
Francis of Assisi: My little sisters, the birds 122
John Huss: You are now going to burn a goose 122

Part 4: The Sixteenth Century
Thomas More: The King's good servant, but God's first 127
Martin Luther: The Ninety-Five Theses 127

Martin Luther: My conscience is captive to the word of God 139
Martin Luther: Preface to Romans 143
Philip Melancthon: The circumstances of Luther's death 160
Philip Melancthon: Elegy for Martin Luther 163
Philip Melancthon: A funeral oration for Martin Luther 163
Hugh Latimer: Who art thou? 175
Hugh Latimer: We shall this day light such a candle 182
William Tyndale: Lord, open the King of England's eyes! 182
William Tyndale: Can the church err? 183
Thomas Cranmer: I recant of my recantations 184
The Book of Homilies: Holy Scripture – a fountain of truth 187
The Book of Homilies: Homily for Whitsunday 187
John Knox: Temptation 187
Richard Hooker: A learned discourse of justification 190

Part 5: The Seventeenth Century

John Donne: Death's duel 199
William Laud: I am coming, O Lord, as quickly as I can 205
The Mayflower Compact 206
John Winthrop: We shall be as a city upon a hill 207
Charles I: I go from a corruptible to an incorruptible crown 209
Samuel Rutherford: The worst that the enemies of the Kirk can do 210
James Renwick: I die a Presbyterian Protestant 212
Thomas Ken: Jesus is Lord 215
Thomas Boston: Of the providence of God 216
George Frederic Handel: I did think I did see all Heaven before me 221

Part 6: The Eighteenth Century

Jonathan Edwards: Sinners in the hands of an angry God 225
Jonathan Edwards: True grace distinguished from the experience of devils 229
Jonathan Edwards: The future glorious state of Christ's Church 234
Jonathan Edwards: A faithful narrative of the surprising work of God 239
Samuel Johnson: Commemorating the death of Christ 256
John Wesley: Now the Lord is that Spirit 257
John Wesley: By grace are ye saved through faith 273
John Wesley: On the death of George Whitefield 284
George Whitefield: This spake he of the Spirit 303
William Wilberforce: The total Abolition ought to take place 318
John Wesley: Letter to William Wilberforce 320
Charles Finney: How to overcome sin 321

Part 7: The Nineteenth Century

Lucretia Mott: Likeness to Christ rather than notions of Christ 325
E. B. Pusey: The presence of God 332
Antony Ashley Cooper: These covetous and cruel practices 332
Abraham Lincoln: As God gives us the right 333
Abraham Lincoln's lying in state: I charge this murder where it belongs, on Slavery 335
Abraham Lincoln's funeral: He is dead, but the God in whom he trusted lives 352
William Booth: God has had all there was of me 363
William Booth: In Darkest England 363
Hudson Taylor: Spiritual revival 372
C. H. Spurgeon: For by grace are ye saved 373
C. H. Spurgeon: Teaching children 378

C. H. Spurgeon: Let the wicked forsake his way 384
Charles Dickens: Many a poor child, sick and neglected 392
Robert Murray M'Cheyne: The cry for revival 397
Robert Murray M'Cheyne: Christ, the Way, the Truth and the Life 403
David Livingstone: Diffusing the blessings of Christianity 408
J. C. Ryle: Are you born again? 410
J. C. Ryle: Holiness 416
Charles Kingsley: Look to the cross this day! 425
Alexander Maclaren: The Cross: the proof of the love of God 426
Alexander Whyte: Look to your motives 430
D. L. Moody: Pentecost isn't over yet! 431

Part 8: The Twentieth Century

R. A. Torrey: The Holy Spirit says, Today 437
Martyn Lloyd-Jones: Jonathan Edwards and the crucial importance of revival 446
Dietrich Bonhoeffer: This is the end, but also the beginning 455
Billy Graham: I'm here to represent Jesus Christ 456
John Stott: Make friends with unbelievers 459
Martin Luther King: I have a dream 469

Introduction

The Oral History of Christianity is a collection of some of the most significant public utterances in the Christian tradition. From Moses to Martin Luther King Jr and from the Beatitudes to Billy Graham, this compilation rangers over the first two millennia of Christianity as well as dipping into some of the speeches recorded in the Old Testament. It gives snapshots of orthodox Christian teaching from different centuries, as the Church fought against the heresies of the day. Seeing the false ideas which attempted to undermine Christianity in the past enables us to put into perspective today's theological battles.

Some of the most poignant entries in this compilation come from the lips of heroic Christian martyrs as they faced their last agonizing hours on this earth. Some dying words of Polycarp, Alban, John Huss, Nicholas Ridley, William Tyndale, Thomas Cranmer, James Renwick and Dietrich Bonhoeffer are brought together in these pages. This compilation also includes the orations given at the funerals of leading Christians such as Martin Luther, George Whitefield and Abraham Lincoln.

As well as some of the most well-known documents in Christian history – such as the Nicene Creed, Martin Luther's Ninety-Five Theses, the Mayflower Compact and Martin Luther King's 'I have a dream' speech – there are also a few less well-known gems, such as Charles Dickens' speech on behalf of poor children, Charles Kingsley's devotional sermon on the cross of Jesus, and Lucretia Mott's address, 'It is time that Christians were judged more by their likeness to Christ than their notions of Christ.'

One of the constant themes in this book is spiritual revival, and a number of famous sermons preached by John Wesley,

George Whitefield and Jonathan Edwards during the Great Awakening in America are recorded here, as well as sermons from D. L. Moody and R. A. Torrey.

I hope that this compilation will help to make the wonderful oral heritage of Christianity more accessible to the reader.

Owen Collins
1998

PART 1

The Bible

All of the biblical quotations in Part 1 are taken from the Authorized Version.

Moses

Before the Red Sea

And Moses said unto the people, 'Fear ye not, stand still, and see the salvation of the LORD, which he will shew to you to day: for the Egyptians whom ye have seen to day, ye shall see them again no more for ever. The LORD shall fight for you, and ye shall hold your peace.'

Exodus 14:13–14

Moses

After crossing the Red Sea

Then sang Moses and the children of Israel this song unto the LORD, and spake, saying, 'I will sing unto the Lord, for he hath triumphed gloriously: the horse and his rider hath he thrown into the sea. The LORD is my strength and song, and he is become my salvation: he is my God, and I will prepare him an habitation; my father's God, and I will exalt him.

'The LORD is a man of war: the LORD is his name. Pharaoh's chariots and his host hath he cast into the sea: his chosen captains also are drowned in the Red sea. The depths have covered them: they sank into the bottom as a stone.

'Thy right hand, O LORD, is become glorious in power: thy right hand, O LORD, hath dashed in pieces the enemy. And in the greatness of thine excellency thou hast overthrown them that rose up against thee: thou sentest forth thy wrath, which consumed them as stubble. And with the blast of thy nostrils the waters were gathered together, the floods stood upright as an heap, and the depths were congealed in the heart of the sea.

'The enemy said, "I will pursue, I will overtake, I will divide the spoil; my lust shall be satisfied upon them; I will draw my sword, my hand shall destroy them." Thou didst blow with thy wind, the sea covered them: they sank as lead in the mighty waters.

'Who is like unto thee, O LORD, among the gods? who is like thee, glorious in holiness, fearful in praises, doing wonders? Thou stretchedst out thy right hand, the earth swallowed them. Thou in thy mercy hast led forth the people which thou hast redeemed: thou hast guided them in thy strength unto thy holy habitation.

'The people shall hear, and be afraid: sorrow shall take hold on the inhabitants of Palestina. Then the dukes of Edom shall be amazed; the mighty men of Moab, trembling shall take hold upon them; all the inhabitants of Canaan shall melt away. Fear and dread shall fall upon them; by the greatness of thine arm they shall be as still as a stone; till thy people pass over, O LORD, till the people pass over, which thou hast purchased.

'Thou shalt bring them in, and plant them in the mountain of thine inheritance, in the place, O LORD, which thou hast made for thee to dwell in, in the Sanctuary, O LORD, which thy hands have established. The LORD shall reign for ever and ever.'

Exodus 15:1–18

Moses

The Ten Commandments

And God spake all these words, saying, 'I am the LORD thy God, which have brought thee out of the land of Egypt, out of the house of bondage.

'Thou shalt have no other gods before me. Thou shalt not make unto thee any graven image, or any likeness of any thing that is in heaven above, or that is in the earth beneath, or that is in the water under the earth. Thou shalt not bow down thyself to them, nor serve them: for I the L{\sc ord} thy God am a jealous God, visiting the iniquity of the fathers upon the children unto the third and fourth generation of them that hate me; And shewing mercy unto thousands of them that love me, and keep my commandments.

'Thou shalt not take the name of the L{\sc ord} thy God in vain; for the L{\sc ord} will not hold him guiltless that taketh his name in vain.

'Remember the sabbath day, to keep it holy. Six days shalt thou labour, and do all thy work: But the seventh day is the sabbath of the L{\sc ord} thy God: in it thou shalt not do any work, thou, nor thy son, nor thy daughter, thy manservant, nor thy maidservant, nor thy cattle, nor thy stranger that is within thy gates: For in six days the L{\sc ord} made heaven and earth, the sea, and all that in them is, and rested the seventh day: wherefore the L{\sc ord} blessed the sabbath day, and hallowed it.

'Honour thy father and thy mother: that thy days may be long upon the land which the L{\sc ord} thy God giveth thee.

'Thou shalt not kill.

'Thou shalt not commit adultery.

'Thou shalt not steal.

'Thou shalt not bear false witness against thy neighbour.

'Thou shalt not covet thy neighbour's house, thou shalt not covet thy neighbour's wife, nor his manservant, nor his maidservant, nor his ox, nor his ass, nor any thing that is thy neighbour's.'

Exodus 20:1–17

Moses

The offer of life or death

For this commandment which I command thee this day, it is not hidden from thee, neither is it far off. It is not in heaven, that thou shouldest say, 'Who shall go up for us to heaven, and bring it unto us, that we may hear it, and do it?' Neither is it beyond the sea, that thou shouldest say, 'Who shall go over the sea for us, and bring it unto us, that we may hear it, and do it?' But the word is very nigh unto thee, in thy mouth, and in thy heart, that thou mayest do it.

See, I have set before thee this day life and good, and death and evil; In that I command thee this day to love the LORD thy God, to walk in his ways, and to keep his commandments and his statutes and his judgments, that thou mayest live and multiply: and the LORD thy God shall bless thee in the land whither thou goest to possess it.

But if thine heart turn away, so that thou wilt not hear, but shalt be drawn away, and worship other gods, and serve them; I denounce unto you this day, that ye shall surely perish, and that ye shall not prolong your days upon the land, whither thou passest over Jordan to go to possess it.

I call heaven and earth to record this day against you, that I have set before you life and death, blessing and cursing: therefore choose life, that both thou and thy seed may live: That thou mayest love the LORD thy God, and that thou mayest obey his voice, and that thou mayest cleave unto him: for he is thy life, and the length of thy days: that thou mayest dwell in the land which the LORD sware unto thy fathers, to Abraham, to Isaac, and to Jacob, to give them.

Deuteronomy 30:11–20

David

I come to thee in the name of the Lord of hosts
And the Philistine came on and drew near unto David; and the man that bare the shield went before him. And when the Philistine looked about, and saw David, he disdained him: for he was but a youth, and ruddy, and of a fair countenance. And the Philistine said unto David, 'Am I a dog, that thou comest to me with staves?' And the Philistine cursed David by his gods. And the Philistine said to David, 'Come to me, and I will give thy flesh unto the fowls of the air, and to the beasts of the field.'

Then said David to the Philistine, 'Thou comest to me with a sword, and with a spear, and with a shield: but I come to thee in the name of the LORD of hosts, the God of the armies of Israel, whom thou hast defied. This day will the LORD deliver thee into mine hand; and I will smite thee, and take thine head from thee; and I will give the carcases of the host of the Philistines this day unto the fowls of the air, and to the wild beasts of the earth; that all the earth may know that there is a God in Israel. And all this assembly shall know that the LORD saveth not with sword and spear: for the battle is the LORD's, and he will give you into our hands.'

And it came to pass, when the Philistine arose, and came, and drew nigh to meet David, that David hastened, and ran toward the army to meet the Philistine. And David put his hand in his bag, and took thence a stone, and slang it, and smote the Philistine in his forehead, that the stone sunk into his forehead; and he fell upon his face to the earth.

1 Samuel 17:41–49

Jesus Christ

The Sermon on the Mount

And seeing the multitudes, he went up into a mountain: and when he was set, his disciples came unto him: And he opened his mouth, and taught them, saying,

'Blessed are the poor in spirit: for theirs is the kingdom of heaven.

'Blessed are they that mourn: for they shall be comforted.

'Blessed are the meek: for they shall inherit the earth.

'Blessed are they which do hunger and thirst after righteousness: for they shall be filled.

'Blessed are the merciful: for they shall obtain mercy.

'Blessed are the pure in heart: for they shall see God.

'Blessed are the peacemakers: for they shall be called the children of God.

'Blessed are they which are persecuted for righteousness' sake: for theirs is the kingdom of heaven.

'Blessed are ye, when men shall revile you, and persecute you, and shall say all manner of evil against you falsely, for my sake.

'Rejoice, and be exceeding glad: for great is your reward in heaven: for so persecuted they the prophets which were before you.

'Ye are the salt of the earth: but if the salt have lost his savour, wherewith shall it be salted? it is thenceforth good for nothing, but to be cast out, and to be trodden under foot of men.

'Ye are the light of the world. A city that is set on an hill cannot be hid. Neither do men light a candle, and put it under a bushel, but on a candlestick; and it giveth light unto all that are in the house. Let your light so shine before men, that they may see your good works, and glorify your Father which is in heaven.

'Think not that I am come to destroy the law, or the prophets: I am not come to destroy, but to fulfil. For verily I say unto you, Till heaven and earth pass, one jot or one tittle shall in no wise pass from the law, till all be fulfilled.

'Whosoever therefore shall break one of these least commandments, and shall teach men so, he shall be called the least in the kingdom of heaven: but whosoever shall do and teach them, the same shall be called great in the kingdom of heaven.

'For I say unto you, That except your righteousness shall exceed the righteousness of the scribes and Pharisees, ye shall in no case enter into the kingdom of heaven.

'Ye have heard that it was said of them of old time, "Thou shalt not kill; and whosoever shall kill shall be in danger of the judgment": But I say unto you, That whosoever is angry with his brother without a cause shall be in danger of the judgment: and whosoever shall say to his brother, "Raca," shall be in danger of the council: but whosoever shall say, "Thou fool," shall be in danger of hell fire.

'Therefore if thou bring thy gift to the altar, and there rememberest that thy brother hath ought against thee; Leave there thy gift before the altar, and go thy way; first be reconciled to thy brother, and then come and offer thy gift.

'Agree with thine adversary quickly, whiles thou art in the way with him; lest at any time the adversary deliver thee to the judge, and the judge deliver thee to the officer, and thou be cast into prison. Verily I say unto thee, Thou shalt by no means come out thence, till thou hast paid the uttermost farthing.

'Ye have heard that it was said by them of old time, "Thou shalt not commit adultery": But I say unto you, That whosoever looketh on a woman to lust after her hath committed adultery with her already in his heart.

'And if thy right eye offend thee, pluck it out, and cast it from thee: for it is profitable for thee that one of thy members should perish, and not that thy whole body should be cast into hell.

'And if thy right hand offend thee, cut it off, and cast it from thee: for it is profitable for thee that one of thy members should perish, and not that thy whole body should be cast into hell.

'It hath been said, "Whosoever shall put away his wife, let him give her a writing of divorcement": But I say unto you, That whosoever shall put away his wife, saving for the cause of fornication, causeth her to commit adultery: and whosoever shall marry her that is divorced committeth adultery.

'Again, ye have heard that it hath been said by them of old time, "Thou shalt not forswear thyself, but shalt perform unto the Lord thine oaths": But I say unto you, Swear not at all; neither by heaven; for it is God's throne: Nor by the earth; for it is his footstool: neither by Jerusalem; for it is the city of the great King. Neither shalt thou swear by thy head, because thou canst not make one hair white or black. But let your communication be, "Yea, yea"; "Nay, nay": for whatsoever is more than these cometh of evil.

'Ye have heard that it hath been said, "An eye for an eye, and a tooth for a tooth": But I say unto you, That ye resist not evil: but whosoever shall smite thee on thy right cheek, turn to him the other also. And if any man will sue thee at the law, and take away thy coat, let him have thy cloke also. And whosoever shall compel thee to go a mile, go with him twain. Give to him that asketh thee, and from him that would borrow of thee turn not thou away.

'Ye have heard that it hath been said, "Thou shalt love thy neighbour, and hate thine enemy." But I say unto you, Love your enemies, bless them that curse you, do good to them that hate you, and pray for them which despitefully use you, and persecute you; That ye may be the children of your Father which is in heaven: for he maketh his sun to rise on the evil and on the good, and sendeth rain on the just and on the unjust.

'For if ye love them which love you, what reward have ye? do not even the publicans the same? And if ye salute your brethren only, what do ye more than others? do not even the publicans so? Be ye therefore perfect, even as your Father which is in heaven is perfect.

'Take heed that ye do not your alms before men, to be seen of them: otherwise ye have no reward of your Father which is in heaven. Therefore when thou doest thine alms, do not sound a trumpet before thee, as the hypocrites do in the synagogues and in the streets, that they may have glory of men. Verily I say unto you, They have their reward. But when thou doest alms, let not thy left hand know what thy right hand doeth: That thine alms may be in secret: and thy Father which seeth in secret himself shall reward thee openly.

'And when thou prayest, thou shalt not be as the hypocrites are: for they love to pray standing in the synagogues and in the corners of the streets, that they may be seen of men. Verily I say unto you, They have their reward.

'But thou, when thou prayest, enter into thy closet, and when thou hast shut thy door, pray to thy Father which is in secret; and thy Father which seeth in secret shall reward thee openly.

'But when ye pray, use not vain repetitions, as the heathen do: for they think that they shall be heard for their much speaking. Be not ye therefore like unto them: for your Father knoweth what things ye have need of, before ye ask him. After this manner therefore pray ye:

'Our Father which art in heaven, Hallowed be thy name. Thy kingdom come. Thy will be done in earth, as it is in heaven. Give us this day our daily bread. And forgive us our debts, as we forgive our debtors. And lead us not into temptation, but deliver us from evil: For thine is the kingdom, and the power, and the glory, for ever. Amen.

'For if ye forgive men their trespasses, your heavenly Father will also forgive you: But if ye forgive not men their trespasses, neither will your Father forgive your trespasses.

'Moreover when ye fast, be not, as the hypocrites, of a sad countenance: for they disfigure their faces, that they may appear unto men to fast. Verily I say unto you, They have their reward. But thou, when thou fastest, anoint thine head, and wash thy face; That thou appear not unto men to fast, but unto thy Father which is in secret: and thy Father, which seeth in secret, shall reward thee openly.

'Lay not up for yourselves treasures upon earth, where moth and rust doth corrupt, and where thieves break through and steal: But lay up for yourselves treasures in heaven, where neither moth nor rust doth corrupt, and where thieves do not break through nor steal: For where your treasure is, there will your heart be also.

'The light of the body is the eye: if therefore thine eye be single, thy whole body shall be full of light. But if thine eye be evil, thy whole body shall be full of darkness. If therefore the light that is in thee be darkness, how great is that darkness!

'No man can serve two masters: for either he will hate the one, and love the other; or else he will hold to the one, and despise the other. Ye cannot serve God and mammon.

'Therefore I say unto you, Take no thought for your life, what ye shall eat, or what ye shall drink; nor yet for your body, what ye shall put on. Is not the life more than meat, and the body than raiment?

'Behold the fowls of the air: for they sow not, neither do they reap, nor gather into barns; yet your heavenly Father feedeth them. Are ye not much better than they? Which of you by taking thought can add one cubit unto his stature? And why take ye thought for raiment? Consider the lilies of the field, how they grow; they toil not, neither do they spin: And yet I say unto you, That even Solomon in all his glory was not arrayed like one of these. Wherefore, if God so clothe the grass of the field, which to day is, and to morrow is cast into the oven, shall he not much more clothe you, O ye of little faith?

'Therefore take no thought, saying, "What shall we eat?" or, "What shall we drink?" or, "Wherewithal shall we be clothed?" (For after all these things do the Gentiles seek:) for your heavenly Father knoweth that ye have need of all these things. But seek ye first the kingdom of God, and his righteousness; and all these things shall be added unto you.

'Take therefore no thought for the morrow: for the morrow shall take thought for the things of itself. Sufficient unto the day is the evil thereof.

'Judge not, that ye be not judged. For with what judgment ye judge, ye shall be judged: and with what measure ye mete, it shall be measured to you again.

'And why beholders thou the mote that is in thy brother's eye, but considerest not the beam that is in thine own eye? Or how wilt thou say to thy brother, "Let me pull out the mote out of thine eye"; and, behold, a beam is in thine own eye? Thou hypocrite, first cast out the beam out of thine own eye; and then shalt thou see clearly to cast out the mote out of thy brother's eye.

'Give not that which is holy unto the dogs, neither cast ye your pearls before swine, lest they trample them under their feet, and turn again and rend you.

'Ask, and it shall be given you; seek, and ye shall find; knock, and it shall be opened unto you: For every one that asketh receiveth; and he that seeketh findeth; and to him that knocketh it shall be opened.

'Or what man is there of you, whom if his son ask bread, will he give him a stone? Or if he ask a fish, will he give him a serpent? If ye then, being evil, know how to give good gifts unto your children, how much more shall your Father which is in heaven give good things to them that ask him?

'Therefore all things whatsoever ye would that men should do to you, do ye even so to them: for this is the law and the prophets.

'Enter ye in at the strait gate: for wide is the gate, and broad is the way, that leadeth to destruction, and many there be which go in thereat: Because strait is the gate, and narrow is the way, which leadeth unto life, and few there be that find it.

'Beware of false prophets, which come to you in sheep's clothing, but inwardly they are ravening wolves. Ye shall know them by their fruits. Do men gather grapes of thorns, or figs of thistles? Even so every good tree bringeth forth good fruit; but a corrupt tree bringeth forth evil fruit. A good tree cannot bring forth evil fruit, neither can a corrupt tree bring forth good fruit. Every tree that bringeth not forth good fruit is hewn down, and cast into the fire. Wherefore by their fruits ye shall know them.

'Not every one that saith unto me, "Lord, Lord," shall enter into the kingdom of heaven; but he that doeth the will of my Father which is in heaven. Many will say to me in that day, "Lord, Lord, have we not prophesied in thy name? and in thy name have cast out devils? and in thy name done many wonderful works?" And then will I profess unto them, "I never knew you: depart from me, ye that work iniquity."

'Therefore whosoever heareth these sayings of mine, and doeth them, I will liken him unto a wise man, which built his house upon a rock: And the rain descended, and the floods came, and the winds blew, and beat upon that house; and it fell not: for it was founded upon a rock.

'And every one that heareth these sayings of mine, and doeth them not, shall be likened unto a foolish man, which built his house upon the sand: And the rain descended, and the floods came, and the winds blew, and beat upon that house; and it fell: and great was the fall of it.'

And it came to pass, when Jesus had ended these sayings, the people were astonished at his doctrine: For he taught them as one having authority, and not as the scribes.

Matthew 5–7

Jesus Christ

The parable of the Good Samaritan

And, behold, a certain lawyer stood up, and tempted him, saying, 'Master, what shall I do to inherit eternal life?'

He said unto him, 'What is written in the law? how readest thou?'

And he answering said, 'Thou shalt love the Lord thy God with all thy heart, and with all thy soul, and with all thy strength, and with all thy mind; and thy neighbour as thyself.'

And he said unto him, 'Thou hast answered right: this do, and thou shalt live.'

But he, willing to justify himself, said unto Jesus, 'And who is my neighbour?'

And Jesus answering said, 'A certain man went down from Jerusalem to Jericho, and fell among thieves, which stripped him of his raiment, and wounded him, and departed, leaving him half dead.

'And by chance there came down a certain priest that way: and when he saw him, he passed by on the other side.

'And likewise a Levite, when he was at the place, came and looked on him, and passed by on the other side.

'But a certain Samaritan, as he journeyed, came where he was: and when he saw him, he had compassion on him, And went to him, and bound up his wounds, pouring in oil and wine, and set him on his own beast, and brought him to an inn, and took care of him.

'And on the morrow when he departed, he took out two pence, and gave them to the host, and said unto him, "Take care of him; and whatsoever thou spendest more, when I come again, I will repay thee."

'Which now of these three, thinkest thou, was neighbour unto him that fell among the thieves?'

And he said, 'He that shewed mercy on him' Then said Jesus unto him, 'Go, and do thou likewise.'

Luke 10:25–37

Jesus Christ

The parable of the Prodigal Son

A certain man had two sons: And the younger of them said to his father, 'Father, give me the portion of goods that falleth to me.' And he divided unto them his living. And not many days after the younger son gathered all together, and took his journey into a far country, and there wasted his substance with riotous living.

And when he had spent all, there arose a mighty famine in that land; and he began to be in want. And he went and joined himself to a citizen of that country; and he sent him into his fields to feed swine. And he would fain have filled his belly with the husks that the swine did eat: and no man gave unto him.

And when he came to himself, he said, 'How many hired servants of my father's have bread enough and to spare, and I perish with hunger! I will arise and go to my father, and will say unto him, "Father, I have sinned against heaven, and before thee, And am no more worthy to be called thy son: make me as one of thy hired servants."'

And he arose, and came to his father. But when he was yet a great way off, his father saw him, and had compassion, and ran, and fell on his neck, and kissed him.

And the son said unto him, 'Father, I have sinned against heaven, and in thy sight, and am no more worthy to be called thy son.'

But the father said to his servants, 'Bring forth the best robe, and put it on him; and put a ring on his hand, and shoes on his feet: And bring hither the fatted calf, and kill it; and let us eat, and be merry: For this my son was dead, and is alive again; he was lost, and is found.' And they began to be merry.

Now his elder son was in the field: and as he came and drew nigh to the house, he heard musick and dancing. And he called one of the servants, and asked what these things meant. And he said unto him, 'Thy brother is come; and thy father hath killed the fatted calf, because he hath received him safe and sound.'

And he was angry, and would not go in: Therefore came his father out, and intreated him. And he answering said to his father, 'Lo, these many years do I serve thee, neither transgressed I at any time thy commandment: and yet thou never gavest me a kid, that I might make merry with my friends: But as soon as this thy son was come, which hath devoured thy living with harlots, thou hast killed for him the fatted calf.'

And he said unto him, 'Son, thou art ever with me, and all that I have is thine. It was meet that we should make merry, and be glad: for this thy brother was dead, and is alive again; and was lost, and is found.'

Luke 15:11–37

The apostle Peter

Ye shall receive the gift of the Holy Ghost

But Peter, standing up with the eleven, lifted up his voice, and said unto them, 'Ye men of Judaea, and all ye that dwell at Jerusalem, be this known unto you, and hearken to my words: For these are not drunken, as ye suppose, seeing it is but the third hour of the day.

'But this is that which was spoken by the prophet Joel; "And it shall come to pass in the last days, saith God, I will pour out of my Spirit upon all flesh: and your sons and your daughters shall prophesy, and your young men shall see visions, and your old men shall dream dreams: And on my servants and on my handmaidens I will pour out in those days of my Spirit; and they shall prophesy: And I will shew wonders in heaven above, and signs in the earth beneath; blood, and fire, and vapour of smoke: The sun shall be turned into darkness, and the moon into blood, before the great and notable day of the Lord come: And it shall come to pass, that whosoever shall call on the name of the Lord shall be saved."

'Ye men of Israel, hear these words; Jesus of Nazareth, a man approved of God among you by miracles and wonders and signs, which God did by him in the midst of you, as ye yourselves also know: Him, being delivered by the determinate counsel and foreknowledge of God, ye have taken, and by wicked hands have crucified and slain: Whom God hath raised up, having loosed the pains of death: because it was not possible that he should be holden of it.

'For David speaketh concerning him, "I foresaw the Lord always before my face, for he is on my right hand, that I should not be moved: Therefore did my heart rejoice, and my tongue was glad; moreover also my flesh shall rest in hope: Because thou wilt not leave my soul in hell, neither wilt thou suffer thine Holy One to see corruption. Thou hast made known to me the ways of life; thou shalt make me full of joy with thy countenance."

'Men and brethren, let me freely speak unto you of the patriarch David, that he is both dead and buried, and his sepulchre is with us unto this day. Therefore being a prophet, and knowing that God had sworn with an oath to him, that of the fruit of his loins, according to the flesh, he would raise up Christ to sit on his throne; He seeing this before spake of the resurrection of Christ, that his soul was not left in hell, neither his flesh did see corruption. This Jesus hath God raised up, whereof we all are witnesses.

'Therefore being by the right hand of God exalted, and having received of the Father the promise of the Holy Ghost, he hath shed forth this, which ye now see and hear. For David is not ascended into the heavens: but he saith himself, "The Lord said unto my Lord, Sit thou on my right hand, Until I make thy foes thy footstool." Therefore let all the house of Israel know assuredly, that God hath made the same Jesus, whom ye have crucified, both Lord and Christ.

Now when they heard this, they were pricked in their heart, and said unto Peter and to the rest of the apostles, 'Men and brethren, what shall we do?'

Then Peter said unto them, 'Repent, and be baptized every one of you in the name of Jesus Christ for the remission of sins, and ye shall receive the gift of the Holy Ghost. For the promise is unto you, and to your children, and to all that are afar off, even as many as the Lord our God shall call.'

And with many other words did he testify and exhort, saying, 'Save yourselves from this untoward generation.' Then they that gladly received his word were baptized: and the same day there were added unto them about three thousand souls.

Acts 2:14–41

The apostle Paul

I saw in the way a light from heaven

Then Agrippa said unto Paul, 'Thou art permitted to speak for thyself.'

Then Paul stretched forth the hand, and answered for himself: 'I think myself happy, king Agrippa, because I shall answer for myself this day before thee touching all the things whereof I am accused of the Jews: Especially because I know thee to be expert in all customs and questions which are among the Jews: wherefore I beseech thee to hear me patiently.

'My manner of life from my youth, which was at the first among mine own nation at Jerusalem, know all the Jews; Which knew me from the beginning, if they would testify, that after the most straitest sect of our religion I lived a Pharisee. And now I stand and am judged for the hope of the promise made of God, unto our fathers: Unto which promise our twelve tribes, instantly serving God day and night, hope to come. For which hope's sake, king Agrippa, I am accused of the Jews.

'Why should it be thought a thing incredible with you, that God should raise the dead? I verily thought with myself, that I ought to do many things contrary to the name of Jesus of

Nazareth. Which thing I also did in Jerusalem: and many of the saints did I shut up in prison, having received authority from the chief priests; and when they were put to death, I gave my voice against them. And I punished them oft in every synagogue, and compelled them to blaspheme; and being exceedingly mad against them, I persecuted them even unto strange cities.

'Whereupon as I went to Damascus with authority and commission from the chief priests, At midday, O king, I saw in the way a light from heaven, above the brightness of the sun, shining round about me and them which journeyed with me. And when we were all fallen to the earth, I heard a voice speaking unto me, and saying in the Hebrew tongue, "Saul, Saul, why persecutest thou me? it is hard for thee to kick against the pricks."

'And I said, "Who art thou, Lord?"

'And he said, "I am Jesus whom thou persecutest. But rise, and stand upon thy feet: for I have appeared unto thee for this purpose, to make thee a minister and a witness both of these things which thou hast seen, and of those things in the which I will appear unto thee; Delivering thee from the people, and from the Gentiles, unto whom now I send thee, To open their eyes, and to turn them from darkness to light, and from the power of Satan unto God, that they may receive forgiveness of sins, and inheritance among them which are sanctified by faith that is in me."

'Whereupon, O king Agrippa, I was not disobedient unto the heavenly vision: But shewed first unto them of Damascus, and at Jerusalem, and throughout all the coasts of Judaea, and then to the Gentiles, that they should repent and turn to God, and do works meet for repentance. For these causes the Jews caught me in the temple, and went about to kill me.

'Having therefore obtained help of God, I continue unto this day, witnessing both to small and great, saying none other things than those which the prophets and Moses did say should come: That Christ should suffer, and that he should be the first that should rise from the dead, and should shew light unto the people, and to the Gentiles.'

And as he thus spake for himself, Festus said with a loud voice, 'Paul, thou art beside thyself; much learning doth make thee mad.'

But he said, 'I am not mad, most noble Festus; but speak forth the words of truth and soberness. For the king knoweth of these things, before whom also I speak freely: for I am persuaded that none of these things are hidden from him; for this thing was not done in a corner. King Agrippa, believest thou the prophets? I know that thou believest.'

Then Agrippa said unto Paul, 'Almost thou persuadest me to be a Christian.'

And Paul said, 'I would to God, that not only thou, but also all that hear me this day, were both almost, and altogether such as I am, except these bonds.'

And when he had thus spoken, the king rose up, and the governor, and Bernice, and they that sat with them: And when they were gone aside, they talked between themselves, saying, 'This man doeth nothing worthy of death or of bonds.'

Then said Agrippa unto Festus, 'This man might have been set at liberty, if he had not appealed unto Caesar.'

Acts 26:1–32

PART 2

The First Century to the Fifth Century

Polycarp

Eighty and six years have I served him

Polycarp (c. 69–155), Bishop of Smyrna in Asia Minor, fought against various heresies for over 40 years. In the end he died as a martyr, being burned alive at a public festival.

Then, when he had been brought in, the proconsul asked him if he was Polycarp. And when he confessed, he would have persuaded him to deny, saying, 'Have respect unto thine age,' and other things like these, as is their custom to say: 'Swear by the fortunes of Caesar'; 'Repent'; 'Say, "Away with the Atheists."' But Polycarp, when he had looked with a grave face at all the multitude of lawless heathen in the arena, having beckoned unto them with his hand, sighed, and looking up unto heaven, said, 'Away with the Atheists!'

And when the proconsul pressed him, and said, 'Swear, and I will release thee, revile Christ'; Polycarp said, 'Eighty and six years have I served him, and in nothing hath he wronged me; and how, then, can I blaspheme my King, who saved me?' ...

The proconsul said unto him, 'I have wild beasts; I will deliver thee unto them, unless thou repentest.' But he said, 'Call them, for repentance from the better to the worse is impossible for us; but it is a good thing to change from evil deeds to just ones.'

But he said again unto him, 'I will cause thee to be consumed by fire if thou despisest the wild beasts, unless thou repentest.' But Polycarp said, 'Thou threatenest me with fire that burneth but for a season, and is soon quenched. For thou art ignorant of the fire of the judgment to come, and of the eternal punishment reserved for the wicked. But why delayest thou? Bring whatever thou wishest.'

The multitude quickly collecting logs and brushwood from the workshops and baths, the Jews especially lending their services zealously for this purpose, as is their custom.

But when the pyre was ready, having put off all his garments, and having loosed his girdle, he essayed to take off his shoes; not being in the habit of doing this previously, because each of the faithful used to strive which should be the first to touch his body, for, on account of his good conversation, he was, even before his martyrdom, adorned with every good gift.

Straightway, therefore, there were put around him the implements prepared for the pyre. And when they were about besides to nail him to it, he said, 'Suffer me thus, for he who gave me to abide the fire will also allow me, without the security of your nails, to remain on the pyre without moving.'

They, therefore, did not nail him, but bound him. But he, having placed his hands behind him, and being bound, like a notable ram appointed for offering out of a great flock, prepared as a whole burnt-offering acceptable unto God, having looked up unto heaven, said:

'O Lord God Almighty, Father of thy beloved and blessed Son Jesus Christ, through whom we have received our knowledge concerning thee, the God of angels and powers, and of the whole creation, and of all the race of the just who lived before thee, I thank thee that thou hast deemed me worthy of this day and hour, that I should have my portion in the number of the martyrs, in the cup of thy Christ, unto the resurrection of eternal life, both of the soul and body, in the incorruptibility of the Holy Spirit. Among these may I be received before thee this day as a rich and acceptable sacrifice, even as thou hast prepared and made manifest beforehand, and hast fulfilled, thou who art the unerring and true God.

'On this account, and concerning all things, I praise thee, I bless thee, I glorify thee, together with the eternal and heavenly

Jesus Christ thy beloved Son, with whom to thee and the Holy Spirit be glory both now and for ever. Amen.'

And when he had uttered the Amen, and had finished his prayer, the men who superintended the fire kindled it...

We pray, brethren, that you may fare well, walking by the word of the gospel of Jesus Christ, with whom be glory to God and the Father, and the Holy Spirit, for the salvation of the holy elect, even as the blessed Polycarp hath born witness, in whose steps may we be found in the kingdom of Jesus Christ.

From The Martyrdom of Polycarp

Justin Martyr

This crucified Christ

Justin (c. 100–165) was the first Christian writer to try to reconcile faith and reason. He was killed for his faith in Rome, and so is known as Justin Martyr.

While I was going about one morning in the walks of the Xystus, a certain man, with others in his company, having met me, and said, 'Hail, O philosopher!' And immediately after saying this, he turned round and walked along with me; his friends likewise followed him. And I in turn having addressed him, said, 'What is there important?' ...

'There will be no other God, O Trypho, nor was there from eternity any other existing' (I thus addressed him), 'but He who made and disposed all this universe. Nor do we think that there is one God for us, another for you, but that He alone is God who led your fathers out from Egypt with a strong hand and a high arm. Nor have we trusted in any other (for there is no other), but in Him in whom you also have trusted, the God of Abraham, and of Isaac, and of Jacob. But we do not trust through Moses or through the law; for then we would do the same as yourselves ... For we have been led to God through this crucified Christ.'

Then Trypho remarked, 'Be assured that all our nation waits for Christ; and we admit that all the Scriptures which you have quoted refer to Him. But whether Christ should be so shamefully crucified, this we are in doubt about. For whosoever is crucified is said in the law to be accursed, so that I am exceedingly incredulous on this point. It is quite clear, indeed, that the Scriptures announce that Christ had to suffer; but we wish to learn if you can prove it to us whether it was by the suffering cursed in the law.'

I replied to him, 'If Christ was not to suffer, and the prophets had not foretold that He would be led to death on account of the sins of the people, and be dishonoured and scourged, and reckoned among the transgressors, and as a sheep be led to the slaughter, whose generation, the prophet says, no man can declare, then you would have good cause to wonder. But if these are to be characteristic of Him and mark Him out to all, how is it possible for us to do anything else than believe in Him most confidently? And will not as many as have understood the writings of the prophets, whenever they hear merely that He was crucified, say that this is He and no other?

'And we who are filled full of war, and slaughter one of another, and every kind of evil, have from out of the whole earth each changed our weapons of war, our swords into ploughshares and our pikes into farming tools, and we farm piety, righteousness, the love of mankind, faith, and hope, which comes from the father himself through him who was crucified, each of us dwelling under his own vine, that is, each enjoying only his own wedded wife ... No one makes us afraid or leads us into captivity as we have set our faith on Jesus. For though we are beheaded, and crucified, and exposed to beasts and chains and fire and all other forms of torture, it is plain that we do not forsake the confession of our faith, but the more things of this kind which happen to us the more are there others who become believers and truly religious through the name of Jesus.

'Just as when one cuts away the parts of a vine that have borne fruit, it so bursts forth that other flourishing and fruit bearing branches shoot up – in that same way it is also with us. For the vine that has been planted by God, and Christ the Saviour, is his people.'

From *Dialogue with Trypho*

Hippolytus

Whatsoever ... the Holy Scriptures do preach
Hippolytus (c. 160–236) was a Greek theologian and martyr.

There is one God, Whom we do not otherwise acknowledge, brethren, but out of the Holy Scriptures. For as he that would profess the wisdom of this world cannot otherwise attain hereunto, unless he read the doctrine of the philosophers, so whosoever of us will exercise piety toward God, cannot learn this elsewhere but out of the Holy Scriptures. Whatsoever, therefore, the Holy Scriptures do preach, that let us know; and whatsoever they teach, that let us understand.

Homily against the Heresy of Noetus

Origen

The eternal generation of the Son

Origen (c. 185–254) became the head of the Catechetical School at Alexandria, where he led an ascetic life.

So, if I call your attention to the case of the Saviour, that the Father did not beget the Son and release him from his generation but ever is begetting him, I shall present a similar statement in the case of the just man also. But let us see who the Saviour is. He is 'the effulgence of his [i.e. the Father's] glory' (Hebrews 1:3). The 'effulgence of glory' has not once been begotten and is no longer begotten. But as far as the light is productive of the effulgence, to so great an extent the effulgence of the glory of God is being begotten. Our Saviour is the 'wisdom of God' (1 Corinthians 1:24). And wisdom is the 'effulgence of eternal light' (Wisdom 7:26). If therefore the Saviour is ever being begotten, and for this reason says, but 'before all hills he begets me' (Proverbs 8:25) – not 'before all hills he has begotten me', but 'before all hills he begets me' and the Saviour is ever being begotten of the Father, so you also if you have the 'spirit of adoption' (Romans 8:15), does God ever beget in himself according to each word, according to each thought, and thus being begotten you are ever being begotten a son of God in Jesus Christ.

From *Homilies on Jeremiah*

Athanasius

The Holy Scriptures and truth
Athanasius (c. 296–373), bishop of Alexandria, was a supporter of the doctrines of the Trinity and the Incarnation.

The Holy Scriptures given by inspiration of God are of themselves sufficient to the discovery of truth.

From the *Oration Against the Gentiles*

Alban

I confess Jesus Christ
Alban, the first British martyr, is now thought to have died on 22 June 309. When asked to offer sacrifices to Jupiter and Apollo, Alban replied:

I confess Jesus Christ, the son of God, with my whole being. Those whom you call gods are idols; they are made by hands.

Alban was then scourged and beheaded.

The First Council of Nicaea

We believe in one God
The Church Council of Nicaea (325), called by the Roman emperor Constantine, condemned the Arian heresy and upheld the doctrine of the Trinity.

We believe in one God, the Father Almighty, maker of all things visible and invisible; and in one Lord Jesus Christ, the Son of God, the only-begotten of his Father, of the substance of the

Father, God of God, Light of Light, very God of very God, begotten, not made, being of one substance [Greek: *homoousion*; Latin: *consubstantialis*] with the Father. By whom all things were made, both which be in heaven and in earth. Who for us men and for our salvation came down [from heaven] and was incarnate and was made man. He suffered and the third day he rose again, and ascended into heaven. And he shall come again to judge both the quick and the dead. And [we believe] in the Holy Ghost. And whosoever shall say that there was a time when the Son of God was not, or that before he was begotten he was not, or that he was made of things that were not, or that he is of a different substance or essence [from the Father] or that he is a creature, or subject to change or conversion – all that so say, the Catholic and Apostolic Church anathematizes them.

The Nicene Creed

Cyril of Jerusalem

Great is the Baptism that lies before you

Cyril (c. 313 – c. 386) was bishop of Jerusalem from about 350 onwards, but was often exiled. In 348 he delivered his celebrated *Catechetical Lectures* to those seeking baptism.

Already there is an odour of blessedness upon you, O ye who are soon to be enlightened: already ye are gathering the spiritual flowers, to weave heavenly crowns: already the fragrance of the Holy Spirit has breathed upon you: already ye have gathered round the vestibule of the King's palace; may ye be led in also by the King! For blossoms now have appeared upon the trees; may the fruit also be found perfect!... For he lieth not who said, that 'to them that love God all things work together for good.' God is lavish in beneficence, yet He waits for each man's genuine will: therefore the Apostle added and said, 'to them that are called according to a purpose.' The honesty of purpose makes thee called: for if thy body be here but not thy mind, it profiteth thee nothing.

Even Simon Magus once came to the Laver: he was baptized, but was not enlightened; and though he dipped his body in water, he enlightened not his heart with the Spirit: his body went down and came up, but his soul was not buried with Christ, nor raised with Him. Now I mention the statements of [men's] falls, that thou mayest not fall: for these things happened to them by way of example, and they are written for the admonition of those who to this day draw near...

A certain man in the Gospels once pried into the marriage feasts, and took an unbecoming garment, and came in, sat down, and ate: for the bridegroom permitted it. But when he saw them all dressed in white, he ought to have worn a garment of the same kind himself: whereas he partook of the like food, but was unlike them in fashion and in purpose. The bridegroom, however, though bountiful, was not undiscerning: and in going round to each of the guests and observing them (for his care was not for their eating, but for their seemly behaviour), he saw a stranger not having on a wedding garment, and said to him, 'Friend, how camest thou in hither? In what a colour! With what a conscience!' ... So he commands the servants, 'Bind his feet, which daringly intruded: bind his hands, which knew not how to put a bright garment around him: and cast him into the outer darkness; for he is unworthy of the wedding torches.' Thou seest what happened to that man: make thine own condition safe...

If the fashion of thy soul is avarice, put on another fashion and come in. Put off thy former fashion, cloke it not up. Put off, I pray thee, fornication and uncleanness, and put on the brightest robe of chastity. This charge I give thee, before Jesus the Bridegroom of souls come in and see their fashions. A long notice is allowed thee; thou hast forty days for repentance: thou hast full opportunity both to put off, and wash, and to put on and enter. But if thou persist in an evil purpose, the speaker is blameless, but thou must not look for the grace: for the water will receive, but the Spirit will not accept thee. If any one is conscious of his wound, let him take the salve; if any has fallen, let him arise. Let there be no Simon among you, no hypocrisy, no idle curiosity about the matter...

We may not receive Baptism twice or thrice; else it might be said, 'Though I have failed once, I shall set it right a second time': whereas if thou fail once, the thing cannot be set right; for there is one Lord, and one faith, and one baptism: for only the heretics are re-baptized, because the former was no baptism.

For God seeks nothing else from us, save a good purpose. Say not, 'How are my sins blotted out?' I tell thee, By believing. What can be shorter than this?... Cease from this day from every evil deed. Let not thy tongue speak unseemly words, let thine eye abstain from sin, and from roving after things unprofitable.

Let thy feet hasten to the catechisings; receive with earnestness the exorcisms: whether thou be breathed upon or exorcised, the act is to thee salvation. Suppose thou hast gold unwrought and alloyed, mixed with various substances, copper, and tin, and iron, and lead: we seek to have the gold alone; can gold be purified from the foreign substances without fire? Even so without exorcisms the soul cannot be purified; and these exorcisms are divine, having been collected out of the divine Scriptures.

Look upward; that is what thy present hour needeth. Be still, and know that I am God ... Let your mind be refined as by fire unto reverence; let your soul be forged as metal: let the stubbornness of unbelief be hammered out: let the superfluous scales of the iron drop off, and what is pure remain; let the rust of the iron be rubbed off, and the true metal remain ... Then may you receive the name of Christ, and the power of things divine...

Great is the Baptism that lies before you: a ransom to captives; a remission of offences; a death of sin; a new-birth of the soul; a garment of light; a holy indissoluble seal; a chariot to heaven; the delight of Paradise; a welcome into the kingdom; the gift of adoption! ... Guard thine own soul, that thou be not ensnared, to the end that abiding in hope thou mayest become an heir of everlasting salvation.

The race is for our soul: our hope is of things eternal: and God, who knoweth your hearts, and observeth who is sincere, and who a hypocrite, is able both to guard the sincere, and to give faith to the hypocrite: for even to the unbeliever, if only he give his heart, God is able to give faith. So may He blot out the handwriting that is against you, and grant you forgiveness of your former trespasses; may He plant you into His Church, and enlist you in His own service, and put on you the armour of righteousness: may He fill you with the heavenly things of the New Covenant, and give you the seal of the Holy Spirit indelible throughout all ages, in Christ Jesus Our Lord: to whom be the glory for ever and ever! Amen.

Prologue to the *Catechetical Lectures*

Cyril of Jerusalem

Of faith

Now faith is the substance of things hoped for, the evidence of things not seen. For by it the elders obtained a good report.
Hebrews 11:1-2

How great a dignity the Lord bestows on you in transferring you from the order of Catechumens to that of the Faithful, the Apostle Paul shews, when he affirms, 'God is faithful, by whom ye were called into the fellowship of His Son Jesus Christ.' For since God is called Faithful, thou also in receiving this title receivest a great dignity. For as God is called Good, and Just, and Almighty, and Maker of the Universe, so is He also called Faithful. Consider therefore to what a dignity thou art rising, seeing thou art to become partaker of a title of God.

Here then it is further required, that each of you be found faithful in his conscience: for a faithful man it is hard to find: not that thou shouldest shew thy conscience to me, for thou art not to be judged of man's judgment; but that thou shew the sincerity of thy faith to God, who tests the hearts, and knoweth the thoughts of men...

The lesson also which was read to-day invites you to the true faith, by setting before you the way in which you also must please God: for it affirms that without faith it is impossible to please Him ... Faith is an eye that enlightens every conscience, and imparts understanding. Faith stoppeth the mouths of lions, as in Daniel's case...

There is much to tell of faith, and the whole day would not be time sufficient for us to describe it fully. Yea, so much power hath faith, that not the believer only is saved, but some have been saved by others believing. The paralytic in Capernaum was not a believer, but they believed who brought him, and let him down through the roof: for the sick man's soul shared the sickness of his body. And think not that I accuse him without cause: the Gospel itself says, when Jesus saw, not his faith, but their faith, He saith to the sick of the palsy, 'Arise!' The bearers believed, and the sick of the palsy enjoyed the blessing of the cure ... Even if thou be faithless, or of little faith, the Lord is loving unto man; He condescends to thee on thy repentance: only on thy part say with honest mind, 'Lord, I believe, help thou mine unbelief' ...

The name of Faith is in the form of speech as one, but has two distinct senses. For there is one kind of faith, the dogmatic, involving an assent of the soul on some particular point: and it is profitable to the soul, as the Lord saith: 'He that heareth My words, and believeth Him that sent Me, hath everlasting life, and cometh not into judgment' ... But there is a second kind of faith, which is bestowed by Christ as a gift of grace. For to one is given through the Spirit the word of wisdom, and to another the word of knowledge according to the same Spirit: to another faith, by the same Spirit, and to another gifts of healing. This faith then which is given of grace from the Spirit is not merely doctrinal, but also worketh things above man's power. For whosoever hath this faith, shall say to this mountain, 'Remove hence to yonder place,' and it shall remove. For whenever any one shall say this in faith, believing that it cometh to pass, and shall not doubt in his heart, then receiveth he the grace...

And just as the mustard seed in one small grain contains many branches, so also this Faith has embraced in few words all the knowledge of godliness in the Old and New Testaments. Take heed then, brethren, and hold fast the traditions which ye now receive, and write them on the table of your heart. Guard them with reverence, lest per chance the enemy despoil any who have grown slack; or lest some heretic pervert any of the truths delivered to you. For faith is like putting money into the bank, even as we have now done; but from you God requires the accounts of the deposit. I charge you, as the Apostle saith, before God, who quickeneth all things, and Christ Jesus, who before Pontius Pilate witnessed the good confession, that ye keep this faith which is committed to you, without spot, until the appearing of our Lord Jesus Christ. A treasure of life has now been committed to thee, and the Master demandeth the deposit at His appearing, which in His own times He shall shew, Who is the blessed and only Potentate, the King of kings, and Lord of lords; Who only hath immortality, dwelling in light which no man can approach unto; Whom no man hath seen nor can see. To Whom be glory, honour, and power for ever and ever. Amen.

Catechetical Lectures, Lecture 5

Cyril of Jerusalem

The Creed of Jerusalem

The Creed of Jerusalem is based on Cyril's *Catechetical Lectures*.

We believe in one God, Father almighty, Maker of heaven and earth, of all things visible and invisible; And in one Lord Jesus Christ, the only-begotten Son of God, who was begotten from the Father as true God before all ages, through whom all things came into being, who was incarnate and became man, who was crucified and buried and rose again from the dead on the third day, and ascended to the heavens, and sat down at the right hand of the Father, and is coming in glory to judge living and dead, of whose kingdom there will not be an end; And in one Holy Spirit, the Paraclete, who spoke in the prophets, and in one baptism of repentance to the remission of sins, and in one holy Catholic Church, and in the resurrection of the flesh, and in life everlasting.

Hilary

We need humble faith

Hilary (315–67) was bishop of Poitiers.

> *O Lord, my heart is not exalted, neither have mine eyes been lifted up.*
>
> Psalm 131:1

This Psalm, a short one, which demands an analytical rather than a homiletical treatment, teaches us the lesson of humility and meekness.... We are bound to bear in mind how much we need humble faith when we listen to the Prophet thus speaking about it as equivalent to the performance of the highest works: 'O Lord, my heart is not exalted.' For a troubled heart is the noblest sacrifice in the eyes of God. The heart, therefore, must not be lifted up by prosperity, but humbly kept within the bounds of meekness through the fear of God.

'Neither have mine eyes been lifted up.' The strict sense of the Greek here conveys a different meaning: the eyes have not been lifted up from one object to look on another. Yet the eyes must be lifted up in obedience to the Prophet's words: 'Lift up your eyes and see who hath displayed all these things.' And the Lord says in the gospel: 'Lift up your eyes, and look on the fields, that they are white unto harvest.' The eyes, then, are to be lifted up: not, however, to transfer their gaze elsewhere, but to remain fixed once for all upon that to which they have been raised.

Then follows: 'Neither have I walked amid great things, nor amid wonderful things that are above me.' It is most dangerous to walk amid mean things, and not to linger amid wonderful things. God's utterances are great; He Himself is wonderful in the highest: how then can the psalmist pride himself as on a good work for not walking in the middle of great and wonderful things? It is the addition of the words, 'which are above me', that show that the walking is not with those things which men commonly regard as great and wonderful. For David, prophet and king as he was, once was humble and despised and unworthy to sit at his father's table; but he found favour with God, he was anointed to be king, he was inspired to prophesy. His kingdom did not make him haughty, he was not moved by hatreds: he loved those that persecuted him, he paid honour to his dead enemies, he spared his incestuous and murderous children. In his capacity of sovereign he was despised, in that of father he was wounded, in that of prophet he was afflicted; yet he did not call for vengeance as a prophet might, nor exact punishment as a father, nor requite insults as a sovereign. And so he did not walk amid things great and wonderful which were above him.

Next, we see: 'If I was not humble-minded but have lifted up my soul.' What inconsistency on the Prophet's part! He does not lift up his heart: he does lift up his soul. He does not walk among things great and wonderful that are above him; yet his thoughts are not mean. He is exalted in mind and cast down in heart. He is humble in his own affairs: but he is not humble in his thought. For his thought reaches to heaven his soul is lifted up on high. But his heart, out of which proceed, according to the Gospel, evil thoughts, murders, adulteries, fornications, thefts, false witness, railings, is humble, pressed down beneath the gentle yoke of meekness. We must strike a middle course, then, between humility and exaltation, so that we may be humble in heart but lifted up in soul and thought.

Then he goes on: 'Like a weaned child upon his mother's breast, so will thou reward my soul.' We are told that when Isaac was weaned Abraham made a feast because now that he was weaned he was on the verge of boyhood and was passing beyond milk food. The Apostle feeds all that are imperfect in the faith and still babes in the things of God with the milk of knowledge. Thus to cease to need milk marks the greatest possible advance. Abraham proclaimed by a joyful feast that his son had come to stronger meat, and the Apostle refuses bread to the carnal-minded and those that are babes in Christ. And so the Prophet prays that God, because he has not lifted up his heart, nor walked among things great and wonderful that are above him, because he has not been humble-minded but did lift up his soul, may reward his soul, lying like a weaned child upon his mother: that is to say that he may be deemed worthy of the reward of the perfect, heavenly and living bread, on the ground that by reason of his works already recorded he has now passed beyond the stage of milk.

But he does not demand this living bread from heaven for himself alone, he encourages all mankind to hope for it by saying: 'Let Israel hope in the Lord from henceforth and for evermore.' He sets no temporal limit to our hope, he bids our faithful expectation stretch out into infinity. We are to hope for ever and ever, winning the hope of future life through the hope of our present life which we have in Christ Jesus our Lord, Who is blessed for ever and ever. Amen.

From *Homilies on the Psalms*

Basil the Great

Render due praise to the Creator
Basil (330–79), bishop of Caesarea, fought against the Arian heresy and founded the ideal of monastic community life.

In the Beginning God made the Heaven and the Earth.
Genesis 1:1

It is right that any one beginning to narrate the formation of the world should begin with the good order which reigns in visible things. I am about to speak of the creation of heaven and earth, which was not spontaneous, as some have imagined, but drew its origin from God. What ear is worthy to hear such a tale? How earnestly the soul should prepare itself to receive such high lessons! ... Let us listen then to these words of truth written without the help of the 'enticing words of man's wisdom' by the dictation of the Holy Spirit; words destined to produce not the applause of those who hear them, but the salvation of those who are instructed by them.

'In the beginning God created the heaven and the earth.' I stop struck with admiration at this thought. What shall I first say? Deceived by their inherent atheism it appeared to the philosophers of Greece that nothing governed or ruled the universe, and that everything was ruled by chance. To guard us against this error the writer on the creation, from the very first words, enlightens our understanding with the name of God; 'In the beginning God created.' What a glorious order! He first establishes a beginning, so that it might not be supposed that the world never had a beginning. Then he adds 'Created' to show that which was made was a very small part of the power of the Creator. In the same way that the potter, after having made with equal pains a great number of vessels, has not exhausted either his art or his talent; thus the Maker of the Universe, whose creative power, far from being bounded by one world, could extend to the infinite, needed only the impulse of His will to bring the immensities of the visible world into being. If then the world has a beginning, and if it has been created, enquire who gave it this beginning, and who was the Creator: or rather, in the fear that human reasonings may make you wander from the truth, Moses has anticipated enquiry by engraving in our hearts, as a seal and a safeguard, the awful name of God: 'In the beginning God created' – It is He, beneficent Nature, Goodness without measure, a worthy object of love for all beings endowed with reason, the beauty the most to be desired, the origin of all that exists, the source of life, intellectual light, impenetrable wisdom, it is He who 'in the beginning created heaven and earth.'

Do not then imagine, O man, that the visible world is without a beginning ... If there has been a beginning do not doubt of the end. Of what use to men are geometry – the calculations of arithmetic – the study of solids and far-famed astronomy, this laborious vanity, if those who pursue them imagine that this visible world is co-eternal with the Creator of all things, with God Himself; if they attribute to this limited world, which has a material body, the same glory as to the incomprehensible and invisible nature; if they cannot conceive that a whole, of which the parts are subject to corruption and change, must of necessity end by itself submitting to the fate of its parts? But they have become 'vain in their imaginations and their foolish heart was darkened. Professing themselves to be wise, they became fools.' Some have affirmed that heaven co-exists with God from all eternity; others that it is God Himself without beginning or end, and the cause of the particular arrangement of all things.

One day, doubtless, their terrible condemnation will be the greater for all this worldly wisdom, since they have wilfully shut their eyes to the knowledge of the truth. These men who measure the distances of the stars and describe them, both those of the North, always shining brilliantly in our view, and those of the southern pole visible to the inhabitants of the South, but unknown to us; these men, I say, have discovered all except one thing: the fact that God is the Creator of the universe, and the just Judge.

It appears, indeed, that even before this world an order of things existed of which our mind can form an idea, but of which we can say nothing, because it is too lofty a subject for men who are but beginners and are still babes in knowledge. The birth of the world was preceded by a condition of things suitable for the exercise of supernatural powers, outstripping the limits of time, eternal and infinite. They fill the essence of this invisible world, as Paul teaches us. 'For by him were all things created that are in heaven, and that are in earth, visible and invisible whether they be thrones or dominions or principalities or powers.' To this world at last it was necessary to add a new world, both a school and training place where the souls of men should be taught and a home for beings destined to be born and to die. The first movement is called beginning. 'To do right is the beginning of the good way' ...

To show that the world is a work of art displayed for the beholding of all people; to make them know Him who created it, Moses does say: 'In the beginning, God created.' He does not say 'God worked,' 'God formed,' but 'God created.' Among those who have imagined that the world co-existed with God from all eternity, many have denied that it was created by God, but say that it exists spontaneously, as the shadow of this power. God, they say, is the cause of it, but an involuntary cause, as the body is the cause of the shadow and the flame is the cause of the brightness. It is to correct this error that the prophet states, with so much precision, 'In the beginning God created.'

'In the beginning God made heaven and earth.' By naming the two extremes, he suggests the substance of the whole world, according to heaven the privilege of seniority, and putting earth in the second rank. All intermediate beings were created at the same time as the extremities....

Let us say with Moses 'God created the heavens and the earth.' Let us glorify the supreme Artificer for all that was wisely and skilfully made; by the beauty of visible things let us raise ourselves to Him who is above all beauty; by the grandeur of bodies, sensible and limited in their nature, let us conceive of the infinite Being whose immensity and omnipotence surpass all the efforts of the imagination. Because, although we ignore the nature of created things, the objects which on all sides attract our notice are so marvellous, that the most penetrating mind cannot attain to the knowledge of the least of the phenomena of the world, either to give a suitable explanation of it or to render due praise to the Creator, to Whom belong all glory, all honour and all power world without end. Amen.

Homily 1

Gregory of Nyssa

We needed a God put to death

Gregory of Nyssa (c. 335–95), theologian and bishop of Nazianzen in Cappadocia, helped to ensure the victory of Nicene orthodoxy over the Arian heresy.

'I will stand upon my watch,' saith the venerable Habakkuk (2:1); and I will take my post beside him today on the authority and observation which was given me of the Spirit; and I will look forth, and will observe what shall be said to me. Well, I have taken my stand, and looked forth; and behold a man riding on the clouds and he is very high, and his countenance is as the countenance of an Angel, and his vesture as the brightness of piercing lightning; and he lifts his hand toward the East, and cries with a loud voice. His voice is like the voice of a trumpet; and round about Him is as it were a multitude of the Heavenly Host; and he saith: 'Today is salvation come unto the world, to that which is visible, and to that which is invisible. Christ is risen from the dead, rise ye with Him. Christ is returned again to Himself, return ye. Christ is freed from the tomb, be ye freed from the bond of sin. The gates of hell are opened, and death is destroyed, and the old Adam is put aside, and the New is fulfilled; if any man be in Christ he is a new creature; be ye renewed.'

Thus he speaks; and the rest sing out, as they did before when Christ was manifested to us by His birth on earth, their 'glory to God in the highest, on earth, peace, goodwill among men.'

And with them I also utter the same words among you. And would that I might receive a voice that should rank with the Angel's, and should sound through all the ends of the earth!

The Lord's Passover, the Passover, and again I say the Passover to the honour of the Trinity! This is to us a Feast of feasts and a Solemnity of solemnities as far exalted above all others, not only those which are merely human and creep on the ground, but even those which are of Christ Himself, and are celebrated in His honour, as the Sun is above the stars. Beautiful indeed yesterday was our splendid array, and our illumination, in which both in public and private we associated ourselves, every kind of men, and almost every rank, illuminating the night with our crowded fires, formed after the fashion of that great light, both that with which the heaven above us lights its beacon fires, and that which is above the heavens, amid the angels, and that which is in the Trinity, from which all light derives its being, parted from the undivided light and honoured.

But today's is more beautiful and more illustrious; inasmuch as yesterday's light was a forerunner of the rising of the Great Light, and as it were a kind of rejoicing in preparation for the Festival; but today we are celebrating the Resurrection itself, no longer as an object of expectation, but as having already come to pass, and gathering the whole world unto itself...

We were created that we might be made happy. We were made happy when we were created. We were entrusted with Paradise that we might enjoy life. We received a Commandment that we might obtain a good repute by keeping it; not that God did not know what would take place, but because He had laid down the law of Free Will. We were deceived because we were the objects of envy. We were cast out because we transgressed. We fasted because we refused to fast, being overpowered by the Tree of Knowledge. For the Commandment was ancient, and was a kind of education of our souls and curb of luxury, to which we were reasonably made subject, in order that we might recover by keeping it that which we had lost by not keeping it. We needed an Incarnate God, a God put to death, that we might live. We were put to death together with Him, that we might be cleansed; we rose again with Him because we were put to death with Him; we were glorified with Him, because we rose again with Him.

Many indeed are the miracles of that time: God crucified; the sun darkened and again rekindled; for it was fitting that the creatures should suffer with their Creator; the veil rent; the Blood and Water shed from His Side; the one as from a man, the other as above man; the rocks rent for the Rock's sake; the dead raised for a pledge of the final Resurrection of all men; the Signs at the Sepulchre and after the Sepulchre, which none can worthily celebrate; and yet none of these equal to the Miracle of my salvation. A few drops of Blood recreate the whole world, and become to all men what rennet is to milk, drawing us together and compressing us into unity.

But, O Pascha, great and holy and purifier of all the world – O Word of God and Light and Life and Wisdom and Might – for I rejoice in all Thy names – Offspring and Expression and Signet of the Great Mind; O Word conceived and Man contemplated, Who bearest all things, binding them by the Word of Thy power; receive this discourse.

From Gregory's Second Paschal Oration

Gregory of Nyssa

What have you to say about the Holy Ghost?

People ask: What have you to say about the Holy Ghost? From whence are you bringing in upon us this strange God, of Whom Scripture is silent? ...

Those people then who are angry with us on the ground that we are bringing in a strange or interpolated God, i.e. the Holy Ghost, and who fight so very hard for the letter, should know that they are afraid where no fear is. We have so much confidence in the Deity of the Spirit Whom we adore, that we will begin our teaching concerning His Godhead by fitting to Him the Names which belong to the Trinity, even though some persons may think us too bold. The Father was the True Light which lighteneth every man coming into the world. The Son was the True Light which lighteneth every man coming into the world. The Other Comforter was the True Light which lighteneth every man coming into the world, Was and Was and Was, but Was One Thing. Light thrice repeated; but One Light and One God. This was what David represented to himself long before when he said, 'In Thy Light shall we see Light.' And now we have both seen and proclaim concisely and simply the doctrine of God the Trinity, comprehending out of Light (the Father), Light (the Son), in Light (the Holy Ghost)...

If ever there was a time when the Father was not, then there was a time when the Son was not. If ever there was a time when the Son was not, then there was a time when the Spirit was not. If the One was from the beginning, then the Three were so too. If you throw down the One, I am bold to assert that you do not set up the other Two. For what profit is there in an imperfect Godhead? Or rather, what Godhead can there be if It is not perfect? And how can that be perfect which lacks something of perfection? And surely there is something lacking if it hath not the Holy, and how would it have this if it were without the Spirit? For either holiness is something different from Him, and if so let some one tell me what it is conceived to be; or if it is the same, how is it not from the beginning, as if it were better for God to be at one time imperfect and apart from the Spirit? If He is not from the beginning, He is in the same rank with myself, even though a little before me; for we are both parted from Godhead by time. If He is in the same rank with myself, how can He make me God, or join me with Godhead? ...

What then? Is the Spirit God? Most certainly. Well then, is He Consubstantial? Yes, if He is God...

But, my opponents say, who in ancient or modern times ever worshipped the Spirit? Who ever prayed to Him? Where is it written that we ought to worship Him, or to pray to Him, and whence have you derived this tenet of yours? It is sufficient to say that it is the Spirit in Whom we worship, and in Whom we pray. For Scripture says, 'God is a Spirit, and they that worship Him must worship Him in Spirit and in truth.' And again, 'We know not what we should pray for as we ought; but the Spirit Itself maketh intercession for us with groanings which cannot be uttered; and I will pray with the Spirit and I will pray with the understanding also'; – that is, in the mind and in the Spirit. Therefore to adore or to pray to the Spirit seems to me to be simply Himself offering prayer or adoration to Himself. And what godly or learned man would disapprove of this, because in fact the adoration of One is the adoration of the Three, because of the equality of honour and Deity between the Three? ...

Our argument has now come to its principal point; and I am grieved that a problem that was long dead, and that had given way to faith, is now stirred up afresh; yet it is necessary to stand against these praters, and not to let judgment go by default, when we have the Word on our side, and are pleading the cause of the Spirit. If, say they, there is God and God and God, how is it that there are not Three Gods, or how is it that what is glorified is not a plurality of Principles? Who is it who say this? ... What I have to say in answer to these is as follows: What right have you who worship the Son, even though you have revolted from the Spirit, to call us Tritheists? ... To us there is One God, for the Godhead is One, and all that proceedeth from Him is referred to One, though we believe in Three Persons. For one is not more and another less God; nor is One before and another after; nor are They divided in will or parted in power; nor can you find here any of the qualities of divisible things; but the Godhead is, to speak concisely, undivided in separate Persons; and there is one mingling of Light, as it were of three suns joined to each other. When then we look at the Godhead, or the

First Cause ... that which we conceive is One; but when we look at the Persons in Whom the Godhead dwells, and at Those Who timelessly and with equal glory have their Being from the First Cause – there are Three Whom we worship...

Look at these facts: – Christ is born; the Spirit is His Forerunner. He is baptized; the Spirit bears witness. He is tempted; the Spirit leads Him up. He works miracles; the Spirit accompanies them. He ascends; the Spirit takes His place. What great things are there in the idea of God which are not in His power? What titles which belong to God are not applied to Him, except only Unbegotten and Begotten? For it was needful that the distinctive properties of the Father and the Son should remain peculiar to Them, lest there should be confusion in the Godhead Which brings all things, even disorder itself, into due arrangement and good order.

Indeed I tremble when I think of the abundance of the titles, and how many Names they outrage who fall foul of the Spirit. He is called the Spirit of God, the Spirit of Christ, the Mind of Christ, the Spirit of The Lord, and Himself The Lord, the Spirit of Adoption, of Truth, of Liberty; the Spirit of Wisdom, of Understanding, of Counsel, of Might, of Knowledge, of Godliness, of the Fear of God. For He is the Maker of all these, filling all with His Essence, containing all things, filling the world in His Essence, yet incapable of being comprehended in His power by the world; good, upright, princely, by nature not by adoption; sanctifying, not sanctified; measuring, not measured; shared, not sharing; filling, not filled; containing, not contained; inherited, glorified, reckoned with the Father and the Son; held out as a threat; the Finger of God; fire like God; to manifest, as I take it, His consubstantiality; the Creator-Spirit, Who by Baptism and by Resurrection creates anew; the Spirit That knoweth all things, That teacheth, That bloweth where and to what extent He listeth; That guideth, talketh, sendeth forth, separateth, is angry or tempted; That revealeth, illumineth, quickeneth, or rather is the very Light and Life; That maketh Temples; That deifieth; That perfecteth so as even to anticipate Baptism, yet after Baptism to be sought as a separate gift. That doeth all things that God doeth; divided into fiery tongues; dividing gifts; making Apostles, Prophets, Evangelists, Pastors, and Teachers; understanding manifold, clear, piercing, undefiled, unhindered, which is the same thing as Most wise and varied in His actions; and making all things clear and plain; and of independent power, unchangeable, Almighty, all-seeing, penetrating all spirits that are intelligent, pure, most subtle...

I have very carefully considered this matter in my own mind, and have looked at it in every point of view, in order to find some illustration of this most important subject, but I have been unable to discover any thing on earth with which to compare the nature of the Godhead. For even if I did happen upon some tiny likeness it escaped me for the most part, and left me down below with my example. I picture to myself an eye, a fountain, a river, as others have done before, to see if the first might be analogous to the Father, the second to the Son, and the third to the Holy Ghost. For in these there is no distinction in time, nor are they torn away from their connexion with each other, though they seem to be parted by three personalities. But I was afraid in the first place that I should present a flow in the Godhead, incapable of standing still; and secondly that by this figure a numerical unity would be introduced. For the eye and the spring and the river are numerically one, though in different forms...

Again I thought of the sun and a ray and light. But here again there was a fear lest people should get an idea of composition in the Uncompounded Nature, such as there is in the Sun and the things that are in the Sun. And in the second place lest we should give Essence to the Father but deny Personality to the Others, and make Them only Powers of God, existing in Him and not Personal. For neither the ray nor the light is another sun, but they are only effulgences from the Sun, and qualities of His essence. And lest we should thus, as far as the illustration goes, attribute both Being and Not-being to God, which is even more monstrous. I have also heard that some one has suggested an illustration of the following kind. A ray of the Sun flashing upon a wall and trembling with the movement of the moisture which the beam has taken up in mid air, and then, being checked by the hard body, has set up a strange quivering. For it quivers with many rapid movements, and is not one rather than it is many, nor yet many rather than one; because by the swiftness of its union and separating it escapes before the eye can see it.

But it is not possible for me to make use of even this... Finally, then, it seems best to me to use the guidance of the Holy Ghost, keeping to the end as my genuine comrade and companion the enlightenment which I have received from Him, and passing through this world to persuade all others also to the best of my power to worship Father, Son, and Holy Ghost, the One Godhead and Power. To Him belongs all glory and honour and might for ever and ever. Amen.

From *The Fifth Theological Oration: On the Holy Spirit*

Gregory of Nyssa

The war of heresy surrounds us
A funeral oration for Melitus, bishop of Antioch.

The number of the Apostles has been enlarged for us by this our late Apostle being reckoned among their company. These Holy ones have drawn to themselves one of like conversation; those athletes a fellow athlete; those crowned ones another crowned like them; the pure in heart one chaste in soul: those ministers of the Word another herald of that Word. Most blessed, indeed, is our Father for this his joining the Apostolic band and his departure to Christ. We are to be pitied for the unseasonableness of our orphaned condition. For him, indeed, better it was by his departure hence to be with Christ, but it was a grievous thing for us to be severed from his fatherly guidance. Behold, it is a time of need for counsel; and our counsellor is silent. War, the war of heresy, surrounds us, and our leader is no more. The general body of the Church labours under disease, and we find not the physician. Oh! that it were possible I could nerve my weakness, and rising to the full proportions of our loss, burst out with a voice of lamentation adequate to the greatness of the distress, as these excellent preachers of yours have done, who have bewailed with loud voice the misfortune that has befallen them in this loss of their father. But what can I do? How can I force my tongue to the service of the theme, thus heavily weighted, and shackled, as it were, by this calamity? How shall I open my mouth thus subdued to speechlessness? How shall I give free utterance to a voice now habitually sinking to the pathetic tone of lamentations? How can I lift up the eyes of my soul, veiled as I am with this darkness of misfortune? Who will pierce for me this deep dark cloud of grief, and light up again, as out of a clear sky, the bright ray of peace? From what quarter will that ray shine forth, now that our star has set?... Lend me, oh lend me, my brethren, the tear of sympathy. When you were glad we shared your gladness. Repay us, therefore, this sad recompense. 'Rejoice with them that do rejoice.' This we have done. It is for you to return it by 'weeping with them that weep'...

To you, the city of Antioch, I address my words. I pity you for this sudden reversal. How has your beauty been despoiled! How have you been robbed of your ornaments! How suddenly has the flower faded! 'Verily the grass withereth and the flower thereof falleth away'...

You have heard the whole series of his labours, what he was in the first, what in the middle, and what in the last. I deem it superfluous to repeat what has been so well described. Yet it may not be out of place to add just so much as this. When that Church, so sound in the faith, at the first beheld the man, she saw features truly formed after the image of God, she saw love welling forth, she saw grace poured around his lips, a consummate perfection of humility beyond which it is impossible to conceive any thing further, a gentleness like that of David, the understanding of Solomon, a goodness like that of Moses, a strictness as of Samuel, a chastity as of Joseph, the skill of a Daniel, a zeal for the faith such as was in the great Elijah, a purity of body like that of the lofty-minded John, an unsurpassable love as of Paul. She saw the concurrence of so many excellences in one soul, and, thrilled with a blessed affection, she loved him, her own bridegroom, with a pure and virtuous passion...

Up to this point how bright and happy is our narrative. What a blessed thing it were with this to bring our sermon to an end. But after these things what follows? 'Call for the mourning women,' as says the prophet Jeremiah ... When I see the confusion of heresy, this confusion is Babylon, and when I see the flood of trials that pours in upon us from this confusion, I say that these are 'the waters of Babylon by which we sit down, and weep' because there is no one to guide us over them ... But let me have all tears wiped away, for I feel that I am indulging more than is right in this womanish sorrow for our loss.

Our Bridegroom has not been taken from us. He stands in our midst, though we see him not. The Priest is within the holy place. He is entered into that within the veil, whither our forerunner Christ has entered for us. He has left behind him the curtain of the flesh. No longer does he pray to the type or shadow of the things in heaven, but he looks upon the very embodiment of these realities. No longer through a glass darkly does he intercede with God, but face to face he intercedes with Him... 'Precious in the sight of the Lord is the death' of such a man, or rather it is not death, but the breaking of bonds, as it is said, 'Thou hast broken my bonds asunder.' Simeon has been let depart. He has been freed from the bondage of the body ... He has entered upon the land of promise, and holds high converse with God upon the mount. He has loosed the sandal of his soul, that with the pure step of thought he may set foot upon that holy land where there is the Vision of God. Having therefore, brethren, this consolation, do ye, who are conveying the bones of our Joseph to the place of blessing, listen to the exhortation of Paul: 'Sorrow not as others who have no hope.' Speak to the people there; relate the glorious tale; speak of the incredible wonder, how the people in their myriads, so densely crowded together as to look like a sea of heads, became all one continuous body, and like some watery flood surged around the procession bearing his remains. Tell them how the fair David distributed himself, in divers ways and manners, among innumerable ranks of people, and danced before that ark in the midst of men of the same and of different language...

Let it be added to your narration how the Emperor showed in his countenance his sorrow for this misfortune, and rose from his throne, and how the whole city joined the funeral procession of the Saint. Moreover console each other with the following words; it is a good medicine that Solomon has for sorrow; for he bids wine be given to the sorrowful; saying this to us, the labourers in the vineyard: 'Give,' therefore, 'your wine to those that are in sorrow,' not that wine which produces drunkenness, plots against the senses, and destroys the body, but such as gladdens the heart, the wine which the Prophet recommends when he says: 'Wine maketh glad the heart of man.' Pledge each other in that liquor undiluted and with the unstinted goblets of the word, that thus our grief may be turned to joy and gladness, by the grace of the Only-begotten Son of God, through Whom be glory to God, even the Father, for ever and ever. Amen.

Ambrose

There is nothing therefore for you to fear
Ambrose (340–97) was bishop of Milan and a hymn-writer. The following extract is from his sermon against Auxentius on the imperial decree ordering the giving up of the basilicas.

I see that you are unusually disturbed, and that you are closely watching me. I wonder what the reason is? Is it that you saw or heard that I had received an imperial order at the hands of the tribunes, to the effect that I was to go hence, whither I would, and that all who wished might follow me? Were you afraid that I should desert the Church and forsake you in fear for my own safety? But you could note the message I sent, that the wish to desert the Church had never entered my mind; for I feared the Lord of the universe more than an earthly emperor; and if force were to drag me from the Church, my body indeed could be driven out, but not my mind. I was ready, if he were to do what royal power is wont to do, to undergo the fate a priest has to bear.

Why, then, are you disturbed? I will never willingly desert you, though if force is used, I cannot meet it. I shall be able to grieve, to weep, to groan; against weapons, soldiers, Goths, my tears are my weapons, for these are a priest's defence. I ought not, I cannot resist in any other way; but to fly and forsake the Church is not my way; lest any one should suppose I did so from fear of some heavier punishment. You yourselves know that I am wont to show respect to our emperors, but not to yield to them, to offer myself freely to punishment, and not to fear what is prepared for me.

Would that I were sure the Church would never be given over to heretics. Gladly would I go to the Emperor's palace, if this but fitted the office of a priest, and so hold our discussion in the palace rather than the church. But in the consistory Christ is not wont to be the accused but the judge. Who will deny that the cause of faith should be pleaded in the church? If any one has confidence let him come hither; let him not seek the judgment of the Emperor, which already shows its bias, which clearly proves by the law that is passed that he is against the faith; neither let him seek the expected goodwill of certain people who want to stand well with both sides. I will not act in such a way as to give any one the chance of making money out of a wrong to Christ.

The soldiers around, the clash of the arms wherewith the church is surrounded, do not alarm my faith, but they disquiet me from fear that in keeping me here you might meet with some danger to your lives. For I have learnt by now not to be afraid, but I do begin to have more fear for you. Allow, I beg you, your bishop to meet his foes. We have an adversary who assails us, for our adversary 'the devil goeth about, as a roaring lion, seeking whom he may devour,' as the Apostle said. He has received, no doubt, the power to tempt in this way, in case I might perhaps by the wounds of my body be drawn away from the earnestness of my faith.

When it was suggested that I should give up the vessels of the Church, I gave the following answer: I will willingly give up whatever of my own property is demanded, whether it is estates, or house, or gold, or silver – anything, in fact, which is in my power. But I cannot take anything away from the temple of God; nor can I give up what I have received to guard and not to give up. In doing this I am acting for the Emperor's good, for it would neither be right for me to give it up, nor for him to receive it. Let him listen to the words of a free-spoken bishop, and if he wishes to do what is best for himself, let him cease to do wrong to Christ.

These words are full of humility, and as I think of that spirit which a bishop ought to show towards the Emperor. But since 'our contest is not against flesh and blood,' but also 'against spiritual wickedness in high places,' that tempter the devil makes the struggle harder by means of his servants, and thinks to make trial of me by the wounds of my flesh. I know, my brethren, that these wounds which we receive for Christ's sake are not wounds that destroy life, but rather extend it. Allow, I pray, the contest to take place. It is for you to be the spectators. Reflect that if a city has an athlete, or one skilled in some other noble art, it is eager to bring him forward for a contest. Why do you refuse to do in a more important matter what you are wont to wish in smaller affairs? He fears not weapons nor barbarians who fears not death, and is not held fast by any pleasures of the flesh.

And indeed if the Lord has appointed me for this struggle, in vain have you kept sleepless watch so many nights and days. The will of Christ will be fulfilled. For our Lord Jesus is almighty, this is our faith: and so what He wills to be done will be fulfilled, and it is not for us to thwart the divine purpose. 'To depart and be with Christ is much better, though to abide in the flesh is more needful for you.' There is nothing therefore for you to fear, beloved brethren. For I know that whatever I may suffer, I shall suffer for Christ's sake. And I have read that I ought not to fear those that can kill the flesh. And I have heard One Who says: 'He that loseth his life for My sake shall find it.'

John Chrysostom

Is there anyone who is a devout lover of God?

John Chrysostom (347–407) was the greatest of the Greek Fathers of the Church. This Easter sermon was preached in about 400, while he was Pastor of Constantinople.

Is there anyone who is a devout lover of God?
Let them enjoy this beautiful bright festival!
Is there anyone who is a grateful servant?
Let them rejoice and enter into the joy of their Lord!

Are there any weary with fasting?
Let them now receive their wages!
If any have toiled from the first hour,
let them receive their due reward;
If any have come after the third hour,
let him with gratitude join in the Feast!
And he that arrived after the sixth hour,
let him not doubt; for he too shall sustain no loss.
And if any delayed until the ninth hour,
let him not hesitate; but let him come too.
And he who arrived only at the eleventh hour,
let him not be afraid by reason of his delay.

For the Lord is gracious and receives the last even as the first.
He gives rest to him that comes at the eleventh hour,
as well as to him that toiled from the first.
To this one He gives, and upon another He bestows.
He accepts the works as He greets the endeavour.
The deed He honours and the intention He commends.

Let us all enter into the joy of the Lord!
First and last alike receive your reward;
rich and poor, rejoice together!
Sober and slothful, celebrate the day!

You that have kept the fast, and you that have not,
rejoice today for the Table is richly laden!
Feast royally on it, the calf is a fatted one.
Let no one go away hungry. Partake, all, of the cup of faith.
Enjoy all the riches of His goodness!

Let no one grieve at his poverty,
for the universal kingdom has been revealed.
Let no one mourn that he has fallen again and again;
for forgiveness has risen from the grave.
Let no one fear death, for the Death of our Saviour has set us
    free.
He has destroyed it by enduring it.

He destroyed Hades when He descended into it.
He put it into an uproar even as it tasted of His flesh.
Isaiah foretold this when he said,
'You, O Hell, have been troubled by encountering Him below.'

Hell was in an uproar because it was done away with.
It was in an uproar because it is mocked.
It was in an uproar, for it is destroyed.
It is in an uproar, for it is annihilated.
It is in an uproar, for it is now made captive.
Hell took a body, and discovered God.
It took earth, and encountered Heaven.
It took what it saw, and was overcome by what it did not see.
O death, where is thy sting?
O Hades, where is thy victory?

Christ is Risen, and you, o death, are annihilated!
Christ is Risen, and the evil ones are cast down!
Christ is Risen, and the angels rejoice!
Christ is Risen, and life is liberated!
Christ is Risen, and the tomb is emptied of its dead;
for Christ having risen from the dead,
is become the first-fruits of those who have fallen asleep.

To Him be Glory and Power forever and ever. Amen!

John Chrysostom

Rejoice in all things which befall us

Let us not be disturbed, neither dismayed, when trials befall us. For if the gold refiner sees how long he ought to leave the piece of gold in the furnace, and when he ought to draw it out, and does not allow it to remain in the fire until it is destroyed and burnt up: much more does God understand this, and when He sees that we have become more pure, He releases us from our trials so that we may not be overthrown and cast down by the multiplication of our evils. Let us then not be faint-hearted, when some unexpected thing befalls us; for He does this for a useful purpose and with a view to benefit those who are tried.

On this account a certain wise man admonishes us saying 'My Son, if thou come to serve the Lord prepare thy soul for temptation, set thy heart aright and constantly endure and make not haste in time of trouble'; 'yield to Him' he says, 'in all things,' for He knoweth exactly when it is right to pluck us out of the furnace of evil. We ought therefore everywhere to yield to Him and always to give thanks, and to bear all things contentedly, whether He bestows benefits or chastisement upon us, for this also is a species of benefit. For the doctor, not only when he bathes and nourishes the patient and conducts him into pleasant gardens, but also when he uses the knife, is a doctor all the same: and a father not only when he caresses his son, but also when he expels him from his house, and when he chides and scourges him, is a father all the same, no less than when he praises him. Knowing therefore that God is more tenderly loving than all doctors, do not enquire too curiously concerning His treatment nor demand an account of it from Him, but whether He is pleased to let us go free or whether He punishes, let us offer ourselves for either alike; for He seeks by means of each to lead us back to health, and to communion with Himself, and He knows our several needs, and what is expedient for each one, and how and in what manner we ought to be saved, and along that path He leads us. Let us then follow wherever He bids us, and let us not too carefully consider whether He commands us to go by a smooth and easy path, or by a difficult and rugged one: as in the case of this paralytic. It was one sort of benefit indeed that his soul should be purged by the long duration of his suffering, being delivered to the fiery trial of affliction as to a kind of furnace; but it was another benefit no less than this that

God was present with him in the midst of the trials, and afforded him great consolation. He it was who strengthened him, and upheld him, and stretched forth a hand to him, and suffered him not to fall. But when you hear that it was God Himself do not deprive the paralytic of his reward of praise, neither him nor any other man who is tried and yet steadfastly endures.

For even if we are infinitely wise, even if we are mightier and stronger than all men, yet in the absence of His grace we shall not be able to withstand even the most ordinary temptation. And why do I speak of such insignificant and abject beings as we are? For even if one were a Paul, or a Peter, or a James, or a John, yet if he should be deprived of the divine help he would easily be put to shame, overthrown, and laid prostrate. And on behalf of these I will read you the words of Christ Himself: for He saith to Peter 'Behold Satan hath asked to have you that he may sift you as wheat, but I have prayed for thee that thy faith fail not.' What is the meaning of 'sift'? To turn and twist, and shake and stir and shatter, and worry, which is what takes place in the case of things which are winnowed: but He says have restrained him, knowing that you are not able to endure the trial, for the expression 'that thy faith fail not' is the utterance of one who signifies that if he had permitted it his faith would have failed. Now if Peter who was such a fervent lover of Christ and exposed his life for Him countless times and sprang into the foremost rank in the Apostolic band, and was pronounced blessed by his Master, and called Peter on this account because he kept a firm and inflexible hold of the faith, would have been carried away and fallen from profession if Christ had permitted the devil to try him as much as he desired, what other man will be able to stand, apart from His help?

Therefore also Paul saith 'But God is faithful, who will not suffer you to be tempted above that ye are able, but will with the temptation also make the way of escape that ye may be able to bear it.' For not only does He say that He does not suffer a trial to be inflicted beyond our strength, but is in proportion to our strength, and He is present carrying us through it, and bracing us up, if only we ourselves first of all contribute the means which are at our disposal, such as zeal, hope in Him, thanksgiving, endurance, patience. For not only in the dangers which are beyond our strength, but in those which are proportioned to it, we need the divine assistance, if we are to make a brave stand; for elsewhere also it is said 'even as the sufferings of Christ abound to us, even so our comfort also aboundeth through Christ, that we may be able to comfort those who are in any trouble, by the comfort wherewith we ourselves are comforted of God.'

So then he who comforted this man is the same who permitted the trial to be inflicted upon him. And now observe after the cure what tenderness He displays. For He did not leave him and depart, but having found him in the temple he saith 'behold! thou art made whole; sin no more lest some worse thing happen unto thee.' For had He permitted the punishment because He hated him He would not have released him, He would not have provided for his future safety: but the expression 'lest some worse thing happen unto thee' is the utterance of one who would check coming evils beforehand. He put an end to the disease, but did not put an end to the struggle: He expelled the infirmity but did not expel the dread of it, so that the benefit which had been wrought might remain unmoved. This is the part of a tender-hearted doctor, not only to put an end to present pains, but to provide for future security, which also Christ did, bracing up his soul by the recollection of past events. For after the things which distress us have left, the recollection of them often departs with them. He wishing it to abide continually, saith 'sin no more lest some worse thing happen unto thee' ...

See moreover He makes a second proof of His power of forgiving sins. For to forgive sins is a very much greater act than to heal the body, greater in proportion as the soul is greater than the body. For as paralysis is a disease of the body, even so sin is a disease of the soul: but although this is the greater it is not palpable: whereas the other although it be less is manifest. Since then He is about to use the less for a demonstration of the greater, proving that He acted thus on account of their weakness, and by way of condescension to their feeble condition, He says 'whether is easier? to say thy sins are forgiven thee or to say arise and walk?' For what reason then should He address Himself to the lesser act on their account? Because that which is manifest presents the proof in a more distinct form. Therefore He did not enable the man to rise until He had said to them 'But that ye may know that the Son of man hath power on earth to forgive sins, (then saith He to the sick of the palsy) arise and walk:' as if He had said: forgiveness of sins is indeed a greater sign: but for your sakes I add the less also since this seems to you to be a proof of the other. For as in another case when He praised the centurion for saying 'speak the word only and my servant shall be healed: for I also say to this man go and he goeth and to the other come and he cometh' He confirmed promising that which belongs only to the Father. He having upbraided and accused them and proved by His deeds that He did not blaspheme supplied us with indisputable evidence that He could do the same things as the Father who begat Him. Observe at least the manner in which He pleases to establish the fact that what belongs to the Father only, belongs also to Himself: for He did not simply enable the paralytic to get up, but also said 'but that ye may know that the Son of man hath power on earth to forgive sins:' thus it was his endeavour and earnest desire to prove above all things that He had the same authority as the Father.

Let us then beseech God that these lessons may abide immoveably in our heart, and let us contribute zeal on our side, and constantly meet in this place. For in this way we shall preserve the truths which have been formerly spoken, and we shall add others to our store; and if any of them slip from our memory through the lapse of time we shall easily be able to recover them by the aid of continual teaching. And not only will the doctrines abide sound and uncorrupt but our course of life will have the benefit of much diligent care and we shall be able to pass through this present state of existence with pleasure and cheerfulness. For whatever kind of suffering is oppressing our soul when we come here will easily be got rid of: seeing that now also Christ is present, and he who approaches Him with faith will readily receive healing from Him.

Suppose some one is struggling with perpetual poverty, and at a loss for necessary food, and often goes to bed hungry, if he has come in here, and heard Paul saying that he passed his time in hunger and thirst and nakedness, and that he experienced this not on one or two or three days, but constantly.

Or another having been subjected to false accusation has acquired a bad reputation with the public, and this is continually vexing and gnawing his soul: he enters this place and hears 'Blessed are ye when men shall reproach you and say all manner of evil against you falsely: rejoice ye and be exceeding glad for great is your reward in Heaven:' then he will lay aside all despondency and receive every kind of pleasure: for it is written 'leap for joy, and be exceeding glad when men cast out your name as evil.' In this manner then God comforts those that are evil spoken of, and them that speak evil He puts in fear after another manner saying 'every evil word which men shall speak they shall give an account thereof whether it be good or evil.'

Another perhaps has lost a little daughter or a son, or a relative, and he also having come here listens to Paul groaning over this present life and longing to see that which is to come, and oppressed by his sojourn in this world, and he will go away with a sufficient remedy for his grief when he has heard him say 'Now concerning them that are asleep I would not have you ignorant, brethren, that ye sorrow not even as others who have no hope.' He did not say concerning 'the dying,' but 'concerning them that are asleep,' proving that death is a sleep. As then if we see any one sleeping we are not disturbed or distressed, expecting that he will certainly get up: even so when we see any one dead, let us not be disturbed or dejected for this also is a sleep, a longer one indeed, but still a sleep. By calling it sleep He comforted the mourners and overthrew the accusation of the unbelievers. If you mourn immoderately over him who has departed you will be like that unbeliever who has no hope of a resurrection. He indeed does well to mourn, inasmuch as he cannot exercise any spiritual wisdom concerning things to come: but thou who hast received such strong proofs concerning the future life, why dost thou sink into the same weakness with him? Therefore it is written 'now concerning them that are asleep we would not have you ignorant that ye sorrow not even as others who have no hope' ...

And you have a convincing example in the case of Job, and of the Apostle, who having for God's sake despised the troubles of this world, obtained the everlasting blessings. Let us then be trustful and in all things which befall us let us rejoice and give thanks to the merciful God, that we may pass through this present life with serenity, and obtain the blessings to come, by the grace and loving kindness of our Lord Jesus Christ to whom be glory, honour and might always, now and ever, world without end. Amen.

From *The Homily on the Paralytic Let Down Through the Roof*

John Chrysostom

Eulogy for the martyr Ignatius

Ignatius, a second-century archbishop of Antioch, was martyred in Rome.

Sumptuous and splendid entertainers give frequent and constant entertainments, alike to display their own wealth, and to show goodwill to their acquaintance. So also the grace of the Spirit, affording us a proof of his own power, and displaying much goodwill towards the friends of God, sets before us successively and constantly the tables of the martyrs...

He presided over the Church among us nobly, and with such carefulness as Christ desires. For that which Christ declared to be the highest standard and rule of the Episcopal office, did this man display by his deeds. For having heard Christ saying, 'The good shepherd layeth down his life for the sheep,' with all courage he did lay it down for the sheep.

He held true converse with the apostles and drank of spiritual fountains. What kind of person then is it likely that he was who had been reared, and who had everywhere held converse with them, and had shared with them truths both lawful and unlawful to utter, and who seemed to them worthy of so great a dignity? The time again came on, which demanded courage; and a soul which despised all things present, glowed with Divine love, and valued things unseen before the things which are seen; and he lay aside the flesh with as much ease as one would put off a garment. What then shall we speak of first? The teaching of the apostles which he gave proof of throughout, or his indifference to this present life, or the strictness of his virtue, with which he administered his rule over the Church; which shall we first call to mind? The martyr or the bishop or the apostle. For the grace of the spirit having woven a threefold crown, thus bound it on his holy head, yea rather a manifold crown. For if any one will consider them carefully, he will find each of the crowns, blossoming with other crowns for us...

For now, by the grace of God, there is no danger for bishops, but deep peace on all sides, and we all enjoy a calm, since the Word of piety has been extended to the ends of the world, and our rulers keep the faith with strictness. But then there was nothing of this, but wherever any one might look, precipices and pitfalls, and wars, and fightings, and dangers; both rulers, and kings, and people and cities and nations, and men at home and abroad, laid snares for the faithful.

And this was not the only serious thing, but also the fact that many of the believers themselves, inasmuch as they tasted for the first time strange doctrines, stood in need of great indulgence, and were still in a somewhat feeble condition and were often upset. And this was a thing which used to grieve the teachers, no less than the fightings without, nay rather much more. For the fightings without, and the plottings, afforded much pleasure to them on account of the hope of the rewards awaiting them.

On this account the apostles returned from the presence of the Sanhedrin rejoicing because they had been beaten; and Paul cries out, saying: 'I rejoice in my sufferings,' and he glories in his afflictions everywhere. But the wounds of those at home, and the failings of the brethren, do not suffer them to breathe again, but always, like some most heavy yoke, continually oppress and afflict the neck of their soul. Hear at least how Paul, thus rejoicing in sufferings, is bitterly pained about these. 'For who, saith he, is weak, and I am not weak? who is offended, and I burn not?' and again, 'I fear lest when I come I shall find you not such as I would, and I be found of you such as ye would not,' and a little afterwards, 'Lest when I come again to you, God humble me, and I shall mourn many of those who have sinned before, and have not repented, of their uncleanness, and wantonness, and fornication which they have committed.' And throughout thou seest that he is in tears and lamentations on account of members of the household, and evermore fearing and trembling for the believers...

For if the oversight of the Church now furnishes much weariness and work to those who govern it, consider how double and treble and manifold was the work then, when there were dangers and fighting and snares, and fear continually. It is not possible to set forth in words the difficulty which those saints then encountered, but he alone will know it who comes to it by experience.

Not only to-day, therefore, but every day let us go forth to him, plucking spiritual fruits from him. For it is, it is possible for him who comes hither with faith to gather the fruit of many good things ... Wherefore I beseech you all, if any is in despondency, if in disease, if under insult, if in any other circumstance of this life, if in the depth of sins, let him come hither with faith, and he will lay aside all those things, and will return with much joy, having procured a lighter conscience from the sight alone. But more, it is not only necessary that those who are in affliction should come hither, but if any one be in cheerfulness, in glory, in power, in much assurance towards God, let not this man despise the benefit. For coming hither and beholding this saint, he will keep these noble possessions unmoved, persuading his own soul to be moderate by the recollection of this man's mighty deeds, and not suffering his conscience by the mighty deeds to be lifted up to any self conceit. And it is no slight thing for those in prosperity not to be puffed up at their good fortune, but to know how to bear their prosperity with moderation, so that the treasure is serviceable to all, the resting place is suitable, for the fallen, in order that they may escape from their temptations, for the fortunate, that their success may remain secure, for those in weakness indeed, that they may return to health, and for the healthy, that they may not fall into weakness. Considering all which things, let us prefer this way of spending our time, to all delight, all pleasure, in order that rejoicing at once, and profiting, we may be able to become partakers with these saints, both of their dwelling and of their home ... through the grace and loving kindness of our Lord Jesus Christ, with whom be glory to the Father with the Holy Spirit, now and always forever and ever, amen.

From *Homilies on Ignatius*

Augustine

Renewal does not happen in one moment of conversion
Augustine (354–430) was bishop of Hippo in North Africa and is revered as a pre-eminent theologian by Protestants and Catholics alike.

Renewal does not happen in one moment of conversion ... It is one thing to throw off a fever, another to recover from the weakness which the fever leaves behind it; it is one thing to remove from the body a missile stuck in it, another to heal the wound it made with a complete cure. The first stage of the cure is to remove the cause of the debility, and this is done by pardoning all sins; the second stage is curing the debility itself, and this is done gradually by making steady progress in the renewal of this image. These two stages are seen in Psalm 103:3, where we read, 'who forgives all your sins,' which happens at baptism, 'and heals all your diseases,' which happens by daily advances while the image is being renewed. The apostle Paul speaks about this quite clearly in 2 Corinthians 4:16: 'Though outwardly we are wasting away, yet inwardly we are being renewed day by day.'

From *Sermons*, Psalm 103

Augustine

In fearing not to fear, and in not fearing to fear
The following is an extract from a sermon preached on a Festival of Martyrs.

> *Be not afraid of them that kill the body.*
> Matthew 10:28

The Divine oracles which have just been read teach us in fearing not to fear, and in not fearing to fear. Ye observed when the Holy Gospel was being read, that our Lord God before He died for us, would have us to be firm; and this by admonishing us 'not' to fear, and withal to fear. For he said, 'Fear not them which kill the body, but are not able to kill the soul.' See where He advised us not to fear. See now where He advised us to fear. 'But,' said he, 'fear Him who hath power to destroy both body and soul in hell.' Let us fear therefore, that we may not fear. Fear seems to be linked to cowardice. It seems to be the character of the weak, not the strong. But see what said the Scripture, 'The fear of the Lord is the hope of strength.' Let us then fear, that we may not fear; that is, let us fear prudently, that we may not fear vainly. The holy martyrs on the occasion of whose solemnity this lesson was read out of the Gospel, in fearing, feared not; because in fearing God, they did not regard men.

For what need a man fear from man? And what is that whereby one man should cause another fear, since both of them are men? ... For he is but a man, and he threatens another man, a creature, another creature; only the one puffed up under his Creator's eye, and the other fleeing for refuge to the same Creator.

Let the stout Martyr then, as he stands a man before another man, say; 'I do not fear, because I fear.' Thou canst not do what thou art threatening, unless He will; but what He threateneth, none can hinder Him from doing ... Behold (I am using the words of a Martyr), behold, I say, not even on account of my body do I fear thy threats. My body indeed is subject to thy power; but even the hairs of my head are numbered by my Creator. Why should I fear lest I lose my body, who cannot even lose a hair? How shall he not have a care of my body, to whom my meanest things are so well known? This body which may be wounded and slain will for a time be ashes, but it will be for ever immortal. But to whom shall this be? To whom shall the body be restored for life eternal, even though it have been slain, destroyed, and scattered to the winds? To whom shall it be so restored? To him who has not been afraid to lay down his own life, since he does not fear, lest his body should be slain...

The body is dead without the soul, and that the soul is dead without God. Every man without God hath a dead soul. Thou dost bewail the dead: bewail the sinner rather, bewail rather the ungodly man, bewail the unbeliever. It is written, 'The mourning for the dead is seven days; for a fool and an ungodly man all the days of his life.' What, is there no of Christian compassion in thee; that thou mournest for a body from which the soul is gone, and mournest not for the soul, from which God is departed? Let the Martyr remembering this make answer to him that threatens him, 'Why dost thou force me to deny Christ?' Wouldest thou then force me to deny the truth? And if I will not, what wilt thou do? Thou wilt assault my body, that my soul shall depart from it; but this same soul of mine has its body only for the soul's sake. It is not so foolish or unwise. Thou wouldest wound my body; but wouldest thou, that through fear lest thou shouldest wound my body, and my soul, should depart from it, I should wound mine own soul, and my God should depart from it? Fear not then, O Martyr, the sword of thy executioner; fear only thine own tongue, lest thou do execution upon thine own self, and slay, not thy body, but thy soul. Fear for thy soul, lest it die in hell-fire.

Therefore said the Lord, 'Who hath power to slay both body and soul in hell-fire.' How? when the ungodly shall be cast into hell-fire, will his body and his soul burn there? Everlasting punishment will be the death of the body; the absence of God will be the death of the soul. Wouldest thou know what the death of the soul is? Understand the Prophet who said, 'Let the ungodly be taken away, that he may not see the glory of the Lord.' Let the soul then fear its proper death, and not fear the death of its body. Because if it fear its own death, and so live in its God, by not offending and thrusting Him away from him, it will be found worthy to receive its body again at the end; not unto everlasting punishment, as the ungodly, but unto life eternal, as the righteous. By fearing this death, and loving that life, did the Martyrs, in hope of the promises of God, and in contempt of the threats of persecutors, attain themselves to be crowned with God, and have left to us the celebration of these solemnities.

Augustine

Our hearts are restless until they find their rest in Thee

Come unto me, all ye that labour and are heavy laden, and I will give you rest.

Matthew 11:28

It seems strange to some, Brethren, when they hear the Lord say, 'Come unto Me, all ye that labour and are heavy laden, and I will refresh you. Take my yoke upon you and learn of Me, for I am meek and lowly in heart, and ye shall find rest unto your souls. For My yoke is easy and My burden is light.' And they consider that they who have fearlessly bowed their necks to this yoke, and have with much submission taken this burden upon their shoulders, are tossed about and exercised by so great difficulties in the world, that they seem not to be called from labour to rest, but from rest to labour rather; since the Apostle also saith, 'All who will live godly in Christ Jesus, shall suffer persecution.' So one will say, 'How is the yoke easy, and the burden light,' when to bear this yoke and burden is nothing else, but to live godly in Christ? And how is it said, 'Come unto Me, all ye that labour and are heavy laden, and I will refresh you'? and not rather said, 'Come ye who are at ease and idle, that ye may labour.' For so he found those men idle and at ease, whom he hired into the vineyard, that they might bear the heat of the day. And we hear the Apostle under that easy yoke and light burden say, 'In all things approving ourselves as the ministers of God, in much patience, in afflictions, in necessities, in distresses, in stripes,' etc., and in another place of the same Epistle, 'Of the Jews five times received I forty stripes save one. Thrice was I beaten with rods, once was I stoned, thrice have I suffered shipwreck, a night and a day have I been in the deep:' and the rest of the perils, which may be enumerated indeed, but endured they cannot be but by the help of the Holy Spirit.

All these grievous and heavy trials which he mentioned, did he very frequently and abundantly sustain; but in very deed the Holy Spirit was with him in the wasting of the outward man, to renew the inner man from day to day, and by the taste of spiritual rest in the affluence of the delights of God to soften down by the hope of future blessedness all present hardships, and to alleviate all heavy trials. Lo, how sweet a yoke of Christ did he bear, and how light a burden; so that he could say that all those hard and grievous sufferings at the recital of which as just above for us, shall Himself deliver us from sin. Let us not despair of ourselves, brethren...

God is loving to man, and loving in no small measure. For say not, 'I have committed fornication and adultery: I have done dreadful things, and not once only, but often: will He forgive? Will He grant pardon?' Hear what the Psalmist says: 'How great is the multitude of Thy goodness, O Lord!' Thine accumulated offences surpass not the multitude of God's mercies: thy wounds surpass not the great Physician's skill. Only give thyself up in faith: tell the Physician thine ailment: say thou also, like David: 'I said, I will confess me my sin unto the Lord': and the same shall be done in thy case, which he says forthwith: 'And thou forgavest the wickedness of my heart.'

Wouldest thou see the loving-kindness of God, O thou that art lately come to the catechising? Wouldest thou see the loving-kindness of God, and the abundance of His long-suffering? Come with me now to those who were saved by repentance. But perhaps even among women some one will say, 'I have committed fornication, and adultery, I have defiled my body by excesses of all kinds: is there salvation for me?' Turn thine eyes, O woman, upon Rahab, and look thou also for salvation; for if she who had been openly and publicly a harlot was saved by repentance, is not she who on some one occasion before receiving grace committed fornication to be saved by repentance and fasting? For inquire how she was saved: this only she said: 'For your God is God in heaven and upon earth.' 'Your God'; for her own she did not dare to say, because of her wanton life. And if you wish to receive Scriptural testimony of her having been saved, you have it written in the Psalms: 'I will make mention of Rahab and Babylon among them that know me.' O the greatness of God's loving-kindness, making mention even of harlots in the Scriptures. There is then in the case of the salvation which is ushered in by repentance...

Take heed lest without reason thou mistrust the power of repentance. Wouldst thou know what power repentance has? Wouldst thou know the strong weapon of salvation, and learn what the force of confession is? Hezekiah by means of confession routed a hundred and eighty-five thousand of his enemies. A great thing verily was this, but still small in comparison with what remains to be told: the same king by repentance obtained the recall of a divine sentence which had already gone forth. For when he had fallen sick, Isaiah said to him, 'Set thine house in order; for thou shalt die, and not live.' What expectation remained, what hope of recovery, when the Prophet said, 'for thou shalt die'? Yet Hezekiah did not desist from repentance; but remembering what is written, 'When thou shalt turn and lament, then shalt thou be saved,' he turned to the wall, and from his bed lifting his mind to heaven, for thickness of walls is no hindrance to prayers sent up with devotion, he said, 'Remember me, O Lord, for it is sufficient for my healing that Thou remember me. Thou art not subject to times, but art Thyself the giver of the law of life. For our life depends not on a nativity, nor on a conjunction of stars, as some idly talk; but both of life and its duration. Then art Thyself the Lawgiver according to Thy Will.' And he, who could not hope to live because of the prophetic sentence, had fifteen years added to his life.

The Lord is loving unto man, and swift to pardon, but slow to punish. Let no man therefore despair of his own salvation. Peter, the leading Apostle, denied the Lord three times in front of a servant girl: but he repented, and wept bitterly. Now weeping shows the repentance of the heart: and therefore he not only received forgiveness for his denial, but also retained his apostolic position.

Having therefore, brethren, many examples of those who have sinned and repented and been saved, do ye also heartily make confession unto the Lord, that ye may both receive the forgiveness of your former sins, and be counted worthy of the heavenly gift, and inherit the heavenly kingdom with all the saints in Christ Jesus; to Whom is the glory for ever and ever. Amen.

Cyril of Alexandria

The Son of God was begot of the very essence of the Father
To the Most Pious and Devout fellow minister Nestorius Cyril and the co-assembled Synod in Alexandria from out of the Province of Egypt, greeting in the Lord.

Whereas our Saviour saith in plain terms, 'He that loveth father or mother above Me is not worthy of Me, and he that loveth son or daughter above Me is not worthy of Me' (Matthew 10:37): what shall be our lot, from whom thy piety claims to be loved in higher degree than Christ the Saviour of us all? who shall have power to aid us in the Day of Doom, or what defence shall we find, after prizing such long silence at the blasphemies which have been done against Him by thee? And if thou wert injuring thyself alone, in thinking and teaching such things, the concern thereat had been less: but since thou offendest the Church and hast cast the leaven of an unwonted and strange heresy among the people (yea and not thither alone, but to those every where were the books of thy commentaries carried round), what answer will any longer suffice for our silence? or how must one not needs remember Christ Who says, 'Think not that I came to cast peace over the earth, I came not to cast peace but a sword; for I came to sever a man against his father and the daughter against her mother'? [Matthew 10:34–35].

Lo then together with the holy Synod that has been gathered together in Great Rome, under the presidency of the Most holy and Most devout our brother and co-minister the Bishop Celestine, we do testify to thee in this third Letter too, counselling thee to refrain from the so crooked and perverted doctrines which thou both holdest and teachest, and to choose in place of them the Right Faith which was delivered to the Churches from the beginning through the holy Apostles and Evangelists who have been both eye-witnesses and ministers of the word [Luke 1:2]. Or if thy Piety do not so, according to the ordinance set forth in the Letters of the afore-mentioned most holy and most pious Bishop and our co-minister of the church of the Romans, Celestine, know that thou hast no lot with us, nor place nor rank among the Priests of God and His Bishops. For neither is it possible for us to overlook the Churches thus harassed and the people offended, and the Right Faith rejected and the flocks torn in pieces by thee who oughtest to preserve them, if thou wert as we a lover of right doctrine, tracking the piety of the holy Fathers. And all who have been by thy Piety severed for the Faith's sake, or deposed, both lay and Cleric, all we are in communion with; for it is not just that they who know to think aright should be wronged by thy decrees, because they doing well have contradicted thee. For this very thing thou hast notified in the Letter written by thee to our most holy brother-bishop of Great Rome, Celestine.

And it will not be enough for thy Piety to confess only the symbol of the Faith which was put forth in its time in the Holy Ghost by the holy and Great Synod gathered together in the City of the Niceans (for thou hast understood and interpret it not aright but rather perversely, even though thou confess the formula with thy mouth): but it will be meet that thou confess in writing and on oath that thou both anathematizest thine own foul and profane dogmas, and that thou wilt hold and teach the things which we all do, the Bishops and Teachers and leaders of the people throughout the West and East. And both the holy Synod at Rome and all of us have consented to the Letters written to thy Piety by the Church of the Alexandrians, as right and irreproachable.

We have subjoined to this our letter the things which thou must hold and teach and those from which thou must abstain: for this is the Faith of the Catholic and Apostolic Church, to which all the Orthodox Bishops throughout the West and East adhere.

We believe in One God the Father Almighty, Maker of all things both visible and invisible, and in One Lord Jesus Christ, the Son of God, the Only-Begotten begot of the Father, that is of the Essence of the Father, God of God, Light of Light, Very God of Very God, Begotten not made, consubstantial with the Father, through Whom all things were made, both that are in Heaven and that are on earth, Who for us men and for our salvation came down and was made flesh and made man, suffered and rose on the third day, went up into the Heavens, cometh to judge quick and dead; and in the Holy Ghost.

And those that say, There was a time when He was not and, Before He was begotten He was not, and that He was made of things that are not, or that say that the Son of God is of some other Hypostasis or Essence, or is subject to change or variation, these the Catholic and Apostolic Church anathematizes.

Following in all respects the confessions of the holy Fathers which they have made through the Holy Ghost speaking in them, and tracking out the aim of their ideas, and going as it were along the royal road, we say that the Only Begotten Son of God Himself, Who was begot of the Very Essence of the Father, Who is Very God of Very God, Light of Light, He through Whom all things were made, both those in Heaven and those on earth, having for our salvation come down and abased Himself unto emptiness, was both made flesh and made man, that is, having taken Flesh of the holy Virgin and made it His own from the womb, He underwent birth as we, and proceeded Man of a woman, not losing what He was, but even though He assumed flesh and blood, thus too abiding what He was, God that is by Nature and in truth: (And neither do we say that the Flesh was turned into the Nature of Godhead nor yet that the Ineffable Nature of God the Word was borne aside into the nature of the flesh; for It is Unchangeable and Invariable, ever abiding wholly the same, according to the Scriptures:) and seen, and a Babe, and in swaddling clothes, being yet in the lap of the Virgin that bare Him, He was filling the Creation as God and co-sitting with the Father. For the Godhead is without quantity and size and endures not to be bounded.

And confessing that the Word was united Personally to flesh, we worship One Son and Lord Jesus Christ, neither putting apart and sundering Man and God, as though they were connected one with another by the unity of dignity and authority (for this were empty speech and nought else), nor yet calling the Word of God Christ by Himself and likewise him born of the woman by himself as though he were another Christ: but knowing One Only Christ, the word of God the Father with His own Flesh (for then was He anointed as Man with us, albeit Himself giveth the Spirit to them that are worthy it, and that not by measure [John 3:34], as saith the blessed Evangelist John), nor yet do we say this that the word of God dwelt in him that was born of the holy Virgin as in a mere man, lest Christ be conceived of as a God-clad man. For even though the Word tabernacled in us [John 1:14], and in Christ too it is said that all the fulness of the Godhead dwelt bodily [Colossians 2:9], yet do we conceive that when He was made Flesh, not as He is said to dwell in the Saints, in like wise do we define that in Him too was the Indwelling, but united according to Nature and not turned into flesh, He made Indwelling of such a kind as the soul of man too may be said to have in regard to its own body.

There is therefore One Christ and Son and Lord not as though man had connection simply with God as by unity of dignity or of authority (for equality of honour doth not unite natures. And verily Peter and John were of equal honour one with another, in that they were both Apostles and holy disciples, yet were not the two one), nor yet do we deem of the mode of connecting [as being] by juxta-position (for this suffices not unto unity of nature), nor yet in the way of an external participation, as we too being joined to the Lord [1 Corinthians 6:17], as it is written, are one spirit with Him; yea rather we refuse the term connection as insufficient to express the Union. But neither do we call the Word of God the Father the God or Lord of Christ, lest again we openly sever into two the One Christ and Son and Lord, and incur the charge of blasphemy, making Him God and Lord of Himself. For the Word of God united (as we already before said) to Flesh Personally, is God of all, ruleth over every thing, but is Himself neither servant nor lord of Himself (for it were silly, yea rather blasphemous also, so to think or say). For he called the Father His God [John 20:17], albeit He is God by Nature and of His Essence: yea, we are not ignorant that together with being God, He became also Man who is under God, according to the Law that befits the nature of the humanity: but how can He be God or Lord of Himself? Therefore as, being Man and as far as pertains to what befits the measures of the emptiness, He says that He is with us under God: so hath He been made under the Law too, albeit Himself spake the Law and is Lawgiver as God.

And we refuse to say of Christ, 'For the sake of Him that wore I reverence that which is worn, for the sake of the Invisible

I worship the seen.' It is besides an awful thing to say, 'He that is assumed shares the Name of God with Him That assumed him.' For he that says thus severs again into two christs, and puts man apart by himself and God likewise: for he denies manifestly the Union, whereby not as one in another is any co-worshipped nor co-named God, but One Christ Jesus is conceived of, the Only Begotten Son, worshipped with one worship together with His own flesh. But we confess that the Son begotten of God the Father and Only-Begotten God Himself, albeit Impassible in His own Nature, hath suffered in the flesh [1 Peter 4:1] for us according to the Scriptures, and was in His crucified body making His own in an Impassible manner the Sufferings of His own Flesh. And by the grace of God He tasted death [Hebrews 2:9] even for every one, albeit by Nature Life and Himself the Resurrection [John 11:25]. For in order that, with Ineffable Might having trodden down death in His own flesh first, He might become the Firstborn of the Dead [Colossians 1:18] and First fruits of them that slept [1 Corinthians 15:20], and might make a way to the nature of man for a return to incorruption, by the grace of God, as we said just now, He tasted death for every man, and lived again after three days having spoiled Hades; so that even though the Resurrection of the Dead [1 Corinthians 15:21] be said to be through man, yet we do conceive of the Word of God made Man and that through Him has the Might of Death been undone and He shall come in His time as one Son and Lord in the glory of the Father to judge the world in righteousness [Acts 17:31], as it is written.

And of necessity will we add this too: Declaring the Death in the Flesh of the Only-Begotten Son of God, that is Jesus Christ, and confessing His living again from the dead and His Assumption into Heaven, we celebrate the Unbloody Service in the churches, and thus approach to the Mystic Blessings, and are sanctified, rendered partakers of the Holy Flesh and Precious Blood of Christ the Saviour of us all. And not as though we were receiving common flesh (God forbid) nor yet that of a man sanctified and connected with the Word by unity of dignity, or as having a Divine Indwelling, but as truly quickening and the own Flesh of the Word Himself. For being by Nature Life as God, since He became One with His own Flesh, He rendered it Life-giving. So that even though He say to us, 'Verily, verily, I say unto you, Except ye eat the Flesh of the Son of Man, and drink His blood' [John 6:53], we shall not account it also as that of one of us (for how will a man's flesh be life-giving in its own nature?) but as having truly become the own Flesh of Him Who for our sakes both became and was called Son of Man.

And the words of our Saviour in the Gospels we apportion neither to two Hypostases nor Persons (for neither is the One and Only Christ two-fold, even though He be conceived to have been out of two diverse things gathered unto an inseverable Unity just as Man too is conceived of as of soul and body, and is not two-fold but one out of both) but thinking aright we shall maintain that both the human and besides the Divine expressions have been said by One. For when He says in God-befitting manner of Himself, 'He that hath seen Me hath seen the Father' [John 14:9], and, 'I and the Father are One' [John 10:30], we conceive of His Divine and Ineffable Nature, wherein He is even One with His own Father by reason of Identity of Essence, and the Image and Impress and Brightness of His Glory [Hebrews 1:3]; but when despising not the measure of the human nature, He addresses the Jews, 'Now are ye seeking to slay Me, a Man which have told you the truth' [John 8:40], we recognize no less the Very God the Word in the Equality and Likeness of the Father, even by the measures of His Manhood. For if it be needful to believe that being God by Nature He have been made

Flesh, or Man ensouled with a reasonable soul, what excuse will any one's being ashamed of His words, if they are made in a man-befitting manner, have? For if He should refuse words befitting man, who compelled Him to become Man as we? and He Who abased Himself for our sakes unto voluntary emptiness, why should He refuse words befitting that emptiness? To one Person therefore must we attribute all the words in the Gospels, to One Incarnate Hypostasis of the Word: for there is One Lord Jesus Christ, according to Scriptures.

And if He be called both Apostle and High Priest of our confession [Hebrews 3:1], as ministering to God the Father the Confession of our faith offered by us to Him and through Him to God the Father and unto the Holy Ghost, we say again that He is the by Nature Only Begotten Son of God and we do not apportion unto a man other than He the name of priesthood and its reality. For He became the Mediator of God and Man [1 Timothy 2:5], and the Reconciler unto Peace, offering Himself to God the Father for an odour of a sweet smell. Wherefore He also saith, 'Sacrifice and offering Thou wouldest not, whole burnt sacrifices and for sin Thou tookest not pleasure in, but a Body preparedst Thou Me: then I said, Lo I come (in the section of the Book hath it been written of Me) to do Thy Will, O God' [Hebrews 10:5-7, from Psalm 40:6-8]. For He offered in our behalf His own Body for an odour of a sweet smell and not rather on His own behalf: for what offering or sacrifice would He need for His own Self, Who is superior to all sin, as God? For if all sinned and are short of God's glory [Romans 3:23], inasmuch as we are apt to go aside, and man's nature is sick of the disease of sin, but Himself not so, and we have therefore come short of His Glory: how will there yet be any doubt that for us and in our behalf hath the Very Lamb been sacrificed? And to say that He hath offered Himself for both Himself and us, will on no account fail of the charge of blasphemy: for in no wise hath He transgressed nor did He sin; what offering then would He need, when there is no sin to which offering full rightly appertains?

And when He says of the Spirit, 'He shall glorify Me' [John 16:14], we conceiving aright say that not as lacking glory from another did the One Christ and Son receive Glory from the Holy Ghost, since neither is His Spirit superior to Him and above Him: but since for demonstration of His Godhead He was using His own Spirit for mighty deeds, He says that He is glorified by Him. Just as if one of us were to say of his own strength (for example) or understanding in regard to ought, 'They will glorify me.' For even though the Spirit exist in His Own Person, and is conceived of by Himself, inasmuch as He is the Spirit and not the Son, yet is He not therefore alien from Him; for He is called the Spirit of truth [John 15:26], and Christ is the Truth [John 14:6], and He proceedeth from Him, just as from God the Father. The Spirit therefore working miracles by the hand too of the holy Apostles after that our Lord Jesus Christ had gone up into Heaven, glorified Him; for He Himself again working through His own Spirit, was believed in, that He is God by Nature. Wherefore He said also, 'He shall receive of Mine and declare it unto you' [John 16:14]. And we do not say that by participation is the Spirit both wise and mighty (for He is All-perfect) but since He is the Spirit of the Father's Might and Wisdom, i.e., the Son, He is Wisdom and Might's Very Self.

And since the holy Virgin hath borne after the Flesh God united Personally to the Flesh, therefore we do say that she is also Mother of God, not as though the Nature of the Word had the beginning of Its existence from flesh, for It was in the beginning and the Word was God, and the Word was with God [John

1:1], and is Himself the Maker of the ages, Co-eternal with the Father and Creator of all things: but (as we have already said) seeing that He united human nature to Himself Personally and underwent fleshly birth from the very womb, not as though by any necessity or for the sake of His own Nature needing the Birth in time and in the last times of the world, but in order to bless the very beginning of our being and that, because a woman bare Him united to the flesh, the curse against our whole race might at length be stopped, the curse which sends to death our bodies of earth, and the words, 'in sorrows shalt thou bear children' [Genesis 3:16], through Him abolished, He might manifest that truth which is uttered by the Prophet's voice, 'Death in its might is swallowed up, and God again removed every tear from off every face' [Isaiah 25:8 LXX]. For this reason do we say that He economically blessed marriage itself also and when bidden in Cana of Galilee went thither together with the holy Apostles.

These things have we been taught to hold by the holy Apostles and Evangelists and the whole God-inspired Scripture, and by the true Confession of the blessed Fathers: to all of them must thy Piety too assent and consent without any guile.

The things which it is necessary that thy Piety anathematize have been annexed to this our Letter:

1. If any one confess not that Emmanuel is in truth God and that the holy Virgin is therefore Mother of God, for she bare after the flesh the Word of God made Flesh, be he anathema.

2. If any one confess not that the Word of God the Father hath been Personally united to Flesh and that He is One Christ with His own Flesh, the Same (that is) God alike and Man, be he anathema.

3. If any one sever the Persons of the One Christ after the Union, connecting them with only a connection of dignity or authority or sway, and not rather with a meeting unto Unity of Nature, be he anathema.

4. If any one allot to two Persons or Hypostases, the words in the Gospel and Apostolic writings, said either of Christ by the saints or by Him of Himself, and ascribe some to a man conceived of by himself apart from the Word That is of God, others as God-befitting to the Word alone That is of God the Father, be he anathema.

5. If any one dare to say, that Christ is a God-clad man, and not rather that He is God in truth as being the One Son and That by Nature, in that the Word hath been made Flesh, and hath shared like us in blood and flesh [Hebrews 2:14], be he anathema.

6. If any one say that the Word That is of God the Father is God or Lord of Christ and do not rather confess that the Same is God alike and Man, in that the Word hath been made flesh, according to the Scriptures, be he anathema.

7. If anyone say that Jesus hath been wrought-in as man by God the Word and that the Glory of the Only-Begotten hath been put about Him, as being another than He, be he anathema.

8. If any one dare to say that the man that was assumed ought to be co-worshipped with God the Word and co-glorified and co-named God as one in another (for the co-, constantly appended, compels us thus to deem) and does not rather honour Emmanuel with One worship and attribute to Him One Doxology, inasmuch as the Word has been made Flesh, be he anathema.

9. If any one say that the One Lord Jesus Christ hath been glorified by the Spirit, using His Power as though it were Another's, and from Him receiving the power of working against unclean spirits and of accomplishing Divine signs upon men; and does not rather say that His own is the Spirit, through Whom He hath wrought the Divine signs, be he anathema.

10. The Divine Scripture says that Christ hath been made the High Priest and Apostle of our confession [Hebrews 3:1] and

He hath offered Himself for us for an odour of a sweet smell to God the Father. If any one therefore say that not the Very Word of God was made our High Priest and Apostle when He was made Flesh and man as we, but that man of a woman apart from himself as other than He, was [so made]: or if any one say that in His own behalf also He offered the Sacrifice and not rather for us alone (for He needed not offering Who knoweth not sin), be he anathema.

11. If any one confess not that the Flesh of the Lord is Life-giving and that it is the own Flesh of the Word Himself That is from God the Father, but say that it belongs to another than He, connected with Him by dignity or as possessed of Divine Indwelling only and not rather that it is Life-giving (as we said) because it hath been made the own Flesh of the Word Who is mighty to quicken all things, be he anathema.

12. If any one confess not that the Word of God suffered in the Flesh and hath been crucified in the Flesh and tasted death in the Flesh and hath been made First-born of the Dead, inasmuch as He is both Life and Life-giving as God, be he anathema.

Third letter to Nestorius

Cyril of Alexandria

A Christmas homily

This extract from a sermon on Luke 2:4–8 is part of a series of sermons on Luke's Gospel which Cyril probably preached during or after the Nestorian controversy.

Christ, therefore, was born in Bethlehem at the time when Augustus Caesar gave orders that the first enrolment should be made. But what necessity was there, some one may perhaps say, for the very wise Evangelist to make special mention of this? Yes, I answer: it was both useful and necessary for him to mark the period when our Saviour was born; for it was said by the voice of the Patriarch: 'The head shall not depart from Judah, nor a governor from his thighs until He come, for Whom it is laid up: and He is the expectation of the Gentiles' [Genesis 49:10]. That we might learn that the Israelites then had no king of the tribe of David, and that their own native governors had failed, with good reason he mentions the decrees of Caesar, as now having Judea and the rest of the nations beneath his sceptre, for it was as their ruler that he commanded the census to be made.

Because he was of the house and lineage of David.

Luke 2:4

The book of the sacred Gospels referring the genealogy to Joseph, who was descended from David's house, has proved through him that the Virgin also was of the same tribe as David, inasmuch as the Divine law commanded that marriages should be confined to those of the same tribe; and the interpreter of the heavenly doctrines, the great apostle Paul, clearly declares the truth, bearing witness that the Lord arose out of Judea [Hebrews 7:14]. The natures, however, which combined unto this union were different, but from the two together is one God the Son, without the diversity of the natures being destroyed by the union. For a union of two natures was made, and therefore we confess One Christ, One Son, One Lord. And it is with reference to this notion of a union without confusion that we proclaim the holy Virgin to be the mother of God, because God the Word was made flesh and became man, and by the act of conception united to Himself the temple that He received from her. For we perceive that two natures, by an inseparable union, met together in Him without confusion, and indivisibly. For the flesh is flesh, and not deity, even though it became the flesh of God; and in like manner also the Word is God, and not flesh, though for the dispensation's sake He made the flesh His own. But although the natures which concurred in forming the union are both different and unequal to one another, yet He Who is formed from them both is only One; nor may we separate the One Lord Jesus Christ into man severally and God severally, but we affirm that Christ Jesus is One and the Same, acknowledging the distinction of the natures, and preserving them free from confusion with one another.

With Mary, his espoused wife, being great with child.
                                                                Luke 2:5

The sacred Evangelist says that Mary was betrothed to Joseph, to show that the conception had taken place upon her betrothal solely, and that the birth of the Emmanuel was miraculous, and not in accordance with the laws of nature. For the holy Virgin did not bear from man's seed. And what, therefore, was the reason for this? Christ, Who is the first-fruits of all, the second Adam according to the Scriptures, was born of the Spirit, that he might transmit the grace (of the spiritual birth) to us also; for we too were intended no longer to bear the name of sons of men, but of God rather, having obtained the new birth of the Spirit in Christ first, that he might be foremost among all [Colossians 1:15], as the most wise Paul declares.

And the occasion of the census most opportunely caused the holy Virgin to go to Bethlehem, that we might see another prophecy fulfilled. For it is written, 'And thou Bethlehem, house of Ephratah, art very small to be among the thousands of Judah: from thee shall come forth for me to be Ruler in Israel!' [Micah 5:2].

But in answer to those who argue that, if He were brought forth in the flesh, the Virgin was corrupted; and if she were not corrupted, that He was brought forth only in appearance, we say, the prophet declares, 'the Lord, the God of Israel, hath entered in and gone out, and the gate remaineth closed' [Ezekiel 44:2]. If, moreover, the Word was made flesh without sexual intercourse, being conceived altogether without seed, then He was born without injury to her virginity...

> *And she laid him in the manger [because there was no room for them in the inn].*
>
> Luke 2:7

He found man reduced to the level of the beasts; therefore is He placed like fodder in a manger, that we, having left off our bestial life, might mount up to that degree of intelligence which befits man's nature; and whereas we were brutish in soul, by now approaching the manger, even His own table, we find no longer fodder, but the bread from heaven, which is the body of life.

Homily 1

Nestorius

Neglect of the Holy Communion

Nestorius (c. 381–c. 452), a monk from Antioch, became bishop of Constantinople and a famous preacher.

There is something wrong with you which I want to draw your attention to with a few words and induce you to change your ways. For you are quick to discern what is seemly. What, then, is it that is amiss? By and by the holy rites are set before the faithful, a king's gift of food to his soldiers. But by then the crowds of the faithful are nowhere to be seen but they are blown away, like chaff, by the wind of indifference, when the catechumens leave ... This is a grievous fault – betrayal of Christ when there is no persecution, desertion of the flesh of the Master by believers under no stress of war. What is the cause for their desertion? Is it urgent business? Why, what business is more binding than one that has to do with God's service, and one, too, that takes but little time? Is it because you are afraid of your sins? ... We ought to tremble at the Master's words adjuring us: 'Verily, verily, I say to you, except you eat the flesh of the Son of Man and drink his blood, you have not life in yourselves.' We ought to be afraid of his rebuking us too and saying to us from heaven: 'Were you not able to stay with me one hour?'

From *Sermons on Hebrews*

Leo I

Partakers in Christ's resurrection life

Leo (d. 461), known as Leo the Great, was pope from 440. The following sermon on Christ's resurrection was delivered on Holy Saturday in the vigil of Easter.

We must all be partakers in Christ's Resurrection life. In my last sermon, dearly-beloved, we explained to you our participation in the cross of Christ, whereby the life of believers contains in itself the mystery of Easter, and thus what is honoured at the feast is celebrated by our practice. And how useful this is you yourselves have proved, and by your devotion have learnt, how your souls and bodies greatly benefit from longer fasts, more frequent prayers, and more liberal alms ... Since, therefore, by our forty days' observance we have wished to bring about this effect, that we should feel something of the Cross at the time of the Lord's Passion, we must strive to be found partakers also of Christ's Resurrection, and 'pass from death unto life,' while we are in this body ... We must die, therefore, to the devil and live to God: we must perish to iniquity that we may rise to righteousness. Let the old sink, that the new may rise; and since, as says the Truth, 'no one can serve two masters,' let not him be lord who has caused the overthrow of those that stood, but Him Who has raised the fallen to victory.

God did not leave His soul in hell, nor suffer His flesh to see corruption. Accordingly, since the Apostle says, 'the first man is of the earth earthy, the second man is from heaven heavenly. As is the earthy, such also are they that are earthy; and as is the heavenly, such also are they that are heavenly. As we have borne the image of the earthy, so let us also bear the image of Him Who is from heaven,' we must greatly rejoice over this change, whereby we are translated from earthly degradation to heavenly dignity through His unspeakable mercy. The Saviour's resurrection did not long keep His soul in Hades, nor His flesh in the tomb.

Christ's manifestation after the Resurrection showed that His Person was essentially the same as before. And then there followed many proofs, whereon the authority of the Faith to be preached through the whole world might be based. And although the rolling away of the stone, the empty tomb, the arrangement of the linen cloths, and the angels who narrated the whole deed by themselves fully built up the truth of the Lord's Resurrection, yet did He often appear plainly to the eyes both of the women and of the Apostles not only talking with them, but also remaining and eating with them, and allowing

Himself to be handled by the eager and curious hands of those whom doubt assailed. For to this end He entered when the doors were closed upon the disciples, and gave them the Holy Spirit by breathing on them, and after giving them the light of understanding opened the secrets of the Holy Scriptures, and again Himself showed them the wound in the side, the prints of the nails, and all the marks of His most recent Passion, whereby it might be acknowledged that in Him the properties of the Divine and Human Nature remained undivided, and we might in such sort know that the Word was not what the flesh is, as to confess God's only Son to be both Word and Flesh.

Being saved by hope, we must not fulfil the lusts of the flesh. Let us not then be taken up with the appearances of worldly matters, neither let our contemplations be diverted from heavenly to earthly things.

Our godly resolutions must continue all the year round, not be confined to Easter only. Let God's people then recognize that they are a new creation in Christ, and with all vigilance understand by Whom they have been adopted and Whom they have adopted. Let not the things, which have been made new, return to their ancient instability; and let not him who has 'put his hand to the plough' forsake his work, but rather attend to that which he sows than look back to that which he has left behind. Let no one fall back into that from which he has risen, but, even though from bodily weakness he still languishes under certain maladies, let him urgently desire to be healed and raised up. For this is the path of health through imitation of the Resurrection begun in Christ, whereby, notwithstanding the many accidents and falls to which in this slippery life the traveller is liable, his feet may be guided from the quagmire on to solid ground, for, as it is written, 'the steps of a man are directed by the Lord, and He will delight in his way. When the just man falls he shall not be overthrown, because the Lord will stretch out His hand.' These thoughts, dearly-beloved, must be kept in mind not only for the Easter festival, but also for the sanctification of the whole life, and to this our present exercise ought to be directed, that what has delighted the souls of the faithful by the experience of a short observance may pass into a habit and remain unalterably, and if any fault creep in, it may be destroyed by speedy repentance. And because the cure of old-standing diseases is slow and difficult, remedies should be applied early, when the wounds are fresh, so that rising ever anew from all downfalls, we may deserve to attain to the incorruptible Resurrection of our glorified flesh in Christ Jesus our Lord, Who lives and reigns with the Father and the Holy Ghost for ever and ever. Amen.

Leo I

All share in the joy of Christmas

Our Saviour, dearly-beloved, was born today: let us be glad. For there is no proper place for sadness, when we keep the birthday of the Life, which destroys the fear of mortality and brings to us the joy of promised eternity. No one is kept from sharing in this happiness. There is for all one common measure of joy, because as our Lord the destroyer of sin and death finds none free from charge, so is He come to free us all. Let the saint exult in that he draws near to victory. Let the sinner be glad in that he is invited to pardon. Let the gentile take courage in that he is called to life. For the Son of God in the fullness of time which the inscrutable depth of the divine counsel has determined, has taken on him the nature of man, thereby to reconcile it to its Author: in order that the inventor of death, the devil, might be conquered. And in this conflict undertaken for us, the fight was fought on great and wondrous principles of fairness; for the Almighty Lord enters the lists with His savage foe not in His own majesty but in our humility, opposing him with the same form and the same nature, which shares indeed our mortality, though it is free from all sin.

Truly foreign to this nativity is what we read about all others, 'no one is clean from stain, not even the infant who has lived but one day upon earth.' Nothing therefore of the lust of the flesh has passed into that peerless nativity, nothing of the law of sin has entered. A royal Virgin of the stem of David is chosen, to be impregnated with the sacred seed and to conceive the Divinely-human offspring in mind first and then in body. And lest in ignorance of the heavenly counsel she should tremble at so strange a result, she learns from speaking with the angel what is to be born in her is of the Holy Ghost. Nor does she believe it loss of honour that she is soon to be the Mother of God. For why should she be in despair over the novelty of such conception, to whom the power of the most High has promised to effect it? Her implicit faith is confirmed also by the witness of a previous miracle, and Elizabeth receives unexpected fertility: in order that there might be no doubt that He who had given conception to the barren, would give it even to a virgin.

The mystery of the Incarnation is a fitting theme for joy both to angels and to men

Therefore the Word of God, Himself God, the Son of God who 'in the beginning was with God,' through whom 'all things were made' and 'without' whom 'was nothing made,' with the purpose of delivering man from eternal death, became man: so bending Himself to take on Him our humility without decrease in His own majesty, that remaining what He was and assuming what He was not, He might unite the true form of a slave to that form in which He is equal to God the Father, and join both natures together by such a compact that the lower should not be swallowed up in its exaltation nor the higher impaired by its new associate. Without detriment therefore to the properties of either substance which then came together in one person, majesty took on humility, strength weakness, eternity mortality: and for the paying off of the debt, belonging to our condition, inviolable nature was united with possible nature, and true God and true man were combined to form one Lord, so that, as suited the needs of our case, one and the same Mediator between God and men, the Man Christ Jesus, could both die with the one and rise again with the other.

Rightly therefore did the birth of our salvation impart no corruption to the Virgin's purity, because the bearing of the Truth was the keeping of honour. Such, then, beloved, was the nativity which became the Power of God and the Wisdom of God, even Christ, whereby He might be one with us in manhood and surpass us in Godhead. For unless He were true God, He would not bring us a remedy; unless He were true Man, He would not give us an example. Therefore the exulting angel's song when the Lord was born is this, 'Glory to God in the Highest,' and their message, 'peace on earth to men of good will.' For they see that the heavenly Jerusalem is being built up out of all the nations of the world: and over that indescribable work of the Divine love how ought the humbleness of men to rejoice, when the joy of the lofty angels is so great?

Christians then must live worthily of Christ their Head
Let us then, dearly beloved, give thanks to God the Father, through His Son, in the Holy Spirit, Who 'for His great mercy, wherewith He has loved us,' has had pity on us: and 'when we were dead in sins, has quickened us together in Christ,' that we

might be in Him a new creation. Let us put off then the old man with his deeds: and having obtained a share in the birth of Christ let us renounce the works of the flesh. Christian, acknowledge thy dignity, and becoming a partner in the Divine nature, refuse to return to the old baseness by degenerate conduct. Remember the Head and the Body of which thou art a member. Recollect that you were rescued from the power of darkness and brought out into God's light and kingdom. By the mystery of Baptism you were made the temple of the Holy Ghost: do not put such a denizen to flight from thee by base acts, and subject thyself once more to the devil's thraldom: because your purchase money is the blood of Christ, because He shall judge you in truth who ransomed you in mercy, who with the Father and the Holy Spirit reigns for ever and ever. Amen.

From *Sermon 21: On the feast of the Nativity*

Ephraem the Syrian

How merciful is God

Ephraem lived in the fourth and fifth centuries and cared for the poor at Edessa in Syria.

Hear and be comforted, beloved, how merciful is God. To the sinful woman He forgave her offences; yea, He upheld her when she was afflicted. With clay He opened the eyes of the blind, so that the eyeballs beheld the light ... And to us He has given the pearls; His holy Body and Blood. He brought His medicines secretly; and with them He heals openly. And He wandered round in the land of Judea, like a physician, bearing his medicines. Simon invited Him to the feast, to eat bread in his house. The sinful woman rejoiced when she heard that He sat and was feasting in Simon's house; her thoughts gathered together like the sea, and like the billows her love surged. She beheld the Sea of Grace, how it had forced itself into one place; and she resolved to go and drown all her wickedness in its billows.

She bound her heart, because it had offended, with chains and tears of suffering; and she began weeping: 'What avails me this fornication? What avails this lewdness? I have defiled the innocent ones without shame; I have corrupted the orphan; and without fear I have robbed the merchants of merchandise, and my rapacity was not satisfied ... Why did I not win me one man, who might have corrected my lewdness? For one man is of God, but many are of Satan.'

These things she said secretly; then began to do openly. She took up the gold in her palm, and carried the alabaster box in her hands. Then hastily went she forth in sadness to the perfumer ... 'Take thee the gold,' she said to the perfumer, 'as much as thou demandest, and give me the precious ointment; take thee that which endures not and give me that which endures; and I will go to Him who endures, and will buy that which endures ... A Man has met me today Who bears riches in abundance. He has robbed me and I have robbed Him; He has robbed me of my transgressions and sins, and I have robbed Him of His wealth ...' She took up the ointment and went forth...

The sinful woman full of transgressions stood clinging by the door. She clasped her arms in prayer, and thus she spake beseeching: 'Blessed Son Who hast descended to earth for the sake of man's redemption, close not Thy door in my face; for Thou hast called me and lo! I come. I know that Thou hast not rejected me; open for me the door of Thy mercy, that I may come in, O my Lord, and find refuge in Thee, from the Evil One and his hosts! I was a sparrow, and the hawk pursued me, and I have fled and taken refuge in Thy nest. I was a heifer, and the yoke galled me, and I will turn back my wanderings to Thee. Lay upon me the shoulder of Thy yoke that I may take it on me, and work with Thy oxen.' Thus did the harlot speak at the door with much weeping.

The master of the house looked and saw her, and the colour of his visage was changed; and he began thus to address her, the harlot: 'Depart thou hence, O harlot, for this man who abides in our house is a man that is righteous, and they that are of his companions are blameless. Is it not enough for thee, harlot, that thou hast corrupted the whole town? Thou hast corrupted the chaste without shame; thou hast robbed the orphans, and hast not blushed, and hast plundered the merchants' wares, and thy countenance is not abashed. From him thou labourest to take his heart. But from him thy net takes no spoil. For this man is righteous indeed, and they of his company are blameless.'

The sinful woman answered and said to him, even to Simon when he had ceased, 'Thou surely art the guardian of the door, O thou that knowest things that are secret. I will propose the matter in the feast, and thou shall be free from blame. And if there be any that wills me to come in, he will bid me and I will come in.' Simon ran and closed the door, and approached and stood afar off. And he tarried a long time and proposed not the matter in the feast. But He, Who knows what is secret, beckoned to Simon and said to him: 'Come hither, Simon, I bid thee; does any one stand at the door? Whosoever he be, open to him that he may come in; let him receive what he needs, and go. If he be hungry and hunger for bread, lo! in thy house is the table of life; and if he be thirsty, and thirst for water, lo! the blessed fountain is in thy dwelling. And if he be sick and ask for healing, lo! the great Physician is in thy house. Suffer sinners to look upon Me, for their sakes have I abased Myself. I will not ascend to heaven, to the dwelling whence I came down, until I bear back the sheep that has wandered from its Father's house, and lift it up on My shoulders and bear it aloft to heaven.'

Simon answered and thus he said to Jesus, when He had done speaking: 'My Lord, this woman that stands in the doorway is a harlot: she is lewd and not free-born, polluted from her childhood. And Thou, my Lord, art a righteous man, and all are eager to see Thee; and if men see Thee having speech with the harlot, all men will flee from beside Thee, and no man will salute Thee.' Jesus answered, and thus He said to Simon when he was done speaking: 'Whosoever it be, open for him to come in, and thou shall be free from blame; and though his offences be many, without rebuke I bid thee receive him.'

Simon approached and opened the door, and began thus to speak: 'Come, enter, fulfil that thou willest, to him who is even as thou.' The sinful woman, full of transgressions, passed forward and stood by His feet, and clasped her arms in prayer, and with these words she spake: 'Mine eyes have become watercourses that cease not from watering the fields, and today they wash the feet of Him Who follows after sinners. This hair, abundant in locks from my childhood till this day, let it not grieve Thee that it should wipe this holy body. The mouth that has kissed the lewd, forbid it not to kiss the body that remits transgressions and sins.'

These things the harlot spake to Jesus, with much weeping. And Simon stood afar off to see what He would do to her. But He Who knows the things that are secret, beckoned to Simon and said to him: 'Lo! I will tell thee, O Simon, what thy meditation is, concerning the harlot. Within thy mind thou imaginest and within thy soul thou saidst, "I have called this man righteous, but lo! the harlot kisses Him. I have called Him to bless my possessions, and lo! the harlot embraces Him." O Simon, there were two debtors, whose creditor was one only; one owed him five-hundred pence, and the other owed fifty. And when the creditor saw that neither of these two had aught, the creditor pardoned and forgave them both their debt. Which of them ought to render the greater thanks? He who was forgiven five hundred, or he who was forgiven fifty?'

Simon answered, and thus he said to Jesus, when He had done speaking: 'He who was forgiven five hundred ought to render the greater thanks.'

Jesus answered and thus He said: 'Thou art he that owes five hundred, and this woman owes fifty. Lo! I came into thy house, O Simon; and water for My feet thou broughtest not; and this woman, of whom thou saidst that she was an harlot, one from her childhood defiled, has washed My feet with her tears, and with her hair she has wiped them. Ought I to send her away, O Simon, without receiving forgiveness? Verily, verily, I say unto thee, I will write of her in the Gospel. Go, O woman, thy sins are forgiven thee and all thy transgression is covered; henceforth and to the end of the world.'

May our Lord account us worthy of hearing this word of His: 'Come, enter, ye blessed of My Father, inherit the kingdom made ready for all who shall do My will, and observe all My commandments.' To Him be glory; on us be mercy; at all times. Amen! Amen!

Sermon on the sinful woman

PART 3

The Sixth Century to the Fifteenth Century

The Rule of St Columba

Be single-minded in your imitation of Christ

Columba (521–97) was an Irish abbot and a missionary to pagan Scotland. In 563 he founded a monastery on the island of Iona. The following rule is attributed to him and reflects the spirit of early Irish monasticism.

Be alone in a separate place near a chief city, if thy conscience is not prepared to be in common with the crowd.

Be always single-minded in your imitation of Christ and the Evangelists.

Whatsoever little or much thou possessest of anything, whether clothing, or food, or drink, let it be at the command of the senior and at his disposal, for it is not befitting a religious to have any distinction of property with his own free brother.

Let a fast place, with one door, enclose thee.

A few religious men to converse with thee of God and his Testament; to visit thee on days of solemnity; to strengthen thee in the Testaments of God, and the narratives of the Scriptures.

A person too who would talk with thee in idle words, or of the world; or who murmurs at what he cannot remedy or prevent, but who would distress thee more should he be a tattler between friends and foes, thou shalt not admit him to thee, but at once give him thy benediction should he deserve it.

Let thy servant be a discreet, religious, not tale-telling man, who is to attend continually on thee, with moderate labour of course, but always ready.

Yield submission to every rule that is of devotion.

A mind prepared for red martyrdom [that is, death for the faith].

A mind fortified and steadfast for white martyrdom [that is, ascetic practices]. Forgiveness from the heart of every one. Constant prayers for those who trouble thee.

Fervour in singing the office for the dead, as if every faithful dead was a particular friend of thine.

Hymns for souls to be sung standing.

Let thy vigils be constant from eve to eve, under the direction of another person.

Three labours in the day, viz., prayers, work, and reading.

The work to be divided into three parts, viz., thine own work, and the work of thy place, as regards its real wants; secondly, thy share of the brethren's work; lastly, to help the neighbours, viz., by instruction or writing, or sewing garments, or whatever labour they may be in want of, as the Lord says, 'You shall not appear before me empty.'

Everything in its proper order; For no one is crowned except he who has striven lawfully.

Follow alms-giving before all things.

Take not of food till thou art hungry.

Sleep not till thou feelest desire.

Speak not except on business.

Every increase which comes to thee in lawful meals, or in wearing apparel, give it for pity to the brethren that want it, or to the poor in like manner.

The love of God with all thy heart and all thy strength; the love of thy neighbour as thyself.

Abide in the Testament of God throughout all times.

Thy measure of prayer shall be until thy tears come; or thy measure of thy work of labour till thy tears come; or thy measure of thy work of labour ... until thy perspiration often comes, if thy tears are not free.

Based on *Councils and Ecclesiastical Documents Relating to Great Britain and Ireland*, II, i

Isaac the Syrian

A Christmas sermon

Isaac the Syrian was a seventh-century bishop of Nineveh.

This [Christmas] night bestowed peace on the whole world; so, let no one threaten; this is the night of the Most Gentle One –

let no one be cruel; this is the night of the most Humble One – let no one be proud. Now is the day of joy – let us not revenge; now is the day of good will – let us not be mean. In this day of peace let us not be conquered by anger ... Today the Bountiful impoverished Himself for our sake; so, the rich one, invite the poor to your table. Today we received a gift, for which we did not ask; so let us give alms to those, who implore us and beg. This present day cast open the heavenly door to our prayers: let us open our door to those who ask our forgiveness. Now the Divine Being took upon Himself the seal of humanity, in order for humanity to be decorated by the seal of Divinity.

Isaac the Syrian

Be a herald of God's goodness

Be a herald of God's goodness, for God rules over you, unworthy though you are; for although your debt to Him is so great, yet He is not seen exacting payment from you, and from the small works you do, He bestows great rewards upon you. Do not call God just, for His justice is not manifest in the things concerning you. And if David calls Him just and upright (cf. Psalms 24:8; 144:17), His Son revealed to us that He is good and kind. He is good, He says, to the evil and to the impious (cf. Luke 6:35). How can you call God just when you come across the Scriptural passage on the wage given to the workers? Friend, I do thee no wrong; I will give unto this last even as unto thee. Is thine eye evil because I am good? (Matthew 10:12–15). How can a man call God just when he comes across the passage on the prodigal son who wasted his wealth with riotous living, how for the compunction alone which he showed, the father ran and fell upon his neck and gave him authority over all his wealth? (Luke

15:11 ff.). None other but His very Son said these things concerning Him, lest we doubt it; and thus He bare witness concerning Him. Where, then, is God's justice, for whilst we are sinners Christ died for us! (cf. Romans 5:8). But if here He is merciful, we may believe that He will not change.

Far be it that we should ever think such an iniquity that God could become unmerciful! For the property of Divinity does not change as do mortals. God does not acquire something which He does not have, nor lose what He has, nor supplement what He does have, as do created beings. But what God has from the beginning, He will have and has until the end, as the blest Cyril wrote in his commentary on Genesis. Fear God, he says, out of love for Him, and not for the austere name that He has been given. Love Him as you ought to love Him; not for what He will give you in the future.

O the wondrous mercy of God! O the astonishment at the bounty of our God and Creator! O might for which all is possible! O the immeasurable goodness that brings our nature again, sinners though we be, to His regeneration and rest! Who is sufficient to glorify Him? He raises up the transgressor and blasphemer.

Come, men of discernment, and be filled with wonder! Whose mind is sufficiently wise and marvellous to wonder worthily at the bounty of our Creator? His recompense of sinners who have repented is, that instead of a just recompense, He rewards them with resurrection, and instead of those bodies with which they trampled upon His law, He robes them with perfect glory and incorruption. Behold, Lord, the waves of Thy grace close my mouth with silence, and there is not a thought left in me before the face of Thy thanksgiving. What mouths can confess Thy praise, O Good King, Thou Who lovest our life? Glory be to Thee for the two worlds which Thou hast created for our growth and delight, leading us by all things which Thou didst fashion to the knowledge of Thy glory, from now and unto ages of ages. Amen.

Homily 60

Methodius

The cross and the passion of Christ

Bishop Methodius (c. 826–85) and his brother Cyril (827–69) were known as the 'Apostles to the Slavs'. Below are two fragments from Methodius' homily on the cross and the passion of Christ.

Fragment 1

Methodius, Bishop, to those who say: What doth it profit us that the Son of God was crucified upon earth, and made man? And wherefore did He endure to suffer in the manner of the cross, and not by some other punishment? And what was the advantage of the cross?

Christ, the Son of God, by the command of the Father, became conversant with the visible creature, in order that, by overturning the dominion of the tyrants, the demons, that is, He might deliver our souls from their dreadful bondage, by reason of which our whole nature, intoxicated by the draughts of iniquity, had become full of tumult and disorder, and could by no means return to the remembrance of good and useful things. Wherefore, also, it was the more easily carried away to idols, inasmuch as evil had overwhelmed it entirely, and had spread over all generations, on account of the change which had come over our fleshy tabernacles in consequence of disobedience; until Christ, the Lord, by the flesh in which He lived and appeared, weakened the force of Pleasure's onslaughts, by means of which the infernal powers that were in arms against us reduced our minds to slavery, and freed mankind from all their evils. For with this end the Lord Jesus both wore our flesh, and became man, and by the divine dispensation was nailed to the cross; in order that by the flesh in which the demons had proudly and falsely feigned themselves gods, having carried our souls captive unto death by deceitful wiles, even by this they might be overturned, and discovered to be no gods. For he prevented their arrogance from raising itself higher, by becoming man; in order that by the body in which the race possessed of reason had become estranged from the worship of the true God, and had suffered injury, even by the same receiving into itself in an ineffable manner the Word of Wisdom, the enemy might be discovered to be the destroyers and not the benefactors of our souls. For it had not been wonderful if Christ, by the terror of His divinity, and the greatness of His invincible power, had reduced to weakness the adverse nature of the demons. But since this was to cause them greater grief and torment, for they would have preferred to be overcome by one stronger than themselves, therefore it was that by a man He procured the safety of the race; in order that men, after that very Life and Truth had entered into them in bodily form, might be able to return to the form and light of the Word, overcoming the power of the enticements of sin; and that the demons, being conquered by one weaker than they, and thus brought into contempt, might desist from their overbold confidence, their hellish wrath being repressed.

It was for this mainly that the cross was brought in, being erected as a trophy against iniquity, and a deterrent from it, that henceforth man might be no longer subject to wrath, after that he had made up for the defeat which, by his disobedience, he had received, and had lawfully conquered the infernal powers, and by the gift of God had been set free from every debt. Since, therefore, the first-born Word of God thus fortified the manhood in which He tabernacled with the armour of righteousness, He overcame, as has been said, the powers that enslaved us by the figure of the cross, and showed forth man, who had been oppressed by corruption, as by a tyrant power, to be free, with unfettered hands. For the cross, if you wish to define it, is the confirmation of the victory, the way by which God to man descended, the trophy against material spirits, the repulsion of death, the foundation of the ascent to the true day; and the ladder for those who are hastening to enjoy the light that is there, the engine by which those who are fitted for the edifice of the Church are raised up from below, like a stone four square, to be compacted on to the divine Word. Hence it is that our kings, perceiving that the figure of the cross is used for the dissipating of every evil. Hence the sea, yielding to this figure, makes itself navigable to men. For every creature, so to speak, has, for the sake of liberty, been marked with this sign; for the birds which fly aloft, form the figure of the cross by the expansion of their wings; and man himself, also, with his hands outstretched, represents the same. Hence, when the Lord had fashioned him in this form, in which He had from the beginning flamed him, He joined on his body to the Deity, in order that it might be henceforth an instrument consecrated to God, freed from all discord and want of harmony. For man cannot, after that he has been formed for the worship of God, and hath sung, as it were, the incorruptible song of truth, and by this hath been made capable of holding the Deity, being fitted to the lyre of life as the chords and strings, he cannot, I say, return to discord and corruption...

Fragment 2

Some think that God also, whom they measure with the measure of their own feelings, judges the same thing that wicked and foolish men judge to be subjects of praise and blame, and that He uses the opinions of men as His rule and measure, not taking into account the fact that, by reason of the ignorance that is in them, every creature falls short of the beauty of God. For He draws all things to life by His Word, from their universal substance and nature. For whether He would have good, He Himself is the Very Good, and remains in Himself; or, whether the beautiful is pleasing to Him, since He Himself is the Only Beautiful, He beholds Himself, holding in no estimation the things which move the admiration of men. That, verily, is to be accounted as in reality the most beautiful and praiseworthy, which God Himself esteems to be beautiful, even though it be contemned and despised by all else – not that which men fancy to be beautiful. Whence it is, that although by this figure He hath willed to deliver the soul from corrupt affections, to the signal putting to shame of the demons, we ought to receive it, and not to speak evil of it, as being that which was given us to deliver us, and set us free from the chains which for our disobedience we incurred. For the Word suffered, being in the flesh affixed to the cross, that He might bring man, who had been deceived by error, to His supreme and godlike majesty, restoring him to that divine life from which he had become alienated. By this figure, in truth, the passions are blunted; the passion of the passions having taken place by the Passion, and the death of death by the death of Christ, He not having been subdued by death, nor overcome by the pains of the Passion. For neither did the Passion cast Him down from His equanimity, nor did death hurt Him, but He was in the passible remaining impassible, and in the mortal remaining immortal, comprehending all that the air, and this middle state, and the heaven above contained, and attempering the mortal to the immortal divinity. Death was vanquished entirely; the flesh being crucified to draw forth its immortality.

Bernard of Clairvaux

If you love Christ tenderly

Bernard (1090–1153) was abbot of the monastery at Clairvaux and was the author of several mystical works and of a monastic rule. His sermons are among the most beautiful examples of medieval scriptural exegesis. The following extract is from his sermon on the Song of Songs.

It has been said that Christ's love is tender, wise and strong. 'I say that it is tender, since he has taken on himself our human nature; wise because he has kept himself free from all sin; and strong because he came to the point of enduring death.'

From the way in which Christ lived you can learn, Christian friend, how you should love Christ. Learn to love him tenderly, to love him wisely and to love him with strong powerful love. If you love Christ tenderly you will not be enticed away from him; if you love Christ wisely you will not be deceived and so drawn away from him; if you love Christ powerfully nothing will be able to separate you from him. Take delight in Christ for he is wisdom above everything else. Then human glory and sinful human passions will not take you away from him. Let Christ, who is the truth, so enlighten you that you are not drawn away from him by any false spirit.

Let Christ, who is the power of God, strengthen you so that you are not overcome by any enemies. Let Christian love strengthen your desire to do good; let Christ's wisdom rule you and direct your life and let steadfastness make you persevere in this. Your Christian love must not be lukewarm, timid or indiscreet. This is what is laid down in the Law, when God says, 'Love the Lord your God with all your heart and with all your soul and with all your strength' (Deuteronomy 6:5).

It seems to me that the best way to make this distinction between the different ways to love God is as follows: the love of the heart concerns your feelings, the love of the soul centres on the decisions of your mind and the love of your strength focuses on the steadfastness of your mind. So you must love the Lord your God wholeheartedly, single-mindedly and sacrificially. As it is written in the Song of Songs (8:6), 'love is as strong as death, its jealousy unyielding as the grave'...

Devotion to the humanity of Christ is a great gift from the Holy Spirit. And yet I have to label this love as sinful human desire when it is compared with other more spiritual desires. For it is possible to seek after Christian graces, such as wisdom, righteousness, holiness and goodness, in the power of mere human effort. The way to remedy this is to recall these words of Paul, 'It is because of him that you are in Christ Jesus, who has become for us wisdom from God – that is, our righteousness, holiness and redemption' (1 Corinthians 1:30)...

When we love God's Son so strongly, through the help of the powerful Holy Spirit, that we do not stop seeking God's righteousness in the middle of troubles, sufferings or the threat of death, then we are loving God with all our strength. This love is spiritual love. Spiritual love is a particularly apt name to give this kind of love because its characteristic is the fullness of the Spirit. I think that this is all I need to say about the bride's words, 'No wonder the maidens love you!' (Song of Songs 1:3).

Francis of Assisi

My little sisters, the birds
Francis of Assisi (1181–1226) was the founder of the Franciscan order of friars.

My little sisters, the birds, much bounden are ye unto God, your creator, and always in every place ought ye to praise him, for that he hath given you liberty to fly about everywhere, and hath also given you double and triple raiment; moreover he preserved your seed in the ark of Noah, that your race might not perish out of the world; still more are ye beholden to him for the element of the air which he hath appointed for you; beyond all this, ye sow not, neither do you reap; and God feedeth you, and giveth you the streams and fountains for your drink; the mountains and valleys for your refuge and the high trees whereon to make your nests; and because ye know not how to spin or sow, God clotheth you, you and your children; wherefore your creator loveth you much, seeing that he hath bestowed on you so many benefits; and therefore, my little sisters, beware of the sin of ingratitude, and study always to give praises unto God.

Canticles

John Huss

You are now going to burn a goose
John Huss (c. 1372–1415) was a Bohemian theologian and martyr.

Huss received the sentence without the slightest emotion; and then knelt down, lifted up his eyes towards heaven, exclaiming, with the magnanimity of a primitive martyr, 'May thy infinite mercy, O my God! pardon this injustice of mine enemies. Thou knowest the injustice of my accusations: how deformed with crimes I have been represented; how I have been oppressed with worthless witnesses, and a false condemnation; yet, O my God! let that mercy of thine, which no tongue can express, prevail with thee not to avenge my wrongs.'

But these excellent sentences were received as so many expressions of treason, and only tended to inflame his adversaries. Accordingly, the bishops appointed by the council stripped him of his priestly garments, degraded him, and put a paper mitre on his head, on which they painted three devils, with this inscription: 'Heresiarch' [Heretic]. This mockery was received by the martyr with an air of unconcern, and seemed to give him dignity rather than disgrace. A serenity appeared in his looks, which indicated that his soul was approaching the realms of everlasting happiness; and when the bishop urged him to recant, he turned to the people and addressed them thus.

'These lords and bishops do counsel me that I should confess before you all that I have erred; which thing, if it might be done with the infamy and reproach of many only, they might, peradventure, easily persuade me to do; but now I am in the sight of the Lord my God, without whose great displeasure I could not do that which they require. For I well know that I never taught any of those things which they have falsely accused me of, but I have always preached, taught, written, and thought contrary thereunto. Should I by this my example trouble so many consciences, endued with the most certain knowledge of the Scriptures and of the gospel of our Lord Jesus Christ? I will never do it, neither commit any such offence, that I should seem to esteem this vile carcass appointed unto death more than their health and salvation.'

At this most godly word he was forced again to hear that he did obstinately persevere in his pernicious errors.

After the ceremony of degradation the bishops delivered him to the emperor, who handed him over to the Duke of Bavaria. His books were burnt at the gates of the church; and on July 6th he was led to the suburbs of Constance to be burnt alive.

Having reached the place of execution, he fell on his knees, sung several portions from the Psalms, and looked steadfastly towards heaven, saying, 'Into thy hands, O Lord! do I commit my spirit: thou hast redeemed me, O most good and faithful God.'

As soon as the chain was put around him at the stake, he said, with a smiling countenance, 'My Lord Jesus Christ was bound with a harder chain than this for my sake: why, then, should I be ashamed of this old rusty one?' Then he prayed: 'Lord Jesus Christ, it is for the sake of the gospel and the preaching of the word that I patiently undergo this ignominious death.'

When the faggots were piled around him, the Duke of Bavaria was officious as to desire him to abjure. 'No,' he said, 'I never preached any doctrine of an evil tendency; and what I taught with my lips I now seal with my blood.' He then said to the executioner, 'You are now going to burn a goose [the meaning of Huss's name in Bohemian], but in a century you will have a swan whom you can neither roast nor boil.' If this were spoken in prophecy, he must have alluded to Martin Luther, who came about a hundred years after him, and had a swan for his arms.

As soon as the faggots were lighted, the martyr sang a hymn, with so cheerful a voice, that he was heard above the cracklings of the fire and the noise of the multitude. At length his voice was interrupted by the flames, which soon put an end to his existence. His ashes were collected, and, by order of the council, thrown into the Rhine, lest his adherents should honour them as relics.

John Foxe's *Book of Martyrs*

PART 4

The Sixteenth Century

Thomas More

The King's good servant, but God's first

Thomas More (1478–1535), English statesman and scholar, was executed for refusing to take the oath of supremacy recognizing Henry VIII as the head of the Church in England.

As More was led to the scaffold he had a joke with the Master Lieutenant, and said to him, 'I pray you, Master Lieutenant, see me safe up, and for my coming down, let me shift for myself.' More was allowed to say little. He simply asked for the prayers of the spectators, and that they should pray for the King, recited Psalm 51, and assured the crowd that he died for the Catholic faith and that he died 'the King's good servant, but God's first.' To the executioner he said, 'Thou wilt give me this day a greater benefit than ever any mortal man can be able to give me. Pluck up thy spirits, man, and be not afraid to do thine office. My neck is very short: take heed, therefore, thou strike not awry for saving of thine honesty.' The executioner severed More's head from his body in a single blow.

Martin Luther

The Ninety-Five Theses

Martin Luther (1483–1546) was the German monk and theologian who led the Reformation. His Ninety-Five Theses were his arguments against the sale of indulgences.

Disputation of Doctor Martin Luther on the Power and Efficacy of Indulgences (31 October 1517)

Out of love for the truth and the desire to bring it to light, the following propositions will be discussed at Wittenberg, under the presidency of the Reverend Father Martin Luther, Master of Arts and of Sacred Theology, and Lecturer in Ordinary on the same at that place. Wherefore he requests that those who are unable to be present and debate orally with us, may do so by letter. In the Name our Lord Jesus Christ. Amen.

1. Our Lord and Master Jesus Christ, when He said *Poenitentiam agite*, willed that the whole life of believers should be repentance.

2. This word cannot be understood to mean sacramental penance, i.e. confession and satisfaction, which is administered by the priests.

3. Yet it means not inward repentance only; nay, there is no inward repentance which does not outwardly work divers mortifications of the flesh.

4. The penalty of sin, therefore, continues so long as hatred of self continues; for this is the true inward repentance, and continues until our entrance into the kingdom of heaven.

5. The pope does not intend to remit, and cannot remit any penalties other than those which he has imposed either by his own authority or by that of the Canons.

6. The pope cannot remit any guilt, except by declaring that it has been remitted by God and by assenting to God's remission;

though, to be sure, he may grant remission in cases reserved to his judgment. If his right to grant remission in such cases were despised, the guilt would remain entirely unforgiven.

7. God remits guilt to no one whom He does not, at the same time, humble in all things and bring into subjection to His vicar, the priest.

8. The penitential canons are imposed only on the living, and, according to them, nothing should be imposed on the dying.

9. Therefore the Holy Spirit in the pope is kind to us, because in his decrees he always makes exception of the article of death and of necessity.

10. Ignorant and wicked are the doings of those priests who, in the case of the dying, reserve canonical penances for purgatory.

11. This changing of the canonical penalty to the penalty of purgatory is quite evidently one of the tares that were sown while the bishops slept.

12. In former times the canonical penalties were imposed not after, but before absolution, as tests of true contrition.

13. The dying are freed by death from all penalties; they are already dead to canonical rules, and have a right to be released from them.

14. The imperfect health of the soul, that is to say, the imperfect love, of the dying brings with it, of necessity, great fear; and the smaller the love, the greater is the fear.

15. This fear and horror is sufficient of itself alone, to say nothing of other things, to constitute the penalty of purgatory, since it is very near to the horror of despair.

16. Hell, purgatory, and heaven seem to differ as do despair, almost-despair, and the assurance of safety.

17. With souls in purgatory it seems necessary that horror should grow less and love increase.

18. It seems unproved, either by reason or Scripture, that they are outside the state of merit, that is to say, of increasing love.

19. Again, it seems unproved that they, or at least that all of them, are certain or assured of their own blessedness, though we may be quite certain of it.

20. Therefore by 'full remission of all penalties' the pope means not actually 'of all', but only of those imposed by himself.

21. Therefore those preachers of indulgences are in error, who say that by the pope's indulgences a man is freed from every penalty, and saved;

22. Whereas he remits to souls in purgatory no penalty which, according to the canons, they would have had to pay in this life.

23. If it is at all possible to grant to any one the remission of all penalties whatsoever, it is certain that this remission can be granted only to the most perfect, that is, to the very fewest.

24. It must needs be, therefore, that the greater part of the

people are deceived by that indiscriminate and high-sounding promise of release from penalty.

25. The power which the pope has, in a general way, over purgatory, is just like the power which any bishop or curate has, in a special way, within his own diocese or parish.

26. The pope does well when he grants remission to souls in purgatory, not by the power of the keys, which he does not possess, but by way of intercession.

27. They preach man who say that so soon as the penny jingles into the money-box, the soul flies out of purgatory.

28. It is certain that when the penny jingles into the money-box, gain and avarice can be increased, but the result of the intercession of the Church is in the power of God alone.

29. Who knows whether all the souls in purgatory wish to be bought out of it, as in the legend of Sts Severinus and Paschal.

30. No one is sure that his own contrition is sincere; much less that he has attained full remission.

31. Rare as is the man that is truly penitent, so rare is also the man who truly buys indulgences, i.e. such men are most rare.

32. They will be condemned eternally, together with their teachers, who believe themselves sure of their salvation because they have letters of pardon.

33. Men must be on their guard against those who say that the

pope's pardons are that inestimable gift of God by which man is reconciled to Him;

34. For these 'graces of pardon' concern only the penalties of sacramental satisfaction, and these are appointed by man.

35. They preach no Christian doctrine who teach that contrition is not necessary in those who intend to buy souls out of purgatory or to buy *confessionalia*.

36. Every truly repentant Christian has a right to full remission of penalty and guilt, even without letters of pardon.

37. Every true Christian, whether living or dead, has part in all the blessings of Christ and the Church; and this is granted him by God, even without letters of pardon.

38. Nevertheless, the remission and participation, in the blessings of the Church, which are granted by the pope are in no way to be despised, for they are, as I have said, the declaration of divine remission.

39. It is most difficult, even for the very keenest theologians, at one and the same time to commend to the people the abundance of pardons and the need of true contrition.

40. True contrition seeks and loves penalties, but liberal pardons only relax penalties and cause them to be hated, or at least, furnish an occasion for hating them.

41. Apostolic pardons are to be preached with caution, lest the people may falsely think them preferable to other good works of love.

42. Christians are to be taught that the pope does not intend the buying of pardons to be compared in any way to works of mercy.

43. Christians are to be taught that he who gives to the poor or lends to the needy does a better work than buying pardons;

44. Because love grows by works of love, and man becomes better; but by pardons man does not grow better, only more free from penalty.

45. Christians are to be taught that he who sees a man in need, and passes him by, and gives [his money] for pardons, purchases not the indulgences of the pope, but the indignation of God.

46. Christians are to be taught that unless they have more than they need, they are bound to keep back what is necessary for their own families, and by no means to squander it on pardons.

47. Christians are to be taught that the buying of pardons is a matter of free will, and not of commandment.

48. Christians are to be taught that the pope, in granting pardons, needs, and therefore desires, their devout prayer for him more than the money they bring.

49. Christians are to be taught that the pope's pardons are useful, if they do not put their trust in them; but altogether harmful, if through them they lose their fear of God.

50. Christians are to be taught that if the pope knew the exactions of the pardon-preachers, he would rather that St Peter's

church should go to ashes, than that it should be built up with the skin, flesh and bones of his sheep.

51. Christians are to be taught that it would be the pope's wish, as it is his duty, to give of his own money to very many of those from whom certain hawkers of pardons cajole money, even though the church of St Peter might have to be sold.

52. The assurance of salvation by letters of pardon is vain, even though the commissary, nay, even though the pope himself, were to stake his soul upon it.

53. They are enemies of Christ and of the pope, who bid the Word of God be altogether silent in some Churches, in order that pardons may be preached in others.

54. Injury is done the Word of God when, in the same sermon, an equal or a longer time is spent on pardons than on this Word.

55. It must be the intention of the pope that if pardons, which are a very small thing, are celebrated with one bell, with single processions and ceremonies, then the Gospel, which is the very greatest thing, should be preached with a hundred bells, a hundred processions, a hundred ceremonies.

56. The 'treasures of the Church', out of which the pope grants indulgences, are not sufficiently named or known among the people of Christ.

57. That they are not temporal treasures is certainly evident, for many of the vendors do not pour out such treasures so easily, but only gather them.

58. Nor are they the merits of Christ and the Saints, for even without the pope, these always work grace for the inner man, and the cross, death, and hell for the outward man.

59. St Lawrence said that the treasures of the Church were the Church's poor, but he spoke according to the usage of the word in his own time.

60. Without rashness we say that the keys of the Church, given by Christ's merit, are that treasure;

61. For it is clear that for the remission of penalties and of reserved cases, the power of the pope is of itself sufficient.

62. The true treasure of the Church is the Most Holy Gospel of the glory and the grace of God.

63. But this treasure is naturally most odious, for it makes the first to be last.

64. On the other hand, the treasure of indulgences is naturally most acceptable, for it makes the last to be first.

65. Therefore the treasures of the Gospel are nets with which they formerly were wont to fish for men of riches.

66. The treasures of the indulgences are nets with which they now fish for the riches of men.

67. The indulgences which the preachers cry as the 'greatest graces' are known to be truly such, in so far as they promote gain.

68. Yet they are in truth the very smallest graces compared with the grace of God and the piety of the cross.

69. Bishops and curates are bound to admit the commissaries of apostolic pardons, with all reverence.

70. But still more are they bound to strain all their eyes and attend with all their ears, lest these men preach their own dreams instead of the commission of the pope.

71. He who speaks against the truth of apostolic pardons, let him be anathema and accursed!

72. But he who guards against the lust and license of the pardon-preachers, let him be blessed!

73. The pope justly thunders against those who, by any art, contrive the injury of the traffic in pardons.

74. But much more does he intend to thunder against those who use the pretext of pardons to contrive the injury of holy love and truth.

75. To think the papal pardons so great that they could absolve a man even if he had committed an impossible sin and violated the Mother of God – this is madness.

76. We say, on the contrary, that the papal pardons are not able to remove the very least of venial sins, so far as its guilt is concerned.

77. It is said that even St Peter, if he were now Pope, could not

bestow greater graces; this is blasphemy against St Peter and against the pope.

78. We say, on the contrary, that even the present pope, and any pope at all, has greater graces at his disposal; to wit, the Gospel, powers, gifts of healing, etc., as it is written in 1 Corinthians 12.

79. To say that the cross, emblazoned with the papal arms, which is set up through the preachers of indulgences, is of equal worth with the Cross of Christ, is blasphemy.

80. The bishops, curates and theologians who allow such talk to be spread among the people, will have to give an account of their actions.

81. This unbridled preaching of pardons makes it no easy matter, even for learned men, to rescue the reverence due to the pope from slander, or even from the shrewd questionings of the laity.

82. To wit: 'Why does not the pope empty purgatory, for the sake of holy love and of the dire need of the souls that are there, if he redeems an infinite number of souls for the sake of miserable money with which to build a Church? The former reasons would be most just; the latter is most trivial.'

83. Again: 'Why are mortuary and anniversary masses for the dead continued, and why does he not return or permit the withdrawal of the endowments founded on their behalf, since it is wrong to pray for the redeemed?'

84. Again: 'What is this new piety of God and the pope, that for money they allow a man who is impious and their enemy to buy

out of purgatory the pious soul of a friend of God, and do not rather, because of that pious and beloved soul's own need, free it for pure love's sake?'

85. Again: 'Why are the penitential canons long since in actual fact and through disuse abrogated and dead, now satisfied by the granting of indulgences, as though they were still alive and in force?'

86. Again: 'Why does not the pope, whose wealth is to-day greater than the riches of the richest, build just this one church of St Peter with his own money, rather than with the money of poor believers?'

87. Again: 'What is it that the pope remits, and what participation does he grant to those who, by perfect contrition, have a right to full remission and participation?'

88. Again: 'What greater blessing could come to the Church than if the pope were to do a hundred times a day what he now does once, and bestow on every believer these remissions and participations?'

89. 'Since the pope, by his pardons, seeks the salvation of souls rather than money, why does he suspend the indulgences and pardons granted heretofore, since these have equal efficacy?'

90. To repress these arguments and scruples of the laity by force alone, and not to resolve them by giving reasons, is to expose the Church and the pope to the ridicule of their enemies, and to make Christians unhappy.

91. If, therefore, pardons were preached according to the spirit and mind of the pope, all these doubts would be readily resolved; nay, they would not exist.

92. Away, then, with all those prophets who say to the people of Christ, 'Peace, peace,' and there is no peace!

93. Blessed be all those prophets who say to the people of Christ, 'Cross, cross,' and there is no cross!

94. Christians are to be exhorted that they be diligent in following Christ, their Head, through penalties, deaths, and hell;

95. And thus be confident of entering into heaven rather through many tribulations, than through the assurance of peace.

Martin Luther

My conscience is captive to the word of God

Luther appeared before the Emperor Charles V at the Diet of Worms on 18 April 1521. He had expected that he would be called on to defend certain articles of faith; instead he was simply called on to recant. In response he made the following great oration, first in German and then in Latin. After Worms the die was cast for the Reformation in Germany.

Most Serene Emperor, Most Illustrious Princes, Most Clement Lords! At the time fixed yesterday I obediently appear, begging for the mercy of God, that your Most Serene Majesty and your Illustrious Lordships may deign to hear this cause, which I hope may be called the cause of justice and truth, with clemency; and if, by my inexperience, I should fail to give anyone the titles due to him, or should sin against the etiquette of the court, please forgive me, as a man who has not lived in courts but in monastic nooks, one who can say nothing for himself but that he has hitherto tried to teach and to write with a sincere mind and single eye to the glory of God and the edification of Christians.

Most Serene Emperor, Most Illustrious Princes! Two questions were asked me yesterday. To the first, whether I would recognize that the books published under my name were mine, I gave a plain answer, to which I hold and will hold for ever, namely, that the books are mine, as I published them, unless perchance it may have happened that the guile or meddlesome wisdom of my opponents has changed something in them. For I only recognize what has been written by myself alone, and not the interpretation added by another.

In reply to the second question I beg your Most Sacred Majesty and your lordships to be pleased to consider that all my books are not of the same kind.

In some I have treated piety, faith, and morals so simply and evangelically that my adversaries themselves are forced to confess that these books are useful, innocent, and worthy to be read by Christians. Even the bull, though fierce and cruel, states that some things in my books are harmless, although it condemns them by a judgement simply monstrous. If, therefore, I should undertake to recant these, would it not happen that I alone of all men should damn the truth which all, friends and enemies alike, confess?

The second class of my works inveighs against the papacy as against that which both by precept and example has laid waste all Christendom, body and soul. No one can deny or dissemble this fact, since general complaints witness that the consciences of all believers are snared, harassed, and tormented by the laws of the Pope and the doctrines of men, and especially that the goods of this famous German nation have been and are devoured in numerous and ignoble ways. Yet the Canon Law provides that the laws and doctrines of the Pope contrary to the gospel and the Fathers are to be held erroneous and rejected. If, therefore, I should withdraw these books, I would add strength to tyranny and open windows and doors to their impiety, which would then flourish and burgeon more freely than it ever dared before. It would come to pass that their wickedness would go unpunished, and therefore would become more licentious on account of my recantation, and their government of the people, thus confirmed and established, would become intolerable, especially if they could boast that I had recanted with the full authority of your Sacred and Most Serene Majesty and of the whole Roman Empire. Good God! In that case I would be the tool of iniquity and tyranny.

In a third sort of books I have written against some private individuals who tried to defend the Roman tyranny and tear down my pious doctrine. In these I confess I was more bitter than is becoming to a minister of religion. For I do not pose as a saint, nor do I discuss my life but the doctrine of Christ. Yet neither is it right for me to recant what I have said in these, for then tyranny and impiety would rage and reign against the people of God more violently than ever by reason of my acquiescence.

As I am a man and not God, I wish to claim no other defence for my doctrine than that which the Lord Jesus put forward when he was questioned before Annas and smitten by a servant: he then said: 'If I have spoken evil, bear witness of the evil.' If the Lord himself, who knew that he could not err, did not scorn to hear testimony against his doctrine from a miserable servant, how much more should I, the dregs of men, who can do nothing but err, seek and hope that someone should bear witness against my doctrine. I therefore beg by God's mercy that if your

Majesty or your illustrious Lordships, from the highest to the lowest, can do it, you should bear witness and convict me of error and conquer me by proofs drawn from the gospels or the prophets, for I am most ready to be instructed and when convinced will be the first to throw my books into the fire.

From this I think it is sufficiently clear that I have carefully considered and weighed the discords, perils, emulation, and dissension excited by my teaching, concerning which I was gravely and urgently admonished yesterday. To me the happiest side of the whole affair is that the Word of God is made the object of emulation and dissent. For this is the course, the fate, and the result of the Word of God, as Christ says: 'I am come not to send peace but a sword, to set a man against his father and a daughter against her mother.' We must consider that our God is wonderful and terrible in his counsels. If we should begin to heal our dissensions by damning the word of God, we should only turn loose an intolerable deluge of woes. Let us take care that the rule of this excellent youth, Prince Charles (in whom, next to God, there is much hope), does not begin inauspiciously. For I could show by many examples drawn from scripture that when Pharaoh and the king of Babylon and the kings of Israel thought to pacify and strengthen their kingdoms by their own wisdom, they really only ruined themselves. For he taketh the wise in their own craftiness and removeth mountains and they know it not. We must fear God. I do not say this as though your lordships needed either my teaching or my admonition, but because I could not shirk the duty I owed Germany. With these words I commend myself to your Majesty and your Lordships, humbly begging that you will not let my enemies make me hateful to you without cause. I have spoken.

Eck replied: Luther, you have not answered the point. You ought not to call in question what has been decided and condemned by councils. Therefore I beg you to give a simple, unsophisticated answer without horns (*non cornutum*). Will you recant or not?

Luther replied: Since your Majesty and your Lordships ask for a plain answer, I will give you one without either horns or teeth. Unless I am convicted by scripture or by right reason (for I trust neither in popes nor in councils, since they have often erred and contradicted themselves) – unless I am thus convinced, I am bound by the texts of the Bible, my conscience is captive to the word of God, I neither can nor will recant anything, since it is neither safe nor right to act against conscience. God help me. Amen.

Martin Luther

Preface to Romans

Below is the Preface to Luther's commentary on Paul's letter to the Romans. The commentary was based on the lectures which he gave to his theological students at Wittenberg in 1515.

This letter is truly the most important piece in the New Testament. It is purest Gospel. It is well worth a Christian's while not only to memorize it word for word but also to occupy himself with it daily, as though it were the daily bread of the soul. It is impossible to read or to meditate on this letter too much or too well. The more one deals with it, the more precious it becomes and the better it tastes. Therefore I want to carry out my service and, with this preface, provide an introduction to the letter, insofar as God gives me the ability, so that every one can gain the fullest possible understanding of it. Up to now it has been darkened by glosses and by many a useless comment, but it is in itself a bright light, almost bright enough to illumine the entire Scripture.

To begin with, we have to become familiar with the vocabulary of the letter and know what St Paul means by the words law, sin, grace, faith, justice, flesh, spirit, etc. Otherwise there is no use in reading it.

You must not understand the word law here in human fashion, i.e., a regulation about what sort of works must be done or must not be done. That's the way it is with human laws: you satisfy the demands of the law with works, whether your heart is in it or not. God judges what is in the depths of the heart. Therefore his law also makes demands on the depths of the heart and doesn't let the heart rest content in works; rather it punishes as hypocrisy and lies all works done apart from the depths of the heart. All human beings are called liars (Psalm 116), since none of them keeps or can keep God's law from the depths of the heart. Everyone finds inside himself an aversion to good and a craving for evil. Where there is no free desire for good, there the heart has not set itself on God's law. There also sin is surely to be found and the deserved wrath of God, whether a lot of good works and an honourable life appear outwardly or not.

Therefore in chapter 2, St Paul adds that the Jews are all sinners and says that only the doers of the law are justified in the sight of God. What he is saying is that no one is a doer of the law by works. On the contrary, he says to them, 'You teach that one should not commit adultery, and you commit adultery. You judge another in a certain matter and condemn yourselves in that same matter, because you do the very same thing that you judged in another.' It is as if he were saying, 'Outwardly you live quite properly in the works of the law and judge those who do not live the same way; you know how to teach everybody. You see the speck in another's eye but do not notice the beam in your own.'

Outwardly you keep the law with works out of fear of punishment or love of gain. Likewise you do everything without free desire and love of the law; you act out of aversion and force. You'd rather act otherwise if the law didn't exist. It follows, then, that you, in the depths of your heart, are an enemy of the law. What do you mean, therefore, by teaching another not to steal, when you, in the depths of your heart, are a thief and would be one outwardly too, if you dared. (Of course, outward work doesn't last long with such hypocrites.) So then, you teach others but not yourself; you don't even know what you are teaching. You've never understood the law rightly. Furthermore, the law increases sin, as St Paul says in chapter 5. That is because a person becomes more and more an enemy of the law the more it demands of him what he can't possibly do.

In chapter 7, St Paul says, 'The law is spiritual.' What does that mean? If the law were physical, then it could be satisfied by works, but since it is spiritual, no one can satisfy it unless everything he does springs from the depths of the heart. But no one can give such a heart except the Spirit of God, who makes the person be like the law, so that he actually conceives a heartfelt longing for the law and henceforward does everything, not through fear or coercion, but from a free heart. Such a law is spiritual since it can only be loved and fulfilled by such a heart and such a spirit. If the Spirit is not in the heart, then there remain sin, aversion and enmity against the law, which in itself is good, just and holy.

You must get used to the idea that it is one thing to do the works of the law and quite another to fulfil it. The works of the law are every thing that a person does or can do of his own free will and by his own powers to obey the law. But because in doing such works the heart abhors the law and yet is forced to obey it, the works are a total loss and are completely useless.

That is what St Paul means in chapter 3 when he says, 'No human being is justified before God through the works of the law.' From this you can see that the scholastic theologians and sophists are seducers when they teach that you can prepare yourself for grace by means of works. How can anybody prepare himself for good by means of works if he does no good work except with aversion and constraint in his heart? How can such a work please God, if it proceeds from an averse and unwilling heart?

But to fulfil the law means to do its work eagerly, lovingly and freely, without the constraint of the law; it means to live well and in a manner pleasing to God, as though there were no law or punishment. It is the Holy Spirit, however, who puts such eagerness of unconstrained love into the heart, as Paul says in chapter 5. But the Spirit is given only in, with, and through faith in Jesus Christ, as Paul says in his introduction. So, too, faith comes only through the word of God, the Gospel, that preaches Christ: how he is both Son of God and man, how he died and rose for our sake. Paul says all this in chapters 3, 4 and 10.

That is why faith alone makes someone just and fulfils the law; faith it is that brings the Holy Spirit through the merits of Christ. The Spirit, in turn, renders the heart glad and free, as the law demands. Then good works proceed from faith itself. That is what Paul means in chapter 3 when, after he has thrown out the works of the law, he sounds as though the wants to abolish the law by faith. No, he says, we uphold the law through faith, i.e. we fulfil it through faith.

Sin in the Scriptures means not only external works of the body but also all those movements within us which bestir themselves and move us to do the external works, namely, the depth of the heart with all its powers. Therefore the word *do* should refer to a person's completely falling into sin. No external work of sin happens, after all, unless a person commit himself to it completely, body and soul. In particular, the Scriptures see into the heart, to the root and main source of all sin: unbelief in the depth of the heart. Thus, even as faith alone makes just and brings the Spirit and the desire to do good external works, so it is only unbelief which sins and exalts the flesh and brings desire to do evil external works. That's what happened to Adam and Eve in Paradise (cf. Genesis 3).

That is why only unbelief is called sin by Christ, as he says in John, chapter 16, 'The Spirit will punish the world because of sin, because it does not believe in me.' Furthermore, before good or bad works happen, which are the good or bad fruits of the heart, there has to be present in the heart either faith or unbelief, the root, sap and chief power of all sin. That is why, in the Scriptures, unbelief is called the head of the serpent and of the ancient dragon which the offspring of the woman, i.e. Christ, must crush, as was promised to Adam (cf. Genesis 3). Grace and gift differ in that grace actually denotes God's kindness or favour which he has toward us and by which he is disposed to pour Christ and the Spirit with his gifts into us, as becomes clear from chapter 5, where Paul says, 'Grace and gift are in Christ, etc.' The gifts and the Spirit increase daily in us, yet they are not complete, since evil desires and sins remain in us which war against the Spirit, as Paul says in chapter 7, and in Galatians, chapter 5. And Genesis, chapter 3, proclaims the enmity between the offspring of the woman and that of the serpent. But grace does do this much: that we are accounted completely just before God. God's grace is not divided into bits and pieces, as are the gifts, but grace takes us up completely into God's favour for the sake of Christ, our intercessor and mediator, so that the gifts may begin their work in us.

In this way, then, you should understand chapter 7, where St Paul portrays himself as still a sinner, while in chapter 8 he says that, because of the incomplete gifts and because of the Spirit, there is nothing damnable in those who are in Christ. Because our flesh has not been killed, we are still sinners, but because we believe in Christ and have the beginnings of the Spirit, God so shows us his favour and mercy, that he neither notices nor judges such sins. Rather he deals with us according to our belief in Christ until sin is killed.

Faith is not that human illusion and dream that some people think it is. When they hear and talk a lot about faith and yet see that no moral improvement and no good works result from it, they fall into error and say, 'Faith is not enough. You must do works if you want to be virtuous and get to heaven.' The result is that, when they hear the Gospel, they stumble and make for themselves with their own powers a concept in their hearts which says, 'I believe.' This concept they hold to be true faith. But since it is a human fabrication and thought and not an experience of the heart, it accomplishes nothing, and there follows no improvement.

Faith is a work of God in us, which changes us and brings us to birth anew from God (cf. John 1). It kills the old Adam, makes us completely different people in heart, mind, senses, and all our powers, and brings the Holy Spirit with it. What a living, creative, active powerful thing is faith! It is impossible that faith ever stop doing good. Faith doesn't ask whether good works are to be done, but, before it is asked, it has done them. It is always active. Whoever doesn't do such works is without faith; he gropes and searches about him for faith and good works but doesn't know what faith or good works are. Even so, he chatters on with a great many words about faith and good works.

Faith is a living, unshakeable confidence in God's grace; it is so certain, that someone would die a thousand times for it. This kind of trust in and knowledge of God's grace makes a person joyful, confident, and happy with regard to God and all creatures. This is what the Holy Spirit does by faith. Through faith, a person will do good to everyone without coercion, willingly and happily; he will serve everyone, suffer everything for the love and praise of God, who has shown him such grace. It is as impossible to separate works from faith as burning and shining from fire. Therefore be on guard against your own false ideas and against the chatterers who think they are clever enough to make judgements about faith and good works but who are in reality the biggest fools. Ask God to work faith in you; otherwise you will remain eternally without faith, no matter what you try to do or fabricate.

Now justice is just such a faith. It is called God's justice or that justice which is valid in God's sight, because it is God who gives it and reckons it as justice for the sake of Christ our Mediator. It influences a person to give to everyone what he owes him. Through faith a person becomes sinless and eager for God's commands. Thus he gives God the honour due him and pays him what he owes him. He serves people willingly with the means available to him. In this way he pays everyone his due. Neither nature nor free will nor our own powers can bring about such a justice, for even as no one can give himself faith, so too he cannot remove unbelief. How can he then take away even the smallest sin? Therefore everything which takes place outside faith or in unbelief is lie, hypocrisy and sin (Romans 14), no matter how smoothly it may seem to go.

You must not understand flesh here as denoting only unchastity or spirit as denoting only the inner heart. Here St Paul calls flesh (as does Christ in John 3) everything born of flesh, i.e. the whole human being with body and soul, reason and senses, since everything in him tends toward the flesh. That is why you should know enough to call that person 'fleshly' who, without grace, fabricates, teaches and chatters about high spiritual matters. You can learn the same thing from Galatians, chapter 5, where St Paul calls heresy and hatred works of the flesh. And in Romans, chapter 8, he says that, through the flesh, the law is weakened. He says this, not of unchastity, but of all sins, most of all of unbelief, which is the most spiritual of vices.

On the other hand, you should know enough to call that person 'spiritual' who is occupied with the most outward of works as was Christ, when he washed the feet of the disciples, and Peter, when he steered his boat and fished. So then, a person is 'flesh' who, inwardly and outwardly, lives only to do those things which are of use to the flesh and to temporal existence. A person is 'spirit' who, inwardly and outwardly, lives only to do those things which are of use to the spirit and to the life to come.

Unless you understand these words in this way, you will never understand either this letter of St Paul or any book of the Scriptures. Be on guard, therefore against any teacher who uses these words differently, no matter who he be, whether Jerome, Augustine, Ambrose, Origen or anyone else as great as or greater than they. Now let us turn to the letter itself.

The first duty of a preacher of the Gospel is, through his revealing of the law and of sin, to rebuke and to turn into sin everything in life that does not have the Spirit and faith in Christ as its base. Thereby he will lead people to a recognition of their miserable condition, and thus they will become humble and yearn for help. This is what St Paul does. He begins in chapter 1 by rebuking the gross sins and unbelief which are in plain view, as were (and still are) the sins of the pagans, who live without God's grace. He says that, through the Gospel, God is revealing his wrath from heaven upon all mankind because of the godless and unjust lives they live. For, although they know and recognize day by day that there is a God, yet human nature in itself, without grace, is so evil that it neither thanks nor honours God. This nature blinds itself and continually falls into wickedness, even going so far as to commit idolatry and other horrible sins and vices. It is unashamed of itself and leaves such things unpunished in others.

In chapter 2, St Paul extends his rebuke to those who appear outwardly pious or who sin secretly. Such were the Jews, and such are all hypocrites still, who live virtuous lives but without eagerness and love; in their heart they are enemies of God's law and like to judge other people. That's the way with hypocrites: they think that they are pure but are actually full of greed, hate, pride and all sorts of filth (cf. Matthew 23). These are they who despise God's goodness and, by their hardness of heart, heap wrath upon themselves. Thus Paul explains the law rightly when he lets no one remain without sin but proclaims the wrath of God to all who want to live virtuously by nature or by free will. He makes them out to be no better than public sinners; he says they are hard of heart and unrepentant.

In chapter 3, Paul lumps both secret and public sinners together: the one, he says, is like the other; all are sinners in the sight of God. Besides, the Jews had God's word, even though many did not believe in it. But still God's truth and faith in him are not thereby rendered useless. St Paul introduces, as an aside, the saying from Psalm 51, that God remains true to his words. Then he returns to his topic and proves from Scripture that they are all sinners and that no one becomes just through the works of the law but that God gave the law only so that sin might be perceived.

Next St Paul teaches the right way to be virtuous and to be saved; he says that they are all sinners, unable to glory in God. They must, however, be justified through faith in Christ, who has merited this for us by his blood and has become for us a mercy seat [cf. Exodus 25:17; Leviticus 16:14ff.; John 2:2] in the presence of God, who forgives us all our previous sins. In so doing, God proves that it is his justice alone, which he gives through faith, that helps us, the justice which was at the appointed time revealed through the Gospel and, previous to that, was witnessed to by the Law and the Prophets. Therefore the law is set up by faith, but the works of the law, along with the glory taken in them, are knocked down by faith.

In chapters 1 to 3, St Paul has revealed sin for what it is and has taught the way of faith which leads to justice. Now in chapter 4 he deals with some objections and criticisms. He takes up first the one that people raise who, on hearing that faith make just without works, say, 'What? Shouldn't we do any good works?' Here St Paul holds up Abraham as an example. He says, 'What did Abraham accomplish with his good works? Were they all good for nothing and useless?' He concludes that Abraham was made righteous apart from all his works by faith alone. Even before the 'work' of his circumcision, Scripture praises him as being just on account of faith alone (cf. Genesis 15). Now if the work of his circumcision did nothing to make him just, a work that God had commanded him to do and hence a work of obedience, then surely no other good work can do anything to make a person just. Even as Abraham's circumcision was an outward sign with which he proved his justice based on faith, so too all good works are only outward signs which flow from faith and are the fruits of faith; they prove that the person is already inwardly just in the sight of God.

St Paul verifies his teaching on faith in chapter 3 with a powerful example from Scripture. He calls as witness David, who says in Psalm 32 that a person becomes just without works but doesn't remain without works once he has become just. Then Paul extends this example and applies it against all other works of the law. He concludes that the Jews cannot be Abraham's heirs just because of their blood relationship to him and still less because of the works of the law. Rather, they have to inherit Abraham's faith if they want to be his real heirs, since it was prior to the Law of Moses and the law of circumcision that Abraham became just through faith and was called a father of all believers. St Paul adds that the law brings about more wrath than grace, because no one obeys it with love and eagerness. More disgrace than grace come from the works of the law. Therefore faith alone can obtain the grace promised to Abraham. Examples like these are written for our sake, that we also should have faith.

In chapter 5, St Paul comes to the fruits and works of faith, namely: joy, peace, love for God and for all people; in addition: assurance, steadfastness, confidence, courage, and hope in sorrow and suffering. All of these follow where faith is genuine, because of the overflowing good will that God has shown in Christ: he had him die for us before we could ask him for it, yes, even while we were still his enemies. Thus we have established that faith, without any good works, makes just. It does not follow from that, however, that we should not do good works; rather it means that morally upright works do not remain lacking. About such works the 'works-holy' people know nothing; they invent for themselves their own works in which are neither peace nor joy nor assurance nor love nor hope nor steadfastness nor any kind of genuine Christian works or faith.

Next St Paul makes a digression, a pleasant little side-trip, and relates where both sin and justice, death and life come from. He opposes these two: Adam and Christ. What he wants to say is that Christ, a second Adam, had to come in order to make us heirs of his justice through a new spiritual birth in faith, just as the old Adam made us heirs of sin through the old fleshy birth.

St Paul proves, by this reasoning, that a person cannot help himself by his works to get from sin to justice any more than he can prevent his own physical birth. St Paul also proves that the divine law, which should have been well-suited, if anything was, for helping people to obtain justice, not only was no help at all when it did come, but it even increased sin. Evil human nature, consequently, becomes more hostile to it; the more the law forbids it to indulge its own desires, the more it wants to. Thus the law makes Christ all the more necessary and demands more grace to help human nature.

In chapter 6, St Paul takes up the special work of faith, the struggle which the spirit wages against the flesh to kill off those sins and desires that remain after a person has been made just. He teaches us that faith doesn't so free us from sin that we can be idle, lazy and self-assured, as though there were no more sin in us. Sin is there, but, because of faith that struggles against it, God does not reckon sin as deserving damnation. Therefore we have in our own selves a lifetime of work cut out for us; we have to tame our body, kill its lusts, force its members to obey the spirit and not the lusts. We must do this so that we may conform to the death and resurrection of Christ and complete our Baptism, which signifies a death to sin and a new life of grace. Our aim is to be completely clean from sin and then to rise bodily with Christ and live forever.

St Paul says that we can accomplish all this because we are in grace and not in the law. He explains that to be 'outside the law' is not the same as having no law and being able to do what you please. No, being 'under the law' means living without grace, surrounded by the works of the law. Then surely sin reigns by means of the law, since no one is naturally well-disposed toward the law. That very condition, however, is the greatest sin. But grace makes the law lovable to us, so there is then no sin any more, and the law is no longer against us but one with us.

This is true freedom from sin and from the law; St Paul writes about this for the rest of the chapter. He says it is a freedom only to do good with eagerness and to live a good life without the coercion of the law. This freedom is, therefore, a spiritual freedom which does not suspend the law but which supplies what the law demands, namely eagerness and love. These silence the law so that it has no further cause to drive people on and make demands of them. It's as though you owed something to a moneylender and couldn't pay him. You could be rid of him in one of two ways: either he would take nothing from you and would tear up his account book, or a pious man would pay for you and give you what you needed to satisfy your debt. That's exactly how Christ freed us from the law. Therefore our freedom is not a wild, fleshy freedom that has no obligation to do anything. On the contrary, it is a freedom that does a great deal, indeed everything, yet is free of the law's demands and debts.

In chapter 7, St Paul confirms the foregoing by an analogy drawn from married life. When a man dies, the wife is free; the one is free and clear of the other. It is not the case that the woman may not or should not marry another man; rather she is now for the first time free to marry someone else. She could not do this before she was free of her first husband. In the same way, our conscience is bound to the law so long as our condition is that of the sinful old man. But when the old man is killed by the spirit, then the conscience is free, and conscience and law are quit of each other. Not that conscience should now do nothing; rather, it should now for the first time truly cling to its second husband, Christ, and bring forth the fruit of life.

Next St Paul sketches further the nature of sin and the law. It is the law that makes sin really active and powerful, because the old man gets more and more hostile to the law since he can't pay the debt demanded by the law. Sin is his very nature; of himself he can't do otherwise. And so the law is his death and torture. Now the law is not itself evil; it is our evil nature that cannot tolerate that the good law should demand good from it. It's like the case of a sick person, who cannot tolerate that you demand that he run and jump around and do other things that a healthy person does.

St Paul concludes here that, if we understand the law properly and comprehend it in the best possible way, then we will see that its sole function is to remind us of our sins, to kill us by our sins, and to make us deserving of eternal wrath. Conscience learns and experiences all this in detail when it comes face to face with the law. It follows, then, that we must have something else, over and above the law, which can make a person virtuous and cause him to be saved. Those, however, who do not understand the law rightly are blind; they go their way boldly and think they are satisfying the law with works. They don't know how much the law demands, namely, a free, willing, eager heart. That is the reason that they don't see Moses rightly before their eyes. For them he is covered and concealed by the veil.

Then St Paul shows how spirit and flesh struggle with each other in one person. He gives himself as an example, so that we may learn how to kill sin in ourselves. He gives both spirit and flesh the name 'law', so that, just as it is in the nature of divine law to drive a person on and make demands of him, so too the flesh drives and demands and rages against the spirit and wants to have its own way. Likewise the spirit drives and demands against the flesh and wants to have its own way. This feud lasts in us for as long as we live, in one person more, in another less, depending on whether spirit or flesh is stronger. Yet the whole human being is both: spirit and flesh. The human being fights with himself until he becomes completely spiritual.

In chapter 8, St Paul comforts fighters such as these and tells them that this flesh will not bring them condemnation. He goes on to show what the nature of flesh and spirit are. Spirit, he says, comes from Christ, who has given us his Holy Spirit; the Holy Spirit makes us spiritual and restrains the flesh. The Holy Spirit assures us that we are God's children no matter how furiously sin may rage within us, so long as we follow the Spirit and struggle against sin in order to kill it. Because nothing is so effective in deadening the flesh as the cross and suffering, Paul comforts us in our suffering. He says that the Spirit, love and all creatures will stand by us; the Spirit in us groans and all creatures long with us that we be freed from the flesh and from sin. Thus we see that these three chapters, 6, 7 and 8, all deal with the one work of faith, which is to kill the old Adam and to constrain the flesh.

In chapters 9, 10 and 11, St Paul teaches us about the eternal providence of God. It is the original source which determines who would believe and who wouldn't, who can be set free from sin and who cannot. Such matters have been taken out of our hands and are put into God's hands so that we might become virtuous. It is absolutely necessary that it be so, for we are so weak and unsure of ourselves that, if it depended on us, no human being would be saved. The devil would overpower all of us. But God is steadfast; his providence will not fail, and no one can prevent its realization. Therefore we have hope against sin.

But here we must shut the mouths of those sacrilegious and arrogant spirits who, mere beginners that they are, bring their reason to bear on this matter and commence, from their exalted position, to probe the abyss of divine providence and uselessly trouble themselves about whether they are predestined or not. These people must surely plunge to their ruin, since they will either despair or abandon themselves to a life of chance.

You, however, follow the reasoning of this letter in the order in which it is presented. Fix your attention first of all on Christ and the Gospel, so that you may recognize your sin and his grace. Then struggle against sin, as chapters 1–8 have taught you to. Finally, when you have come, in chapter 8, under the shadow of the cross and suffering, they will teach you, in chapters 9–11, about providence and what a comfort it is. Apart from suffering, the cross and the pangs of death, you cannot come to grips with providence without harm to yourself and secret anger against God. The old Adam must be quite dead before you can endure this matter and drink this strong wine. Therefore make sure you don't drink wine while you are still a babe at the breast. There is a proper measure, time and age for understanding every doctrine.

In chapter 12, St Paul teaches the true liturgy and makes all Christians priests, so that they may offer, not money or cattle, as priests do in the Law, but their own bodies, by putting their desires to death. Next he describes the outward conduct of Christians whose lives are governed by the Spirit; he tells how they teach, preach, rule, serve, give, suffer, love, live and act toward friend, foe and everyone. These are the works that a Christian does, for, as I have said, faith is not idle.

In chapter 13, St Paul teaches that one should honour and obey the secular authorities. He includes this, not because it makes people virtuous in the sight of God, but because it does insure that the virtuous have outward peace and protection and that the wicked cannot do evil without fear and in undisturbed peace. Therefore it is the duty of virtuous people to honour secular authority, even though they do not, strictly speaking, need it. Finally, St Paul sums up everything in love and gathers it all into the example of Christ: what he has done for us, we must also do and follow after him.

In chapter 14, St Paul teaches that one should carefully guide those with weak conscience and spare them. One shouldn't use Christian freedom to harm but rather to help the weak. Where that isn't done, there follows dissension and despising of the Gospel, on which everything else depends. It is better to give way a little to the weak in faith until they become stronger than to have the teaching of the Gospel perish completely. This work is a particularly necessary work of love especially now when people, by eating meat and by other freedoms, are brashly, boldly and unnecessarily shaking weak consciences which have not yet come to know the truth.

In chapter 15, St Paul cites Christ as an example to show that we must also have patience with the weak, even those who fail by sinning publicly or by their disgusting morals. We must not cast them aside but must bear with them until they become better. That is the way Christ treated us and still treats us every day; he puts up with our vices, our wicked morals and all our imperfection, and he helps us ceaselessly. Finally Paul prays for the Christians at Rome; he praises them and commends them to God. He points out his own office and the message that he preaches. He makes an unobtrusive plea for a contribution for the poor in Jerusalem. Unalloyed love is the basis of all he says and does.

The last chapter consists of greetings. But Paul also includes a salutary warning against human doctrines which are preached alongside the Gospel and which do a great deal of harm. It's as though he had clearly seen that out of Rome and through the Romans would come the deceitful, harmful Canons along with the entire brood and swarm of human laws and commands that is now drowning the whole world and has blotted out this letter and the whole of the Scriptures, along with the Spirit and faith. Nothing remains but the idol Belly, and St Paul depicts those people here as its servants. God deliver us from them. Amen.

We find in this letter, then, the richest possible teaching about what a Christian should know: the meaning of law, Gospel, sin, punishment, grace, faith, justice, Christ, God, good works, love, hope and the cross. We learn how we are to act toward everyone, toward the virtuous and sinful, toward the strong and the weak, friend and foe, and toward ourselves. Paul bases everything firmly on Scripture and proves his points with examples from his own experience and from the Prophets, so that nothing more could be desired. Therefore it seems that St Paul, in writing this letter, wanted to compose a summary of the whole of Christian and evangelical teaching which would also be an introduction to the whole Old Testament. Without doubt, whoever takes this letter to heart possesses the light and power of the Old Testament. Therefore each and every Christian should make this letter the habitual and constant object of his study. God grant us his grace to do so. Amen.

Philip Melancthon

The circumstances of Luther's death

Philip Melancthon (1497–1560), whose real name was Philip Schwarzerd, was a German Protestant scholar who helped Martin Luther to prepare a German translation of the New Testament.

To the Students in The University of Wittenburg, on the death of Luther, 1546 on our assembling to hear the Epistle of Paul to the Romans, at nine o'clock in the forenoon, Dr Philip Melancthon publicly recited to us the following address; saying at the same time, that he was induced to do so at the suggestion of some learned professors, and that we being in possession of the true state of things, might be prepared to reject any incorrect statements which he foresaw would be in circulation after Luther's death.

'Most Noble Youths,

'We have undertaken as you know, to deliver a critical exposition of the Epistle to the Romans, wherein is contained the true doctrine of the Son of God, which our Heavenly Father has in peculiar mercy, laid open to us, at this time, through our revered Father and Preceptor, Dr Martin Luther.

'But now alas, so deep a shade of sorrow is cast over these writings, which but augment my grief, that I know not whether I shall be able hereafter to pursue the study of them in our college. I am anxious however, at the request of my friends of the University, and that you may have a right understanding of the circumstances of Luther's death, to communicate to you the following particulars, in order that you may not even entertain, much less circulate, reports which, as is so often the case, will probably now be current in society. On the 17th of February, our Master and Teacher, a little before supper, was attacked by his usual complaint to which I remember he had occasionally been subject. After supper a recurrence of the disorder took place, under the influence of which he requested permission to withdraw into an adjoining room, where he lay for nearly two hours, until his sufferings increased. Doctor Jonas sleeping in the same room with him, Doctor Martin called him hastily, requesting him to rise and give orders that Ambrosius, the servant who attended on the children, should make his private apartment warm: and having retired into it, Albert, the illustrious Count of Mansfield, with his Countess, and many others, entered, the names of whom for brevity's sake, we omit. At length when he found that the close of his life was approaching, before four o'clock on the following day, the 18th of February, he commended himself to God in the following prayer:

"'My heavenly Father, eternal and merciful God! Thou has revealed unto me Thy dear Son, our Lord Jesus Christ, whom I have learned – whom I have proclaimed to be my Lord – whom I love and whom I honour, as my precious Saviour and Redeemer – whom the ungodly persecute, dishonour, and blaspheme; take Thou my soul unto Thyself."

'Three times he expressed these words. "Into Thy hands I commit my spirit. Thou hast redeemed me, O God of Truth!" "And God so loved the world," etc. Amid these prayers occasionally repeated, he was called to the one eternal assembly and to everlasting bliss, in which he is now enjoying the presence of the Father, of the Son, and of the Holy Ghost, with that of all the Prophets and Apostles. Alas, for the chariot of Israel and the horsemen thereof! Our Elijah is no more, he who guided and governed the Church in this decrepitude of the world. Human sagacity could not have discovered the doctrines of the remission of sins, and of faith in the Son of God; but He has been pleased to reveal them to us through the medium of this, His servant, whom also we see that God has taken unto himself. Let us therefore cherish his memory with that of the peculiar doctrine which he delivered to us, and let us be the more humbled in our spirits when we contemplate the great calamities and the mighty revolutions which will probably follow this event. I beseech Thee, O Son of God! Thou who wast crucified for us, and art now the risen Emmanuel, that Thou wilt govern, preserve, and defend Thy Church. Amen.'

Philip Melancthon

Elegy for Martin Luther

Since Luther is no more, his cherished name shall from our hearts, a deathless tribute claim. We hailed him minister of Christ, the Lord, Jesus he preached, with faith, and taught his word.

Luther is dead, and now the church in tears
A mourner clothed in saddest garb appears.
She weeps her loved preceptor now no more,
Honoured and dear, a father's name he bore.
Fallen on the field the mighty chieftain lies,
And Israel's voice proclaims his obsequies.
Then let us bathe in tears the muse's lay
And publish forth our sorrows to the day.
It thus becomes us well to weep and mourn
Whilst, orphans in our grief, we dress affection's urn.

Philip Melancthon

A funeral oration for Martin Luther

Although amid this universal grief, my voice is impeded by sorrow and by tears, yet since in so large an assembly, we are called upon for some expression of our feelings; let it not be after the manner of the heathen, a declamation in praise of the departed one, but rather a commemoration in the audience of those now present of the wonderful pilotage of the church in all her perils; that we may call to mind on what account it behoves us to mourn, what purposes we should ourselves most diligently pursue, and in what manner we should order our lives. For although irreligious men conceive that the interests of this world are borne along in a giddy tide of confusion and uncertainty, yet, reassured as we are by the many indubitable testimonies of God, we make a wide distinction between the church and the profane multitude, and we believe that she is indeed governed and upheld by the power of God: we clearly discern his polity – we acknowledge the true helmsmen, and we watch their course – we choose also for ourselves, befitting leaders and teachers whom we devotedly follow and revere.

On these so weighty matters, it is necessary both to think and to speak, as often as mention is made of that revered man Dr Martin Luther, our beloved father and teacher; and whilst he has been the object of most cruel hatred to many, let us who know that he was a divinely inspired minister of the gospel, regard his memory with love and esteem, and let us gather such testimonies as prove that his teaching was by no means a blind dissemination of seditious opinions, as the Epicureans give out, but a demonstration of the will and of the true worship of God, an unfolding of the sacred records and a declaration of the word of God, that is of the gospel of Jesus Christ. In orations such as the present, much is usually said of the individual excellencies of those whom we wish to commend; passing however, in silence over this part of my theme, it is my design to dwell principally on that main point, the call to gospel ministry; and here we may unite in opinion with all just thinkers, that if Luther has illustrated a wholesome and necessary doctrine in the church, we ought to return thanks unto God, that He has been pleased to raise him up to this work, whilst his personal labours, his faith, his constancy, and his other virtues are to be commended, and his memory to be held most dear by all good men. Let this therefore be the beginning, of our oration.

The Son of God, as Paul says, sits on the right hand of the Eternal Father, and gives gifts unto men; these gifts are the voice of the Gospel and of the Holy Spirit, with which, as He imparts them, He inspires Prophets, Apostles, Pastors and Teachers, and selects them from this our assembly, that is to say, from those who are yet in the rudiments of divine knowledge, who read, who hear, and who love the prophetic and apostolic writings; nor does he often call to this warfare those who are in the exercise of established power, but it even pleases him to wage war on these very men through leaders chosen from other ranks. It is cheering and instructive to take a retrospect of the church throughout all past ages, and to contemplate the goodness of God who has sent out from its bosom gifted ministers in so unbroken a series, that as the first of these have passed away, others have pressed closely in their footsteps. The line of the first fathers is well worthy of our consideration. Adam, Seth, Enoch, Methuselah, Noah, and Abraham, who was raised up to be a fellow-helper of Sem and his associate in the all-important work of spreading true religion; and although at this time Sem was still dwelling in the neighbourhood of Sodom, the people had lost the recollection both of his precepts and those of Noah, and were altogether abandoned to the worship of idols. To Abraham succeeded law and Jacob; next Joseph – who kindled the light of truth throughout all Egypt, at that time the most flourishing kingdom in the world. After these, we read of Moses, Joshua, Samuel, and David; then Elisha, of whose ministry the prophet Isaiah was a partaker; then ... John the Baptist: and lastly, Christ and His Apostles.

It is delightful to behold this unbroken chain, which is a clear testimony to the presence of God in his church. After the Apostles followed a band, which although somewhat weaker, was nevertheless honoured with the blessing of God. Polycarp, Irenaeus, Gregory the Niocaesarien, Basilius, Augustinus, Prosper, Maximus, Hugo, Bernardus, Taulerus, and others;

and although this later age has become more corrupt, yet God has always preserved a remnant of the faithful, whilst it is evident that the light of the gospel has now been peculiarly manifested through the preaching of Luther. He is therefore to be numbered with that blessed company, the excellent of the earth, whom God has sent forth for the gathering together and the building up of his church, and whom we truly recognize as ornaments of the human race. Solon, Themistocles, Scipio, Augustus, and others were indeed great men, who founded states, or ruled over vast empires; yet do they rank far below our spiritual leaders, Isaiah, John the Baptist, Paul and Luther. It is also well that we should regard the grand disputations which have existed in the church, and in connection with this subject let us look at those themes of deep and high import which have been brought to light by Luther, and which evince that the tenor of his life was worthy of our highest approbation. It is true that many exclaim 'the church is in confusion', saying that inextricable controversies are engendered in it; to these I answer, such is the mode of divine Government, for when the Holy Spirit convicts the world, dissensions arise through the pertinacity of the wicked; and the guilt is on those who refuse to listen to the Son of God, and of whom our Heavenly Father says, 'Hear Him.'

That Luther illustrated the essential truths of the Gospel is manifest, as the deepest shades had previously veiled its doctrines, in dispersing these he clearly proved to us the nature of sincere repentance, he showed us in whom we must seek refuge, and what is the sure consolation of the mind that trembles under a sense of the wrath of God. He elucidated the doctrine of Paul which says, that man is justified by faith; he showed the difference between the Law and the Gospel, between Spiritual righteousness and the Moral law; he pointed out the nature of true prayer, and he called back the church universal from that heathen madness which teaches that God, is to be invoked even when the mind, oppressed with metaphysical doubts, is flying far from Him: he enforced on us the conviction that prayer is to be made in faith, and in a good conscience, and he led us to the Mediator, the Son of God sitting at the right hand of the Eternal Father, and interceding for us; not to those images and departed mortals, to whom the ungodly world, with awful infatuation, is wont to perform its devotions. He also pointed out other sacred duties which are acceptable to God, whilst he was himself careful to adorn and to preserve inviolate the institutions of civil life as no preceding writers had done; he also drew a line of distinction between works necessary to be performed, and the puerile observances of human ceremonies, including their rights and established laws which impede the offering of the heart to God. In order that this heavenly teaching might be transmitted unimpaired to posterity, he translated the prophetic and apostolic writings into German, which work he executed with such perspicuity, that this version alone imparts more light to the mind of the reader, than the perusal of many commentaries would do.

To this he added various expositions which, as Erasmus was accustomed to say, were far superior to any others then extant; and as it is related of the builders of Jerusalem, that they wrought with one hand and held the sword in the other, so was he at the same time contending with the enemies of truth, and composing expositions fraught with divine philosophy; whilst by his pious counsels he strengthened the minds of many. Since the mystery of godliness lies far beyond the reach of human vision, as for instance, the doctrines of Faith, and of the Remission of Sins, we are constrained to acknowledge that Luther was taught of God; and how many of us have witnessed the wrestlings in which he was himself instructed, and by which we must be convinced that through faith alone we also can be heard and accepted of God. Therefore shall His people to all eternity celebrate the blessings which He has conferred on the church by this His servant: first they will offer up thanksgivings to God, then they will acknowledge that they owe much to the labours of this our friend and brother; although the irreligious who deride the church in general, say that these good deeds are but idle pastime or intoxicating madness. Let it not be said that endless disputations have been raised, or that the apple of discord has been thrown by the church, as some falsely assert; nor have the enigmas of the Sphynx been propounded by her, for to men of sense and piety who can give a candid judgment, it is by no means difficult on comparing opinions, to distinguish those which accord from those which do not accord with heavenly doctrine; and indeed there is no doubt that in these controversies we discover the revelation of Himself. For since it has pleased God to manifest Himself and His holy will in prophetic and apostolic writ, in which he has revealed himself, we cannot suppose that His word is ambiguous like the leaves of the Sybil, 'Which flit abroad, the sport of playful winds.'

Others however, without any evil design, have complained that Luther was unduly severe; I do not myself offer an opinion on this subject, but answer I them in the words of Erasmus: 'God has administered to us of the present age, a bitter draught, on account of our abounding infirmities.' But when he is pleased to raise up such an instrument against the shameless and insolent enemies of truth, as when the Lord said to Jeremiah, 'Behold I have given my words into thy mouth, that thou shouldest destroy and build up,' and when it is His pleasure to set as it were, His Gorgons in array against them, then it is a vain thing that they should expostulate with Him; for He governs His church not by human counsels, neither truly are His ways our ways. It is however, no uncommon thing for minds of limited scope to undervalue the more powerful energies with which others may be endowed, whether directed to good or evil purposes; thus it was with emotion that Aristides beheld Themistocles undertaking and bringing to a happy issue, vast enterprises; and although he rejoiced in the felicity of the state, he was earnest to arrest that ardent spirit in its career. Nor do I deny that strong and lively impulse often leads astray, since none who are subject to the infirmities of our nature, are without fault. If however, there be any living of whom we may say as the ancients did of Hercules, Cimon and others, 'Unadorned indeed, but in all important points a good man,' then was Luther a just man, and his name of good report; for in the church, if, as the apostle Paul says, 'he wars a good warfare, holding faith and a good conscience,' then he pleases God and is to be revered by us. And such we know Luther to have been, for whilst he steadfastly maintained sound doctrine he preserved the integrity of his own conscience: and who that has known him can be ignorant with what large benevolence he was endowed, or forget his suavity in the intercourse of private life, and how far removed he was from contention and strife, whilst to all his actions lie imparted the gravity that became his character, as is depicted in the following passage; 'His manner was dignified, and his discourse familiar;' or rather, all with him was in accordance with the language of Paul, 'Whatsoever things are true, whatsoever things are honest, whatsoever things are just, whatsoever things are of good report;' so that the asperity of which we have spoken, appears to have arisen from the love of truth, not from a factious spirit, or from bitterness of feeling: of these things both we and many others have been witnesses.

But if I were to undertake an eulogium on the remaining points of Luther's life, a life which until the age of 63 was absorbed in subjects of the highest interest, and was passed in the pursuit of piety and of all that is noble and good, in what lofty strains of eloquence might I not indulge. His was a mind in which we never traced the inroads of wandering lusts; no seditious counsels held their seat there, on the contrary he rather advocated the laying down of arms, as he was unwilling to mingle with the interests of the church, schemes for the aggrandizement either of himself or his friends. Indeed, I esteem his wisdom and his virtue at so high a price as to feel assured that human efforts alone could never have attained to them. Thus it is essential that spirits bold, lofty, and ardent, such as every thing proves Luther's to have been, should be restrained by a power from on high. And now what shall I say of his other virtues? I have myself often surprised him, when with weeping he has been engaged in offering up prayers for the whole church. He devoted almost daily, a portion of time to the repetition of certain psalms with which amid his sighs and tears, he mingled his prayers; and he often said that he felt indignant against those who through slothfulness of spirit, or on account of worldly occupations, say that the prayer of a single sigh is enough. He considered therefore, that forms of prayer are prescribed to us by divine counsel, and that a perusal of them animates our minds even as our voices acknowledge the God whom we worship. And often when weighty deliberations have arisen on the danger of the state, we have seen him endowed with a mighty potency of soul, unmoved by fear and unsubdued by terror, for he leaned on that sacred anchor which is the power of God; nor did he allow his faith therein to be shaken.

He was also distinguished for the acuteness of his perceptions, as by his own independent judgment he could readily perceive the course to be pursued in cases of difficulty. Nor was he as many think, negligent of the public weal, or inadvertent to the interests of others; on the contrary he could fully appreciate the welfare of the community, whilst he most sagaciously perceived the sentiments and wishes of those with whom he mingled in social life. And although the genius of his mind was of a lively order, he read with avidity ecclesiastical writings as well as history in general, from which, with a peculiar dexterity, he derived precedents adapted to the present occasion.

Of his eloquence we possess enduring monuments, for in this science he undoubtedly equalled those to whom the highest palm in oratory has been conceded. We do then for our own sakes, justly mourn that such a man, endowed with the loftiest grade of intellect, instructed in wisdom, matured by long experience, adorned with many excellent and heroic virtues, and chosen by God for the building up of his church; that he who has embraced us all with a father's love, should have been thus called away from our earthly fellowship. For we are like orphans deprived of an excellent and faithful parent; but whilst we bow to the will of God, let us not in the memory of our friend allow his virtues, and the benefits which we have derived from his society to perish from amongst us. Let us rather bid him joy that he is now participating in sweet and unrestrained communion with God, and with his Son our Lord Jesus Christ, and with the Prophets and Apostles; which fellowship he ever sought and waited for through faith in the Son of God. In that blessed state he now receives the approval of God on the labours which he here sustained in the propagation of the gospel, with the testimony also of the Church universal in heaven; there, set free from the shackles of mortality as from a prison, and having joined that company which is perfected in wisdom, he now sees, not as in a glass darkly, the essential character of God, the union of the two natures in His Son, and the whole assembly of the gathered and redeemed Church; whilst those divine real ties which he here knew but in part, which he briefly demonstrated, and which in faith he contemplated, he now beholds with open face, and moved with ecstatic joy, in all the ardour of his soul he gives God thanks for his unspeakable gift. He learns why the Son of God is called the Word, and the likeness of the Eternal Father; and in what way the Holy Spirit is the bond of mutual love, not only between the Eternal Father and the Son, but also between them and the Church. He had learned whilst here on earth which be the first principles of the oracles of God and often did he most wisely and weightily descant on these highest themes; on the distinction between true and false prayer, and on the knowledge of God and of divine manifestations; also on distinguishing the true God from false deities.

There are many in this assembly, who in times past, have heard him thus express himself, 'You shall see the heavens opened, and the angels of God ascending and descending upon the Son of Man.' Thus he delighted first to instil into the minds of his hearers this most full consolation, which declares that heaven is opened, that is to say, that there is a way made for us to God, that the barrier of divine wrath is removed as we flee for refuge to his Son; that God holds near communion with us, and that those who seek him in prayer are received, governed and kept by him. Luther admonished us that this divine promise, which infidels declare to be fabulous, is and must be opposed to human doubts, and to those fears which deter diffident minds from venturing to call upon God, or to put their trust in him; for he said that the angels ascending and descending on the body of Christ, are the ministers of the gospel who with Christ for their leader, first ascend to God and receive from him the gifts of the Gospel, and of the Holy Spirit, and afterwards descend, that is to fulfil their duty of teaching amongst men. He also added this interpretation, that those heavenly spirits themselves, whom we usually call angels, beholding the Son are enabled to comprehend and to rejoice in the mysterious union of the two natures, and as they are soldiers of their Lord in defence of His Church, so are they guided and governed as by the signal of His hand. Now is our departed friend himself a spectator of these most sublime visions, and as he once among the ministers of the Gospel, ascended and descended with Christ for his leader, so now he descries angels sent on embassies by their Lord, and enjoys in common with them, the absorbing contemplation of divine wisdom and of the works of God.

Let us call to mind with what delight he has recited to us the polity, the purposes, the dangers, and the deliverances of the prophets, and with what erudition he was wont to trace the history of the Church in all ages; thus it is evident that his heart glowed with no common emotion when speaking of those favoured servants of the Lord. The spirits of these he now embraces, with delight he listens to their living words, and with them he speaks face to face, whilst they with transport hail him as their fellow, and with one heart and one voice give thanks unto God for having thus gathered and preserved his Church. Therefore we doubt not that Luther is happy: we do indeed, mourn our bereavement, and whilst we bow to the fiat which has called him hence, we know it to be the will of God that we retain in our memories the virtues and the benefactions of this his servant.

Let us now be faithful to our trust. We must acknowledge that he was a hallowed instrument of God. Let us then devotedly embrace his doctrines, and strive to resemble him in those graces which are essential to our more humble walk, the fear of God, faith and fervency in prayer, soundness in ministry, purity, vigilance in avoiding seditious counsels, and an ardent thirst for knowledge. And as we are called upon to turn our thoughts with intentness and frequency towards those leaders in the Church whose histories have been transmitted to us, as Jeremiah, John the Baptist, and Paul, so let us often dwell on the doctrine and experience of Luther. Let us now add the tribute of thanksgiving and prayers which are due from this assembly, and let us all unite in this devotion:

'We give thanks unto Thee, oh omnipotent God! the eternal Father of our Lord Jesus Christ and Founder of Thy Church, with Thy co-eternal Son our Lord Jesus Christ and the Holy Spirit, wise, good, merciful, a true Judge, powerful and uncontrolled; in that Thou art by Thy dear Son, gathering unto Thyself an inheritance from amongst the human race, and art preserving the ministry of Thy gospel, for which Thou hast at this time raised up Luther. We beseech Thee that thou wilt henceforth sustain and govern thy Church, and that thou wilt seal in us the true doctrine, as Isaiah prayed for his disciples. Deign Thou to quicken our hearts by Thy Holy Spirit, that we may offer prayer acceptably unto Thee, and that we may order our lives in Thy fear.'

In conclusion, as we are aware that the loss from amongst us of those who have directed us in our earthly course, often proves to survivors, the watchword of impending calamities: I would myself, with all to whom is committed the gift of teaching, implore you to consider to what the world now stands exposed. On the one hand the Turks are ravaging, on the other contending parties threaten us with a civil war; every where indeed, we trace the empire of misrule; and now that the enemies of the Church no longer fear the power of Luther, they will doubtless with the greater daring, lay waste the doctrine which has been delivered to us by divine authority. That God may avert these evils, let us be more diligent in regulating our lives and directing our pursuits, and let us ever hold this sentiment fixed in our minds, so that whilst we retain, hear, learn, and love the pure truths of the Gospel, we may ourselves constitute the house and Church of God: as the Son of God himself says, 'If any man love me, he will keep my word, and my Father will love him, and we will come unto him and make our abode with him.' Encouraged by this cheering promise of our blessed Lord, let us incite one another to the acquiring of heavenly wisdom, and let us not forget that human interests and human institutions are to be respected for the sake of his Church. Let us realize to our minds, that future eternity to which God has called us, who indeed has not in vain revealed Himself to us by such illustrious testimonies, neither has he sent his Son in vain, but He truly loves and preserves those who magnify His grace. Amen.

Hugh Latimer

Who art thou?

Bishop Hugh Latimer (c. 1485–1555) was converted to Protestantism in 1524. In the reign of the Catholic Queen Mary he was burned at the stake for his faith. Below is an extract from a sermon which he preached in Cambridge in about 1529, quoted by John Foxe in his *Book of Martyrs*.

Tue quis es? Which words are as much to say in English, 'Who art thou?' These be the words of the Pharisees, which were sent by the Jews unto St John the Baptist in the wilderness, to have knowledge of him who he was; which words they spake unto him of an evil intent, thinking that he would have taken on him to be Christ, and so they would have had him done by their good wills, because they knew that he was more carnal and given to their laws than Christ indeed should be, as they perceived by their old prophecies: and also, because they marvelled much at his great doctrine, preaching, and baptizing, they were in doubt whether he was Christ or not; wherefore they said unto him, 'Who art thou?' Then answered St John, and confessed that he was not Christ.

Now then, according to the preacher, let every man and woman, of a good and simple mind, contrary to the Pharisees' intent, ask this question, 'Who art thou?' This question must be moved to themselves, what they be of themselves, on this fashion: 'What art thou of thy only and natural generation between father and mother, when thou camest into the world? What substance, what virtue, what goodness art thou of thyself?' Which question, if thou rehearse oftentimes to thyself, thou shalt well perceive and understand how thou shalt reply, which must be made like this: 'I am of myself, and by myself, coming from my natural father and mother, the child of anger and indignation of God, the true inheritor of hell, a lump of sin, and working nothing of myself, but all towards hell, except I have better help of another than I have of myself.' Now we may see in what state we enter into this world, that we be of ourselves the true and just inheritors of hell, the children of the ire and indignation of Christ, working all towards hell, whereby we deserve of ourselves perpetual damnation by the right judgement of God, and the true claim of ourselves: which unthrifty state that we be born unto is come unto us for our own deserts, as proveth well this example following:

Let it be admitted for the probation of this, that it might please the king's grace now being, to accept into his favour a mean man of simple degree and birth, not born to any possession; whom the king's grace favoureth, not because this person hath of himself deserved any such favour, but that the king casteth his favour unto him of his own mere motion and fancy: and because the king's grace will more declare his favour unto him, he giveth unto this said man a thousand pounds in lands, to him and his heirs, on this condition, that he shall take upon him to be the chief captain and defender of his town of Calais, and to be true and faithful to him in the custody of the same, against the Frenchmen especially above all other enemies.

This man taketh on him this charge, promising this fidelity thereunto. It chanceth in process of time, that by the singular acquaintance and frequent familiarity of this captain with the Frenchmen, these Frenchmen give unto the said captain of Calais a great sum of money, so that he will be but content and agreeable that they may enter into the said town of Calais by force of arms, and so thereby possess the same unto the crown of France. Upon this agreement the Frenchmen do invade the said town of Calais, only by the negligence of this captain.

Now the king hearing of this invasion, cometh with a great puissance to defend this his said town, and so by good policy of war overcometh the said Frenchmen, and entereth again into his town of Calais. Then he being desirous to know how these enemies of his came thither, maketh strict search and inquiry by whom this treason was conspired; but this search was known, and found by his own captain to be the very author and the beginner of the betraying of it. The king, seeing the great infidelity of this person, dischargeth this man of his office, and taketh from him and his heirs this thousand pounds' possession. Think you not that the king doth use justice unto him, and all his posterity and heirs? Yes truly; the said captain cannot deny himself but that he had true justice, considering how unfaithfully he behaved himself to his prince, contrary to his own fidelity and promise. So likewise it was of our first father Adam: he had given him the spirit and science of knowledge, to work all goodness therewith; this said spirit was not given only to him, but unto all his heirs and posterity. He had also delivered him the town of Calais, that is to say, Paradise in earth, the most strong and fairest town in the world, to be in his custody: he, nevertheless, by the instigation of these Frenchmen, that is, the temptation of the fiend, did consent unto their desire, and so he broke his promise and fidelity, the commandment of the everlasting King, his master, in eating of the apple by him prohibited.

Now then, the King, seeing this great treason in his captain, dispossessed him of the thousand pounds of lands, that is to say, from everlasting life and glory, and all his heirs and posterity: for likewise as he had the spirit of science and knowledge for him and his heirs, so in like manner when he lost the same, his heirs also lost it by him, and in him. So now this example proveth that by our father Adam we had once in him the very inheritance of everlasting joy; and by him and in him again we lost the same.

And now the world standing in this damnable state, cometh in the occasion of the incarnation of Christ; the Father in heaven perceiving the frail nature of man, that he by himself and of himself could do nothing for himself, by his prudent wisdom sent down the second person in the Trinity, his Son Jesus Christ, to declare unto man his pleasure and commandment: and so at the Father's will Christ took on him human nature, being willing to deliver man out of this miserable way, and was content to suffer cruel passion in shedding his blood for all mankind; and so left behind, for our safeguard, laws and ordinances, to keep us always in the right path to everlasting life, as the gospels, the sacraments, the commandments etc., which if we keep and observe according to our profession, we shall answer better the question 'Who art thou?' than we did before: for before thou didst enter into the sacrament of baptism, thou wert but a natural man, or a natural woman; as I might say, a man, a woman; but after thou takest on thee Christ's religion, thou hast a longer name, for then thou art a Christian man, a Christian woman.

Now then, seeing thou art a Christian man, what shall be the answer to this question, 'Who art thou?'

The answer to this question is, when I ask it of myself, I must say that I am a Christian man, a Christian woman, the child of everlasting joy, through the merits of the bitter passion of Christ. This is a joyful answer. Here we may see how much we are bound and indebted to God, that hath revived us from death to life, and saved us that were damned: which great benefit we cannot well consider, unless we remember what we were of ourselves before we meddled with him or his laws: and the more we know our feeble nature, and set less by it, the more we shall conceive and know in our hearts what God hath done for us; and the more we know what God hath done for us, the less we shall set by ourselves, and the more we shall love and please God; so that in no condition we shall either know ourselves of God, except we utterly confess ourselves to be mere vileness and corruption. Well, now it is come to this point, that we are Christian men, Christian women, I pray you, what does Christ require of a Christian man, or of a Christian woman? Christ requireth nothing else of a Christian man or woman but that they will observe his rule.

[*John Foxe writes:*] To relate the noise and alarm the preaching of these sermons occasioned at Cambridge would require too much time and space.

First came out the prior of Black Friars, named Buckenham, who attempted to prove that it was not expedient for the Scriptures to be in English, lest the ignorant and vulgar sort might be running into some inconvenience: as for example:

The ploughman, when he heareth this in the gospel, 'No man that layeth his hand on the plough and looketh back, is meet for the kingdom of God,' might, peradventure, cease from his plough. Likewise a baker, when he hears that a little leaven corrupteth a whole lump of dough, may perchance leave our bread unleavened, and so our bodies shall be unseasoned. Also the simple man, when he heareth in the Gospel, 'If thine eye offend thee, pluck it out, and cast if from thee,' may make himself blind, and so fill the world with beggars.

Mr Latimer, being thus persecuted by the friars, doctors, and masters of that university, about the year 1529, continued, notwithstanding the malice of these adversaries, preaching in Cambridge for about three years. Mr Latimer and Mr Bilney conferred together so frequently, that the field wherein they walked was called 'The Heretics' Hill'.

Mr Latimer was, at length, cited before the cardinal for heresy. He was brought to London, where he was greatly molested, and detained a long time from his cure, being summoned thrice every week before the said bishops, to vindicate his preaching, and to subscribe to certain articles or propositions, devised by the instigation of his enemies. The following curious incident was related by himself, in a sermon preached at Stamford, October 9, 1550, and the following are his words:

I was once in examination before five or six bishops, where I had much trouble: thrice every week I came to examinations, and many snares and traps were laid to get something. Now God knoweth I was ignorant of the law, but that God gave me wisdom what I should speak; it was God indeed, or else I had never escaped them. At last I was brought forth to be examined into a chamber hung with arras [a wall hanging of heavy woven fabric], where I was wont to be examined; but now at this time the chamber was somewhat altered. For now the fire was taken away, and an arras hung over the chimney, and the table stood near the fireplace.

There was among the bishops who examined me one with whom I have been very familiar, and took him for my great friend, an aged man, and he sat next to the table's end.

Then among all other questions, he put forth a very subtle and crafty one, and such a one, indeed, as I could not think so great danger in. And when I should make answer, 'I pray you, Mr Latimer,' said one, 'speak out; I am very thick of hearing, and here may be many that sit far off.' I marvelled at this, that I was bid to speak out, and began to suspect, and give an ear to the chimney; and there I heard a pen writing in the chimney behind the cloth. They had appointed one there to write all mine answers, for they made sure that I should not start from them; and there was no starting from them. God was my good Lord, and gave me answer, else I could never have escaped.

Mr Latimer continued in his laborious episcopal functions until the passing of the Six Articles. Being then much distressed through the straitness of the times, he felt that he must either sacrifice a good conscience or else forsake his bishopric; accordingly he did the latter. When he visited London, he was imprisoned in the Tower, where he remained until King Edward came to the crown, when the golden mouth of this English Chrysostom was opened again. He often affirmed that the preaching of the Gospel would cost him his life, for which he was cheerfully prepared; for after the death of King Edward, and not long after Mary had been proclaimed queen, Mr Latimer was arrested and brought to London.

Hugh Latimer

We shall this day light such a candle

In 1555 the Protestant clerics Hugh Latimer and Nicholas Ridley were burned at the stake on the orders of the Catholic Queen Mary. As a faggot was set on fire at his feet Latimer said to Ridley:

Be of good comfort, Mr Ridley, and play the man! We shall this day light such a candle, by God's grace, in England, as I trust never shall be put out.

In his *Book of Martyrs* John Foxe wrote:

On the 17th October, 1555, those two pillars of Christ's church, Dr Nicholas Ridley, Bishop of London, and Mr Hugh Latimer, sometime Bishop of Worcester, were burnt in one fire at Oxford – men ever memorable for their piety, learning, and incomparable ornaments and gifts of grace, joined with no less commendable sincerity of life.

William Tyndale

Lord, open the King of England's eyes!

William Tyndale (c. 1494–1536) was a Protestant Bible translator. His work was later used as the basis for the New Testament in the Authorized Version. He was martyred at Vilvorde in Belgium.

William Tyndale was brought up in the University of Oxford, where he studied the liberal arts and the Scriptures. He then moved to Cambridge, and then to Gloucestershire where he became tutor to a knight called Welch. To this gentleman's table several abbots, deans, and other beneficed men used to go, with whom Tyndale talked about learned men, especially Luther and Erasmus, and about questions concerning the Scriptures.

Not long after, Tyndale happened to be in the company of a certain divine, and in their discussion pressed him so hard that the doctor burst out with these blasphemous words: 'We were better to be without God's laws than the Pope.'

Tyndale, full of godly zeal, replied: 'I defy the Pope and all his laws.' He added that if God spared him life, ere many years, he would cause a boy who drives the plough to know more of the Scriptures than he did. Tyndale felt moved, by God's Spirit, to translate the Scriptures into his mother tongue for the benefit of the uneducated people in England. The English church leaders had persuaded the king to issue a proclamation which condemned and forbad Tyndale's translation of the New Testament. Not content with this they plotted to see how they could kill the author. Tyndale was taken to be executed and as he was being tied to the stake, he cried with a loud and earnest voice, 'Lord, open the King of England's eyes!' He was then strangled, and his remains burnt to ashes.

John Foxe's Book of Martyrs

William Tyndale

Can the church err?

The church of Christ is the multitude of all those who believe in Christ for the remission of sins, and who are thankful for that mercy and who love the law of God purely, and who hate the sin in this world and long for the life to come. This is the church that cannot err damnably, nor for any length of time, nor all of them. But as soon as any question arises, the truth of God's promise stirs someone up to teach them the truth about everything that is necessary for salvation, from God's word. This enlightens the hearts of the other genuine members, to see the same, and to agree with it.

From *Exposition on Matthew 5–7*

Thomas Cranmer

I recant of my recantations

Thomas Cranmer (1489–1556), Archbishop of Canterbury under Henry VIII, was the main compiler of the *Book of Common Prayer*. During the reign of Queen Mary he was executed for his Protestant faith. Before his execution he had signed recantations of his beliefs, but when he was about to be burned at the stake he insisted, 'I recant of my recantations.' Below is an account of his martyrdom.

'Good people – my dearly beloved brethren in Christ, I beseech you most heartily to pray for me to Almighty God, that he will forgive me all my sins and offences, which are without number, and great above measure. But yet one thing grieveth my conscience more than all the rest, whereof, God willing, I intend to speak more hereafter. But how great and how many soever my sins be, I beseech you to pray to God of his mercy to pardon and forgive them all.' And here, kneeling down, he said the following prayer:

'O Father of heaven, O Son of God, Redeemer of the world, O Holy Ghost, three persons and one God, have mercy upon me, most wretched caitiff and miserable sinner. I have offended both against heaven and earth more than my tongue can express. Whither, then, may I go, or whither shall I flee? To heaven I may be ashamed to lift up mine eyes, and in earth I find no place of refuge or succour. To thee, therefore, O Lord, do I run; to thee do I humble myself, saying, O Lord my God, my sins be great, but yet have mercy upon me for thy great mercy. The great mystery that God became man was not wrought for little or few offences. Thou didst not give thy Son, O heavenly Father, unto death for small sins only, but for all the greatest sins of the world, so that the sinner return to thee with his whole heart, as I do at this present. Wherefore have mercy on me, O God, whose property is always to have mercy; have mercy upon me, O Lord, for thy great mercy. I crave nothing for mine own merits, but for thy name's sake. And now, O Father of heaven, hallowed be thy name.' And after repeating the Lord's Prayer, he continued:

'Every man, good people, desireth at the time of his death to give some good exhortation, that others may remember the same before their death, and be the better thereby; so I beseech God grant me that I may speak something at this my departing, whereby God may be glorified, and you edified.

'First, it is a heavy cause to see that so many folk so much dote upon the love of this false world, and be so careful for it, that of the love of God, or the world to come, they seem to care very little or nothing. Therefore, this shall be my first exhortation: That you set not your minds over much upon this deceitful world, but upon God, and upon the world to come, and to learn to know what this lesson meaneth which St John teacheth, that the love of this world is hatred against God.

'The second exhortation is, That next unto God you obey your King and Queen, willingly and gladly.

'The third exhortation is, That you love altogether like brethren and sisters.

'The fourth exhortation shall be to them that have great substance and riches of this world, That they will well consider and weigh Luke 18:24, 1 John 3:17 and James 5:1–3. Let them that be rich ponder well these three sentences; for if they ever had occasion to show their charity, they have it now at this present, the poor people being so many, and victuals so dear.

'And now, forasmuch as I am come to the last end of my life, whereupon hangeth all my life past and all my life to come, either to live with my master Christ for ever in joy, or else to be in pain for ever with wicked devils in hell, and I see before my eyes presently either heaven ready to receive me, or else hell ready to swallow me up; I shall therefore declare to you my very faith how I believe, without any colour of dissimulation, for now is no time to dissemble, whatsoever I have said or written in times past.

'First, I believe in God the Father Almighty, maker of heaven and earth etc. And I believe every article of the catholic faith, every word and sentence taught by our Saviour Jesus Christ, his apostles and prophets, in the New and Old Testament.

'And now I come to the great thing, that so much troubleth my conscience, more than any thing that ever I did or said in my whole life; and this is the setting abroad of a writing contrary to the Truth; which now here I renounce and refuse, as things written with my hand, contrary to the truth which I thought in my heart, and written for fear of death, and to save my life, if it might be; and that is, all such bills and papers which I have written or signed with my hand since my degradation, wherein I have written many things untrue. And forasmuch as my hand offended, writing contrary to my heart, my hand shall first be punished therefore; for, may I come to the fire it shall be first burned.'

John Foxe's *Book of Martyrs*

The Book of Homilies

Holy Scripture – a fountain of truth

Below is an excerpt from the *Book of Homilies*, first published in July 1547, which disaffected and unlearned English clergy were obliged to read out to their congregations.

There can be nothing either more necessary or profitable, than the knowledge of Holy Scripture. And there is no truth nor doctrine, necessary for our justification and everlasting salvation, but that is, or may be, drawn out of that fountain and well of truth.

The Book of Homilies

Homily for Whitsunday

It is not the duty and part of any Christian, under the pretence of the Holy Ghost, to bring in his own dreams and fantasies into the church; but he must diligently provide that his doctrine and decrees be agreeable to Christ's Holy Testament; otherwise, in making the Holy Ghost the Author thereof, he doth blaspheme and belie the Holy Ghost to his own condemnation.

John Knox

Temptation

John Knox (1531–72), a Scottish Protestant Reformer, was the founder of the Church of Scotland. Below is an excerpt from one of his sermons, preached in 1556.

Then Jesus was led by the Spirit into the desert that he should be tempted of the devil.

Matthew 4:1

The cause moving me to treat this place of scripture is, that such as by the inscrutable providence of God do fall in diverse temptations, judge not themselves by reason thereof less acceptable in God's presence; but, rather the opposite, having the way prepared to victory by Christ Jesus, shall not fear above measure the crafty assaults of that subtle serpent Satan; but with joy and bold courage, having such a Guide as here is pointed forth, such a Champion, and such weapons as here are to be found, may assure ourselves of God's present favour, and of final victory, by the means of him, who, for our safeguard and deliverance, entered in the battle, and triumphed over his adversary...

Temptation, or to tempt, in the scriptures of God, is called to try, to prove, or to assault the valour, the power, the will, the pleasure, or the wisdom, whether it be of God, or of creatures. And it is taken sometimes in good part, as when it is said that 'God tempted Abraham', 'God tempted the people of Israel' (Genesis 22:1; Deuteronomy 8:2, 16; 13:3): that is, God did try and examine, not for his own knowledge, to whom nothing is hid, but for the certification of others, how obedient Abraham was to God's commandment, and how weak and infirm the Israelites were in their journey towards the promised land. And this temptation is always good, because it proceeds immediately from God, to open and make manifest the secret thoughts of men's hearts, the power of God's word, and the great lenity and gentleness of God towards the sins and rebellions of those whom he has received into his regimen and care...

Otherwise temptation, or to tempt, is taken in evil part: that is, he that does assault or assail intends destruction and confusion to him that is assaulted – as when Satan tempted the woman in the garden, Job by diverse tribulations, and David by adultery. The scribes and Pharisees tempted Christ by diverse means, questions, and subtleties. And of this matter, says St James, 'God tempteth no man' (James 1:13): that is, by temptation proceeding immediately from him, he intends no man's destruction. And here you shall note, that albeit Satan sometimes appears to prevail against God's elect, yet he is ever frustrated of his final purpose. By temptation he led Eve and David from the obedience of God; but he could not retain them for ever under his thralldom. Power was granted to him to spoil Job of his substance and children, and to strike his body with a plague and sickness most vile and fearful; but he could not compel his mouth to blaspheme God's majesty. And, therefore, albeit we are laid open sometimes, as it were, even to the mouth of Satan, let us not think therefore that God has abjected us, and that he takes no care over us. No, he permits Satan to rage, and as it were to triumph for a time, that when he has poured forth the venom of his malice against God's elect, it may return to his own confusion; and that the deliverance of God's children may be more to his glory and comfort of the afflicted: knowing that his hand is so puissant, his mercy and good-will so prompt, that he delivers his little ones from their cruel enemy, even as David did his sheep and lambs from the mouth of the lion (1 Samuel 17:34–36). For a benefit received in extreme danger more moves us than the preservation from ten thousand perils, so that we fall not to them. And yet to preserve from dangers and perils, so that we fall not to them, whether they are of body or spirit, is no less the work of God, than to deliver from them.

Last, to tempt betokens simply to prove, or try, without any determinate purpose of profit or damage to ensue; as when the mind doubts of anything, and therein desires to be satisfied, without great love or extreme hatred of the thing that is tempted or tried. As the queen of Sheba came to tempt Solomon in subtle questions (1 Kings 10:1, 6–7). David tempted, that is, tried himself if he could go in harness (1 Samuel 17:38–39). And Gideon says, 'Let not thine anger kindle against me, if I tempt thee yet once again' (Judges 6:39). This famous queen, not fully trusting the bruit and fame that was spread of Solomon, by subtle questions desired to prove his wisdom – at the first, neither extremely hating nor fervently loving the person of the king. And David, as a man not accustomed to harness, would try how he was able to go, and behave and fashion himself therein, before he would hazard battle with Goliath. And Gideon, not satisfied in his conscience by the first sign that he received, desired (without contempt or hatred of God) a second time to be certified of his vocation. And in this sense must the apostle be expounded when he commands us to tempt – that is, to try and examine ourselves – if we stand in the faith.

Richard Hooker

A learned discourse of justification

Richard Hooker (c. 1554–1600) was one of the most significant theologians of the sixteenth century. In 1585 he was appointed Master of the Temple in London, and so preached in one of the most important pulpits in England. He aroused the suspicions of the Puritan party when he said, 'I doubt not but God was merciful to save thousands of our fathers living in popish superstitions, inasmuch as they sinned ignorantly.'

Walter Travers, the afternoon lecturer at the Temple, said that since the adherents of the Pope did not believe in justification by faith, they could not be justified by faith, which meant that they could not be justified at all, which meant that they were certainly damned, with no exceptions. The following sermon was Hooker's reply.

> *The wicked doth compass about the righteous; therefore perverse judgment doth proceed.*
>
> Habakkuk 1:4

For better manifestation of the prophet's meaning in this place we are: first, to consider 'the wicked', of whom he saith that they 'compass about the righteous'; secondly, 'the righteous' that are compassed about by them; and, thirdly, that which is inferred, 'therefore perverse judgment proceedeth.' Touching the first, there are two kinds of wicked men, of whom in the fifth of the former to the Corinthians the blessed Apostle speaketh thus: 'Do ye not judge them that are within? But God judgeth them that are without' [1 Corinthians 5:12f.]. There are wicked, therefore, whom the Church may judge, and there are wicked whom God only judgeth, wicked within and wicked without the walls of the Church. If within the Church particular persons, being apparently such, cannot otherwise be reformed, the rule of apostolical judgment is this: 'Separate them from among them you' [1 Corinthians 5:13]; if whole assemblies, this: 'Separate yourselves from among them; for what society hath light with darkness?' [2 Corinthians 6:14]. But the wicked whom the prophet meaneth were Babylonians, and therefore without. For which cause we have heard at large heretofore in what sort he urgeth God to judge them.

Now concerning the righteous, there neither is nor ever was any mere natural man absolutely righteous in himself: that is to say, void of all unrighteousness, of all sin. We dare not except, no not the blessed Virgin herself, of whom although we say with St Augustine, for the honour's sake which we owe to our Lord and

Saviour Christ, we are not willing, in this cause, to move any question of his mother; yet forasmuch as the schools of Rome have made it a question, we must answer with Eusebius Emissenus ... 'The mother of the Redeemer herself, otherwise than by redemption, is not loosed from the band of that ancient sin.' If Christ have paid a ransom for all [1 Timothy 2:6], even for her, it followeth that all without exception were captives. If one have died for all, all were dead, dead in sin [2 Corinthians 5:14f.; Ephesians 2:1, 5]; all sinful, therefore none absolutely righteous in themselves; but we are absolutely righteous in Christ. The world then must show a Christian man, otherwise it is not able to show a man that is perfectly righteous: 'Christ is made unto us wisdom, righteousness, sanctification, and redemption' [1 Corinthians 1:30]: wisdom, because he hath revealed his Father's will; righteousness, or, justice, because he hath offered himself a sacrifice for sin; sanctification, because he hath given us of his Spirit; redemption, because he hath appointed a day to vindicate his children out of the bands of corruption into liberty which is glorious [Romans 8:21]. How Christ is ... made the righteousness of men we are now to declare...

First ... all have sinned.... They teach, as we do, that God doth justify the soul of man alone, without any other coefficient cause of justice; that, in making man righteous none do work efficiently with God, but God [Trent VI, ch. 7]. They teach, as we do, that unto justice, or, righteousness, no man ever attained, but by the merits of Jesus Christ. They teach, as we do, that although Christ as God be the efficient, as man the meritorious, cause of our justice, yet in us also there is something required [Trent VI, chs 4, 5; canons 4, 9]. God is the cause of our natural life; in him we live: but he quickeneth not the body without the soul in the body. Christ hath merited to make us just; but as a medicine which is made for health doth not heal by being made but by being applied, so by the merits of Christ there can be no justification without the application of his merits. Thus far we join hands with the Church of Rome.

Wherein then do we disagree? We disagree about the nature of the very essence of the medicine whereby Christ cureth our disease; about the manner of applying it; about the number and the power of means, which God requireth in us for the effectual applying thereof to our soul's comfort.

When they are required to show what the righteousness is whereby a Christian man is justified, they answer that it is a divine spiritual quality, which quality, received into the soul, doth first make it to be one of them who are born of God; and, secondly, endue it with power to bring forth such works as they do that are born of him; even as the soul of man, being joined unto his body, doth first make him to be in the number of reasonable creatures, and, secondly, enable him to perform the natural functions which are proper to his kind; that it maketh the soul gracious and amiable in the sight of God, in regard whereof it is termed grace; that by it, through the merit of Christ, we are delivered as from sin, so from eternal death and condemnation, the reward of sin. This grace they will have to be applied by infusion, to the end that, as the body is warm by the heat which is in the body, so the soul might be righteous by inherent grace; which grace they make capable of increase; as the body may be more and more warm, so the soul more and more justified, according as grace shall be augmented; the augmentation whereof is merited by good works, as good works are made meritorious by it [Trent VI, ch. 10]. Wherefore the first receipt of grace is in their divinity the first justification; the second thereof, the second justification.

[They teach that] as grace may be increased by the merit of good works, so it may be diminished by the demerit of sins venial; it may be lost by mortal sin [Trent VI, chs 14, 15]. Inasmuch, therefore, as it is needful in the one case to repair, in the other to recover, the loss which is made, the infusion of grace hath her sundry after-meals; for which cause they make many ways to apply the infusion of grace. It is applied unto infants through baptism, without either faith or works, and in them it really taketh away original sin and the punishment due unto it; it is applied unto infidels and wicked men in their first justification through baptism, without works, yet not without faith; and it taketh away both sin actual and original, together with all whatsoever punishment eternal or temporal thereby deserved. Unto such as have attained the first justification, that is to say, the first receipt of grace, it is applied further by good works to the increase of former grace, which is the second justification. If they work more and more, grace doth more and more increase, and they are more and more justified.

To such as have diminished it by venial sins it is applied by holy water, Ave Marias, crossings, papal salutations, and such like, which serve for reparations of grace decayed. To such as have lost it through mortal sin, it is applied by the sacrament (as they term it) of penance; which sacrament hath force to confer grace anew, yet in such sort that, being so conferred, it hath not altogether so much power as at the first. For it only cleanseth out the stain or guilt of sin committed, and changeth the punishment eternal into a temporary satisfactory punishment here, if time do serve, if not, hereafter to be endured, except it be either lightened by masses, works of charity, pilgrimages, fasts, and such like; or else shortened by pardon for term, or by plenary pardon quite removed and taken away [Trent VI, ch. 14].

This is the mystery of the man of sin. This maze the Church of Rome doth cause her followers to tread when they ask her the way of justification. I cannot stand now to unrip this building and to sift it piece by piece; only I will set up a frame of apostolical erection by it in a few words, that it may befall Babylon, in presence of that which God hath builded, as it happened unto Dagon before the ark.

'Doubtless,' saith the Apostle, 'I have counted all things but loss, and I do judge them to be dung, that I may win Christ, and be found in him, not having mine own righteousness, but that which is through the faith of Christ, the righteousness which is of God through faith' [Philippians 3:8f.]. Whether they speak of the first or second justification, they make the essence of it a divine quality inherent, they make it righteousness which is in us. If it be in us, then it is ours, as our souls are ours, though we have them from God and can hold them no longer than pleaseth him; for if he withdraw the breath of our nostrils we fall to dust; but the righteousness wherein we must be found, if we will be justified, is not our own: therefore we cannot be justified by any inherent quality. Christ hath merited righteousness for as many as are found in him. In him God findeth us, if we be faithful, for by faith we are incorporated into him.

Then, although in ourselves we be altogether sinful and unrighteous, yet even the man who in himself is impious, full of iniquity, full of sin, him being found in Christ through faith, and having his sin in hatred through repentance, him God beholdeth with a gracious eye, putteth away his sin by not imputing it, taketh quite away the punishment due thereunto, by pardoning it, and accepteth him in Jesus Christ as perfectly righteous, as if he had fulfilled all that is commanded him in the law: shall I say more perfectly righteous than if he himself had fulfilled the whole law? I must take heed what I say; but the Apostle saith, 'God made him who knew no sin to be sin for us, that we might be made the righteousness of God in him' [2 Corinthians 5:21]. Such we are in the sight of God the Father as is the very Son of

God himself. Let it be counted folly, or whatsoever. It is our wisdom and our comfort; we care for no knowledge in the world but this: that man hath sinned and God hath suffered; that God hath made himself the sin of men, and that men are made the righteousness of God.

You see therefore that the Church of Rome, in teaching justification by inherent grace, doth pervert the truth of Christ, and that by the hands of his Apostles we have received otherwise than she teacheth...

PART 5

The Seventeenth Century

John Donne

Death's duel

John Donne (1571–1631) was brought up in the Roman Catholic faith but later converted to Anglicanism, eventually becoming dean of St Paul's Cathedral. He was also one of the finest poets England has ever produced. The sermon below, preached before King Charles I, was the last that Donne delivered before his death.

To the reader

This sermon was, by sacred authority, styled the author's own funeral sermon, most fitly, whether we respect the time or matter. It was preached not many days before his death, as if, having done this, there remained nothing for him to do but to die; and the matter is of death – the occasion and subject of all funeral sermons. It hath been observed of this reverend man, that his faculty in preaching continually increased, and that, as he exceeded others at first, so at last he exceeded himself. This is his last sermon; I will not say it is therefore his best, because all his were excellent. Yet thus much: a dying man's words, if they concern ourselves, do usually make the deepest impression, as being spoken most feelingly, and with least affectation. Now, whom doth it concern to learn both the danger and benefit of death? Death is every man's enemy, and intends hurt to all, though to many he be occasion of greatest good. This enemy we must all combat dying, whom he living did almost conquer, having discovered the utmost of his power, the utmost of his cruelty. May we make such use of this and other like preparatives, that neither death, whensoever it shall come, may seem terrible, nor life tedious, how long soever it shall last.

And unto God the Lord belong the issues of death [i.e. from death].

Psalm 68:20

Buildings stand by the benefit of their foundations that sustain and support them, and of their buttresses that embrace them. The body of our building is in the former part of this verse. It is this: He that is our God is the God of salvation; *ad salutes*, of salvations in the plural, so it is in the original; the God that gives us spiritual and temporal salvation too.

The issues of death are with God

First, we consider that with God the Lord are the issues of death; and therefore in all our death, and deadly calamities of this life, we may justly hope of a good issue from him ... Here we have no continuing city (Hebrews 13:14), nay, no cottage that continues, nay, no persons, no bodies, that continue. Whatsoever moved Saint Jerome to call the journeys of the Israelites in the wilderness (Exodus 17:1), mansions; the word (the word is nasang) signifies but a journey, [is] but a peregrination. Even the Israel of God hath no mansions, but journeys, pilgrimages in this life. By what measure did Jacob measure his life to Pharaoh? The days of the years of my pilgrimage (Genesis 47:29). And the apostle says that whilst we are in the body we are dead, whilst we are in the body we are but in a pilgrimage, and we are absent from the Lord (2 Corinthians 5:6). He might have said dead, for this whole world is but an universal churchyard, but our common grave, and the life and motion that the greatest persons have in it is but as the shaking of buried bodies in their grave, by an earthquake.

And so have you that that belongs to the first acceptation of these words (unto God the Lord belong the issues of death);

That though from the womb to the grave, we pass from death to death, yet, as Daniel speaks, the Lord our God is able to deliver us, and he will deliver us.

God passes judgment on us at death

And so we pass unto our second accommodation of these words (unto God the Lord belong the issues of death); that it belongs to God, and not to man, to pass a judgment upon us at our death, or to conclude a dereliction on God's part upon the manner thereof.

Those indications which doctors receive, they receive and they give out of the grounds and the rules of their art, but we have no such rule or art to give an opinion about spiritual death and damnation upon any such indication as we see in any dying man. We see often enough to be sorry, but not to despair; we may be deceived both ways. We are used to comforting ourself on the death of a friend, if it be testified that he went away like a lamb, that is, without any reluctance. But God knows that may be accompanied with an insensibility of his present state. Our blessed Saviour suffered great upheavals as he died, and a sadness even in his soul to death, and an agony even to a bloody sweat in his body, and expostulations with God, and exclamations upon the cross. Christ himself hath forbidden us by his own death to make any ill conclusion. He was executed as a malefactor, and no doubt many of them who concurred to his death did believe him to be so. Of sudden death there are scarce examples to be found in the Scriptures upon good men, for death in battle cannot be called sudden death; but God governs not by examples but by rules, and therefore make no ill conclusion upon sudden death nor upon distempers neither, though perchance accompanied with some words of diffidence and distrust in the mercies of God. The tree lies as it falls, it is true, but it is not the last stroke that fells the tree, nor the last word nor gasp that qualifies the soul. Still pray we for a peaceable life against violent death, and for time of repentance against sudden death, and for sober and modest assurance against distempered and diffident death, but never make ill conclusions upon persons overtaken with such deaths. To God the Lord belong the issues of death.

And he received Samson, who went out of this world in such a manner (consider it actively, consider it passively in his own death, and in those whom he slew with himself) as was subject to interpretation hard enough. Yet the Holy Ghost hath moved Saint Paul to celebrate Samson in his great catalogue (Hebrews 11), and so doth all the church. Our critical day is not the very day of our death, but the whole course of our life. I thank him that prays for me when the bell tolls, but I thank him much more that catechizes me, or preaches to me, or instructs me how to live. My security is: do this and thou shalt live. But though I do it, yet I shall die too, die a bodily, a natural death. But God never mentions, never seems to consider that death, the bodily, the natural death. God doth not say, 'Live well, and thou shalt die well,' that is, an easy, a quiet death; but, 'Live well here, and thou shalt live well for ever.' But whether the gate of my prison be opened with an oiled key, by a gentle and preparing sickness, or the gate be hewn down by a violent death, or the gate be burnt down by a raging and frantic fever, a gate into heaven I shall have, for from the Lord is the cause of my life, and with God the Lord are the issues of death. And further we carry not this second acceptation of the words, as this issue of death is freedom in death, God's care that the soul be safe, what agonies soever the body suffers in the hour of death.

We are delivered from death by someone else's death

But pass to our third part and last part: As this issue of death is a deliverance by the death of another. So why did the Lord die? And why did he die in such a way? Saint Augustine, interpreting this text, says, 'What can be more obvious, more manifest than this sense of these words? In the former part of this verse it is said, He that is our God is the God of salvation; the God that must save us. Who can that be, says he, but Jesus?' For therefore that name was given him because he was to save us. And to this Jesus, says he, this Saviour (Matthew 1:21), belong the issues of death. He came into this life in our mortal nature, he could not go out of this life any other way but by death.

From this text doth Saint Isidore prove that Christ was truly man, which as many sects of heretics denied, as that he was truly God, because to him, though he were, God the Lord, yet to him, to God the Lord belonged the issues of death. More cannot be said than Christ himself says of himself; 'These things Christ ought to suffer' (Luke 24:26). He had no other way but death: so then this part of our sermon must needs be a passion sermon, since all his life was a continual passion, all our Lent may well be a continual Good Friday. Christ's painful life took off none of the pains of his death, he felt not the less then for having felt so much before. Nor will any thing that shall be said before lessen, but rather enlarge the devotion, to that which shall be said of his passion at the time of due solemnization thereof. Christ bled not a drop the less at the last for having bled at his circumcision before, nor will you a tear the less then if you shed some now. And therefore be now content to consider with me how to this God the Lord belonged the issues of death. That God, this Lord, the Lord of life, could die, is a strange contemplation; that the Red Sea could be dry, that the sun could stand still, that an oven could be seven times heated and not burn, that lions could be hungry and not bite, is strange, miraculously strange, but super-miraculous that God could die; but that God would die is an exaltation of that. But even of that also it is a super-exaltation, that God should die, must die, for God the Lord had no issue but by death, all this Christ ought to suffer, was bound to suffer.

There was nothing more free, more voluntary, more spontaneous than the death of Christ. It is true, he died voluntarily; but yet when we consider the contract that had passed between his Father and him, there was a kind of necessity upon him: all this Christ ought to suffer. And when shall we date this obligation, this necessity? When shall we say that began? Certainly this decree by which Christ was to suffer all this was an eternal decree, and was there any thing before that that was eternal? Infinite love, eternal love; be pleased to follow this home, and to consider it seriously, that what liberty soever we can conceive in Christ to die or not to die; this necessity of dying, this decree is as eternal as that liberty; and yet how small a matter made he of this necessity and this dying? ...

To us that speak daily of the death of Christ, 'he was crucified, dead, and buried', can the memory or the mention of our own death be irksome or bitter? Take in the whole day from the hour that Christ received the passover upon Thursday unto the hour in which he died the next day. Make this present day that day in thy devotion, and consider what he did, and remember what you have done. Before he instituted and celebrated the sacrament, which was after the eating of the passover, he proceeded to that act of humility, to wash his disciples' feet, even Peter's, who for a while resisted him. In thy preparation to the holy and blessed sacrament, hast thou with a sincere humility sought a reconciliation with all the world, even with those that have been averse from it, and refused that reconciliation from thee? If so, and not else, thou hast spent that first part of his last day in a conformity with him. After the sacrament he spent the time till night in prayer, in preaching, in psalms: hast thou considered that a worthy receiving of the sacrament consists in a continuation of holiness after, as well as in a preparation before? ... If so, thou hast therein also conformed thyself to him; so Christ spent his time till night. At night he went into the garden to pray, and he spent much time in prayer ... He finally placed himself into his Father's hands; for though to this God our Lord belonged these issues of death, it was necessary for him to die. He gave up the ghost; and as God breathed a soul into the first Adam, so this second Adam breathed his soul into God, into the hands of God.

There we leave you in that blessed dependency, to hang upon him that hangs upon the cross, there bathe in his tears, there suck at his wounds, and lie down in peace in his grave, till he vouchsafe you a resurrection, and an ascension into that kingdom which He hath prepared for you with the inestimable price of his incorruptible blood. Amen.

William Laud

I am coming, O Lord, as quickly as I can
William Laud (1573–1645), Archbishop of Canterbury in the reign of Charles I, was martyred on Tower Hill on 10 January 1645.

I forgive all the world; all and every of those bitter enemies which have persecuted me. And I humbly desire to be forgiven – of God first, and then, of every man, whether I have offended him or not: if he do but conceive that I have, Lord, do Thou forgive me, and I do beg forgiveness of him. And so, I heartily bid you join in prayer with me.

O eternal God and merciful Father, look down upon me in mercy; in the riches and fullness of all Thy mercies, look down upon me: but not till Thou hast nailed my sins to the Cross of Christ, not till Thou has bathed me in the Blood of Christ, not till I have hid myself in the wounds of Christ, that so the punishment due unto my sins may pass over me. And since Thou art pleased to try me to the utmost, I humbly beseech Thee, give me now, in this great instant, full patience, proportionable comfort, and a heart ready to die for Thine honour, the Kings's happiness, and the Church's preservation...

I am coming, O Lord, as quickly as I can. I know I must pass through death before I can come to see Thee. But it is only the mere shadow of death; a little darkness upon nature.

Thou, by Thy merits, hast broken through the jaws of death. The Lord receive my soul, and have mercy upon me, and bless this kingdom with peace and plenty, and with brotherly love and charity, that there may not be this effusion of Christian blood among them: for Jesus Christ's sake, if it be Thy will.

Lord, receive my soul.

The Mayflower Compact

Below is the Compact which the Pilgrim Fathers signed on 11 November 1620 after landing at Cape Cod.

In the name of God, Amen. We, whose names are underwritten, the Loyal Subjects of our dread Sovereigne Lord, King James, by the Grace of God, of Great Britaine, France, and Ireland, King, Defender of the Faith, etc.

Having undertaken for the Glory of God, and Advancement of the Christian Faith, and the Honour of our King and Country, a Voyage to plant the first colony in the Northerne Parts of

Virginia; doe, by these Presents, solemnly and mutually in the Presence of God and one of another, covenant and combine ourselves together into a civill Body Politick, for our better Ordering and Preservation, and Furtherance of the Ends aforesaid; And by Virtue hereof do enact, constitute, and frame, such just and equall Laws, Ordinances, Acts, Constitutions, and Offices, from time to time, as shall be thought most meete and convenient for the Generall Good of the Colonie; unto which we promise all due Submission and Obedience.

In Witness whereof we have hereunto subscribed our names at Cape Cod the eleventh of November, in the Raigne of our Sovereigne Lord, King James of England, France, and Ireland, the eighteenth, and of Scotland, the fiftie-fourth, Anno Domini, 1620.

John Winthrop

We shall be as a city upon a hill

John Winthrop (1588–1649), the first Governor of the Massachusetts Bay Colony, is often called 'the first great American'. He grew up in Suffolk, England, in a Puritan family, but went to America to escape religious persecution. Below is an extract from a sermon in which he outlined his ideals for government in the New World. American presidents, such as Reagan and Kennedy, have quoted from this sermon in their own addresses. The section containing the words 'We shall be as a city upon a hill' is carved into a stone monument on Boston Common.

Thus stands the case between God and us. We are entered into a covenant with him for this work. We have taken out a commission. The Lord hath given us leave to draw our own articles. We have professed to enterprise these and those ends, upon these and those accounts. We have hereupon besought of him favour and blessing. Now if the Lord shall please to hear us, and bring us in peace to the place we desire, then hath he ratified this covenant and sealed our commission, and will expect a strict performance of the articles contained in it; but if we shall neglect the observation of these articles which are the ends we have propounded, and, dissembling with our God, shall fall to embrace this present world and prosecute our carnal intentions, seeking great things for ourselves and our prosperity, the Lord will surely break out in wrath against us; be revenged of such a people, and make us know the price of the breach of such a covenant.

Now the only way to avoid this shipwreck, and to provide for our posterity, is to follow the counsel of Micah, to do justly, to love mercy, to walk humbly with our God. For this end, we must be knit together, in this work, as one man. We must entertain each other in brotherly affection. We must be willing to abridge ourselves of our superfluities, for the supply of others' necessities. We must uphold a familiar commerce together in all meekness, gentleness, patience, and liberality. We must delight in each other; make other's conditions our own; rejoice together, always having before our eyes our commission and community in the work, as members of the same body. So shall we keep the unity of the spirit in the bond of peace. The Lord will be our God, and delight to dwell among us, as his own people, and will command a blessing upon us in all our ways. So that we shall see much more of his wisdom, power, goodness and truth, than formerly we have been acquainted with. We shall find that the God of Israel is among us, when ten of us shall be able to resist a thousand of our enemies; when he shall make us a praise and a glory, that men shall say of succeeding plantations, 'The Lord make it like that of New England.' For we must consider that we shall be as a city upon a hill. The eyes of all people are upon us.

So that if we shall deal falsely with our God in this work we have undertaken, and so cause him to withdraw his present help from us, we shall be made a story and a by-word throughout the world. We shall open the mouths of enemies to speak evil of the ways of God, and all professors for God's sake. We shall shame the face of many of God's worthy servants, and cause their prayers to be turned into curses upon us till we be consumed out of the good land whither we are a-going.

I shall shut up this discourse with that exhortation of Moses, that faithful servant of the Lord, in his last farewell to Israel in Deuteronomy chapter 30. Beloved, there is now set before us life and good, death and evil, in that we are commanded this day to love the Lord our God, and to love one another, to walk in his ways and to keep his commandments and his ordinance and his laws, and the articles of our covenant with him, that we may live and be multiplied, and that the Lord our God may bless us in the land whither we go to possess it. But if our hearts shall turn away, so that we will not obey, but shall be seduced, and worship and serve other gods, our pleasure and profits, and serve them; it is propounded to us this day, we shall surely perish out of the good land whither we pass over this vast sea to possess it; therefore let us choose life that we, and our seed may live, by obeying his voice and cleaving to him, for he is our life and our prosperity.

Charles I

I go from a corruptible to an incorruptible crown

King Charles I (1600–49) was beheaded on the orders of Parliament in 1649. Soldiers lined the streets as he walked to the scaffold, and no one was supposed to hear his last words. Nevertheless, two bystanders managed to take down the following words, which were subsequently published in the London newspapers.

'The people's liberty and freedom consist in having government, in having those laws by which their lives and their goods may be most their own. It is not their having a share in the government. If I would have given way to an arbitrary way, to have all laws changed by the power of the sword, I needed not to have come here; and therefore I tell you that I am the martyr of the people.'

At this point he said words to Bishop Jexon which subsequently became very famous: 'I go from a corruptible to an incorruptible crown, where no disturbance can be.'

Samuel Rutherford

The worst that the enemies of the Kirk can do

Samuel Rutherford (c. 1600–61) was a Scottish Presbyterian minister and a member of the Westminster Assembly. Below is an extract from a sermon which he preached on 22 August 1640.

For as yet they did not know the Scripture, that He must rise again from the dead. Then the disciples went away again to their own homes. But Mary stood outside by the tomb weeping, and as she wept she stooped down and looked into the tomb. And she saw two angels in white sitting, one at the head and the other at the feet, where the body of Jesus had lain. Then they said to her, 'Woman, why are you weeping?' She said to them, 'Because they have taken away my Lord, and I do not know where they have laid Him.'

John 20:9–13

In these passages of our Lord's Word, beloved in Him, we have first set down the earthly witnesses that came to the grave to seek our Lord after He was risen from the dead. And they be of two sorts. The first sort of them are public men in a public charge, Peter and John, the Lord's disciples; and how they sought Christ, and what speed they came in seeking Him! The second sort of persons are private persons coming to seek our Lord, Mary Magdalene, out of whom He had before cast seven devils...

First: We observe one thing in the general, that concerns the estate of our Kirk at this time. Herod and Pilate, and Jew and Gentile, they have all joined themselves together at this time to do the worst they can to Christ our Lord, and yet, when they have done all that they can, they cannot mend themselves. For now they had buried Him to hold Him down, and yet for all that that mends them not. The worst that the enemies of the Kirk can do to the Kirk is to put her to death, and yet when they think they have gotten that done, it will not do their turn when all is done. For wherever our Lord's bride be, albeit she were even in the grave, she will rise again, and in a triumph over her enemies. Let our Lord and His Kirk be where they will, He and His Kirk and cause, albeit they were dead, they will live the third day again, as Christ Himself did, according to that triumphant and glorious word which He spake (Revelation 1:17–18): 'Fear not; I am the first and the last: I am He that liveth, and was dead; and, behold, I am alive for evermore.' When John had seen His glory, and fell down dead because he was afraid thereof, He says that to him. There is news to comfort the Kirk of God, and to comfort all those who doubt whether our Lord will lose the battle that He has against His enemies or not. No; He will make good that word that He speaks there of Himself: 'I was dead, but I am alive; and, behold, I am alive for evermore' ... We need not to doubt of it, but the enemies of Christ thought that they were rid of Him now, that He would burden them no more; but it is not so for all that yet, for He shall live when all is done, for all the ill they have done to Him. And within these few years our adversaries, they thought with themselves that long or now they should have been rid of our burden, and that this gospel should been clean borne down long before now. But with their leave Christ is letting us see this day that He will not have it to be so, that He will have that gospel which they thought to bear down so far, to come to some perfection again...

And, oh, that this land would believe this now, that He is our God, and the God of this land ... He is Scotland's Lord, if so be that we will wait upon Him, and trust in Him and in His salvation, it shall be found that it is not a vain thing to do so, but that He shall grant us His salvation who trust in Him.

James Renwick

I die a Presbyterian Protestant

James Renwick (?–1688), a Presbyterian minister, was martyred on 17 February 1688 in the Grassmarket of Edinburgh. Below is an account of his death.

Before he went out of the Tolbooth, he was at dinner with his mother, sisters, and some Christian friends, when the drum beat the first warning of his execution; which so soon as he heard, he leapt up in a ravishment of heavenly joy, saying, 'Let us be glad and rejoice, for the marriage of the Lamb is come;' and I can say, in some measure, 'The bride, the Lamb's wife, hath made himself ready.' And, till dinner was over, he enlarged upon the parallel of a marriage, and invited all of them to come to the wedding, meaning his execution. When he was come to the scaffold, the drums being beat all the while, none of the distant spectators could hear anything that he said; only some very few, that were close by him, did hear it; whereof one has collected the following account. He delivered himself to this effect:

'Spectators, I must tell you I am come here this day to lay down my life for adhering to the truths of Christ, for which I am neither afraid nor ashamed to suffer; nay, I bless the Lord that ever he counted my worthy, or enabled me to suffer anything for him; and I desire to praise his grace that he hath not only kept me free from the gross pollutions of the time, but also from many ordinary pollutions of children; and such as I have been stained with, he hath washen from them in his own blood. I am this day to lay down my life for these three things:

'1. For disowning the usurpations of the tyranny of James Duke of York.

'2. For preaching that it was unlawful to pay the cess expressly exacted for bearing down the Gospel.

'3. For preaching that it was lawful for people to carry arms for defending themselves in their meetings for receiving the persecuted Gospel ordinances.

'I think a testimony for these is worth many lives, and if I had ten thousand I would think it little enough to lay them all down for the same.

'Dear friends, spectators, I must tell you that I die a Presbyterian Protestant.

'I own the Word of God as the rule of Faith and manners; I own the Confession of Faith, Larger and Shorter Catechisms, Sum of Saving Knowledge, Directory for Worship, etc.; Covenants, National and Solemn League; Acts of General Assemblies – and all the faithful contendings that have been for the work of reformation.

'I leave my testimony approving the preaching of the Gospel in the fields, and the defending the same by arms.

'I adjoin my testimony to all that hath been sealed by blood, shed either on scaffolds, fields, or seas, for the cause of Christ.

'I leave my testimony against Popery, Prelacy, Erastianism, etc.; against all profanity, and everything contrary to sound doctrine; particularly against all usurpations made upon Christ's right, who is the Prince of the kings of the earth, who alone must bear the glory of ruling his own kingdom, the church; and, in particular, against the absolute power usurped by this usurper, that belongs to no mortal, but is the incommunicable prerogative of Jehovah, and against this toleration flowing from that absolute power.'

Upon this, he was bid have done. He answered, 'I have near done.'

Then he said, 'Ye that are the people of God, do not weary in maintaining the testimony of the day, in your stations and places; and whatever ye do, make sure an interest in Christ, for there is a storm coming that shall try your foundation. Scotland must be rid of Scotland before the delivery come. And you that are strangers to God, break off from your sins by repentance, else I will be a witness against you in the day of the Lord.'

Here they caused him desist. Upon the scaffold he sung a part of Psalm 103, from the beginning and read chapter 19 of the Revelation.

In prayer he said: 'Lord, I die in the faith that thou wilt not leave Scotland, but that thou wilt make the blood of thy witnesses the seed of thy church, and return again, and be glorious in our land. And now, Lord, I am ready – "the bride, the Lamb's wife, hath made herself ready."'

The napkin then being tied about his face, he said to his friend attending him – 'Farewell. Be diligent in duty. Make your peace with God, through Christ. There is a great trial coming. As to the remnant I leave, I have committed them to God. Tell them from me not to weary, nor be discouraged in maintaining the testimony. Let them not quit nor forego one of these despised truths. Keep your ground, and the Lord will provide you teachers and ministers, and when he comes, he will make these despised truths glorious upon the earth.'

Then he turned over the ladder, with these words in his mouth: 'Lord, into thy hands I commit my spirit, for thou has redeemed me, Lord God of truth.'

And having thus finished his course, served his generation, and witnessed a good confession for his Lord and Master, before many witnesses, by the will of God, he yielded up his spirit into the hands of God who gave it.

He was the last that sealed the testimony of this suffering period in a public way upon a scaffold.

A Cloud of Witnesses, ed. John H. Thomson (Edinburgh, 1781)

Thomas Ken

Jesus is Lord

Thomas Ken (1637–1711) was an English bishop and hymn-writer.

I believe in thee, O Jesus, and I rejoice in thy dear name, which is so full and expressive of thy love.

Thou art Jesus our Saviour, because thou camest into the world to save us from our sins: all love, all glory, be to thee.

O be thou ever Jesus to me; O let me feel the kind force of that sweet name, in which I and all sinners do find our deliverance and our salvation and the remedy for our guilt.

I believe that thou, O Jesus, wast anointed with the Holy Spirit, that all his gifts and graces were poured out, and diffused like a sweet ointment on thy soul, without measure; thou art altogether lovely, O Christ, and of thy fullness we all receive; all love, all glory, be to thee.

By the love of thy cross, O Jesu, I live; in that I will only glory, that above all things will I study, that before all things will I value; by the love of thy cross I will take up my cross daily, and follow thee.

From Sermons

Thomas Boston

Of the providence of God

Thomas Boston (1676–1732) was a Scottish clergyman noted for his preaching and pastoral ministry.

Are not two sparrows sold for a farthing? And one of them shall not fall on the ground without your Father.

Matthew 10:29

Our Lord is here encouraging his disciples against all the troubles and distresses they might meet with in their way, and particularly against the fear of men, by the consideration of the providence of God, which reaches unto the meanest of things, sparrows and the hairs of our head. Sparrows are of a mean price and small value; and yet, for as mean as they are, God preserves them, guides and disposes of all things concerning them, so that one of them cannot fall to the ground by shot or any other way, without his sovereign ordering and disposal.

The instruction deducible from the text is: There is a providence that extends itself to the least of things. In discoursing from this doctrine, I shall: 1. Shew that there is a providence. 2. Consider its object. 3. Explain the acts thereof. 4. Consider its properties. 5. Lastly, make improvement.

1. I am to shew that there is a providence. This appears:

A. From plain scripture-testimonies; as Psalm 103:19, 'His kingdom ruleth over all.' Acts 17:28, 'In him we live, and move, and have our being.' Ephesians 1:11, 'Who worketh all things after the counsel of his own will.'

B. From the nature of God, who being independent, and the first cause of all things, the creatures must needs depend upon him in their being and working. He is the end of all things, wise, knowing how to manage all for the best; powerful to effectuate whatever he has purposed; and faithful to accomplish all he has decreed, promised, or threatened...

2. Let us, in the next place, consider the object of providence, or where it reaches and extends to. And this is all the creatures, and all their actions, Hebrews 1:3, 'Upholding all things by the word of his power'; Psalm 103:19, 'His kingdom ruleth over all.' The angels are subject to this providence, Nehemiah 9:6, 'Thou, even thou art Lord alone, thou hast made heaven, the heaven of heavens, with all their host, the earth and all things that are therein, the seas and all that is therein, and thou preservest them all, and the host of heaven worshippeth thee.' So are also the devils, these infernal spirits, Matthew 8:31, 'If thou cast us out (said they to Jesus), suffer us to go away unto the herd of swine.' It reaches natural things, as clouds, snow, winds, etc. as appears from Psalms 104; 147 and from daily observation. Casual things are ordered by providence, as lots, Proverbs

16:33, 'The lot is cast into the lap: but the whole disposing thereof is of the Lord.' So in the case of accidental manslaughter, Exodus 21:13, 'If a man lie not in wait, and God deliver him into his hand.' There is nothing so mean but providence extends to it, such as the falling of a sparrow, and the numbering of the hairs of our head. It is God that feeds the fowls and the young ravens that cry. He clothes the lilies and grass of the field, that have no hand of man about them. He made lice, frogs, etc. a plague to scourge Pharaoh and his people, and worms to eat up Herod, etc. In a special manner providence is conversant about man, forming him in the womb, 'Hast thou not poured me out as milk (says Job), and curdled me like cheese? Thou hast clothed me with flesh and hast fenced me with bones and sinews,' Job 10:10–11; bringing him forth out of his mother's bowels, and holding him up thereafter, Psalm 71:6. His heart is in the Lord's hand, and all his thoughts and inclinations are under his control, Proverbs 21:1. He directs and orders all his steps. The most free acts of the creature's will are governed by superintending providence. All their good actions, John 15:5, 'Without me ye can do nothing.' So also their evil actions, Acts 4:27–28, 'For of a truth against thy holy child Jesus, whom thou hast anointed, both Herod and Pontius Pilate, with the Gentiles, and the people of Israel, were gathered together, for to do whatsoever thy hand and thy counsel determined before to be done.' Genesis 45:7, 'God sent me before you,' says Joseph to his brethren, though they had wickedly sold him into Egypt.

3. I proceed to consider the acts of providence. They are two, preserving and governing the creatures and their actions.

A. God by his providence preserves all the creatures. This preservation of the creatures is an act of providence, whereby they are preserved in their being and power of acting, Hebrews 1:3,

'Upholding all things by the word of his power.' In this God sometimes makes use of means, and sometimes acts without means. We have both described, Hosea 2:21–22, 'I will hear saith the Lord, I will hear the heavens, and they shall hear the earth, and the earth shall hear the corn, and the wine, and the oil, and they shall hear Jezreel.' He preserves the heavens immediately, the earth, the corn, the wine, and the oil, etc. immediately. And thus by this providence he provides all things necessary for the preservation of all things; Psalm 145:15–16, 'The eyes of all wait upon thee, and thou givest them their meat in due season. Thou openest thine hand, and satisfiest the desire of every living thing.'

B. God does not only preserve the creatures, but governs and manages them, which is the second act of providence; whereby he disposes of all things, persons, and actions, according to his will, Proverbs 21:1, 'The King's heart is in the hand of the Lord, as the rivers of water: he turneth it whithersoever he will.' Proverbs 26:33, 'The lot is cast into the lap: but the whole disposing thereof is of the Lord.' Proverbs 16:9, 'A man's heart deviseth his way; but the Lord directeth his steps.'

4. Our next business is to consider the properties of divine providence.

A. God's providence is most holy, Psalm 145:7, 'The Lord is righteous in all his ways, and holy in all his works.' Even though providence reach to and be conversant in sinful actions, yet it is pure; as the sun contracts no defilement, though it shine on a dunghill.

B. It is most wise, Isaiah 28:29, 'This cometh forth from the Lord of hosts, who is wonderful in counsel, and excellent in working.' Infinite wisdom always proposes the most excellent ends in all its operations, and uses the best methods for accomplishing its ends.

C. Providence is most powerful. Hence the Lord says to Sennacherib, the king of Assyria, 'I will put my hook in thy nose, and my bridle in thy lips, and I will turn thee back by the way by which thou camest,' 2 Kings 19:28. 'The king's heart is in the hand of the Lord, as the rivers of water: he turneth it whithersoever he will.' Who can resist his will which is almighty? He can never fail of his end, but all things fall out according to his decree, which is efficacious and irresistible.

5. I shall conclude with an use of exhortation.

A. Beware of drawing an excuse for your sin from the providence of God; for it is most holy, and has not the least efficiency in any sin you commit. Though he has by a permissive decree allowed moral evil to be in the world, yet that has no influence on the sinner to commit it.

B. Beware of murmuring and fretting under any dispensations of providence that ye meet with; remembering that nothing falls out without a wise and holy providence, which knows best what is fit and proper for you. And in all cases, even amidst the most afflicting incidents that befall you, learn submission to the will of God; as Job did, when he said, in consequence of a train of the heaviest calamities that happened to him, 'The Lord gave, and the Lord hath taken away, blessed be the name of the Lord,' Job 1:21. In the most distressing case say with the disciples, 'The will of the Lord be done,' Acts 21:14.

C. Beware of anxious cares and diffidence about your journey through the world. This our Lord has cautioned his followers against, Matthew 6:31, 'Take no thought (that is, anxious and perplexing thought), saying, What shall we eat? or, What shall we drink? or, Wherewithal shall we be clothed?'

D. Do not slight means, seeing God worketh by them; and he that hath appointed the end orders the means necessary for gaining the end. Do not rely upon means, for they can do nothing without God, Matthew 4:4. Do not despond if there be no means, for God can work without them, as well as with them, Hosea 1:7, 'I will save them by the Lord their God, and will not save them by bow, nor by sword, nor by battle, nor by horses, nor by horsemen.' If the means be unlikely, he can work above them, Romans 4:19, 'He considered not his own body now dead, neither yet the deadness of Sarah's womb.'

E. Lastly, happy is the people whose God the Lord is: for all things shall work together for their good. They may sit secure in exercising faith upon God, come what will. They have ground for prayer; for God is a prayer-hearing God, and will be inquired of by his people as to all their concerns in the world. And they have ground for the greatest encouragement and comfort amidst all the events of providence, seeing they are managed by their covenant God and gracious friend, who will never neglect or overlook his dear people, and whatever concerns them. For he hath said, 'I will never leave thee, nor forsake thee,' Hebrews 13:5.

George Frederic Handel

I did think I did see all Heaven before me

While he was writing the *Messiah*, the composer Handel (1685–1759) stayed in his house for 24 days, completely immersed in his work. As he put the finishing touches to the 'Hallelujah Chorus', he turned to his servant with tears in his eyes and exclaimed:

I did think I did see all Heaven before me, and the great God Himself!

PART 6

The Eighteenth Century

Jonathan Edwards

Sinners in the hands of an angry God

Jonathan Edwards (1703–58) was a philosopher and a revival preacher during the Great Awakening in the United States.

Their foot shall slide in due time.

Deuteronomy 32:35

In this verse is threatened the vengeance of God on the wicked unbelieving Israelites, who were God's visible people, and who lived under the means of grace; but who, notwithstanding all God's wonderful works towards them, remained (as verse 28) void of counsel, having no understanding in them ... The expression I have chosen for my text, 'Their foot shall slide in due time', seems to imply the following things, relating to the punishment and destruction to which these wicked Israelites were exposed.

1. That they were always exposed to destruction; as one that stands or walks in slippery places is always exposed to fall. This is implied in the manner of their destruction coming upon them, being represented by their foot sliding. The same is expressed, Psalm 73:18, 'Surely thou didst set them in slippery places; thou castedst them down into destruction.'

2. It implies, that they were always exposed to sudden unexpected destruction. As he that walks in slippery places is every moment liable to fall, he cannot foresee one moment whether he shall stand or fall the next; and when he does fall, he falls at once without warning: Which is also expressed in Psalm 73:18–19, 'Surely thou didst set them in slippery places; thou castedst them down into destruction: How are they brought into desolation as in a moment!'

3. Another thing implied is, that they are liable to fall of themselves, without being thrown down by the hand of another; as he that stands or walks on slippery ground needs nothing but his own weight to throw him down.

4. That the reason why they are not fallen already, and do not fall now, is only that God's appointed time is not come. For it is said, that when that due time, or appointed time comes, their foot shall slide. Then they shall be left to fall, as they are inclined by their own weight. God will not hold them up in these slippery places any longer, but will let them go; and then, at that very instant, they shall fall into destruction.

The observation from the words that I would now insist upon is this. 'There is nothing that keeps wicked men at any one moment out of hell, but the mere pleasure of God.' The truth of this observation may appear by the following considerations.

1. There is no want of power in God to cast wicked men into hell at any moment. Men's hands cannot be strong when God rises up.

2. They deserve to be cast into hell. The sword of divine justice is every moment brandished over their heads, and it is nothing but the hand of arbitrary mercy, and God's mere will, that holds it back.

3. They are already under a sentence of condemnation to hell ... 'He that believeth not is condemned already' (John 3:18).

4. They are now the objects of that very same anger and wrath of God, that is expressed in the torments of hell...

5. The devil stands ready to fall upon them, and seize them as his own, at what moment God shall permit him...

6. There are in the souls of wicked men those hellish principles reigning, that would presently kindle and flame out into hell fire, if it were not for God's restraints...

7. It is no security to wicked men for one moment, that there are no visible means of death at hand ... The arrows of death fly unseen at noonday; the sharpest sight cannot discern them.

8. Natural men's prudence and care to preserve their own lives, or the care of others to preserve them, do not secure them a moment...

9. All wicked men's pains and contrivance which they use to escape hell, while they continue to reject Christ, and so remain wicked men, do not secure them from hell one moment...

10. God has laid himself under no obligation, by any promise to keep any natural man out of hell one moment...

Application: The use of this awful subject may be for awakening unconverted persons in this congregation. This that you have heard is the case of every one of you that are out of Christ. That world of misery, that lake of burning brimstone, is extended abroad under you ... The wrath of God is like great waters that are damned for the present; they increase more and more, and rise higher and higher, till an outlet is given; and the longer the stream is stopped, the more rapid and mighty is its course, when once it is let loose ... Thus all you that never passed under a great change of heart, by the mighty power of the Spirit of God upon your souls; all you that were never born again, and made new creatures, and raised from being dead in sin, to a state of new, and before altogether unexperienced light and life, are in the hands of an angry God...

O sinner! Consider the fearful danger you are in: it is a great furnace of wrath, a wide and bottomless pit, full of the fire of wrath, that you are held over in the hand of that God, whose wrath is provoked and incensed as much against you, as against many of the damned in hell. You hang by a slender thread, with the flames of divine wrath flashing about it, and ready every moment to singe it, and burn it asunder; and you have no interest in any Mediator, and nothing to lay hold of to save yourself, nothing to keep off the flames of wrath, nothing of your own, nothing that you ever have done, nothing that you can do, to induce God to spare you one moment. And consider here more particularly,

1. Whose wrath it is: it is the wrath of the infinite God... 'And I say unto you, my friends, Be not afraid of them that kill the body, and after that, have no more that they can do. But I will forewarn you whom you shall fear: fear him, which after he hath killed, hath power to cast into hell; yea, I say unto you, Fear him' (Luke 12:4–5).

2. It is the fierceness of his wrath that you are exposed to. We often read of the fury of God; as in Isaiah 59:18, 'According to their deeds, accordingly he will repay fury to his adversaries.' So Isaiah 66:15, 'For behold, the Lord will come with fire, and with his chariots like a whirlwind, to render his anger with fury, and his rebuke with flames of fire' ...

3. The misery you are exposed to is that which God will inflict to that end, that he might show what that wrath of Jehovah is. God hath had it on his heart to show to angels and men, both how excellent his love is, and also how terrible his wrath is... 'And it shall come to pass, that from one new moon to another, and from one sabbath to another, shall all flesh come to worship before me, saith the Lord. And they shall go forth and look upon the carcasses of the men that have transgressed against me; for their worm shall not die, neither shall their fire be quenched, and they shall be an abhorring unto all flesh' (Isaiah 66:23–24).

4. It is everlasting wrath. It would be dreadful to suffer this fierceness and wrath of Almighty God one moment; but you must suffer it to all eternity. There will be no end to this exquisite horrible misery...

And let every one that is yet of Christ, and hanging over the pit of hell, whether they be old men and women, or middle aged, or young people, or little children, now hearken to the loud calls of God's word and providence. This acceptable year of the Lord, a day of such great favours to some, will doubtless be a day of as remarkable vengeance to others. Men's hearts harden, and their guilt increases apace at such a day as this, if they neglect their souls; and never was there so great danger of such persons being given up to hardness of heart and blindness of mind. God seems now to be hastily gathering in his elect in all parts of the land; and probably the greater part of adult persons that ever shall be saved, will be brought in now in a little time, and that it will be as it was on the great outpouring of the Spirit upon the Jews in the apostles' days; the election will obtain, and the rest will be blinded...

Therefore, let every one that is out of Christ, now awake and fly from the wrath to come. The wrath of Almighty God is now undoubtedly hanging over a great part of this congregation: Let every one fly out of Sodom: 'Haste and escape for your lives, look not behind you, escape to the mountain, lest you be consumed.'

Jonathan Edwards

True grace distinguished from the experience of devils

You believe that there is one God. Good! Even the demons believe that – and shudder.

James 2:19

Some people have strong religious experiences, and think of them as proof of God's working in their hearts. Often these experiences give people a sense of the importance of the spiritual world, and the reality of divine things. However, these, too, are no sure proof of salvation. Demons and damned human beings have many spiritual experiences which have a great effect on their heart attitudes. They live in the spiritual world and see firsthand what it is like. Their sufferings show them the worth of salvation and the worth of a human soul in the most powerful way imaginable. The parable in Luke chapter 16 teaches this clearly, as the suffering man asks that Lazarus might be sent to tell his brothers to avoid this place of torment. No doubt people in hell now have a distinct idea of the vastness of eternity, and of the shortness of life. They are completely convinced that all the things of this life are unimportant when compared to the experiences of the eternal world. People now in hell have a great sense of the preciousness of time, and of the wonderful opportunities people have, who have the privilege of hearing the Gospel. They are completely aware of the foolishness of their sin, of neglecting opportunities, and ignoring the warnings of God. When sinners find out by personal experience the final result of their sin there is 'weeping and gnashing of teeth' (Matthew 13:42). So even the most powerful religious experiences are not a sure sign of God's grace in the heart...

When a person comes to see the proper foundation of faith and trust with his own eyes, this is saving faith. 'For my Father's will is that everyone who looks to the Son and believes in him shall have eternal life' (John 6:40). 'I have revealed you to those whom you gave me out of the world. They were yours; you gave them to me and they have obeyed your word. Now they know that everything you have given me comes from you. For I gave them the words you gave me and they accepted them. They knew with certainty that I came from you, and they believed that you sent me' (John 17:6–8).

It is this sight of the divine beauty of Christ that captivates the wills and draws the hearts of men. A sight of the outward greatness of God in His glory may overwhelm men, and be more than they can endure. This will be seen on the day of judgment, when the wicked will be brought before God. They will be overwhelmed, yes, but the hostility of the heart will remain in full strength and the opposition of the will continue. But on the other hand, a single ray of the moral and spiritual glory of God and of the supreme loveliness of Christ shone into the heart overcomes all hostility. The soul is inclined to love God as if by an omnipotent power, so that now not only the understanding, but the whole being receives and embraces the loving Saviour.

This sense of the beauty of Christ is the beginning of true saving faith in the life of a true convert. This is quite different from any vague feeling that Christ loves him or died for him. These sort of feelings can cause a sort of love and joy, because the person feels a gratitude for escaping the punishment of their sin. In actual fact, these feelings are based on self-love, and not on a love for Christ at all. It is a sad thing that so many people are deluded by this false faith. On the other hand, a glimpse of the glory of God in the face of Jesus Christ causes in the heart a supreme genuine love for God. This is because the divine light shows the excellent loveliness of God's nature. A love based on this is far, far above anything coming from self-love, which demons can have as well as men. The true love of God which comes from this sight of His beauty causes a spiritual and holy joy in the soul; a joy in God, and exulting in Him. There is no rejoicing in ourselves, but rather in God alone.

The sight of the beauty of divine things will cause true desires after the things of God. These desires are different from the longings of demons, which happen because the demons know their doom awaits them, and they wish it could somehow be otherwise. The desires that come from this sight of Christ's beauty are natural free desires, like a baby desiring milk. Because these desires are so different from their counterfeits, they help to distinguish genuine experiences of God's grace from the false.

False spiritual experiences have a tendency to cause pride, which is the devil's special sin. 'He must not be a recent convert, or he may become conceited and fall under the same judgment as the devil' (1 Timothy 3:6). Pride is the inevitable result of false spiritual experiences, even though they are often covered with a disguise of great humility. False experience is enamoured with self and grows on self. It lives by showing itself in one way or another. A person can have great love for God, and be proud of the greatness of his love. He can be very humble, and very proud indeed of his humility. But the emotions and experiences that come from God's grace are exactly opposite. God's true working in the heart causes humility. They do not cause any kind of showiness or self-exaltation. That sense of the awesome, holy, glorious beauty of Christ kills pride and humbles the soul. The light of God's loveliness, and that alone, shows the soul its own ugliness. When a person really grasps this, he inevitably begins a process of making God bigger and bigger, and himself smaller and smaller.

Another result of God's grace working in the heart is that the person will hate every evil and respond to God with a holy heart and life. False experiences may cause a certain amount of zeal, and even a great deal of what is commonly called religion. However it is not a zeal for good works. Their religion is not a service of God, but rather a service of self. This is how the apostle James puts it himself in this very context, 'You believe that there is one God. Good! Even the demons believe that – and shudder. You foolish man, do you want evidence that faith without deeds is useless?' (James 2:19–20). So, words, deeds, or good works, are evidence of a genuine experience of God's grace in the heart. 'We know that we have come to know him if we obey his commands. The man who says, "I know him," but does not do what he commands is a liar, and the truth is not in him' (1 John 2:34). When the heart has been ravished by the beauty of Christ, how else can it respond?

How excellent is that inner goodness and true religion that comes from this sight of the beauty of Christ! Here you have the most wonderful experiences of saints and angels in heaven. Here you have the best experience of Jesus Christ Himself. Even though we are mere creatures, it is a sort of participation in God's own beauty. 'Through these he has given us his very great and precious promises, so that through them you may participate in the divine nature' (2 Peter 1:4). 'God disciplines us for our good, that we may share in his holiness' (Hebrews 12:10). Because of the power of this divine working, there is a mutual indwelling of God and His people. 'God is love. Whoever lives in love lives in God, and God in him' (1 John 4:16).

This special relationship has to make the person involved as happy and as blessed as any creature in existence. This is a special gift of God, which he gives only to his special favourites. Gold, silver, diamonds, and earthly kingdoms are given by God to people who the Bible calls dogs and pigs. But this great gift of beholding Christ's beauty, is the special blessing of God to His dearest children. Flesh and blood cannot give this gift: only God can bestow it. This was the special gift which Christ died to obtain for his elect. It is the highest token of his everlasting love, the best fruit of his labours, and the most precious purchase of his blood.

By this gift, more than anything else, the saints shine as lights in the world. This gift, more than anything else, is their comfort. It is impossible that the soul who possesses this gift should ever perish. This is the gift of eternal life. It is eternal life begun: those who have it can never die. It is the dawning of the light of glory. It comes from heaven, it has a heavenly quality, and it will take its bearer to heaven. Those who have this gift may wander in the wilderness or be tossed by waves on the ocean, but they will arrive in heaven at last. There the heavenly spark will be made perfect and increased. In heaven the souls of the saints will be transformed into a bright and pure flame, and they will shine forth as the sun in the kingdom of their Father. Amen.

Jonathan Edwards

The future glorious state of Christ's Church
Below is one of Edwards' sermons from the time of the Great Awakening.

A Humble Attempt to Promote the Agreement and Union of God's People Throughout the World in Extraordinary Prayer for a Revival of Religion and the Advancement of God's Kingdom on Earth, According to Scriptural Promises and Prophecies of the Last Time.

> *This is what the LORD Almighty says: 'Many peoples and the inhabitants of many cities will yet come, and the inhabitants of one city will go to another and say, "Let us go at once to entreat the LORD and seek the LORD Almighty. I myself am going." And many peoples and powerful nations will come to Jerusalem to seek the LORD Almighty and to entreat him.'*
> Zechariah 8:20–22

In Zechariah 8:20–22 we have an account of how this future advancement of the Church should occur. It would come to fruition as multitudes from different towns resolve to unite in extraordinary prayer, seeking God until He manifests Himself and grants the fruits of his presence...

This prophecy gives us a picture of union in prayer being a happy thing. We sense God's pleasure, and the results prove tremendously successful. From the whole of this prophecy we may infer that it is well pleasing to God for many people, in different parts of the world, to voluntarily come into a visible union to pray in an extraordinary way for those great outpourings of the Holy Spirit which shall advance the Kingdom of our Lord Jesus Christ that God has so often promised shall be in the latter ages of the world.

Let me relate a brief history of what has happened in Scotland:

In October of 1744, a number of ministers in Scotland, considering the state of God's Church, and mankind in general, believed that God was calling those concerned for the welfare of the Church to unite in extraordinary prayer. They knew God was the Creator and source of all blessings and benefits in the Church so they earnestly prayed that He would appear in His glory, and strengthen the Church, and manifest His compassion to the world of mankind by an abundant outpouring of His Holy Spirit. They desired a true revival in all parts of Christendom, and to see nations delivered from their great and many calamities, and to bless them with the unspeakable benefits of the Kingdom of our glorious Redeemer, and to fill the whole earth with His glory.

These ministers consulted with one another on this subject and concluded that they were obliged to begin such prayer and attempt to persuade others to do the same. After seeking God for direction, they determined that for the next two years they would set apart some time on Saturday evenings and Sunday mornings every week for prayer as one's other duties would allow. More importantly, it was decided that the first Tuesday of each quarter (beginning with the first Tuesday of November) would be time to be spent in prayer. People were to pray for either the entire day or part of the day, as they found themselves disposed, or as circumstances allowed. They would meet in either private prayer groups or in public meetings, whichever was found to be most convenient.

It was determined that none should make any promises or feel under strict obligation to observe every one of these days without fail; for these days were not holy or established by sacred authority. However, to prevent negligence, and the temptation to make excuses for trivial reasons, it was proposed that if those who resolve to pray cannot take part on the agreed upon day, they would use the next available day for the purpose of prayer.

The primary reason for this cooperation in prayer was to maintain, among the people of God, that necessity of prayer for the coming of Christ's Kingdom, which Christ directed his followers to do. We are, unfortunately, too little inclined to pray because of our laziness and immaturity, or because of the distraction of our own worldly, private affairs. We have prayed at times, but without special seasons for prayer, we are, likely, to neglect it either partially or totally. But when we set aside certain times for prayer, resolving to fulfil this commission unless extraordinarily hindered, we are less likely to neglect it.

The return of each new season will naturally refresh the memory and will cause us to remember these teachings of our Lord Jesus Christ, and the obligations we have as His followers. We will be renewed in the importance, necessity and unspeakable value of the mercy we seek from God, and by frequent renovation, the vision to pray will be kept alive in our hearts at all times.

Therefore, those ministers from Scotland determined that such gatherings would help encourage greater prayerfulness among God's people for revival throughout the year. They also believed that the quarterly gathering would encourage and strengthen people to pray, especially if they knew that many other Christians in so many distant places were praying for the same things at a same time.

It was thought that two years would be a sufficient trial period, after which time would be given to evaluate fruitfulness of the endeavour. It was not known but thought best to allow some time to make some adjustments if necessary. The time period, though short, was thought sufficient to judge its fruitfulness. Those involved would have the opportunity to communicate their thoughts, and perhaps improve, on this manner of prayer.

As for promulgating this concert of prayer, the ministers decided to simply pass the word through personal conversation, and correspondence with others far away, rather than any formal advertisement in the press. At first it was intended that some formal paper outlining the proposal should be sent around for proper amendments and improvements, and then agreement. But after more thoughtful deliberation, it was concluded that this would only give rise to objections which they thought best to avoid in the beginning.

Great success seems to have met their labours for great numbers in Scotland and England, and even some in North America joined with them. As to Scotland, many people in the four chief cities, Edinburgh, Glasgow, Aberdeen, and Dundee joined. There were also many country towns and congregations in various other areas that participated. A Mr Robe, of Kilsyth, stated that 'There were then above thirty societies of young people there, newly erected, some of which consisted of upwards of thirty members.'

The two years ended last November. Just prior to this, a number of ministers in Scotland agreed on a letter, to be printed and sent abroad to their brethren, proposing to them, and requesting of them, to join with them in continuing this concert of prayer, and in the endeavours to promote it. Almost five hundred copies of this letter were sent over to New England, with instructions to distribute them to the Massachusetts Bay area, Connecticut, New Hampshire, Rhode Island, New York, New Jersey, Pennsylvania, Maryland, Virginia, Carolina and Georgia. Most were sent to a congregational minister in Boston along with a letter from twelve ministers in Scotland. Other copies were sent to other ministers in Boston, and some to a minister in Connecticut.

The proposal, dated August 26, 1746, opens with an explanation of the purpose and times for the concerts of prayer, and an entreaty to the ministers to communicate their opinions after the two year period had completed.

The ministers then go on to assure their Bostonian brethren that the concerts are not to be seen as binding; men are not expected to set apart days from secular affairs, or 'fix on any part of ... precise days, whether it be convenient or not.' Nor are they to be seen as 'absolute promises, but as friendly, harmonious resolutions, with liberty to alter circumstances as shall be found expedient.' Because of such liberty these prayer times cannot be judged to infringe upon those 'religious times' appointed by men.

The letter also asked ministers to consider composing and publishing short 'persuasive directions' regarding the necessity of prayer, either by particular authors or several joining together. Without such repeated reminders men are apt to become weary and begin to neglect their duty. Ministers are also asked to preach frequently on the importance and necessity of prayer for the coming of the Lord's Kingdom, particularly near or on the quarterly times.

The Boston ministers are to understand that these prayer concerts are not restricted to any particular denomination, but is extended to all who have 'at heart the interest of vital Christianity, and the power of godliness; and who, however differing about other things, are convinced of the importance of fervent prayer ...'

It was proposed that the prayer should extend for seven more years and the ministers agreed to this. However there was concern that zeal for spreading news of the concert would wane because of the length proposed. Nevertheless, it was agreed that the first period of time (two years) was too short.

If persons who formerly agreed to this concert should discontinue it, would it not look like that fainting in prayer Scripture so ardently warned against? Would this not be particularly unsuitable given the need of public reformation?

Those ministers in Boston said of this proposal: 'The motion seems to come from above, and to be wonderfully spreading in Scotland, England, Wales, Ireland and North America.'

Jonathan Edwards

A faithful narrative of the surprising work of God

Below is Edwards' own account of the spiritual revival in Northampton, Massachusetts and in other nearby communities in the early stages of the Great Awakening.

This work of God, as it was carried on, and the number of true saints multiplied, soon made a glorious alteration in the town of Northampton: so that in the spring and summer following, anno 1735, the town seemed to be full of the presence of God: it never was so full of love, nor of joy, and yet so full of distress, as it was then. There were remarkable tokens of God's presence in almost every house. It was a time of joy in families on account of salvation being brought to them; parents rejoicing over their children as new born, and husbands over their wives, and wives over their husbands. The doings of God were then seen in His sanctuary, God's day was a delight, and His tabernacles were amiable. Our public assemblies were then beautiful: the congregation was alive in God's service, every one earnestly intent on the public worship, every hearer eager to drink in the words of the minister as they came from his mouth; the assembly in general were, from time to time, in tears while the word was preached; some weeping with sorrow and distress, others with joy and love, others with pity and concern for the souls of their neighbour....

When this work first appeared and was so extraordinarily carried on amongst us in the winter, others round about us seemed not to know what to make of it. Many scoffed at and ridiculed it; and some compared what we called conversion, to certain distempers. There were many instances of persons who came from abroad on visits, or on business, who had not been long here, before, to all appearances, they were savingly wrought upon, and partook of that shower of divine blessing which God rained down here, and went home rejoicing; till at length the same work began evidently to appear and prevail in several other towns in the county.

In the month of March, the people in South-Hadley began to be seized with deep concern about the things of religion; which very soon became universal. The work of God has been very wonderful there; not much, if any thing, short of what it has been here, in proportion to the size of the place. About the same time, it began to break forth in the west part of Suffield (where it also has been very great), and soon spread into all parts of the town. It appeared at Sunderland, and soon overspread the town: and I believe was, for a season, not less remarkable than it was here. About the same time it began to appear in a part of Deerfield, called Green River, and afterwards filled the town, and there has been a glorious work there. It began also to be manifest, in the south part of Hatfield, in a place called the Hill, and the whole town, in the second week in April, seemed to be seized, as it were at once, with concern about the things of religion; and the work of God has been great there. There has been also a very general awakening at West-Springfield, and Long Meadow; and in Enfield there was for a time a pretty general concern amongst some who before had been very loose persons. About the same time that this appeared at Enfield, the Rev. Mr Bull, of Westfield, informed me, that there had been a great alteration there, and that more had been done in one week, than in seven years before. Something of this work likewise appeared in the first precinct in Springfield, principally in the north and south extremes of the parish. And in Hadley old town, there gradually appeared so much of a work of God on souls, as at another time would have been thought worthy of much notice. For a short time there was also a very great and general concern, of the like nature, at Northfield. And wherever this concern appeared, it seemed not to be in vain: but in every place God brought saving blessings with Him, and His word attended with His Spirit (as we have all reason to think) returned not void. It might well be said at that time, in all parts of the county, 'Who are these that fly as a cloud, and as doves to their windows?'

This remarkable pouring out in the Spirit of God, which thus extended from one end to the other of this county, was not confined to it, but many places in Connecticut have partaken in the same mercy. There has been a very great ingathering of souls to Christ in that place, and something considerable of the same work began afterwards in East Windsor, my honoured father's parish, which has in times past been a place favoured with mercies of this nature, above any on this western side of New England, excepting Northampton; there having been four or five seasons of the pouring out of the Spirit to the general awakening of the people there, since my father's settlement amongst them.

This has also appeared to be a very extraordinary dispensation, in that the Spirit of God has so much extended not only His awakening, but regenerating influences, both to elderly persons, and also to those who are very young. It has been heretofore rarely heard of, that any were converted past middle age; but now we have the same ground to think that many such have at this time been savingly changed, as that others have been so in more early years. I suppose there were upwards of fifty persons converted in this town above forty years of age; more than twenty of them above fifty; about ten of them above sixty; and two of them above seventy years of age.

This work seemed to be at its greatest height in this town in the former part of the spring, in March and April. At that time God's work in the conversion of souls was carried on amongst us in so wonderful a manner, that, so far as I can judge, it appears to have been at the rate at least of four persons in a day; or near thirty in a week, take one with another, for five or six weeks together. When God in so remarkable a manner took the work into His own hands, there was as much done in a day or two, as at ordinary times, with all endeavours that men can use, and with such a blessing as we commonly have, is done in a year.

The manner of conversion various, yet bearing a great analogy
These awakenings when they have first seized on persons, have had two effects; one was, that they have brought them immediately to quit their sinful practices; and the looser sort have been brought to forsake and dread their former vices and extravagances. When once the Spirit of God began to be so wonderfully poured out in a general way through the town, people had soon done with their old quarrels, backbitings, and intermeddling with other men's matters. The tavern was soon left empty, and persons kept very much at home; none went abroad unless on necessary business, or on some religious account, and every day seemed in many respects like a Sabbath-day. The other effect was, that it put them on earnest application to the means of salvation, reading, prayer, meditation, the ordinances of God's house, and private conference; their cry was, 'What shall we do to be saved?' The place of resort was now altered, it was no longer the tavern, but the minister's house that was thronged far more than ever the tavern had been wont to be.

Some persons who had before, for a long time, been exceedingly entangled with peculiar temptations of one sort or other, unprofitable and hurtful distresses, were soon helped over former stumbling-blocks, that hindered their progress towards saving good; convictions have wrought more kindly, and they have been successfully carried on in the way to life. And thus Satan seemed to be restrained, till towards the latter end of this wonderful time, when God's Holy Spirit was about to withdraw.

Very often, under first awakenings, when they are brought to reflect on the sin of their past lives, and have something of a terrifying sense of God's anger, they set themselves to walk more strictly, and confess their sins, and perform many religious duties, with a secret hope of appeasing God's anger, and making up for the sins they have committed. And oftentimes, at first setting out, their affections are so moved, that they are full of tears, in their confessions and prayers; which they are ready to make very much of, as though they were some atonement, and had power to move correspondent affections in God too. Hence they are for a while big with expectation of what God will do for them; and conceive they grow better apace, and shall soon be thoroughly converted. But these affections are but short-lived; they quickly find that they fail, and then they think themselves to be grown worse again. They do not find such a prospect of being soon converted, as they thought: instead of being nearer, they seem to be further off; their hearts they think are grown harder, and by this means their fears of perishing greatly increase. But though they are disappointed, they renew their attempts again and again; and still as their attempts are multiplied, so are their disappointments. All fails, they see no token of having inclined God's heart to them, they do not see that He hears their prayers at all, as they expected He would; and sometimes there have been great temptations arising hence to leave off seeking, and to yield up the case. But as they are still more terrified with fears of perishing, and their former hopes of prevailing on God to be merciful to them in a great measure fail, sometimes their religious affections have turned into heart risings against God, because He will not pity them, and seems to have little regard to their distress, and piteous cries, and to all the pains they take. They think of the mercy God has shown to others; how soon and how easily others have obtained comfort, and those too who were worse than they, and have not laboured so much as they have done; and sometimes they have had even dreadful blasphemous thoughts, in these circumstances.

There is no one thing that I know of which God has made such a means of promoting His work amongst us, as the news of others' conversion. This has been owned in awakening sinners, engaging them earnestly to seek the same blessing, and in quickening saints. Though I have thought that a minister declaring his judgment about particular persons' experiences, might from these things be justified; yet I often signify to my people how unable man is to know another's heart, and how unsafe it is to depend merely on the judgment of others. I have abundantly insisted, that a manifestation of sincerity in fruits brought forth, is better than any manifestation they can make of it in words alone: and that without this, all pretences to spiritual experiences are vain. This all my congregation can witness. And the people in general have manifested an extraordinary dread of being deceived; being exceeding fearful lest they should build wrong. Some of them have been backward to receive hope, even to a great extreme, which has occasioned me to dwell longer on this part of the narrative.

Many, while their minds have been filled with spiritual delights, have as it were forgot their food; their bodily appetite has failed, while their minds have been entertained with meat to eat that others knew not of. The light and comfort which some of them enjoy, give a new relish to their common blessings, and cause all things about them to appear as it were beautiful, sweet, and pleasant. All things abroad, the sun, moon, and stars, the clouds and sky, the heavens and earth, appear as it were with a divine glory and sweetness upon them. Though this joy includes in it a delightful sense of the safety of their own state, yet frequently, in times of their highest spiritual entertainment, this seems not to be the chief object of their fixed thought and meditation. The supreme attention of their minds is to the glorious excellencies of God and Christ; and there is very often a ravishing sense of God's love accompanying a sense of His excellency. They rejoice in a sense of the faithfulness of God's promises, as they respect the future eternal enjoyment of Him.

This work further illustrated in particular instances

But to give a clear idea of the nature and manner of the operation of God's Spirit, in this wonderful effusion of it, I would give an account of two particular instances. The first is an adult person, a young woman whose name was Abigail Hutchinson. I fix upon her especially, because she is now dead, and so it may be more fit to speak freely of her than of living instances: though I am under far greater disadvantages, on other accounts, to give a full and clear narrative of her experiences, than I might of some others; nor can any account be given but what has been retained in the memories of her friends, of what they have heard her express in her lifetime.

She was of an intelligent family: there could be nothing in her education that tended to enthusiasm, but rather to the contrary extreme. It is in no-wise the temper of the family to be ostentatious of experiences, and it was far from being her temper. She was, before her conversion, to the observation of her neighbours, of a sober and inoffensive conversation; and was a still, quiet, reserved person. She had long been infirm of body, but her infirmity had never been observed at all to incline her to be notional or fanciful, or to occasion any thing of religious melancholy. She was under awakenings scarcely a week, before there seemed to be plain evidence of her being savingly converted.

She was first awakened in the winter season, on Monday, by something she heard her brother say of the necessity of being in good earnest in seeking regenerating grace, together with the news of the conversion of the young woman before mentioned, whose conversion so generally affected most of the young people here. This news wrought much upon her, and stirred up a spirit of envy in her towards this young woman, whom she thought very unworthy of being distinguished from others by such a mercy; but withal it engaged her in a firm resolution to do her utmost to obtain the same blessing. Considering with herself what course she should take, she thought that she had not a sufficient knowledge of the principles of religion to render her capable of conversion; whereupon she resolved thoroughly to search the Scriptures; and accordingly immediately began at the beginning of the Bible, intending to read it through. She continued thus till Thursday: and then there was a sudden alteration, by a great increase of her concern in an extraordinary sense of her own sinfulness, particularly the sinfulness of her nature, and wickedness of her heart. This came upon her, as she expressed it, as a flash of lightning, and struck her into an exceeding terror. Upon which she left off reading the Bible, in course, as she had begun; and turned to the New Testament, to see if she could not find some relief there for her distressed soul.

Her great terror, she said, was, that she had sinned against God: her distress grew more and more for three days; until she saw nothing but blackness of darkness before her, and her very flesh trembled for fear of God's wrath: she wondered and was astonished at herself, that she had been so concerned for her body, and had applied so often to physicians to heal that, and had neglected her soul. Her sinfulness appeared with a very awful aspect to her, especially in three things; viz. her original sin, and her sin in murmuring at God's providence – in the weakness and afflictions she had been under – and in want of duty to parents, though others had looked upon her to excel in dutifulness. On Saturday, she was so earnestly engaged in reading the Bible and other books, that she continued in it, searching for something to relieve her, till her eyes were so dim that she could not know the letters. While she was thus engaged in reading, prayer, and other religious exercises, she thought of those words of Christ, wherein He warns us not to be as the heathen, that think they shall be heard for their much speaking;

which, she said, led her to see that she had trusted to her own prayers and religious performances, and now she was put to a nonplus, and knew not which way to turn herself, or where to seek relief.

While her mind was in this posture, her heart, she said, seemed to fly, to the minister for refuge, hoping that he could give her some relief. She came the same day to her brother, with the countenance of a person in distress, expostulating with him, why he had not told her more of her sinfulness, and earnestly inquiring of him what she should do. She seemed that day to feel in herself an enmity against the Bible, which greatly affrighted her. Her sense of her own exceeding sinfulness continued increasing from Thursday till Monday and she gave this account of it: That it had been her opinion, till now, she was not guilty of Adam's sin, nor any way concerned in it, because she was not active in it; but that now she saw she was guilty of that sin, and all over defiled by it; and the sin which she brought into the world with her, was alone sufficient to condemn her.

On the Sabbath-day she was so ill, that her friends thought it best that she should not go to public worship, of which she seemed very desirous: but when she went to bed on the Sabbath night, she took up a resolution, that she would the next morning go to the minister, hoping to find some relief there. As she awakened on Monday morning, a little before day, she wondered within herself at the easiness and calmness she felt in her mind, which was of that kind she never felt before. As she thought of this, such words as these were in her mind: 'The words of the Lord are pure words, health to the soul, and marrow to the bones': and then these words, 'The blood of Christ cleanses from all sin'; which were accompanied with a lively sense of the excellency of Christ, and His sufficiency to satisfy for the sins of the whole world. She then thought of that expression, 'It is a pleasant thing for the eyes to behold the sun'; which words then seemed to her to be very applicable to Jesus Christ. By these things her mind was led into such contemplations and views of Christ, as filled her exceeding full of joy. She told her brother, in the morning, that she had seen (i.e. in realizing views by faith) Christ the last night, and that she had really thought that she had not knowledge enough to be converted; but, says she, 'God can make it quite easy!' On Monday she felt all day a constant sweetness in her soul. She had a repetition of the same discoveries of Christ three mornings together, and much in the same manner, at each time, waking a little before day; but brighter and brighter every day.

At the last time, on Wednesday morning, while in the enjoyment of a spiritual view of Christ's glory and fullness, her soul was filled with distress for Christless persons, to consider what a miserable condition they were in. She felt a strong inclination immediately to go forth to warn sinners; and proposed it the next day to her brother to assist her in going from house to house; but her brother restrained her, by telling her of the unsuitableness of such a method. She told one of her sisters that day, that she loved all mankind, but especially the people of God. Her sister asked her why she loved all mankind. She replied, 'Because God has made them.' After this, there happened to come into the shop where she was at work, three persons who were thought to have been lately converted: her seeing of them, as they stepped in one after another, so affected her, and so drew forth her love to them, that it overcame her, and she almost fainted. When they began to talk of the things of religion, it was more than she could bear; they were obliged to cease on that account. It was a very frequent thing with her to be overcome with the flow of affection to them whom she thought godly, in conversation with them, and sometimes only at the sight of them.

She had many extraordinary discoveries of the glory of God and Christ; sometimes, in some particular attributes, and sometimes in many. She gave an account, that once, as those four words passed through her mind – wisdom, justice, goodness, and truth – her soul was filled with a sense of the glory of each of these divine attributes, but especially the last. 'Truth,' said she, 'sunk the deepest!' And, therefore, as these words passed, this was repeated, 'truth, truth!' Her mind was so swallowed up with a sense of the glory of God's truth and other perfections, that she said, it seemed as though her life was going, and that she saw it was easy with God to take away her life by discoveries of Himself. Soon after this she went to a private religious meeting, and her mind was full of a sense and view of the glory of God all the time. When the exercise was ended, some asked her concerning what she had experienced, and she began to give an account, but as she was relating it, it revived such a sense of the same things, that her strength failed, and they were obliged to take her and lay her upon the bed. Afterwards she was greatly affected, and rejoiced with these words, 'Worthy is the Lamb that was slain!' She had several days together a sweet sense of the excellency and loveliness of Christ in His meekness, which disposed her continually to be repeating over these words, which were sweet to her, 'meek and lowly in heart, meek and lowly in heart'. She once expressed herself to one of her sisters to this purpose, that she had continued whole days and whole nights, in a constant ravishing view of the glory of God and Christ, having enjoyed as much as her life could bear. Once, as her brother was speaking of the dying love of Christ, she told him, she had such a sense of it, that the mere mentioning of it was ready to overcome her.

Once, when she came to me, she said, that at such and such a time, she thought she saw as much of God, and had as much joy and pleasure, as was possible in this life; and that yet, afterwards, God discovered Himself far more abundantly. She saw the same things as before, yet more clearly, and in a far more excellent and delightful manner; and was filled with a more exceeding sweetness. She likewise gave me such an account of the sense she once had, from day to day, of the glory of Christ, and of God, in His various attributes, that it seemed to me she dwelt for days together in a kind of beatific vision of God; and seemed to have, as I thought, as immediate an intercourse with Him, as a child with a father. At the same time, she appeared most remote from any high thought of herself, and of her own sufficiency; but was like a little child, and expressed a great desire to be instructed, telling me that she longed very often to come to me for instruction, and wanted to live at my house, that I might tell her what was her duty.

She often expressed a sense of the glory of God appearing in the trees, the growth of the fields, and other works of God's hands. She told her sister who lived near the heart of the town, that she once thought it a pleasant thing to live in the middle of the town, but now, says she, 'I think it much more pleasant to sit and see the wind blowing the trees, and to behold in the country what God has made.' She had sometimes the powerful breathings of the Spirit of God on her soul, while reading the Scripture; and would express her sense of the certain truth and divinity thereof. She sometimes would appear with a pleasant smile on her countenance; and once, when her sister took notice of it, and asked why she smiled, she replied, 'I am brim-full of a sweet feeling within.' She often used to express how good and sweet it was to lie low before God, and the lower (says she) the better! and that it was pleasant to think of lying in the dust, all the days of her life, mourning for sin. She was wont to manifest a great sense of her own meanness and dependence. She often expressed an exceeding compassion, and pitiful love, which she found in her heart towards persons in a Christless condition. This was sometimes so strong, that, as she was passing by such in the streets, or those that she feared were such, she would be overcome by the sight of them. She once said, that she longed to have the whole world saved; she wanted, as it were, to pull them all to her, she could not bear to have one lost.

She had great longings to die, that she might be with Christ: which increased until she thought she did not know how to be patient to wait till God's time. But once, when she felt those longings, she thought with herself, 'If I long to die, why do I go to physicians?' Whence she concluded that her longings for death were not well regulated. After this she often put it to herself, which she should choose, whether to live or to die, to be sick or to be well; and she found she could not tell, till at last she found herself disposed to say these words: 'I am quite willing to live, and quite willing to die; quite willing to be sick, and quite willing to be well; and quite willing for any thing that God will bring upon me!' 'And then,' said she, 'I felt myself perfectly easy, in a full submission to the will of God.' She then lamented much, that she had been so eager in her longings for death, as it argued want of such a resignation to God as ought to be. She seemed henceforward to continue in this resigned frame till death.

After this, her illness increased upon her: and once after she had before spent the greater part of the night in extreme pain, she waked out of a little sleep with these words in her heart and mouth; 'I am willing to suffer for Christ's sake, I am willing to spend and be spent for Christ's sake; I am willing to spend my life, even my very life, for Christ's sake!' And though she had an extraordinary resignation with respect to life or death, yet the thoughts of dying were exceeding sweet to her. At a time when her brother was reading in Job, concerning worms feeding on the dead body, she appeared with a pleasant smile; and being asked about it, she said, It was sweet to her to think of her being in such circumstances. At another time, when her brother mentioned the danger there seemed to be, that the illness she laboured under might be an occasion of her death, it filled her with joy that almost overcame her. At another time, when she met a company following a corpse to the grave, she said, it was sweet to her to think that they would in a little time follow her in like manner.

Her illness, in the latter part of it, was seated much in her throat; and an inward swelling filled up the pipe, so that she could swallow nothing but what was perfectly liquid and but very little of that, with great and long strugglings. That which she took in fled out at her nostrils, till at last she could swallow nothing at all. She had a raging appetite for food; so that she told her sister, when talking with her about her circumstances, that the worst bit would be sweet to her; but yet, when she saw that she could not swallow it, she seemed to be as perfectly contented without it, as if she had no appetite. Others were greatly moved to see what she underwent, and were filled with admiration at her unexampled patience. At a time when she was striving in vain to get down a little of something liquid, and was very much spent with it; she looked upon her sister with a smile, saying, 'O sister, this is for my good!' At another time, when her sister was speaking of what she underwent, she told her, that she lived a heaven upon earth for all that. She used sometimes to say to her sister, under her extreme sufferings, 'It is good to be so!' Her sister once asked her, why she said so; 'Why,' says she, 'because God would have it so: it is best that things should be as God would have them: it looks best to me.' After her confinement, as they were leading her from the bed to the door, she seemed overcome by the sight of things abroad, as showing forth the glory of the Being who had made them. As she lay on her death-bed, she would often say these words, 'God is my friend!' And once, looking upon her sister with a smile, said, 'O sister, How good it is! How sweet and comfortable it is to consider, and think of heavenly things!' and used this argument to persuade her sister to be much in such meditations.

She expressed, on her death-bed, an exceeding longing, both for persons in a natural state, that they might be converted, and for the godly, that they might see and know more of God. And when those who looked on themselves as in a Christless state came to see her, she would be greatly moved with compassionate affection. One in particular, who seemed to be in great distress about the state of her soul, and had come to see her from time to time, she desired her sister to persuade not to come any more, because the sight of her so wrought on her compassions, that it overcame her nature. The same week that she died, when she was in distressing circumstances as to her body, some of her neighbours who came to see her, asked if she was willing to die! She replied, that she was quite willing either to live or die; she was willing to be in pain; she was willing to be so always as she was then, if that was the will of God. She willed what God willed. They asked her whether she was willing to die that night. She answered, 'Yes, if it be God's will.' And seemed to speak all with that perfect composure of spirit, and with such a cheerful and pleasant countenance, that it filled them with admiration.

She was very weak a considerable time before she died, having pined away with famine and thirst, so that her flesh seemed to be dried upon her bones; and therefore could say but little, and manifested her mind very much by signs. She said she had matter enough to fill up all her time with talk, if she had but strength. A few days before her death, some asked her, Whether she held her integrity still? Whether she was not afraid of death? She answered to this purpose, that she had not the least degree of fear of death. They asked her why she would be so confident? She answered, 'If I should say otherwise, I should speak contrary to what I know. There is,' said she, 'indeed, a dark entry, that looks something dark, but on the other side there appears such a bright shining light, that I cannot be afraid!' She said not long before she died, that she used to be afraid how she should grapple with death; but, says she, 'God has showed me that He can make it easy in great pain.' Several days before she died, she could scarcely say any thing but just 'Yes', and 'No', to questions that were asked her; for she seemed to be dying for three days together. But she seemed to continue in an admirably sweet composure of soul, without any interruption, to the last, and died as a person that went to sleep, without any struggling, about noon, on Friday, June 27, 1735.

She had long been infirm, and often had been exercised with great pain; but she died chiefly of famine. It was, doubtless, partly owing to her bodily weakness, that her nature was so often overcome, and ready to sink with gracious affection; but yet the truth was, that she had more grace, and greater discoveries of God and Christ, than the present frail state did well consist with. She wanted to be where strong grace might have more liberty, and be without the clog of a weak body; there she longed to be, and there she doubtless now is. She was looked upon amongst us, as a very eminent instance of Christian experience; but this is but a very broken and imperfect account I have given of her: her eminency would much more appear, if her experiences were fully related, as she was wont to express and manifest them, while living. I once read this account to some of her pious neighbours, who were acquainted with her, who said, to this purpose, that the picture fell much short of the life; and particularly that it much failed of duly representing her humility, and that admirable lowliness of heart, that at all times appeared in her. But there are, blessed be God! many living instances, of much the like nature, and in some things no less extraordinary.

Thus, Reverend Sir, I have given a large and particular account of this remarkable affair; and yet, considering how manifold God's works have been amongst us, it is but a very brief one.

Samuel Johnson

Commemorating the death of Christ

The lexicographer Samuel Johnson (1709–84) was eighteenth-century London's leading literary figure. Below is an extract from his sermon on 1 Corinthians 11:28.

By commemorating the death of Christ, as the Redeemer of the world, we confess our belief in him; for why else should we perform so solemn a rite in commemoration of him? To confess our belief in him, is to declare ourselves his followers. We enter into an obligation to perform those conditions upon which he has admitted us to follow him, and to practise all the duties of that religion which he has taught us.

This is implied in the word sacrament, which, being originally used to signify an oath of fidelity taken by the soldiers to their leaders, is now made use of by the church, to import a solemn vow, of unshaken adherence to the faith of Christ.

Thus the sacrament is a kind of repetition of baptism, the means whereby we are readmitted into the communion of the church of Christ, when we have, by sin, been separated from it; for every sin, and much more any habit or course of sin long continued, is, according to the different degrees of guilt, an apostasy or defection from our Saviour; as it is a breach of those conditions upon which we became his followers; and he that breaks the condition of a covenant, dissolves it on his side. Having therefore broken the covenant between us and our Redeemer, we lose the benefits of his death; nor can we have any hopes of obtaining them, while we remain in this state of separation from him.

But vain had been the sufferings of our Saviour, had there not been left means of reconciliation to him; since every man falls away from him occasionally, by sins of negligence at least, and perhaps, by known, deliberate, premeditated offences. So that some method of renewing the covenant between God and man was necessary; and for this purpose this sacrament was instituted; which is therefore a renewal of our broken vows, a re-entrance into the society of the church, and the act, by which we are restored to the benefits of our Saviour's death, upon performance of the terms prescribed by him.

So that this sacrament is a solemn ratification of a covenant renewed; by which, after having alienated ourselves from Christ by sin, we are restored, upon our repentance and reformation, to pardon and favour, and the certain hopes of everlasting life.

John Wesley

Now the Lord is that Spirit

In a career that spanned half a century John Wesley (1703–91), the founder of Methodism, preached the gospel message all over England, often in the open air. Below is the sermon on the Holy Spirit which he preached at St Mary's, Oxford, on Whitsunday 1736.

Now the Lord is that Spirit.

2 Corinthians 3:17

The apostle had been showing how the gospel ministry was superior to that of the law: The time being now come when types and shadows should be laid aside, and we should be invited to our duty by the manly and ingenuous motives of a clear and full revelation, open and free on God's part, and not at all disguised by his ambassadors. But what he chiefly insists upon is, not the manner, but the subject of their ministry: 'Who hath made us able ministers,' saith he, 'of the New Testament: Not of the letter, but of the Spirit: For the letter killeth, but the Spirit giveth life.' Here lies the great difference between the two dispensations: That the law was indeed spiritual in its demands, requiring a life consecrated to God in the observance of many rules; but, not conveying spiritual assistance, its effect was only to kill and mortify man, by giving him to understand, that he must needs be in a state of great depravity, since he found it so difficult to obey God; and that, as particular deaths were by that institution inflicted for particular sins, so death, in general, was but the consequence of his universal sinfulness. But the ministration of the New Testament was that of a 'Spirit which giveth life' – a Spirit, not only promised, but actually conferred; which should both enable Christians now to live unto God, and fulfil precepts even more spiritual than the former; and restore them hereafter to perfect life, after the ruins of sin and death. The incarnation, preaching, and death of Jesus Christ were designed to represent, proclaim, and purchase for us this gift of the Spirit; and therefore says the apostle, 'The Lord is that Spirit,' or the Spirit.

This description of Christ was a proper inducement to Jews to believe on him; and it is still a necessary instruction to

Christians, to regulate their expectations from him. But [we] think this age has made it particularly necessary to be well assured what Christ is to us: When that question is so differently resolved by the pious but weak accounts of some pretenders to faith on one hand, and by the clearer, but not perfectly Christian, accounts of some pretenders to reason on the other: While some derive from him a 'righteousness of God,' but in a sense somewhat improper and figurative; and others no more than a charter of pardon, and a system of morality: While some so interpret the gospel, as to place the holiness they are to be saved by in something divine, but exterior to themselves; and others, so as to place it in things really within themselves, but not more than human. Now, the proper cure of what indistinctness there is one way, and what infidelity in the other, seems to be contained in the doctrine of my text: 'The Lord is that Spirit.' In treating of which words, I will consider:

1. The nature of our fall in Adam; by which it will appear, that if 'the Lord' were not 'that Spirit,' he could not be said to save or redeem us from our fallen condition.

2. I will consider the person of Jesus Christ; by which it will appear that 'The Lord is that Spirit.'

3. I will inquire into the nature and operations of the Holy Spirit, as bestowed upon Christians.

1. I am to consider the nature of our fall in Adam

Our first parents did enjoy the presence of the Holy Spirit; for they were created in the image and likeness of God, which was no other than his Spirit. By that he communicates himself to his creatures, and by that alone they can bear any likeness to him. It is, indeed, his life in them; and so properly divine, that, upon this ground, angels and regenerate men are called his children.

But when man would not be guided by the Holy Spirit, it left him. When he would be wise in his own way, and in his own strength, and did not depend in simplicity upon his heavenly Father, the seed of a superior life was recalled from him. For he was no longer fit to be formed into a heavenly condition, when he had so unworthy a longing for, or rather dependence upon, an earthly fruit, which he knew God would not bless to him; no longer fit to receive supernatural succours, when he could not be content with his happy state towards God, without an over-curious examination into it.

Then he found himself forsaken of God, and left to the poverty, weakness, and misery of his own proper nature. He was now a mere animal, like unto other creatures made of flesh and blood, but only possessed of a larger understanding; by means of which he should either be led into greater absurdities than they could be guilty of, or else be made sensible of his lost happiness, and put into the right course for regaining it; that is, if he continued a careless apostate, he should love and admire the goods of this world, the adequate happiness only of animals; and, to recommend them and dissemble their defects, add all the ornament to them that his superior wit could invent. Or else (which is indeed more above brutes, but no nearer the perfection of man as a partaker of God, than the other) he should frame a new world to himself in theory; sometimes by warm imaginations, and sometimes by cool reasonings, endeavour to aggrandize his condition and defend his practice, or at least divert himself from feeling his own meanness and disorder.

If, on the other hand, he should be willing to find out the miseries of his fall, his understanding might furnish him with reasons for constant mourning, for despising and denying himself; might point out the sad effects of turning away from God and losing his Spirit, in the shame and anguish of a nature at variance with itself; thirsting after immortality, and yet subject to death; approving righteousness, and yet taking pleasure in things inconsistent with it; feeling an immense want of something to perfect and satisfy all its faculties, and yet neither able to know what that mighty thing is, otherwise than from its present defects, nor how to attain it, otherwise than by going contrary to its present inclinations.

Well might Adam now find himself naked; nothing less than God was departed from him. Till then he had experienced nothing but the goodness and sweetness of God; a heavenly life spread itself through his whole frame, as if he were not made of dust; his mind was filled with angelic wisdom; a direction from above took him by the hand; he walked and thought uprightly, and seemed not to be a child or novice in divine things. But now he had other things to experience; something in his soul that he did not find, nor need to fear, while he was carried on straight forward by the gentle gale of divine grace; something in his body that he could not see nor complain of; while that body was covered with glory. He feels there a self-displeasure, turbulence, and confusion; such as is common to other spirits who have lost God: He sees here causes of present shame and a future dissolution; and a strong engagement to that grovelling life which is common to animals that never enjoyed the divine nature.

The general character, therefore, of man's present state is death – a death from God, whereby we no longer enjoy any intercourse with him, or happiness in him; we no longer shine with his glory, or act with his powers. It is true, while we have a being, 'in him we must live, and move, and have our being;' but this we do now, not in a filial way, but only in a servile one, as all, even the meanest creatures, exist in him. It is one thing to receive from God an ability to walk and speak, eat and digest – to be supported by his hand as a part of this earthly creation, and upon the same terms with it, for farther trial or vengeance; and another, to receive from him a life which is his own likeness – to have within us something which is not of this creation, and which is nourished by his own immediate word and power.

Yet this is not the whole that is implied in man's sin. For he is not only inclined himself to all the sottishness of appetite, and all the pride of reason, but he is fallen under the tutorship of the evil one, who mightily furthers him in both. The state he was at first placed in, was a state of the most simple subjection to God, and this entitled him to drink of his Spirit; but when he, not content to be actually in Paradise, under as full a light of God's countenance as he was capable of, must know good and evil, and be satisfied upon rational grounds whether it was best for him to be as he was, or not; when, disdaining to be directed as a child, he must weigh every thing himself; and seek better evidence than the voice of his Maker and the seal of the Spirit in his heart; then he not only obeyed, but became like to, that eldest son of pride, and was unhappily entitled to frequent visits, or rather a continued influence, from him. As life was annexed to his keeping the command, and, accordingly, that Spirit, which alone could form it unto true life, dwelt in his body; so, being sentenced to death for his transgression, he was now delivered unto 'him who has the power of death, that, is, the devil,' whose hostile and unkindly impressions promote death and sin at once.

This being the state of man, if God should send him a Redeemer, what must that Redeemer do for him? Will it be sufficient for him to be the promulgator of a new law – to give us a set of excellent precepts? No: If we could keep them, that alone would not make us happy. A good conscience brings a man the happiness of being consistent with himself; but not that of being raised above himself into God; which every person will find, after all, is the thing he wants. Shall he be the fountain of an imputed righteousness, and procure the tenderest favour to all his followers? This is also not enough. Though a man should be allowed to be righteous, and be exempt from all punishment, yet if he is as really enslaved to the corruptions of nature, as endued with these privileges of redemption, he can hardly make himself easy; and whatever favour he can receive from God, here or hereafter, without a communication of himself; it is neither the cure of a spirit fallen, nor the happiness of one reconciled. Must not then our Redeemer be (according to the character which St John, his forerunner, gave of him) one that 'baptizeth with the Holy Ghost' – the Fountain and Restorer of that to mankind, whereby they are restored to their first estate, and the enjoyment of God? And this is a presumptive argument that 'the Lord is that Spirit.'

2. The person of Jesus Christ; by which it will appear that 'the Lord is that Spirit'

But it will appear more plainly that he is so, from the second thing proposed; which was the consideration of the person of Jesus Christ.

He was one to whom 'God gave not the Spirit by measure: but in him dwelt all the fulness of the Godhead bodily; and of his fulness we have all received, and grace for grace.' Indeed, all the communications of the Godhead, which any creatures could receive, were always from him as the Word of God; but all that mankind now in an earthly state were to receive, must be from him by means of that body, at first mortal, like unto theirs, and then glorious 'in the likeness of God,' which he took upon him for their sake.

In the beginning, the heavenly Word – being a Spirit that issued from the Father, and the Word of his power – made man an image of immortality, according to the likeness of the Father;

but he who had been made in the image of God, afterwards became mortal, when the more powerful Spirit was separated from him. To remedy this, the Word became Man, that man by receiving the adoption might become a son of God once more; that the light of the Father might rest upon the flesh of our Lord, and come bright from thence unto us; and so man, being encompassed with the light of the Godhead, might be carried into immortality. When he was incarnate and became man, he recapitulated in himself all generations of mankind, making himself the centre of our salvation, that what we lost in Adam, even the image and likeness of God, we might receive in Christ Jesus. By the Holy Ghost coming upon Mary, and the power of the highest overshadowing her, the incarnation of Christ was wrought, and a new birth, whereby man should be born of God, was shown; that as by our first birth we did inherit death, so by this birth we might inherit life.

This is no other than what St Paul teaches us: 'The first man, Adam, was made a living soul, but the Second Adam was made a quickening spirit.' All that the first man possessed of himself, all that he has transmitted to us, is 'a living soul;' a nature endued with an animal life, and receptive of a spiritual. But the Second Adam is, and was made to us, 'a quickening spirit;' by a strength from him as our Creator, we were at first raised above ourselves; by a strength from him as our Redeemer, we shall again live unto God.

In him is laid up for us that supplement to our nature, which we shall find the need of sooner or later; and that it cannot be countervailed by any assistance from the creatures, or any improvement of our own faculties: For we were made to be happy only in God; and all our labours and hopes, while we do not thirst after our deified state – to partake as truly of God as we do of flesh and blood, to be glorified in his nature, as we have been dishonoured in our own – are the labours and hopes of those who utterly mistake themselves.

The divine wisdom knew what was our proper consolation, though we did not. What does more obviously present itself in the Saviour of the world, than an union of man with God? – an union attended with all the propriety of behaviour that we are called to, as candidates of the Spirit; such as walking with God in singleness of heart, perfect self-renunciation, and a life of sufferings – an union which submitted to the necessary stages of our progress; where the divine life was hid, for the most part, in the secret of the soul till death; in the state of separation, comforted the soul, but did not raise it above the intermediate region of Paradise; at the resurrection, clothed the body with heavenly qualities, and the powers of immortality; and at last raised it to the immediate presence and right hand of the Father.

Christ is not only God above us; which may keep us in awe, but cannot save; but he is Immanuel, God with us, and in us. As he is the Son of God, God must be where he is; and as he is the Son of man, he will be with mankind; the consequence of this is, that in the future age 'the tabernacle of God will be with men,' and he will show them his glory; and, at present, he will dwell in their hearts by faith in his Son.

I hope it sufficiently appears, that 'the Lord is that Spirit.' Considering what we are, and what we have been, nothing less than the receiving that Spirit again would be redemption to us; and considering who that heavenly person was that was sent to be our Redeemer, we can expect nothing less from him.

3. The nature and operations of the Holy Spirit, as bestowed upon Christians

I proceed now to the third thing proposed, to inquire into the nature and operations of the Holy Spirit, as bestowed upon Christians.

And here I shall pass by the particular extraordinary gifts vouchsafed to the first ages for the edification of the Church and only consider what the Holy Spirit is to every believer, for his personal sanctification and salvation. It is not granted to every one to raise the dead, and heal the sick. What is most necessary is, to be sure, as to ourselves, that we are 'passed from death unto life;' to keep our bodies pure and undefiled, and let them reap that health which flows from a magnanimous patience, and the serene joys of devotion. The Holy Spirit has enabled men to speak with tongues, and to prophesy; but the light that most necessarily attends it is a light to discern the fallacies of flesh and blood, to reject the irreligious maxims of the world, and to practice those degrees of trust in God and love to men, whose foundation is not so much in the present appearances of things, as in some that are yet to come. The object which this light brings us most immediately to know is ourselves; and by virtue of this, one that is born of God, and has a lively hope may indeed see far into the ways of Providence, and farther yet into the holy Scriptures; for the holy Scriptures, excepting some accidental and less necessary parts, are only a history of that new man which he himself is; and Providence is only a wise disposal of events for the awakening of particular persons, and ripening the world in general for the coming of Christ's kingdom.

But I think the true notion of the Spirit is, that it is some portion of, as well as preparation for, a life in God, which we are to enjoy hereafter. The gift of the Holy Spirit looks full to the resurrection; for then is the life of God completed in us.

Then, after man has passed through all the penalties of sin, the drudgery and vanity of human life, the painful reflections of an awakened mind, the infirmities and dissolution of the body, and all the sufferings and mortifications a just God shall lay in his way; when, by this means, he is come to know God and himself, he may safely be entrusted with true life, with the freedom and ornaments of a child of God; for he will no more arrogate anything to himself. Then shall the Holy Spirit be fully bestowed, when the flesh shall no longer resist it, but be itself changed into an angelical condition, being clothed upon with the incorruption of the Holy Spirit; when the body which, by being born with the soul, and living through it, could only be called an animal one, shall now become spiritual, whilst by the Spirit it rises into eternity.

Everything in Christianity is some kind of anticipation of something that is to be at the end of the world. If the apostles were to preach by their Master's command, 'that the kingdom of God drew nigh;' the meaning was, that from henceforth all men should fix their eyes on that happy time, foretold by the Prophets, when the Messiah should come and restore all things; that by renouncing their worldly conversation, and submitting to the gospel institution, they should fit themselves for, hasten, that blessing. 'Now are we the sons of God,' as St John tells us; and yet what he imparts to us at present will hardly justify that title, without taking in that fullness of his image which shall then be displayed in us, when we shall be 'the children of God, by being the children of the resurrection.'

True believers, then, are entered upon a life, the sequel of which they know not; for it is 'a life hid with Christ in God.' He, the forerunner, hath attained the end of it, being gone unto the Father; but we can know no more of it than appeared in him while he was upon earth. And even that, we shall not know but by following his steps; which if we do, we shall be so strengthened and renewed day by day in the inner man, that we shall desire no comfort from the present world through a sense of 'the joy set before us;' though, as to the outward man, we shall be subject to distresses and decays, and treated as the offscouring of all things.

Well may a man ask his own heart, whether it is able to admit the Spirit of God. For where that divine Guest enters, the laws of another world must be observed: The body must be given up to martyrdom, or spent in the Christian warfare, as unconcernedly as if the soul were already provided of its house from heaven; the goods of this world must be parted with as freely, as if the last fire were to seize them to-morrow; our neighbour must be loved as heartily as if he were washed from all his sins, and demonstrated to be a child of God by the resurrection from the dead. The fruits of this Spirit must not be mere moral virtues, calculated for the comfort and decency of the present life; but holy dispositions, suitable to the instincts of a superior life already begun.

Thus to press forward, whither the promise of life calls him – to turn his back upon the world, and comfort himself in God – every one that has faith perceives to be just and necessary, and forces himself to do it: Every one that has hope, does it gladly and eagerly, though not without difficulty; but he that has love does it with ease and singleness of heart.

The state of love, being attended with 'joy unspeakable and full of glory,' with rest from the passions and vanities of man, with the integrity of an unchangeable judgment, and an undivided will, is, in a great measure, its own reward; yet not so as to supersede the desire of another world. For though such a man, having a free and insatiable love of that which is good, may seldom have need formally to propose to himself the hopes of retribution, in order to overcome his unwillingness to do his duty; yet surely he must long for that which is best of all; and feel a plain attraction towards that country in which he has his place and station already assigned him; and join in the earnest expectation of all creatures, which wait for the manifestation of the sons of God. For now we obtain but some part of his Spirit, to model and fit us for incorruption, that we may, by degrees, be accustomed to receive and carry God within us; and, therefore, the Apostle calls it, 'the earnest of the Spirit;' that is, a part of that honour which is promised us by the Lord. If, therefore, the earnest, abiding in us, makes us spiritual even now, and that which is mortal is, as it were, swallowed up of immortality; how shall it be when, rising again, we shall see him face to face? when all our members shall break forth into songs of triumph, and glorify Him who hath raised them from the dead, and granted them everlasting life? For if this earnest or pledge, embracing man into itself, makes him now cry, 'Abba, Father;' what shall the whole grace of the Spirit do, when, being given at length to believers, it shall make us like unto God, and perfect us through the will of the Father?

And thus I have done what was at first proposed: I have considered the nature of our fall in Adam; the person of Jesus Christ; and the operations of the Holy Spirit in Christians.

The only inference I will draw from what has been said, and principally from the account of man's fall, shall be, the reasonableness of those precepts of self-denial, daily suffering, and renouncing the world, which are so peculiar to Christianity, and which are the only foundation whereon the other virtues, recommended in the New Testament, can be practised or attained, in the sense there intended.

This inference is so natural, that I could not help anticipating it in some measure all the while. One would think it should be no hard matter to persuade a creature to abhor the badges of his misery; to dislike a condition or mansion which only banishment and disgrace have assigned him; to trample on the grandeur, refuse the comforts, and suspect the wisdom of a life whose nature it is to separate him from his God.

Your Saviour bids you 'hate your own life.' If you ask the reason, enter into your heart, see whether it be holy, and full of God; or whether, on the other hand, many things that are contrary to him are wrought there, and it is become a plantation of the enemy. Or, if this is too nice an inquiry, look upon your body. Do you find there the brightness of an angel, all the vigour of immortality? If not, be sure your soul is in the same degree of poverty, nakedness, and absence from God. It is true, your soul may sooner be readmitted to some rays of the light of God's countenance, than your body can; but if you would take any step at all towards it, to dislike your present self must be the first.

You want a reason why you should renounce the world. Indeed you cannot see the prince of it walking up and down, 'seeking whom he may devour;' and you may be so far ignorant of his devices, as not to know that they take place, as well in the most specious measures of business and learning, as in the wildest pursuits of pleasure. But this, however, you cannot but see, that the world is not still a paradise of God, guarded and ennobled with the light of glory; it is, indeed, a place where God has determined he will not appear to you at best, but leave you in a state of hope, that you shall see his face when this world is dissolved.

However, there is a way to rescue ourselves, in great measure, from the ill consequences of our captivity; and our Saviour has taught us that way. It is by suffering. We must not only 'suffer many things,' as he did, and so enter into our glory; but we must also suffer many things, that we may get above our corruption at present, and enjoy the Holy Spirit.

The world has no longer any power over us, than we have a quick relish of its comforts; and suffering abates that. Suffering is, indeed, a direct confutation of the pretences which the flattering tempter gains us by: For I am in human life; and if that life contains such soft ease, ravishing pleasure, glorious eminence, as you promise, why am I thus? Is it because I have not yet purchased riches to make me easy, or the current accomplishments to make me considerable. Then I find that all the comfort you propose is by leading me off from myself; but I will rather enter deep into my own condition, bad as it is: Perhaps I shall be nearer to God, the Eternal Truth, in feeling sorrows and miseries that are personal and real, than in feeling comforts that are not so. I begin already to find that all my grievances centre in one point: There is always at the bottom one great loss or defect, which is not the want of friends or gold, of health or philosophy. And the abiding sense of this may possibly become a prayer in the ears of the Most High; – a prayer not resulting from a set of speculative notions, but from the real, undissembled state of all that is within me; nor, indeed, so explicit a prayer as to describe the thing I want, but, considering how strange a want mine is, as explicit a one as I can make. Since, then, suffering opens me a door of hope, I will not put it from me as long as I live: It helps me to a true discovery of one period of my existence, though it is a low one; and bids fairer for having some connexion with a more glorious period that may follow, than the arts of indulgence, the amusements of pride and sloth, and all the dark policy of this world, which wage war with the whole truth, that man must know and feel, before he can look towards God. It may be, while I continue on the cross, I shall, like my Saviour, put off 'principalities and powers;' recover myself more and more from the subjection I am indeed in (which he only seemed to be) to those wicked rulers, and to 'triumph over them in it.'

At least, it shall appear, in the day when God shall visit, that my heart, though grown unworthy of his residence, was too big to be comforted by any of his creatures; and was kept for him, as a place originally sacred, though for the present unclean.

But supposing that our state does require of us to 'die daily' – to sacrifice all that this present life can boast of, or is delighted with, before we give up life itself; supposing also, that in the hour we do somewhat of this kind, we receive light and strength from God, to grow superior to our infirmities, and are carried smoothly towards him in the joy of the Holy Ghost; yet how can a man have such frequent opportunities of suffering? Indeed, martyrdoms do not happen in every age, and some days of our lives may pass without reproaches from men; we may be in health, and not want food to eat and raiment to put on; (though health itself, and nutrition itself, oblige us to the pain of a constant correction of them;) yet still, the love of God and heavenly hope will not want something to oppress them in this world.

Let a man descend calmly into his heart, and see if there be no root of bitterness springing up; whether, at least, his thoughts, which are ever in motion, do not sometimes sally out into projects suggested by pride, or sink into indolent trifling, or be entangled in mean anxiety. Does not he find a motion of anger, or of gaiety, leavening him in an instant throughout; depriving him of the meekness and steady discernment he laboured after? Or, let him but conceive at any time, that unfeigned obedience, and watchful zeal, and dignity of behaviour, which, is suitable, I do not say to an angel, but to a sinner that has 'a good hope through grace,' and endeavour to work himself up to it; and if he find no sort of obstacle to this within him, he has indeed then no opportunity of suffering. In short, if he is such an abject sort of creature, as will, unless grace should do him a perpetual violence, relapse frequently into a course of thinking and acting entirely without God; then he can never want occasions of suffering, but will find his own nature to be the same burden to him, as that 'faithless and perverse generation' was to our Saviour, of whom he said, 'How long shall I be with you? How long shall I suffer you?'

I will conclude all with that excellent Collect of our Church: – 'O God, who in all ages hast taught the hearts of thy faithful people, by sending to them the light of thy Holy Spirit; grant us by the same Spirit to have a right judgment in all things, and evermore to rejoice in his holy comfort, through the merits of Jesus Christ our Saviour; who liveth and reigneth with thee, in the unity of the same Spirit, one God, world without end. Amen.'

John Wesley

By grace are ye saved through faith

Wesley preached the following sermon at St Mary's, Oxford, before the University on 18 June 1738.

By grace are ye saved through faith.

Ephesians 2:8

All the blessings which God hath bestowed upon man are of his mere grace, bounty, or favour; his free, undeserved favour; favour altogether undeserved; man having no claim to the least of his mercies. It was free grace that 'formed man of the dust of the ground, and breathed into him a living soul,' and stamped on that soul the image of God, and 'put all things under his feet.' The same free grace continues to us, at this day, life, and breath, and all things. For there is nothing we are, or have, or do, which can deserve the least thing at God's hand. 'All our works, Thou, O God, hast wrought in us.' These, therefore, are so many more instances of free mercy: and whatever righteousness may be found in man, this is also the gift of God.

Wherewithal then shall a sinful man atone for any the least of his sins? With his own works? No. Were they ever so many or holy, they are not his own, but God's. But indeed they are all unholy and sinful themselves, so that every one of them needs a fresh atonement. Only corrupt fruit grows on a corrupt tree. And his heart is altogether corrupt and abominable; being 'come short of the glory of God,' the glorious righteousness at first impressed on his soul, after the image of his great Creator. Therefore, having nothing, neither righteousness nor works, to plead, his mouth is utterly stopped before God.

If then sinful men find favour with God, it is 'grace upon grace!' If God vouchsafe still to pour fresh blessings upon us, yea, the greatest of all blessings, salvation; what can we say to these things, but, 'Thanks be unto God for his unspeakable gift!' And thus it is. Herein 'God commendeth his love toward us, in that, while we were yet sinners, Christ died' to save us 'By grace,' then, 'are ye saved through faith.' Grace is the source, faith the condition, of salvation.

Now, that we fall not short of the grace of God, it concerns us carefully to inquire:

1. What faith it is through which we are saved?
2. What is the salvation which is through faith?

1. What faith it is through which we are saved?

First, it is not barely the faith of a heathen. Now, God requireth of a heathen to believe, 'that God is; that he is a rewarder of them that diligently seek him;' and that he is to be sought by glorifying him as God, by giving him thanks for all things, and by a careful practice of moral virtue, of justice, mercy, and truth, toward their fellow creatures...

Nor, second, is it the faith of a devil, though this goes much farther than that of a heathen. For the devil believes, not only that there is a wise and powerful God, gracious to reward, and just to punish; but also, that Jesus is the Son of God, the Christ, the Saviour of the world. So we find him declaring, in express terms, 'I know Thee who Thou art; the Holy One of God' (Luke 4:34). Nor can we doubt but that unhappy spirit believes all those words which came out of the mouth of the Holy One, yea, and whatsoever else was written by those holy men of old, of two of whom he was compelled to give that glorious testimony, 'These men are the servants of the most high God, who show unto you the way of salvation.' Thus much, then, the great enemy of God and man believes, and trembles in believing – that God was made manifest in the flesh; that he will 'tread all enemies under his feet;' and that 'all Scripture was given by inspiration of God.' Thus far goes the faith of a devil.

Third. The faith through which we are saved, in that sense of the word which will hereafter be explained, is not barely that which the apostles themselves had while Christ was yet upon earth; though they so believed on him as to 'leave all and follow him;' although they had then power to work miracles, to 'heal all manner of sickness, and all manner of disease;' yea, they had then 'power and authority over all devils;' and, which is beyond all this, were sent by their Master to 'preach the kingdom of God.'

What faith is it then through which we are saved? It may be answered, first, in general, it is a faith in Christ: Christ, and God through Christ, are the proper objects of it. Herein, therefore, it is sufficiently, absolutely distinguished from the faith either of ancient or modern heathens. And from the faith of a devil it is fully distinguished by this: it is not barely a speculative, rational thing, a cold, lifeless assent, a train of ideas in the head; but also a disposition of the heart. For thus saith the Scripture, 'With the heart man believeth unto righteousness;' and, 'If thou shalt confess with thy mouth the Lord Jesus, and shalt believe in thy heart that God hath raised him from the dead, thou shalt be saved.'

And herein does it differ from that faith which the apostles themselves had while our Lord was on earth, that it acknowledges the necessity and merit of his death, and the power of his resurrection. It acknowledges his death as the only sufficient means of redeeming man from death eternal, and his resurrection as the restoration of us all to life and immortality; inasmuch as he 'was delivered for our sins, and rose again for our justification.' Christian faith is then, not only an assent to the whole gospel of Christ, but also a full reliance on the blood of Christ; a trust in the merits of his life, death, and resurrection; a recumbency upon him as our atonement and our life, as given for us, and living in us; and, in consequence hereof, a closing with him, and cleaving to him, as our 'wisdom, righteousness, sanctification, and redemption,' or, in one word, our salvation.

2. What salvation it is, which is through this faith?

And, first, whatever else it imply, it is a present salvation. It is something attainable, yea, actually attained, on earth, by those who are partakers of this faith. For thus saith the apostle to the believers at Ephesus, and through them to the believers of all ages, not, 'Ye shall be' (though that also is true), but, 'Ye are saved through faith.'

'Ye are saved' from sin. This is the salvation which is through faith. This is that great salvation foretold by the angel, before God brought his first-begotten into the world: 'Thou shalt call his name Jesus; for he shall save his people from their sins.' And neither here, nor in other parts of holy writ, is there any limitation or restriction. All his people, or, as it is elsewhere expressed, 'all that believe in him,' he will save from all their sins; from original and actual, past and present sin, 'of the flesh and of the spirit.' Through faith that is in him, they are saved both from the guilt and from the power of it.

First, from the guilt of all past sin. For, whereas all the world is guilty before God, insomuch that should he 'be extreme to mark what is done amiss, there is none that could abide it;' and whereas, 'by the law is' only 'the knowledge of sin,' but no deliverance from it, so that, 'by' fulfilling 'the deeds of the law, no flesh can be justified in his sight': now, 'the righteousness of God, which is by faith of Jesus Christ, is manifested unto all that believe.' Now, 'they are justified freely by his grace, through the redemption that is in Jesus Christ.' 'Him God hath set forth to be a propitiation through faith in his blood, to declare his righteousness for the remission of the sins that are past.' Now hath Christ taken away 'the curse of the law, being made a curse for us.' He hath 'blotted out the handwriting that was against us, taking it out of the way, nailing it to his cross.' 'There is therefore no condemnation now to them which' believe 'in Christ Jesus.'

And being saved from guilt, they are saved from fear. Not indeed from a filial fear of offending; but from all servile fear; from that fear which hath torment; from fear of punishment; from fear of the wrath of God, whom they now no longer regard as a severe Master, but as an indulgent Father. 'They have not received again the spirit of bondage, but the Spirit of adoption, whereby they cry, Abba, Father: the Spirit itself also bearing witness with their spirits, that they are the children of God.' They are also saved from the fear, though not from the possibility, of falling away from the grace of God, and coming short of the great and precious promises. Thus have they 'peace with

God through our Lord Jesus Christ. They rejoice in hope of the glory of God. And the love of God is shed abroad in their hearts, through the Holy Ghost, which is given unto them.' And hereby they are persuaded that 'neither death, nor life, nor things present, nor things to come, nor height, nor depth, nor any other creature, shall be able to separate them from the love of God, which is in Christ Jesus our Lord.'

Again, through this faith they are saved from the power of sin, as well as from the guilt of it. So the apostle declares, 'Ye know that he was manifested to take away our sins; and in him is no sin. Whosoever abideth in him sinneth not.' Again, 'Little children, let no man deceive you. He that committeth sin is of the devil. Whosoever believeth is born of God. And whosoever is born of God doth not commit sin; for his seed remaineth in him: and he cannot sin, because he is born of God.' Once more: 'We know that whosoever is born of God sinneth not; but he that is begotten of God keepeth himself, and that wicked one toucheth him not' (1 John 5:18).

He that is, by faith, born of God sinneth not, by any habitual sin; for all habitual sin is sin reigning. But sin cannot reign in any that believeth. Nor by any wilful sin. For his will, while he abideth in the faith, is utterly set against all sin, and abhorreth it as deadly poison. Nor, by any sinful desire; for he continually desireth the holy and perfect will of God, and any tendency to an unholy desire, he by the grace of God, stifleth in the birth. Nor, doth he sin by infirmities, whether in act, word, or thought; for his infirmities have no concurrence of his will; and without this they are not properly sins. Thus, 'he that is born of God doth not commit sin', and though he cannot say he hath not sinned, yet now 'he sinneth not.'

This, then, is the salvation which is through faith, even in the present world: a salvation from sin, and the consequences of sin, both often expressed in the word 'justification'; which, taken in the largest sense, implies a deliverance from guilt and punishment, by the atonement of Christ actually applied to the soul of the sinner now believing on him, and a deliverance from the power of sin, through Christ 'formed in his heart'. So that he who is thus justified, or saved by faith, is indeed 'born again'. He is 'born again of the Spirit' unto a new life, which 'is hid with Christ in God.' And as a new-born babe he gladly receives the 'sincere milk of the word, and grows thereby;' going on in the might of the Lord his God, from faith to faith, from grace to grace, until at length, he come unto 'a perfect man, unto the measure of the stature of the fullness of Christ.'

The first usual objection to this is, that to preach salvation or justification, by faith only, is to preach against holiness and good works. To which a short answer might be given: 'It would be so, if we spake, as some do, of a faith which was separate from these; but we speak of a faith which is not so, but productive of all good works, and all holiness.'

But it may be of use to consider it more at large; especially since it is no new objection, but as old as St Paul's time. For even then it was asked, 'Do we not make void the law through faith?' We answer, First, all who preach not faith do manifestly make void the law; either directly and grossly, by limitations and comments that eat out all the spirit of the text; or indirectly, by not pointing out the only means whereby it is possible to perform it. Whereas, secondly, 'we establish the law,' both by showing its full extent and spiritual meaning; and by calling all to that living way, whereby 'the righteousness of the law may be fulfilled in them.' These, while they trust in the blood of Christ alone, use all the ordinances which he hath appointed, do all the 'good works which he had before prepared that they should walk therein,' and enjoy and manifest all holy and heavenly tempers, even the same mind that was in Christ Jesus.

But does not preaching this faith lead men into pride? We answer, Accidentally it may: therefore ought every believer to be earnestly cautioned, in the words of the great apostle 'Because of unbelief,' the first branches 'were broken off: and thou standest by faith. Be not high-minded, but fear. If God spared not the natural branches, take heed lest he spare not thee. Behold therefore the goodness and severity of God! On them which fell, severity; but towards thee, goodness, if thou continue in his goodness; otherwise thou also shalt be cut off.' And while he continues therein, he will remember those words of St Paul, foreseeing and answering this very objection (Romans 3:27), 'Where is boasting then? It is excluded. By what law? of works? Nay: but by the law of faith.' If a man were justified by his works, he would have whereof to glory. But there is no glorying for him 'that worketh not, but believeth on him that justifieth the ungodly' (Romans 4:5). To the same effect are the words both preceding and following the text (Ephesians 2:4ff.): 'God, who is rich in mercy, even when we were dead in sins, hath quickened us together with Christ (by grace ye are saved), that he might show the exceeding riches of his grace in his kindness toward us through Christ Jesus. For by grace are ye saved through faith; and that not of yourselves.' Of yourselves cometh neither your faith nor your salvation: 'it is the gift of God;' the free, undeserved gift; the faith through which ye are saved, as well as the salvation which he of his own good pleasure, his mere favour, annexes thereto. That ye believe, is one instance of his grace; that believing ye are saved, another. 'Not of works, lest any man should boast.' For all our works, all our righteousness, which were before our believing, merited nothing of God but condemnation; so far were they from deserving faith, which therefore, whenever given, is not of works. Neither is salvation of the works we do when we believe, for it is then God that worketh in us: and, therefore, that he giveth us a reward for what he himself worketh, only commendeth the riches of his mercy, but leaveth us nothing whereof to glory.

'However, may not the speaking thus of the mercy of God, as saving or justifying freely by faith only, encourage men in sin?' Indeed, it may and will: Many will 'continue in sin that grace may abound:' but their blood is upon their own head. The goodness of God ought to lead them to repentance; and so it will those who are sincere of heart. When they know there is yet forgiveness with him, they will cry aloud that he would blot out their sins also, through faith which is in Jesus. And if they earnestly cry, and faint not, it they seek him in all the means he hath appointed; if they refuse to be comforted till he come; 'he will come, and will not tarry.' And he can do much work in a short time. Many are the examples, in the Acts of the Apostles, of God's working this faith in men's hearts, even like lightning falling from heaven. So in the same hour that Paul and Silas began to preach, the jailer repented, believed, and was baptized; as were three thousand, by St Peter, on the day of Pentecost, who all repented and believed at his first preaching. And, blessed be God, there are now many living proofs that he is still 'mighty to save.'

Yet to the same truth, placed in another view, a quite contrary objection is made: 'If a man cannot be saved by all that he can do, this will drive men to despair.' True, to despair of being saved by their own works, their own merits, or righteousness. And so it ought; for none can trust in the merits of Christ, till he has utterly renounced his own. He that 'goeth about to stablish his own righteousness' cannot receive the righteousness of God. The righteousness which is of faith cannot be given him while he trusteth in that which is of the law.

But this, it is said, is an uncomfortable doctrine. The devil spoke like himself, that is, without either truth or shame, when he dared to suggest to men that it is such. It is the only comfortable one, it is 'very full of comfort,' to all self-destroyed, self-condemned sinners. That 'whosoever believeth on him shall not be ashamed that the same Lord over all is rich unto all that call upon him': here is comfort, high as heaven, stronger than death! What! Mercy for all? For Zacchaeus, a public robber? For Mary Magdalene, a common harlot? Methinks I hear one say 'Then I, even I, may hope for mercy!' And so thou mayest, thou afflicted one, whom none hath comforted! God will not cast out thy prayer. Nay, perhaps he may say the next hour, 'Be of good cheer, thy sins are forgiven thee;' so forgiven, that they shall reign over thee no more; yea, and that 'the Holy Spirit shall bear witness with thy spirit that thou art a child of God.' O glad tidings, tidings of great joy, which are sent unto all people! 'Ho, every one that thirsteth, come ye to the waters: Come ye, and buy, without money and without price.' Whatsoever your sins be, 'though red like crimson,' though more than the hairs of your head, 'return ye unto the Lord, and he will have mercy upon you, and to our God, for he will abundantly pardon.'

When no more objections occur, then we are simply told that salvation by faith only ought not to be preached as the first doctrine, or, at least, not to be preached at all. But what saith the Holy Ghost? 'Other foundation can no man lay than that which is laid, even Jesus Christ.' So then, that 'whosoever believeth on him shall be saved,' is, and must be, the foundation of all our preaching; that is, must be preached first. 'Well, but not to all.' To whom, then are we not to preach it? Whom shall we except? The poor? Nay; they have a peculiar right to have the gospel preached unto them. The unlearned? No. God hath revealed these things unto unlearned and ignorant men from the beginning. The young? By no means. 'Suffer these,' in any wise, 'to come unto Christ, and forbid them not.' The sinners? Least of all. 'He came not to call the righteous, but sinners to repentance.' Why then, if any, we are to except the rich, the learned, the reputable, the moral men. And, it is true, they too often except themselves from hearing; yet we must speak the words of our Lord. For thus the tenor of our commission runs, 'Go and preach the gospel to every creature.' If any man wrest it, or any part of it, to his destruction, he must bear his own burden. But still, 'as the Lord liveth, whatsoever the Lord saith unto us, that we will speak.'

At this time, more especially, will we speak, that 'by grace are ye saved through faith': because, never was the maintaining this doctrine more seasonable than it is at this day. Nothing but this can effectually prevent the increase of the Romish delusion among us. It is endless to attack, one by one, all the errors of that Church. But salvation by faith strikes at the root, and all fall at once where this is established. It was this doctrine, which our Church justly calls 'the strong rock and foundation of the Christian religion', that first drove Popery out of these kingdoms; and it is this alone can keep it out. Nothing but this can give a check to that immorality which hath 'overspread the land as a flood' ... Nothing but this can stop the mouths of those who 'glory in their shame, and openly deny the Lord that bought them.' They can talk as sublimely of the law, as he that hath it written by God in his heart. To hear them speak on this head might incline one to think they were not far from the kingdom of God: but take them out of the law into the gospel; begin with the righteousness of faith; with Christ, 'the end of the law to every one that believeth;' and those who but now appeared almost, if not altogether, Christians, stand confessed the sons of perdition; as far from life and salvation (God be merciful unto them!) as the depth of hell from the height of heaven.

For this reason the adversary so rages whenever 'salvation by faith' is declared to the world: for this reason did he stir up earth and hell, to destroy those who first preached it. And for the same reason, knowing that faith alone could overturn the foundations of his kingdom, did he call forth all his forces, and employ all his arts of lies and calumny, to affright Martin Luther from reviving it. Nor can we wonder thereat; for, as that man of God observes, 'How would it enrage a proud, strong man armed, to be stopped and set at nought by a little child coming against him with a reed in his hand!' especially when he knew that little child would surely overthrow him, and tread him under foot. Even so, Lord Jesus! Thus hath Thy strength been ever 'made perfect in weakness'! Go forth then, thou little child that believest in him, and his 'right hand shall teach thee terrible things'! Though thou art helpless and weak as an infant of days, the strong man shall not be able to stand before thee. Thou shalt prevail over him, and subdue him, and overthrow him and trample him under thy feet. Thou shalt march on, under the great Captain of thy salvation, 'conquering and to conquer,' until all thine enemies are destroyed, and 'death is swallowed up in victory.'

Now, thanks be to God, which giveth us the victory through our Lord Jesus Christ; to whom, with the Father and the Holy Ghost, be blessing, and glory, and wisdom, and thanksgiving, and honour, and power, and might, for ever and ever. Amen.

John Wesley

On the death of George Whitefield

Below is the sermon which Wesley preached at the funeral of his friend and fellow evangelist George Whitefield in November 1770.

Let me die the death of the righteous, and let my last end be like his!

Numbers 23:10

'Let my last end be like his!' How many of you join in this wish? Perhaps there are few of you who do not, even in this numerous congregation! And O that this wish may rest upon your minds! – that it may not die away till your souls also are lodged 'where the wicked cease from troubling, and where the weary are at rest'!

An elaborate exposition of the text will not be expected on this occasion. It would detain you too long from the sadly-pleasing thought of your beloved brother, friend, and pastor; yea, and father too: for how many are here whom he hath 'begotten in the Lord'! Will it not, then, be more suitable to your inclinations, as well as to this solemnity, directly to speak of this man of God, whom you have so often heard speaking in this place? – the end of whose conversation ye know, 'Jesus Christ, the same yesterday, and to-day, and for ever.' And may we not, I. Observe a few particulars of his life and death? II. Take some view of his character? and, III. Inquire how we may improve this awful providence, his sudden removal from us?

I. A few particulars of his life and death

1. He was born at Gloucester, in December, 1714, and put to a grammar-school there, when about twelve years old. When he was seventeen, he began to be seriously religious, and served God to the best of his knowledge. About eighteen he removed to the University, and was admitted at Pembroke College in Oxford; and about a year after he became acquainted with the Methodists (so called), whom from that time he loved as his own soul.

2. By them he was convinced that we 'must be born again,' for outward religion will profit us nothing. He joined with them

in fasting on Wednesdays and Fridays; in visiting the sick and the prisoners; and in gathering up the very fragments of time, that no moment might be lost: and he changed the course of his studies; reading chiefly such books as entered into the heart of religion, and led directly to an experimental knowledge of Jesus Christ, and Him crucified.

3. He was soon tried as with fire. Not only his reputation was lost, and some of his dearest friends forsook him; but he was exercised with inward trials, and those of the severest kind. Many nights he lay sleepless upon his bed; many days, prostrate on the ground. But after he had groaned several months under 'the spirit of bondage,' God was pleased to remove the heavy load, by giving him 'the Spirit of adoption'; enabling him through a living faith, to lay hold on 'the Son of His Love.'

4. However, it was thought needful, for the recovery of his health, which was much impaired, that he should go into the country. He accordingly went to Gloucester, where God enabled him to awaken several young persons. These soon formed themselves into a little society, and were some of the first-fruits of his labour. Shortly after, he began to read, twice or thrice a week, to some poor people in the town; and every day to read to and pray with the prisoners in the county jail.

5. Being now about twenty-one years of age, he was solicited to enter into holy orders. Of this he was greatly afraid, being deeply sensible of his own insufficiency. But the Bishop himself sending for him, and telling him, 'Though I had purposed to ordain none under three-and-twenty, yet I will ordain you whenever you come' – and several other providential circumstances concurring – he submitted, and was ordained on Trinity Sunday, 1736. The next Sunday he preached to a crowded auditory, in the church wherein he was baptized. The week following he returned to Oxford, and took his Bachelor's degree: and he was

now fully employed; the care of the prisoners and the poor lying chiefly on him.

6. But it was not long before he was invited to London, to serve the cure of a friend going into the country. He continued there two months, lodging in the Tower, reading prayers in the chapel twice a week, catechizing and preaching once, beside visiting the soldiers in the barracks and the infirmary. He also read prayers every evening at Wapping chapel, and preached at Ludgate prison every Tuesday. While he was there, letters came from his friends in Georgia, which made him long to go and help them: but not seeing his call clear, at the appointed time he returned to his little charge at Oxford, where several youths met daily at his room, to build up each other in their most holy faith.

7. But he was quickly called from hence again, to supply the cure of Dummer, in Hampshire. Here he read prayers twice a day; early in the morning, and in the evening after the people came from work. He also daily catechized the children, and visited from house to house. He now divided the day into three parts, allotting eight hours for sleep and meals, eight for study and retirement, and eight for reading prayers, catechizing, and visiting the people. Is there a more excellent way for a servant of Christ and His Church? If not, who will 'go and do likewise'?

8. Yet his mind still ran on going abroad; and being now fully convinced he was called of God thereto, he set all things in order, and, in January, 1737, went down to take leave of his friends in Gloucester. It was in this journey that God began to bless his ministry in an uncommon manner. Wherever he preached, amazing multitudes of hearers flocked together, in Gloucester, in Stonehouse, in Bath, in Bristol; so that the heat of the churches was scarce supportable: and the impressions made on the minds of many were no less extraordinary. After his return to London, while he was detained by General

Oglethorpe, from week to week, and from month to month, it pleased God to bless his word still more. And he was indefatigable in his labour: generally on Sunday he preached four times, to exceeding large auditories; beside reading prayers twice or thrice, and walking to and fro often ten or twelve miles.

9. On December 28 he left London. It was on the 29th that he first preached without notes. December 30, he went on board; but it was above a month before they cleared the land. One happy effect of their very slow passage he mentions in April following: 'Blessed be God, we now live very comfortably in the great cabin. We talk of little else but God and Christ; and scarce a word is heard among us when together, but what has reference to our fall in the first, and our new birth in the Second, Adam.' It seems, likewise, to have been a peculiar providence, that he should spend a little time at Gibraltar; where both citizens and soldiers, high and low, young and old, acknowledged the day of their visitation.

10. From Sunday, May 7, 1738, till the latter end of August following, he 'made full proof of his ministry' in Georgia, particularly at Savannah: he read prayers and expounded twice a day, and visited the sick daily. On Sunday he expounded at five in the morning; at ten read prayers and preached, and at three in the afternoon; and at seven in the evening expounded the Church Catechism. How much easier is it for our brethren in the ministry, either in England, Scotland, or Ireland, to find fault: with such a labourer in our Lord's vineyard, than to tread in his steps!

11. It was now that he observed the deplorable condition of many children there; and that God put into his heart the first thought of founding an Orphan-house, for which he determined to raise contributions in England, if God should give him a safe return thither. In December following, he did return to

London; and on Sunday, January 14, 1739, he was ordained priest at Christ Church, Oxford. The next day he came to London again; and on Sunday, the 21st, preached twice. But though the churches were large, and crowded exceedingly, yet many hundreds stood in the churchyard, and hundreds more returned home. This put him upon the first thought of preaching in the open air. But when he mentioned it to some of his friends, they judged it to be mere madness: so he did not carry it into execution till after he had left London. It was on Wednesday, February 21, that, finding all the church doors to be shut in Bristol (beside, that no church was able to contain one half of the congregation), at three in the afternoon he went to Kingswood, and preached abroad to near two thousand people. On Friday he preached there to four or five thousand; and on Sunday too, it was supposed, ten thousand! The number continually increased all the time he stayed at Bristol; and a flame of holy love was kindled, which will not easily be put out. The same was afterwards kindled in various parts of Wales, of Gloucestershire, and Worcestershire. Indeed, wherever he went, God abundantly confirmed the word of his messenger.

12. On Sunday, April 29, he preached the first time in Moorfields, and on Kennington Common; and the thousands of hearers were as quiet as they could have been in a church. Being again detained in England from month to month, he made little excursions into several counties, and received the contributions of willing multitudes for an Orphan-house in Georgia. The embargo which was now laid on the shipping gave him leisure for more journeys through various parts of England, for which many will have reason to bless God to all eternity. At length, on August 14, he embarked: but he did not land in Pennsylvania till October 30. Afterwards he went through Pennsylvania, the Jerseys, New York, Maryland, Virginia, North

and South Carolina; preaching all along to immense congregations, with full as great effect as in England. On January 10, 1740, he arrived at Savannah.

13. January 29, he added three desolate orphans to near twenty which he had in his house before. The next day he laid out the ground for the house, about ten miles from Savannah. February 11, he took in four orphans more; and set out for Frederica, in order to fetch the orphans that were in the southern parts of the colony. In his return he fixed a school, both for children and grown persons, at Darien, and took four orphans thence. March 25, he laid the first stone of the Orphan-house; to which, with great propriety, he gave the name of Bethesda; a work for which the children yet unborn shall praise the Lord. He had now about forty orphans, so that there was near a hundred mouths to be fed daily. But he was 'careful for nothing,' casting his care on Him who feed the young ravens that call upon Him.

14. In April he made another tour through Pennsylvania, the Jerseys, and New York. Incredible multitudes flocked to hear, among whom were abundance of Negroes. In all places the greater part of the hearers were affected to an amazing degree. Many were deeply convinced of their lost state, many truly converted to God. In some places, thousands cried out aloud; many as in the agonies of death; most were drowned in tears; some turned pale as death; others were wringing their hands; others lying on the ground; others sinking into the arms of their friends; almost all lifting up their eyes, and calling for mercy.

15. He returned to Savannah, June 5. The next evening, during the public service, the whole congregation, young and old, were dissolved in tears: after service, several of the parishioners, and all his family, particularly the little children, returned home crying along the street, and some could not help praying

aloud. The groans and cries of the children continued all night, and great part of the next day.

16. In August he set out again, and through various provinces came to Boston. While he was here, and in the neighbouring places, he was extremely weak in body: yet the multitudes of hearers were so great, and the effects wrought on them so astonishing, as the oldest men then alive in the town had never seen before. The same power attended his preaching at New York, particularly on Sunday, November 2: almost as soon as he began, crying, weeping, and wailing were to be heard on every side. Many sank down to the ground, cut to the heart; and many were filled with divine consolation. Toward the close of his journey he made this reflection: 'It is the seventy-fifth day since I arrived at Rhode Island, exceeding weak in body; yet God has enabled me to preach an hundred and seventy-five times in public, besides exhorting frequently in private! Never did God vouchsafe me greater comforts: never did I perform my journeys with less fatigue, or see such a continuance of the divine presence in the congregations to whom I preached.' In December he returned to Savannah, and in the March following arrived in England.

17. You may easily observe, that the preceding account is chiefly extracted from his own journals, which, for their artless and unaffected simplicity, may vie with any writings of the kind. And how exact a specimen is this of his labours both in Europe and America, for the honour of his beloved Master, during the thirty years that followed, as well as of the uninterrupted shower of blessings wherewith God was pleased to succeed his labours! Is it not much to be lamented, that anything should have prevented his continuing this account, till at least near the time when he was called by his Lord to enjoy the fruit of his labour? If he has left any papers of this kind, and his friends account me

worthy of the honour, it would be my glory and joy to methodize, transcribe, and prepare them for the public view.

18. A particular account of the last scene of his life is thus given by a gentleman of Boston: 'After being about a month with us in Boston and its vicinity, and preaching every day, he went to Old York; preached on Thursday, September 27, there; proceeded to Portsmouth, and preached there on Friday. On Saturday morning he set out for Boston; but before he came to Newbury, where he had engaged to preach the next morning, he was importuned to preach by the way. The house not being large enough to contain the people, he preached in an open field. But having been infirm for several weeks, this so exhausted his strength, that when he came to Newbury he could not get out of the ferry-boat without the help of two men. In the evening, however, he recovered his spirits, and appeared with his usual cheerfulness. He went to his chamber at nine, his fixed time, which no company could divert him from, and slept better than he had done for some weeks before. He rose at four in the morning, September 30, and went into his closet; and his companion observed he was unusually long in private. He left his closet, returned to his companion, threw himself on the bed, and lay about ten minutes. Then he fell upon his knees, and prayed most fervently to God that if it was consistent with His will, he might that day finish his Master's work. He then desired his man to call Mr Parsons, the clergyman, at whose house he was; but, in a minute, before Mr Parsons could reach him, died, without a sigh or groan. On the news of his death, six gentlemen set out for Newbury, in order to bring his remains hither: but he could not be moved; so that his precious ashes must remain at Newbury. Hundreds would have gone from this town to attend his funeral, had they not expected he would have been interred here ... May this stroke be sanctified to the Church of God in general, and to this province in particular!'

II. We are, in the second place,
to take some view of his character

1. A little sketch of this was soon after published in the *Boston Gazette*; an extract of which is subjoined. ['Little can be said of him but what every friend to vital Christianity who has sat under his ministry will attest.']

'In his public labours he has, for many years, astonished the world with his eloquence and devotion. With what divine pathos did he persuade the impenitent sinner to embrace the practice of piety and virtue! [Filled with the spirit of grace, he] spoke from the heart, and, with a fervency of zeal perhaps unequalled since the day of the Apostles, [adorned the truths he delivered with the most graceful charms of rhetoric and oratory]. From the pulpit he was unrivalled in the command of an ever-crowded auditory. Nor was he less agreeable and instructive in his private conversation; happy in a remarkable ease of address, willing to communicate, studious to edify. May the rising generation catch a spark of that flame which shone, with such distinguished luster, in the spirit and practice of this faithful servant of the most high God!'

2. A more particular, and equally just, character of him has appeared in one of the English papers. It may not be disagreeable to you to add the substance of this likewise:

'The character of this truly pious person must be [deeply] impressed on the heart of every friend to vital religion. In spite of a tender [and delicate] constitution, he continued to the last day of his life, preaching with a frequency and fervour that seemed to exceed the natural strength of the most robust. Being called to the exercise of his function at an age when most young men are only beginning to qualify themselves for it, he had not time to make a very considerable progress in the learned languages. But this defect was amply supplied by a lively and fertile genius, by fervent zeal, and by a forcible and most persuasive delivery. And though in the pulpit he often found it needful by "the terrors of the Lord" to "persuade men", he had nothing gloomy in his nature; being singularly cheerful, as well as charitable and tender-hearted. He was as ready to relieve the bodily as the spiritual necessities of those that applied to him. It ought also to be observed, that he constantly enforced upon his audience every moral duty; particularly industry in their several callings, and obedience to their superiors. He endeavoured, by the most extraordinary efforts of preaching, in different places, and even in the open fields, to rouse the lower class of people from the least degree of inattention and ignorance to a sense of religion. For this, and his other labours, the name of George Whitefield will long be remembered with esteem and veneration.'

3. That both these accounts are just and impartial, will readily be allowed; that is, as far as they go. But they go little farther than the outside of his character. They show you the preacher, but not the man, the Christian, the saint of God. May I be permitted to add a little on this head, from a personal knowledge of near forty years? Indeed, I am thoroughly sensible how difficult it is to speak on so delicate a subject; what prudence is required to avoid both extremes, to say neither too little nor too much! Nay, I know it is impossible to speak at all, to say either less or more, without incurring from some the former, from others the latter censure. Some will seriously think that too little is said; and others, that it is too much. But without attending to this, I will speak just what I know, before Him to whom we are all to give an account.

4. Mention has already been made of his unparalleled zeal, his indefatigable activity, his tender-heartedness to the afflicted, and charitableness toward the poor. But should we not likewise

mention his deep gratitude to all whom God had used as instruments of good to him? – of whom he did not cease to speak in the most respectful manner, even to his dying day. Should we not mention, that he had a heart susceptible of the most generous and the most tender friendship? I have frequently thought that this, of all others, was the distinguishing part of his character. How few have we known of so kind a temper, of such large and flowing affections! Was it not principally by this, that the hearts of others were so strangely drawn and knit to him? Can anything but love beget love? This shone in his very countenance, and continually breathed in all his words, whether in public or private. Was it not this, which, quick and penetrating as lightning, flew from heart to heart? which gave that life to his sermons, his conversations, his letters? Ye are witnesses!

5. But away with the vile misconstruction of men of corrupt minds, who know of no love but what is earthly and sensual! Be it remembered, at the same time, that he was endued with the most nice and unblemished modesty. His office called him to converse very frequently and largely with women as well as men; and those of every age and condition. But his whole behaviour towards them was a practical comment on that advice of St Paul to Timothy: 'Entreat the elder women as mothers, the younger as sisters, with all purity.'

6. Meantime, how suitable to the friendliness of his spirit was the frankness and openness of his conversation! – although it was as far removed from rudeness on the one hand, as from guile [and disguise] on the other. Was not this frankness at once a fruit and a proof of his courage and intrepidity? Armed with these, he feared not the faces of men, but 'used great plainness of speech' to persons of every rank and condition, high and low, rich and poor; endeavouring only 'by manifestation of the truth to commend himself to every man's conscience in the sight of God.'

7. Neither was he afraid of labour or pain, any more than of 'what man [could] do unto him'; being equally patient in bearing ill and doing well. And this appeared in the steadiness wherewith he pursued whatever he undertook for his Master's sake. Witness one instance for all – the Orphan-house in Georgia; which he began and perfected, in spite of all discouragements. Indeed, in whatever concerned himself he was pliant and flexible. In this case he was 'easy to be entreated'; easy to be either convinced or persuaded. But he was immovable in the things of God, or wherever his conscience was concerned. None could persuade, any more than affright, him to vary, in the least point, from that integrity which was inseparable from his whole character, and regulated all his words and actions. Herein he did 'Stand as an iron pillar strong, And steadfast as a wall of brass.'

8. If it be inquired what was the foundation of this integrity, or of his sincerity, courage, patience, and every other valuable and amiable quality; it is easy to give the answer. It was not the excellence of his natural temper, nor the strength of his understanding; it was not the force of education; no, nor the advice of his friends: it was no other than faith in a bleeding Lord; 'faith of the operation of God.' It was 'a lively hope of an inheritance incorruptible, undefiled, and that fadeth not away.' It was 'the love of God shed abroad in his heart by the Holy Ghost which was given unto him,' filling his soul with tender, disinterested love to every child of man. From this source arose that torrent of eloquence which frequently bore down all before it; from this, that astonishing force of persuasion which the most hardened sinners could not resist. This it was which often made his 'head as waters, and his eyes a fountain of tears.' This it was which enabled him to pour out his soul in prayer, in a manner peculiar to himself, with such fullness and ease united together, with such strength and variety both of sentiment and expression.

9. I may close this head with observing what an honour it pleased God to put upon His faithful servant, by allowing him to declare His everlasting gospel in so many various countries, to such numbers of people, and with so great an effect on so many of their precious souls! Have we read or heard of any person since the Apostles, who testified the gospel of the grace of God through so widely extended a space, through so large a part of the habitable world? Have we read or heard of any person who called so many thousands, so many myriads, of sinners to repentance? Above all, have we read or heard of any who has been a blessed instrument in His hand of bringing so many sinners from 'darkness to light, and from the power of Satan unto God'? It is true, were we to talk thus to the gay world, we should be judged to speak as barbarians. But you understand the language of the country to which you are going, and whither our dear friend is gone a little before us.

III. But how shall we improve this awful providence?
This is the third thing which we have to consider. And the answer to this important question is easy (may God write it in all our hearts!). By keeping close to the grand doctrines which he delivered; and by drinking into his spirit.

1. And, first, let us keep close to the grand scriptural doctrines which he everywhere delivered. There are many doctrines of a less essential nature, with regard to which even the sincere children of God (such is the present weakness of human understanding) are and have been divided for many ages. In these we may think and let think; we may 'agree to disagree'. But, meantime, let us hold fast the essentials of 'the faith which was once delivered to the saints'; and which this champion of God so strongly insisted on, at all times, and in all places!

2. His fundamental point was, 'Give God all the glory of whatever is good in man'; and, 'In the business of salvation, set

Christ as high and man as low as possible.' With this point, he and his friends at Oxford, the original Methodists, so called, set out. Their grand principle was, there is no power (by nature) and no merit in man. They insisted, all power to think, speak, or act aright, is in and from the Spirit of Christ; and all merit is (not in man, how high soever in grace, but merely) in the blood of Christ. So he and they taught: there is no power in man, till it is given him from above, to do one good work, to speak one good word, or to form one good desire. For it is not enough to say, all men are sick of sin: no, we are all 'dead in trespasses and sins'. It follows, that all the children of men are, 'by nature, children of wrath'. We are all 'guilty before God', liable to death temporal and eternal.

3. And we are all helpless, both with regard to the power and to the guilt of sin. 'For who can bring a clean thing out of an unclean?' None less than the Almighty. Who can raise those that are dead, spiritually dead in sin? None but He who raised us from the dust of the earth. But on what consideration will He do this? 'Not for works of righteousness that we have done.' 'The dead cannot praise Thee, O Lord'; nor do anything for the sake of which they should be raised to life. Whatever, therefore, God does, He does it merely for the sake of His well-beloved Son: 'He was wounded for our transgressions, He was bruised for our iniquities.' He Himself 'bore' all 'our sins in His own body upon the tree'. He 'was delivered for our offences, and was raised again for our justification.' Here then is the sole meritorious cause of every blessing we do or can enjoy; in particular of our pardon and acceptance with God, of our full and free justification. But by what means do we become interested in what Christ has done and suffered? 'Not by works, lest any man should boast'; but by faith alone. 'We conclude,' says the Apostle, 'that a man is justified by faith, without the works of the law.'

And 'to as many as' thus 'receive Him, giveth He power to become the sons of God, even to those that believe in His name; who are born, not of the will of man, but of God.'

4. And 'except a man be' thus 'born again, he cannot see the kingdom of God.' But all who are thus 'born of the Spirit' have 'the kingdom of God within them'. Christ sets up His kingdom in their hearts; 'righteousness, peace, and joy in the Holy Ghost'. That 'mind is in them, which was in Christ Jesus', enabling them to 'walk as Christ also walked.' His indwelling Spirit makes them both holy in heart, and 'holy in all manner of conversation'. But still, seeing all this is a free gift, through the righteousness and blood of Christ, there is eternally the same reason to remember, 'He that glorieth, let him glory in the Lord.'

5. You are not ignorant that these are the fundamental doctrines which he everywhere insisted on. And may they not be summed up, as it were, in two words – the new birth, and justification by faith? These let us insist upon with all boldness, at all times, and in all places – in public (those of us who are called thereto), and at all opportunities in private. Keep close to these good, old, unfashionable doctrines, how many soever contradict and blaspheme. Go on, my brethren, in the 'name of the Lord, and in the power of His might'. With all care and diligence, 'keep that safe which is committed to your trust'; knowing that 'heaven and earth shall pass away, but this truth shall not pass away.'

6. But will it be sufficient to keep close to his doctrines, how pure soever they are? Is there not a point of still greater importance than this, namely, to drink into his spirit? – herein to be a follower of him, even as he was of Christ? Without this, the purity of our doctrines would only increase our condemnation. This, therefore, is the principal thing – to copy after his spirit. And allowing that in some points we must be content to admire what we cannot imitate; yet in many others we may, through the

same free grace, be partakers of the same blessing. Conscious then of your own wants and of His bounteous love, who 'giveth liberally and upbraids not', cry to Him that works all in all for a measure of the same precious faith; of the same zeal and activity; the same tender-heartedness, charitableness, bowels of mercies. Wrestle with God for some degree of the same grateful, friendly, affectionate temper; of the same openness, simplicity, and godly sincerity; 'love without dissimulation'. Wrestle on, till the power from on high works in you the same steady courage and patience; and above all, because it is the crown of all, the same invariable integrity!

7. Is there any other fruit of the grace of God with which he was eminently endowed, and the want of which among the children of God he frequently and passionately lamented? There is one, that is, catholic love; that sincere and tender affection which is due to all those who, we have reason to believe, are children of God by faith; in other words, all those, in every persuasion, who 'fear God and work righteousness'. He longed to see all who had 'tasted of the good word', of a true catholic spirit; a word little understood, and still less experienced, by many who have it frequently in their mouth. Who is he that answers this character? Who is the man of a catholic spirit? One who loves as friends, as brethren in the Lord, as joint partakers of the present kingdom of heaven, and fellow heirs of His eternal kingdom, all, of whatever opinion, mode of worship, or congregation, who believe in the Lord Jesus; who love God and man; who, rejoicing to please and fearing to offend God, are careful to abstain from evil, and zealous of good works. He is a man of a truly catholic spirit, who bears all these continually upon his heart; who, having an unspeakable tenderness for their persons, and an earnest desire of their welfare, does not cease to commend them to God in prayer, as well as to plead their cause before men; who

speaks comfortably to them, and labours, by all his words, to strengthen their hands in God. He assists them to the uttermost of his power, in all things, spiritual and temporal; he is ready to 'spend and be spent' for them; yea, 'to lay down his life for his brethren.'

8. How amiable a character is this! How desirable to every child of God! But why is it then so rarely found? How is it that there are so few instances of it? Indeed, supposing we have tasted of the love of God, how can any of us rest till it is our own? Why, there is a delicate device, whereby Satan persuades thousands that they may stop short of it and yet be guiltless. It is well if many here present are not in this 'snare of the devil, taken captive at his will'. 'O yes,' says one, 'I have all this love for those I believe to be children of God; but I will never believe he is a child of God, who belongs to that vile congregation! Can he, do you think, be a child of God, who holds such detestable opinions? or he that joins in such senseless and superstitious, if not idolatrous, worship?' So we may justify ourselves in one sin by adding a second to it! We excuse the want of love in ourselves by laying the blame on others! To colour our own devilish temper, we pronounce our brethren children of the devil! O beware of this! – and if you are already taken in the snare, escape out of it as soon as possible! Go and learn that truly catholic love which 'is not rash', or hasty in judging; that love which 'thinks no evil'; which 'believes and hopes all things'; which makes all the allowances for others that we desire others should make for us! Then we shall take knowledge of the grace of God which is in every man, whatever be his opinion or mode of worship: then will all that fear God be near and dear unto us 'in the bowels of Jesus Christ'.

9. Was not this the spirit of our dear friend? And why should it not be ours? O Thou God of love, how long shall Thy people

be a by-word among the Heathen? How long shall they laugh us to scorn, and say, 'See how these Christians love one another!' When wilt Thou roll away our reproach? Shall the sword devour for ever? How long will it be ere Thou bid Thy people return from 'following each other'? Now, at least, 'let all the people stand still, and pursue after their brethren no more!' But whatever others do, let all of us, my brethren, hear the voice of him that, being dead, yet speaks! Suppose ye hear him say, 'Now, at least, be ye followers of me as I was of Christ! Let brother "no more lift up sword against brother, neither know ye war any more!" Rather put ye on, as the elect of God, bowels of mercies, humbleness of mild, brotherly kindness, gentleness, long-suffering, forbearing one another in love. Let the time past suffice for strife, envy, contention; for biting and devouring one another. Blessed be God, that ye have not long ago been consumed one of another! From henceforth hold ye the unity of the Spirit in the bond of peace.'

10. O God, with Thee no word is impossible! Thou doest whatsoever please Thee! O that Thou would cause the mantle of Thy prophet, whom Thou hast taken up, now to fall upon us that remain! 'Where is the Lord God of Elijah?' Let his spirit rest upon these Thy servants! Show Thou art the God that answers by fire! Let the fire of Thy love fall on every heart! And because we love Thee, let us love one another with a 'love stronger than death'! Take away from us 'all anger, and wrath, and bitterness; all clamour and evil speaking'! Let Thy Spirit so rest upon us, that from this hour we may be 'kind to each other, tenderhearted, forgiving one another, even as God, for Christ's sake hath forgiven us'!

The Eighteenth Century

George Whitefield

This spake he of the Spirit

The English clergyman George Whitefield (1714–70) had a very effective evangelistic career in both Britain and the USA. Many of his meetings were held in the open air and were attended by huge crowds. The sermon below was originally entitled 'The indwelling of the Spirit: the common privilege of all believers'.

> *In the last day, that great [day] of the feast, Jesus stood and cried, saying, 'If any man thirst, let him come unto me, and drink. He that believeth on me, as the scripture hath said, out of his belly shall flow rivers of living water.' But this spake he of the Spirit, which they that believe on him should receive.*
>
> John 7:37–39

Nothing has rendered the cross of Christ of less effect; nothing has been a greater stumbling-block and rock of offense to weak minds, than a supposition, now current among us, that most of what is contained in the gospel of Jesus Christ, was designed only for our Lord's first and immediate followers, and consequently calculated but for one or two hundred years. Accordingly, many now read the life, sufferings, death, and resurrection of Jesus Christ, in the same manner as Caesar's *Commentaries*, or *The Conquests of Alexander* are read: as things rather intended to afford matter for speculation, than to be acted over again in and by us.

As this is true of the doctrines of the gospel in general, so it is of the operation of God's Spirit upon the hearts of believers in particular; for we no sooner mention the necessity of our receiving the Holy Ghost in these last days, as well as formerly, but we are looked upon by some, as enthusiasts and madmen; and by others, represented as willfully deceiving the people, and undermining the established constitution of the church.

Judge ye then, whether it is not high time for the true ministers of Jesus, who have been made partakers of this heavenly gift, to lift up their voices like a trumpet; and if they would not have those souls perish, for which the Lord Jesus has shed his precious blood, to declare, with all boldness, that the Holy Spirit is the common privilege and portion of all believers in all ages; and that we as well as the first Christians, must receive the Holy Ghost, before we can be truly called the children of God.

For this reason (and also that I might answer the design of our church in appointing the present festival [Whitsuntide]), I have chosen the words of the text.

They were spoken by Jesus Christ, when he was at the feast of tabernacles. Our Lord attended on the temple-service in general, and the festivals of the Jewish church in particular. The festival at which he was now present, was that of the feast of tabernacles, which the Jews observed according to God's appointment in commemoration of their living in tents. At the last day of this feast, it was customary for many pious people to fetch water from a certain place, and bring it on their heads, singing this anthem out of Isaiah, 'And with joy shall they draw water out of the wells of salvation.' Our Lord observing this, and it being his constant practice to spiritualize every thing he met with, cries out, 'If any man thirst, let him come unto me (rather than unto that well), and drink. He that believeth on me, as the scripture hath spoken (where it is said, God will make water to spring out of a dry rock, and such-like), out of his belly shall flow rivers of living water.' And that we might know what our Saviour meant by this living water, the Evangelist immediately adds, 'But this spake he of the Spirit, which they that believe on him should receive.'

The last words I shall chiefly insist on in the ensuing discourse, and: First, I shall briefly show, what is meant by the word Spirit. Second, that this Spirit is the common privilege of all believers. Third, I shall show the reason on which this doctrine is founded. I will conclude with a general exhortation to believe on Jesus Christ, whereby alone we can receive the Spirit.

1. First, I am to show, what is meant by the word Spirit

By the Spirit, is evidently to be understood the Holy Ghost, the third person in the ever-blessed Trinity, consubstantial and co-eternal with the Father and the Son, proceeding from, yet equal to them both. For, to use the words of our Church in this day's office, that which we believe of the glory of the Father, the same we believe of the Son, and of the Holy Ghost, without any difference or inequality.

Thus, says St John, in his first epistle, chapter 5, verse 7, 'There are three that bear record in heaven, the Father, the Word, and the Holy Ghost, and these three are one.' And our Lord, when he gave his Apostles commission to go and teach all nations, commanded them to baptize in the name of the Holy Ghost, as well as of the Father and the Son. And St Peter, Acts 5:3, said to Ananias, 'Why hath Satan filled thine heart to lie to the Holy Ghost?' And verse 4 he says, 'Thou hast not lied unto men, but unto God.' From all which passages, it is plain, that the Holy Ghost, is truly and properly God, as well as the Father and the Son. This is an unspeakable mystery, but a mystery of God's revealing, and, therefore, to be assented to with our whole hearts: seeing God is not a man that he should lie, nor the son of man that he should deceive.

2. Second, that this Spirit is the common privilege of all believers

I proceed, secondly, to demonstrate that the Holy Ghost is the common privilege of all believers.

But, here I would not be understood of to receiving the Holy Ghost, as to enable us to work miracles, or show outward signs and wonders. I allow our adversaries, that to pretend to be inspired, in this sense, is being wise above what is written. Perhaps it cannot be proved, that God ever interposed in this extraordinary manner, but when some new revelation was to be established, as at the first settling of the Mosaic and gospel dispensation: and as for my own part, I cannot but suspect the spirit of those who insist upon a repetition of such miracles at this time. For the world being now become nominally Christian (though, God knows, little of the power is left among us), there need not outward miracles, but only an inward co-operation of the Holy Spirit with the word, to prove that Jesus is the Messiah which was to come into the world.

Besides, if it was possible for thee, O man, to have faith, so as to be able to remove mountains, or cast out devils; nay, couldst thou speak with the tongue of men and angels, yea, and bid the sun stand still in the midst of heaven; what would all these gifts of the Spirit avail thee, without being made partaker of his sanctifying graces? Saul had the spirit of government for a while, so as to become another man, and yet probably was a cast-away. And many, who cast out devils, in Christ's name, at the last will be disowned by him. If therefore, thou hast only the gifts, and was destitute of the graces of the Holy Ghost, they would only serve to lead thee with so much the more solemnity to hell.

Here then we join issue with our adversaries, and will readily grant, that we are not in this sense to be inspired, as were our Lord's first Apostles. But unless men have eyes which see not, and ears that hear not, how can they read the latter part of the text, and not confess that the Holy Spirit, in another sense, is the common privilege of all believers, even to the end of the world? 'This spake he of the Spirit, which they that believe on him should receive.' Observe, he does not say, they that believe on him for one or two ages, but they that believe on him in general, or, at all times, and in all places. So that, unless we can prove, that St John was under a delusion when he wrote these words, we must believe that even we also, shall receive the Holy Ghost, if we believe on the Lord Jesus with our whole hearts.

Again, our Lord, just before his bitter passion, when he was about to offer up his soul an offering for the sins of the elect world; when his heart was most enlarged and he would undoubtedly demand the most excellent gift for his disciples, prays, 'That they all may be one, as thou, Father, art in me, and I in thee; that they also may be one in us, I in them, and thou in me; that they may be made perfect in one'; that is, that all his true followers might be united to him by his Holy Spirit, by as real, vital, and mystical an union, as there was between Jesus Christ and the Father. I say all his true followers; for it is evident, from our Lord's own words, that he had us, and all believers, in view, when he put up this prayer; 'Neither pray I for these alone, but for them also which shall believe on me through their word'; so that, unless we treat our Lord as the high priests did, and count him a blasphemer, we must confess, that all who believe in Jesus Christ, through the word, or ministration of his servants, are to be joined to Jesus Christ, by being made partakers of the Holy Spirit.

A great noise hath been made of late, about the word enthusiast, and it has been cast upon the preachers of the gospel, as a term of reproach; but every Christian, in the proper sense of the word, must be an enthusiast; that is, must be inspired of God or have God, by his Spirit, in him. St Peter tells us, 'we have many great and precious promises, that we may be made partakers of the divine nature'; our Lord prays, 'that we may be one, as the Father and he are one'; and our own church, in conformity to these texts of Scripture, in her excellent communion-office, tells us, that those who receive the sacrament worthily, 'dwell in Christ, and Christ in them; that they are one with Christ, and Christ with them.' And yet, Christians must have their names cast out as evil, and ministers in particular, must be looked upon as deceivers of the people, for affirming, that we must be really united to God, by receiving the Holy Ghost. Be astonished, O heavens, at this!

Indeed, I will not say, all our letter-learned preachers deny this doctrine in express words; but however, they do in effect; for they talk professedly against inward feelings, and say, we may have God's Spirit without feeling it, which is in reality to deny the thing itself. And had I a mind to hinder the progress of the gospel, and to establish the kingdom of darkness, I would go about, telling people, they might have the Spirit of God, and yet not feel it.

But to return: When our Lord was about to ascend to his Father and our Father, to his God and our God he gave his apostles this commission, 'Go and teach all nations, baptizing them in the name of the Father, and of the Son, and of the Holy Ghost.' And accordingly, by authority of this commission, we do teach and baptize in this, and every age of the church. And though we translate the words, 'baptizing them in the name'; yet, as the name of God, in the Lord's prayer, and several other places, signifies his nature, they might as well be translated thus, 'baptizing them into the nature of the Father, into the nature of the Son, and into the nature of the Holy Ghost.' Consequently, if we are all to be baptized into the nature of the Holy Ghost, before our baptism be effectual to salvation, it is evident, that we all must actually receive the Holy Ghost, and ere we can say, we truly believe in Jesus Christ. For no one can say, that Jesus is my Lord, but he that has thus received the Holy Ghost.

Numbers of other texts might be quoted to make this doctrine, if possible, still more plain; but I am astonished, that any who call themselves members; much more, that many, who are preachers in the church of England, should dare so much as to open their lips against it. And yet, with grief I speak it, God is my Judge, persons of the established church seem more generally to be ignorant of it, than any dissenters whatsoever.

But, my dear brethren, what have you been doing? How often have your hearts given your lips the lie how often have you offered to God the sacrifice of fools, and had your prayers turned into sin, if you approve of, and use our church-liturgy, and yet deny the Holy Spirit to be the portion of all believers? In the daily absolution, the minister exhorts the people to pray, that 'God would grant them repentance, and his Holy Spirit'; in the Collect for Christmas day, we beseech God, 'that he would daily renew us by his Holy Spirit'; in the last week's Collect, we prayed that 'we may evermore rejoice in the comforts of the Holy Ghost'; and in the concluding prayer, which we put up every day, we pray, not only that the grace of our Lord Jesus Christ, and the love of God, but that 'the fellowship of the Holy Ghost' may be with us all evermore.

But further, a solemn season, to some, is now approaching; I mean the Easter-days, at the end of which, all that are to be ordained to the office of a deacon, are in the sight of God, and in the presence of the congregation, to declare, that 'they trust they are inwardly moved by the Holy Ghost, to take upon them that administration'; and to those, who are to be ordained priests, the bishop is to repeat these solemn words, 'Receive thou the Holy Ghost, now committed unto them, by the imposition of our hands.' And yet, O that I had no reason to speak it, many that use our forms, and many who have witnessed this good confession, yet dare to both talk and preach against the necessity of receiving the Holy Ghost now; and not only so, but cry out against those, who do insist upon it, as madmen, enthusiasts, schismatics, and underminers of the established constitution.

But you are the schismatics, you are the bane of the church of England, who are always crying out, 'the temple of the Lord, the temple of the Lord'; and yet starve the people out of our communion, by feeding them only with the dry husks of dead morality, and not bringing out to them the fatted calf; I mean, the doctrines of the operations of the blessed Spirit of God. But here is the misfortune; many of us are not led by, and therefore no wonder that we cannot talk feelingly of, the Holy Ghost; we subscribe to our articles, and make them serve for a key to get into church-preferment, and then preach contrary to those very articles to which we have subscribed. Far be it from me, to charge all the clergy with this hateful hypocrisy; no, blessed be God, there are some left among us, who dare maintain the doctrines of the Reformation, and preach the truth as it is in Jesus. But I speak the truth in Christ, I lie not; the generality of the clergy are fallen from our articles, and do not speak agreeable to them, or to the form of sound words delivered in the Scriptures; woe be unto such blind leaders of the blind! How can you escape the damnation of hell? It is not all your learning (falsely so called), it is not all your preferments can keep you from the just judgment of God. Yet a little while, and we shall all appear before the tribunal of Christ; there, there will I meet you; there Jesus Christ, the great Shepherd and Bishop of souls, shall determine who are the false prophets; who are the wolves in sheep's clothing. Those who say, that we must now receive and feel the

Holy Ghost, or those who exclaim against it, as the doctrine of devils.

But I can no more; it is an unpleasing talk to censure any order of men, especially those who are in the ministry; nor would any thing excuse it but necessity: that necessity which extorted from our Lord himself so many woes against the Scribes and Pharisees, the letter-learned rulers and teachers of the Jewish church; and surely, if I could bear to see people perish for lack of knowledge, and yet be silent towards those who keep from them the key of true knowledge, the very stones would cry out.

Would we restore the church to its primitive dignity, the only way is to live and preach the doctrine of Christ, and the articles to which we have subscribed; then we shall find the number of dissenters will daily decrease, and the church of England become the joy of the whole earth.

3. Third, I shall show the reason on which this doctrine is founded

I am, in the third place, to show the reasonableness of this doctrine. I say, the reasonableness of this doctrine; for however it may seem foolishness to the natural man, yet to those, who have tasted of the good word of life, and have felt the power of the world to come, it will appear to be founded on the highest reason; and is capable, to those who have eyes to see, even of a demonstration; I say of demonstration: for it stands on this self-evident truth, that we are fallen creatures, or, to use the scripture-expression, 'have all died in Adam'.

I know indeed, it is now no uncommon thing amongst us, to deny the doctrine of original sin, as well as the divinity of Jesus Christ; but it is incumbent on those who deny it, first to disprove the authority of the holy Scriptures; if thou canst prove, thou unbeliever, that the book, which we call The Bible, odes not contain the lively oracles of God; if thou canst show, that holy men of old, did not write this book, as they were inwardly moved by the Holy Ghost, then will we give up the doctrine of original sin; but unless thou canst do this, we must insist upon it, that we are all conceived and born in sin; if for no other, yet for this one reason, because that God, who cannot lie, has told us so.

But what has light to do with darkness, or polite infidels with the Bible? Alas! as they are strangers to the power, so they are generally as great strangers to the word of God. And therefore, if we will preach to them, we must preach to and from the heart: for talking in the language of scripture, to them, is but like talking in an unknown tongue. Tell me then, O man, whosoever thou art, that denied the doctrine of original sin, if thy conscience be not seared as with a hot iron! Tell me, if thou dost not find thyself, by nature, to be a mostly mixture of brute and devil? I know these terms will stir up the whole Pharisee in thy heart; but let not Satan hurry thee hence; stop a little, and let us reason together; dost thou not find, that by nature thou art prone to pride? Otherwise, wherefore art thou now offended? Again, dost not thou find in thyself the seeds of malice, revenge, and all uncharitableness? And what are these but the very tempers of the devil? Again, do we not all by nature follow, and suffer ourselves to be led by our natural appetites, always looking downwards, never looking upwards to that God, in whom we live, move, and have our being? And what is this but the very nature of the beasts that perish? Out of thy own heart, therefore, will I oblige thee to confess, what an inspired apostle has long since told us, that 'the whole world (by nature) lies in the wicked one'; we are no better than those whom St Jude calls 'brute beasts'; for we have tempers in us all by nature, that prove to a demonstration, that we are earthly, sensual, devilish.

And this will serve as another argument, to prove the reality of the operations of the blessed Spirit on the hearts of believers, against those false professors, who deny there is any such thing as influences of the Holy Spirit, that may be felt. For if they will grant that the devil worketh, and so as to be felt in the hearts of the children of disobedience (which they must grant, unless they will give an apostle the lie) where is the wonder that the good Spirit should have the same power over those who are truly obedient to the faith of Jesus Christ?

If it be true then; that we are all by nature, since the fall, a mixture of brute an devil, it is evident, that we all must receive the Holy Ghost, ere we can dwell with and enjoy God.

When you read, how the prodigal, in the gospel, was reduced to so low a condition, as to eat husks with swine, and how Nebuchadnezzar was turned out, to graze with oxen; I am confident, you pity their unhappy state. And when you hear, how Jesus Christ will say, at the last day, to all that are not born again of God, 'Depart from me, ye cursed, into everlasting fire, prepared for the devil and his angels,' do not your hearts shrink within you, with a secret horror? And if creatures, with only our degree of goodness, cannot bear even the thoughts of dwelling with beasts or devils, to whose nature we are so nearly allied, how do we imagine God, who is infinite goodness, and purity itself, can dwell with us, while we are partakers of both their natures? We might as well think to reconcile heaven and hell.

When Adam had eaten the forbidden fruit, he fled and hid himself from God; why? Because he was naked; he was alienated from the life of God, the due punishment of his disobedience. Now, we are all by nature naked and void of God, as he was at that time, and consequently, until we are changed, renewed, and clothed with a divine nature again, we must fly from God also.

Hence then appears the reasonableness of our being obliged

to receive the Spirit of God. It is founded on the doctrine of original sin: and, therefore, you will always find, that those who talk against feeling the operations of the Holy Ghost, very rarely, or slightly at least, mention our fall in Adam; no, they refer St Paul's account of the depravity of unbelievers, only to those of old time. Whereas it is obvious, on the contrary, that we are all equally included under the guilt and consequences of our first parent's sin, even as others; and to use the language of our own church-article, 'bring into the world with us, a corruption, which renders us liable to God's wrath, and eternal damnation.'

Should I preach to you any other doctrine, I should wrong my own soul; I should be found a false witness towards God and you; and he that preaches any other doctrine, howsoever dignified and distinguished, shall bear his punishment, whosoever he be.

From this plain reason then appears the necessity why we, as well as the first apostles, in this sense, must receive the Spirit of God.

For the great work of sanctification, or making us holy, is particularly reserved to the Holy Ghost; therefore, our Lord says, 'Unless a man be born of the Spirit, he cannot enter into the kingdom of God.'

Jesus Christ came down to save us, not only from the guilt, but also from the power of sin: and however often we have repeated our creed, and told God we believe in the Holy Ghost, yet, if we have not believed in him, so as to be really united to Jesus Christ by him, we have no more concord with Jesus Christ than Belial himself.

And now, my brethren, what shall I say more? Tell me, are not many of you offended at what has been said already? Do not some of you think, though I mean well, yet I have carried the point a little too far? Are not others ready to cry out, if this be true, who then can be saved? Is not this driving people into despair?

Yes, I ingenuously confess it is; but into what despair? A despair of mercy through Christ? No, God forbid; but a despair of living with God without receiving the Holy Ghost. And I would to God, that not only all you that hear me this day, but that the whole world was filled with this despair. Believe me, I have been doing no more than you allow your bodily physicians to do every day: if you have a wound, and are in earnest about a cure, you bid the surgeon probe it to the very bottom; and shall not the physician of your souls be allowed the same freedom? What have I been doing but searching your natural wounds, that I might convince you of your danger, and put you upon applying to Jesus Christ for a remedy? Indeed I have dealt with you as gently as I could; and now I have wounded, I will attempt to heal you.

Conclusion

For I was in the last place, to exhort you all to come to Jesus Christ by faith, whereby you, even you also, shall receive the Holy Ghost. 'For this spake he of the Spirit, which they that believe on him should receive.'

This, this is what I long to come to. Hitherto I have been preaching only the law; but behold I bring you glad tidings of great joy. If I have wounded you, be not afraid; behold, I now bring a remedy for all your wounds. Notwithstanding you are sunk into the nature of the beast and devil, yet, if you truly believe on Jesus Christ, you shall receive the quickening Spirit promised in the text, and be restored to the glorious liberties of the sons of God; I say, if you believe on Jesus Christ. 'For by faith we are saved; it is not of works, lest any one should boast.' And, however some men may say, there is a fitness required in the creature, and that we must have a righteousness of our own, before we can lay hold on the righteousness of Christ; yet, if we believe the scripture, salvation is the free gift of God, in Christ Jesus our Lord; and whosoever believeth on him with his whole heart, though his soul be as black as hell itself, shall receive the gift of the Holy Ghost. Behold then, I stand up, and cry out in this great day of the feast, let every one that thirsteth come unto Jesus Christ and drink. 'He that believeth on him, out of his belly shall flow (not only streams of rivulets, but whole) rivers of living water.' This I speak of the Spirit, which they that believe on Jesus shall certainly receive. For Jesus Christ is the same yesterday, today, and for ever; he is the way, the truth, the resurrection, and the life; 'whosoever believeth on him, though he were dead, yet shall he live.' There is no respect of persons with Jesus Christ; high and low, rich and poor, one with another, may come to him with an humble confidence, if they draw near by faith; from him we may all receive grace upon grace; for Jesus Christ is full of grace and truth, and ready to save to the uttermost, all that by a true faith turn unto him. Indeed, the poor generally receive the gospel, and 'God has chosen the poor in this world, rich in faith.' But though not many mighty, not many noble are called; and though it be easier for a camel to go through the eye of a needle, than for a rich man to enter into the kingdom of God, yet, even to you that are rich, do I now freely offer salvation, by Jesus Christ, if you will renounce yourselves, and come to Jesus Christ as poor sinners; I say, as poor sinners; for the 'poor in spirit' are only so blessed, as to have a right to the kingdom of God. And Jesus Christ calls none to him, but those who thirst after his righteousness, and feel themselves weary, and heavy laden with the burden of their sins. Jesus Christ justifies the ungodly; he came not to call the righteous, but sinners to repentance.

Do not then say you are unworthy, for this is a faithful and true saying, and worthy of all men to be received, 'that Jesus

Christ came into the world to save sinners'; and if you are the chief of sinners, if you feel yourselves such, verily Jesus Christ came into the world chiefly to save you. When Joseph was called out of the prison-house to Pharaoh's court, we are told, that he stayed some time to prepare himself; but do you come with all your prison clothes about you; come poor, and miserable, and blind, and naked, as you are, and God the Father shall receive you with open arms, as was the returning prodigal. He shall cover you nakedness with the best robe of his dear Son's righteousness, shall seal you with the signet of his Spirit, and feed you with the fatted calf, even with the comforts of the Holy Ghost. O, let there then be joy in heaven over some of you, as believing; let me not go back to my Master, and say, 'Lord, they will not believe my report.' Harden no longer your hearts, but open them wide, and let the King of glory enter in; believe me, I am willing to go to prison or death for you; but I am not willing to go to heaven without you. The love of Jesus Christ constrains me to lift up my voice like a trumpet. My heart is now full; out of the abundance of the love which I have for your precious and immortal souls, my mouth now speaketh; and I could now not only continue my discourse until midnight, but I could speak until I could speak no more.

And why should I despair of any? No, I can despair of no one, when I consider Jesus Christ has had mercy on such a wretch as I am; but the free grace of Christ prevented me; he saw me in my blood, he passed by me, and said unto me, 'Live'; and the same grace which we sufficient for me, is sufficient for you also; behold, the same blessed Spirit is ready to breathe on all your dry bones, if you will believe on Jesus Christ, whom God has sent; indeed, you can never believe on, or serve a better master, one that is more mighty, or more willing to save; I can say, 'The Lord Christ is gracious, his yoke is easy, his burden exceeding light';

after you have served him many years, like the servants under the law, was he willing to discharge you, you would say, 'We love our Master, and will not go from him.' Come then, my guilty brethren, come and believe on the Lord that bought you with his precious blood; look up by faith, and see him whom you have pierced; behold him bleeding, panting, dying! Behold him with arms stretched out ready to receive you all; cry unto him as the penitent thief did, 'Lord, remember us now thou art in thy kingdom,' and he shall say to your souls, 'Shortly shall you be with me in paradise.' For those whom Christ justified, them he also glorifies, even with that glory which he enjoyed with the Father, before the world began. Do not say, 'I have bought a piece of ground, and must needs go see it'; or 'I have bought a yoke of oxen, and must needs go prove them'; or 'I have married a wife, I am engaged in an eager pursuit after the lust of the eye, and the pride of life, that I therefore cannot come.' Do not fear having your name cast out as evil, or being accounted a fool for Christ's sake; yet a little while, and you shall shine like the stars in the firmament for ever. Only believe, and Jesus Christ shall be to you wisdom, righteousness, sanctification, and eternal redemption; your bodies shall be fashioned like unto his glorious body, and your souls be partakers of all the fullness of God.

William Wilberforce

The total Abolition ought to take place

William Wilberforce (1759–1833), politician and campaigner against slavery, made the following speech in the House of Commons in 1789.

I mean not to accuse anyone but to take the shame upon myself, in common indeed with the whole Parliament of Great Britain, for having suffered this horrid trade to be carried on under their authority. We are all guilty – we ought all to plead guilty, and not to exculpate ourselves by throwing the blame on others...

It is not regulation, it is not mere palliatives, that can cure this enormous evil: total Abolition is the only possible cure for it... I trust I have shown that upon every ground the total Abolition ought to take place ... [Wilberforce then explained his motivation in being an abolitionist.] There is a principle, and I am not ashamed to say. There is a principle above everything that is political. And when I reflect on the command that says, 'Thou shalt do no murder', believing the authority to be divine, how can I dare set up any reasonings of my own against it? And, Sir, when we think of eternity, and of the future consequences of all human conduct, where is there in this life which should make any man contradict the principles of his own conscience, the principles of justice, the laws of religion, and of God?

Sir, the nature and all the circumstances of the Trade are now laid open to us. We can no longer plead ignorance, we cannot evade it, it is now an object placed before us, we cannot pass it. We may spurn it, we may kick it out of our way, but we cannot turn aside so as to avoid seeing it. For it is brought now so directly before our eyes that this House must decide, and must justify to all the world, and to their own consciences, the rectitudes of their grounds and of the principles of their decision ... Let not Parliament be the only body that is insensible to natural justice. Let us make reparation to Africa, so far as we can, by establishing a trade upon true commercial principles, and we shall soon find the rectitude of our conduct rewarded by the benefits of a regular and a growing commerce.

John Wesley

Letter to William Wilberforce

The last letter that John Wesley wrote before his death was to William Wilberforce, who had been converted under his ministry. In the letter, which is printed below, Wesley expresses his opposition to slavery and encourages Wilberforce to carry on campaigning against it. Parliament finally outlawed England's participation in the slave trade in 1807.

Balam, February 24, 1791

Dear Sir:

Unless the divine power has raised you up to be as *Athanasius contra mundum* [Athanasius against the world], I see not how you can go through your glorious enterprise in opposing that execrable villainy which is the scandal of religion, of England, and of human nature. Unless God has raised you up for this very thing, you will be worn out by the opposition of men and devils. But if God be for you, who can be against you? Are all of them together stronger than God? O be not weary of well doing! Go on, in the mane of God and in the power of his might, till even American slavery (the vilest that ever saw the sun) shall vanish away before it.

Reading this morning a tract wrote by a poor African, I was particularly struck by that circumstance that a man who has a black skin, being wronged or outraged by a white man, can have no redress; it being a 'law' in our colonies that the oath of a black against a white goes for nothing. What villainy is this?

That he who has guided you from youth up may continue to strengthen you in this and all things, is the prayer of, dear sir,

Your affectionate servant,
  John Wesley

Charles Finney

How to overcome sin

Charles Finney (1792–1875) was an American revivalist preacher.

> *They said therefore to Him, 'What shall we do, that we may work the works of God?' Jesus answered and said to them, 'This is the work of God, that you believe in Him whom He has sent.'*
>
> John 6:28–29

There are multitudes of anxious Christians who are inquiring what they shall do to overcome the world, the flesh, and the devil. They overlook the fact that 'this is the victory that has overcome the world – our faith' (1 John 5:4), that it is with 'the shield of faith' that they are to 'extinguish all the flaming missiles of the evil one' (Ephesians 6:16). They ask, 'Why am I overcome by sin? Why can't I get above its power? Why am I the slave of my appetites and passions and the sport of the devil?' They look all around them for the cause of all this spiritual wretchedness and death. Sometimes they think they have discovered the answer in the neglect of one duty, and at another time in the neglect of another duty...

But all this only brings us back to the real question again: How are we to overcome this corrupt nature, this wickedness, and our sinful habits? I answer, By faith alone. No works of the law have the least tendency to overcome our sins, but rather they strengthen the soul in self-righteousness and unbelief.

The great and fundamental sin which is at the foundation of all other sin is unbelief.

The first thing to do is to give that up – to believe the Word of God. There is no breaking away from one sin without this.

'Whatever is not of faith is sin' (Romans 14:23). 'Without faith it is impossible to please God' (Hebrews 11:6). Thus we see that the backslider and convicted Christian, when agonizing to overcome sin, will almost always try to use the works of the law to obtain faith. They will fast and pray and read and struggle and outwardly reform, and thus endeavour to obtain grace. But all this is in vain and wrong...

What is 'faith'?

The first element of saving faith is realizing the truth of the Bible. But this alone is not saving faith, for Satan also realizes the truth of the Bible, which makes him tremble (James 2:19). But a second element in saving faith is the agreement of the heart (or will) to the truth understood by the mind...

Faith is the only exercise that receives Christ with all His powerfully sanctifying influences into the heart. The Bible everywhere represents the sanctified soul as being under the influence of an indwelling Christ. Now the exercise of faith is an opening of the door by which Christ is received to reign in the heart. If this is so, the proper direction plainly is to do that which receives Christ. If this is done, all else will be done. If this is neglected, all else will be neglected, of course! ...

My dear friend, you inquire whether you shall obtain holiness by reading the Bible, or by prayer, fasting, or by all these together. Now let this sermon answer you and know that by neither nor by all of these, in the absence of faith, are you to grow any better, or find any relief. You speak of being in darkness and of being discouraged. No wonder you are so, since you have plainly been seeking sanctification by outward works. You have 'stumbled over the stumbling stone' (Romans 9:32). You are in that pit of miry clay. Immediately exercise faith upon the Son of God! It is the first, the only thing you can do to rest your feet upon the Rock – and it will immediately put a new song into your mouth!

PART 7

The Nineteenth Century

Lucretia Mott

Likeness to Christ rather than notions of Christ

Lucretia Mott (1793–1880), an American Quaker minister, was also an anti-slavery campaigner and a women's rights leader. She delivered this address at Philadelphia in September 1849.

It is time that Christians were judged more by their likeness to Christ than their notions of Christ. Were this sentiment generally admitted we should not see such tenacious adherence to what men deem the opinions and doctrines of Christ while at the same time in every day practice is exhibited anything but a likeness to Christ. My reflections in this meeting have been upon the origin, parentage, and character of Jesus. I have thought we might profitably dwell upon the facts connected with his life, his precepts, and his practice in his walks among men. Humble as was his birth, obscure as was his parentage, little known as he seemed to be in his neighbourhood and country, he has astonished the world and brought a response from all mankind by the purity of his precepts, the excellence of his example. Wherever that inimitable sermon on the mount is read, let it be translated into any language and spread before the people, there is an acknowledgement of its truth. When we come to judge the sectarian professors of his name by the true test, how widely do their lives differ from his?

Instead of going about doing good as was his wont, instead of being constantly in the exercise of benevolence and love as was his practice, we find the disposition too generally to measure the Christian by his assent to a creed which had not its sign with him nor indeed in his day. Instead of engaging in the exercise of peace, justice, and mercy, how many of the professors are arrayed against him in opposition to those great principles even as were his opposers in his day. Instead of being the bold nonconformist (if I may so speak) that he was, they are adhering to old church usages, and worn-out forms and exhibiting little of a Christlike disposition and character. Instead of uttering the earnest protests against the spirit of proselytism and sectarianism as did the blessed Jesus – the divine, the holy, the born of God – there is the servile accommodation to this sectarian spirit and an observance of those forms even long after there is any claim of virtue in them; a disposition to use language which shall convey belief that in the inmost heart of many they reject.

Is this honest, is this Christlike? Should Jesus again appear and preach as he did round about Judea and Jerusalem and Galilee, these high professors would be among the first to set him at naught, if not to resort to the extremes which were resorted to in his day. There is no danger of this now, however, because the customs of the age will not bear the bigot out in it, but the spirit is manifest, which led martyrs to the stake, Jesus to the cross, Mary Dyer to the gallows. This spirit is now showing itself in casting out the name one of another, as evil, in brother delivering up brother unto sectarian death. We say if Jesus should again appear – He is here; he has appeared, from generation to generation and his spirit is now as manifest, in the humble, the meek, the bold reformers, even among some of obscure parentage.

His spirit is now going up and down among men seeking their good, and endeavouring to promote the benign and holy principles of peace, justice, and love. And blessing to the merciful, to the peacemaker, to the pure in heart, and the poor in spirit, to the just, the upright, to those who desire righteousness is earnestly proclaimed, by these messengers of the Highest who are now in our midst. These, the preachers of righteousness, are no more acknowledged by the same class of people than was the messiah to the Jews. They are the anointed of God, the inspired preachers and writers and believers of the present time. In the pure example which they exhibit to the nations, they are emphatically the beloved sons of God. It is, my friends, my mission to declare these things among you at the hazard of shocking many prejudices. The testimony of the chosen servants of the Highest in our day is equally divine inspiration with the inspired teaching of those in former times. It is evidence of the superstition of our age, that we can adhere to, yea that we can bow with profound veneration to the records of an Abraham, the sensualist Solomon, and the war-like David, inspired though they may have been (and I am not disposed to doubt it), more than to the equal inspiration of the writers of the present age. Why not acknowledge the inspiration of many of the poets of succeeding ages, as well as Deborah and Miriam in their songs of victory, or Job and David in their beautiful poetry and psalms, or Isaiah and Jeremiah in their scorching rebukes and mournful lamentations? These are beautifully instructive but ought they to command our veneration more than the divine poetic language of many, very many, since their day, who have uttered truth equally precious?

Truth speaks the same language in every age of the world and is equally valuable to us. Are we so blindly superstitious as to reject the one and adhere to the other? How much does this society lose by this undue veneration to ancient authorities, a want of equal respect to the living inspired testimonies of latter time? Christianity requires that we bring into view the apostles of succeeding generations, that we acknowledge their apostleship and give the right hand of fellowship to those who have been and who are sent forth of God with Great truths to declare before the people; and also to practise lives of righteousness, exceeding the righteousness of the scribes and Pharisees, and even of the chosen ones of former times. The people in their childish and dark state, just emerging out of barbarism, were not prepared to exhibit all those great principles in the near approach to fullness, to the perfection that is called for at our hands. There is this continued advance toward perfection from age to age. The records of our predecessors give evidence of such progress. When I quote the language of William Penn, 'it is time for Christians to be judged more by their likeness to Christ than their notions of Christ,' I offer the sentiment of one who is justly held in great regard if not veneration by this people, and whose writings may be referred to with as much profit as those of the servants of God in former ages; and we may well respect the memory of him and his contemporaries as well as of many not limited to our religious society, who have borne testimony to the truth.

It is of importance to us, also, to speak of those whom we know, those whose characters we have fuller acquaintance with, than we can have with such as lived in ages past, that we should bring into view the lives of the faithful of our generation.

Jesus bore his testimony – doing always the things which pleased his Father. He lived his meek, his humble and useful life – drawing his disciples around him, and declaring great truths to the people who gathered to hear him.

His apostles and their successors were faithful in their day – going out into the world, and shaking the nations around them. Reformers since their time have done their work in exposing error and wrong, and calling for priests of righteousness in place of vain forms. The bold utterances of Elias Hicks and his contemporaries aroused the sectarian and theological world in our day. Their demand for a higher righteousness was not in vain. Their examples of self-denials and faithfulness to duty should be held up for imitation. We overestimate those who have lived and laboured in days long past, while we value not sufficiently the labours of those around us, who may have as high a commission as had their predecessors.

Let us not hesitate to regard the utterance of truth in our age, as of equal value with that which is recorded in the scriptures. None can revere more than I do the truths of the Bible. I have read it perhaps as much as any one present, and, I trust, with profit. It has at times been more to me than my daily food. When an attempt was made some twenty years ago to engraft some church dogmas upon this society, claiming this book for authority, it led me to examine, and compare text with the content. In so doing I became so much interested that I scarcely noted the passage of time. Even to this day, when I open this volume, so familiar is almost every chapter that I can sometimes scarcely lay it aside from the interest I feel in its beautiful pages. But I should be recreant to the principle, [if I did not] say, the great error in Christendom is in regarding these scriptures taken as a whole as the plenary inspiration of God, and their authority as supreme. I consider this, as Elias Hicks did, one of the greatest drawbacks, one of the greatest barriers to human progress that there is in the religious world, for while this volume is held as it is, and, by a resort to it, war, and slavery, wine drinking, and other cruel, oppressive, and degrading evils are sustained, pleading the example of the ancients as authority, it serves as a check to human progress, as an obstacle in the way of these great and glorious reformers that are now upon the field. Well did that servant of God, Elias Hicks, warn the people against an undue veneration of the Bible, or of any human authority, any written record or outward testimony. The tendency of his ministry was to lead the mind to the divine teacher, the sublime ruler, that all would find within themselves, which was above men's teaching, human records, or outward authorities. Highly as he valued these ancient testimonies, they were not to take the place of the higher law inwardly revealed, which was and should be, the governing principle of our lives.

One of our early friends, Richard Davies, attended a meeting of the independents, and heard the preacher express the sentiment that the time would come when Christians would have no more need of the Bible than of any other book. He remarked on this saying of the preacher, 'Hast thou not experienced that time already come?' Does not this imply, or may we not infer from this, that our worthy friend has experienced that time already come; was it a greater heresy, than that uttered by the apostle Paul, when he declared that those who had known a birth into the gospel, had no more need of the law? that they were under a higher dispensation than were they who were bound by their statutes and ceremonies? Let us also not hesitate to declare it, and to speak the truth plainly as it is in Jesus, that we believe the time is come when this undue adherence to outward authorities, or to any forms of baptism or of communion of church or sabbath worship, should give place to more practical goodness among men, more love manifested one unto another in our every day life, doing good and ministering to the wants and interests of our fellow beings the world over. If we fully believe this, should we be most honest, did we so far seek to please men, more than to please God, as to fail to utter in our meetings, and whenever we feel called upon to do so in our conversation, in our writings, and to exhibit by example, by a life of non-conformity, in accordance with these views, that we have faith and confidence in our convictions? It needs, my friends, in this day that one should go forth saying neither baptism profiteth anything nor non-baptism, but faith which worketh by love, neither the ordinance of the communion table profiteth anything, nor the absence from the same, but faith which worketh by love.

These things should never be regarded as the test of the worshipper. Neither your sabbath observance profiteth anything, nor the non-observance of the day, but faith which worketh by love. Let all these subjects be held up in their true light. Let them be plainly spoken of – and let our lives be in accordance with our convictions of right, each striving to carry out our principles. Then obscure though we may be, lost sight of almost, in the great and pompous religious associations of the day, we yet shall have our influence and it will be felt. Why do we wish it to be felt? Because we believe it is the testimony of truth, and our duty to spread it far and wide. Because the healthful growth of the people requires that they should come away from their vain oblations, and settle upon the ground of obedience to the requirings of truth.

I desire to speak so as to be understood, and trust there are among you ears blessed that they hear, and that these principles shall be received as the Gospel of the blessed son of God. Happy shall they be, who by observing these, shall come to be divested of the traditions and superstitions which have been clinging to them, leading them to erect an altar 'to the unknown God'.

In the place of this shall an altar be raised where on may be oblations of God's own preparing. Thus may these approach our Father in Heaven and hold communion with him – entering his courts with thanksgiving, and his gates with praise, even though there may be no oral expression. He may unite in prayer and in praise, which will ascend as sweet incense, and the blessing will come which we can scarcely contain.

E. B. Pusey

The presence of God
The English clergyman E. B. Pusey (1800–82) was one of the leaders of the Tractarian (Oxford) Movement.

We cannot picture to ourselves the Presence of God, because we have no faculties to imagine what a spirit is. We are conscious that we have souls. Let materialists say what they will, our consciousness is a witness to us. The blindness of the blind is no evidence against our sight. But in vain we should set ourselves to imagine the Presence of God, who cannot imagine our own souls, which we know that we have. We cannot picture to ourselves spirit, so God speaks to us of himself in holy Scripture under images, taken from what we do know, ourselves, whom he, in some degree, made in his own likeness. But the facts we know. We know that God is close to us, closer to us than any of his creatures which he has made. He surrounds us and penetrates us: he is within us, without us.

From *Parochial and Cathedral Sermons*

Antony Ashley Cooper, seventh Earl of Shaftesbury

These covetous and cruel practices
The seventh Earl of Shaftesbury (1801-1885) was a leading English social reformer. In Parliament he campaigned against the injustices caused by the industrial revolution and introduced laws to provide care for the insane (1845) and to limit child labour (1842).

I have sufficiently proved that there prevails a system of slavery under the sanction of law ... The whole course of our manufacturing system tends to make only criminals and paupers ... My object is to appeal to, and excite the public opinion; where we cannot legislate, we can exhort, and laws may fail, where example will succeed. I must appeal to the bishops and ministers of the Church of England, nay, more to the ministers of every denomination, to urge on the hearts of their hearers, the mischief and the danger of these covetous and cruel practices.

Abraham Lincoln

As God gives us the right

Below is the Second Inaugural Address of President Abraham Lincoln (1809–65), delivered in Washington DC on 4 March 1865. *The London Spectator* wrote about this speech, 'We cannot read it without a renewed conviction that it is the noblest political document known to history ...'

At this second appearing to take the oath of the presidential office, there is less occasion for an extended address than there was at the first. Then a statement, somewhat in detail, of a course to be pursued, seemed fitting and proper. Now, at the expiration of four years, during which public declarations have been constantly called forth on every point and phase of the great contest which still absorbs the attention, and engrosses the energies of the nation, little that is new could be presented. The progress of our arms, upon which all else chiefly depends, is as well known to the public as to myself; and it is, I trust, reasonably satisfactory and encouraging to all. With high hope for the future, no prediction in regard to it is ventured.

On the occasion corresponding to this four years ago, all thoughts were anxiously directed to an impending civil war. All dreaded it – all sought to avert it. While the inaugural [address] was being delivered from this place, devoted altogether to saving the Union without war, insurgent agents were in the city seeking to destroy it without war – seeking to dissolve [the Union], and divide effects, by negotiation. Both parties deprecated war; but one of them would make war rather than let the nation survive; and the other would accept war rather than let it perish. And the war came.

One eighth of the whole population were colored slaves, not distributed generally over the Union, but localized in the Southern part of it. These slaves constituted a peculiar and powerful interest. All knew that this interest was, somehow, the cause of the war. To strengthen, perpetuate, and extend this interest was the object for which the insurgents would rend the Union, even by war; while the government claimed no right to do more than to restrict the territorial enlargement of it. Neither party expected for the war, the magnitude, or the duration, which it has already attained. Neither anticipated that the cause of the conflict might cease with, or even before, the conflict itself should cease. Each looked for an easier triumph, and a result less fundamental and astounding. Both read the same Bible, and pray to the same God; and each invokes His aid against the other. It may seem strange that any men should dare to ask a just God's assistance in wringing their bread from the sweat of other men's faces; but let us judge not that we be not judged. The prayers of both could not be answered; that of neither has been answered fully. The Almighty has his own purposes. 'Woe unto the world because of offences! for it must needs be that offences come; but woe to that man by whom the offence cometh!' If we shall suppose that American Slavery is one of those offences which, in the providence of God, must needs come, but which, having continued through His appointed time, He now wills to remove, and that He gives to both North and South, this terrible war, as the woe due to those by whom the offence came, shall we discern therein any departure from those divine attributes which the believers in a Living God always ascribe to Him? Fondly do we hope – fervently do we pray – that this mighty scourge of war may speedily pass away. Yet, if God wills that it continue, until all the wealth piled by the bond-man's two hundred and fifty years of unrequited toil shall be sunk, and until every drop of blood drawn with the lash, shall be paid by another drawn with the sword, as was said three thousand years ago, so still it must be said 'the judgments of the Lord, are true and righteous altogether.'

With malice toward none; with charity for all; with firmness in the right, as God gives us to see the right, let us strive on to finish the work we are in; to bind up the nation's wounds; to care for him who shall have borne the battle, and for his widow, and his orphan – to do all which may achieve and cherish a just and lasting peace, among ourselves, and with all nations.

Abraham Lincoln's lying in state

I charge this murder where it belongs, on Slavery

After the assassination of Abraham Lincoln his body lay in state in Philadelphia. At that time Phillips Brooks (1835–93), rector of the Church of the Advent in that city, preached the sermon below.

He chose David also His servant, and took him away from the sheepfolds; that he might feed Jacob His people, and Israel

> *His inheritance. So he fed them with a faithful and true heart, and ruled them prudently with all his power.*
>
> Psalm 78:71–73

While I speak to you to-day, the body of the President who ruled this people, is lying, honoured and loved, in our city. It is impossible with that sacred presence in our midst for me to stand and speak of ordinary topics which occupy the pulpit. I must speak of him to-day, and I therefore undertake to do what I had intended to do at some future time, to invite you to study with me the character of Abraham Lincoln, the impulses of his life and the causes of his death. I know how hard it is to do it rightly, how impossible it is to do it worthily. But I shall speak with confidence, because I speak to those who love him, and whose ready love will fill out the deficiencies in a picture which my words will weakly try to draw.

We take it for granted, first of all, that there is an essential connection between Mr Lincoln's character and his violent and bloody death. It is no accident, no arbitrary decree of Providence. He lived as he did, and he died as he did, because he was what he was. The more we see of events, the less we come to believe in any fate or destiny except the destiny of character. It will be our duty, then, to see what there was in the character of our great President that created the history of his life, and at last produced the catastrophe of his cruel death. After the first trembling horror, the first outburst of indignant sorrow, has grown calm, these are the questions which we are bound to ask and answer.

It is not necessary for me even to sketch the biography of Mr Lincoln. He was born in Kentucky fifty-six years ago, when Kentucky was a pioneer State. He lived, as boy and man, the hard and needy life of a backwoodsman, a farmer, a river boatman, and, finally, by his own efforts at self-education, of an active, respected, influential citizen, in the half-organized and manifold interests of a new and energetic community. From his boyhood up he lived in direct and vigorous contact with men and things, not as in older States and easier conditions with words and theories; and both his moral convictions and his intellectual opinions gathered from that contact a supreme degree of that character by which men knew him, that character which is the most distinctive possession of the best American nature, that almost indescribable quality which we call in general clearness or truth, and which appears in the physical structure as health, in the moral constitution as honesty, in the mental structure as sagacity, and in the region of active life as practicalness. This one character, with many sides, all shaped by the same essential force and testifying to the same inner influences, was what was powerful in him and decreed for him the life he was to live and the death he was to die. We must take no smaller view than this of what he was. Even his physical conditions are not to be forgotten in making up his character. We make too little always of the physical; certainly we make too little of it here if we lose out of sight the strength and muscular activity, the power of doing and enduring, which the backwoods-boy inherited from generations of hard-living ancestors, and appropriated for his own by a long discipline of bodily toil. He brought to the solution of the question of labour in this country not merely a mind, but a body thoroughly in sympathy with labour, full of the culture of labour, bearing witness to the dignity and excellence of work in every muscle that work had toughened and every sense that work had made clear and true. He could not have brought the mind for his task so perfectly, unless he had first brought the body whose rugged and stubborn health was always contradicting to him the false theories of labour, and always asserting the true.

As to the moral and mental powers which distinguished him, all embraceable under this general description of clearness of truth, the most remarkable thing is the way in which they blend with one another, so that it is next to impossible to examine them in separation. A great many people have discussed very crudely whether Abraham Lincoln was an intellectual man or not; as if intellect were a thing always of the same sort, which you could precipitate from the other constituents of a man's nature and weigh by itself, and compare by pounds and ounces in this man with another. The fact is, that in all the simplest characters that line between the mental and moral natures is always vague and indistinct. They run together, and in their best combinations you are unable to discriminate, in the wisdom which is their result, how much is moral and how much is intellectual. You are unable to tell whether in the wise acts and words which issue from such a life there is more of the righteousness that comes of a clear conscience, or of the sagacity that comes of a clear brain. In more complex characters and under more complex conditions, the moral and the mental lives come to be less healthily combined. They co-operate, they help each other less. They come even to stand over against each other as antagonists; till we have that vague but most melancholy notion which pervades the life of all elaborate civilization, that goodness and greatness, as we call them, are not to be looked for together, till we expect to see and so do see a feeble and narrow conscientiousness on the one hand, and a bad, unprincipled intelligence on the other, dividing the suffrages of men.

It is the great boon of such characters as Mr Lincoln's, that they reunite what God has joined together and man has put asunder. In him was vindicated the greatness of real goodness and the goodness of real greatness. The twain were one flesh. Not one of all the multitudes who stood and looked up to him for direction with such a loving and implicit trust can tell you today whether the wise judgments that he gave came most from a strong head or a sound heart. If you ask them, they are puzzled. There are men as good as he, but they do bad things. There are men as intelligent as he, but they do foolish things. In him goodness and intelligence combined and made their best result of wisdom. For perfect truth consists not merely in the right constituents of character, but in their right and intimate conjunction. This union of the mental and moral into a life of admirable simplicity is what we most admire in children; but in them it is unsettled and unpractical. But when it is preserved into manhood, deepened into reliability and maturity, it is that glorified childlikeness, that high and reverend simplicity, which shames and baffles the most accomplished astuteness, and is chosen by God to fill his purposes when he needs a ruler for his people, of faithful and true heart, such as he had who was our President.

Another evident quality of such a character as this will be its freshness or newness; if we may so speak. Its freshness or readiness – call it what you will – its ability to take up new duties and do them in a new way, will result of necessity from its truth, and clearness. The simple natures and forces will always be the most pliant ones. Water bends and shapes itself to any channel. Air folds and adapts itself to each new figure. They are the simplest and the most infinitely active things in nature. So this nature, in very virtue of its simplicity, must be also free, always fitting itself to each new need. It will always start from the most fundamental and eternal conditions, and work in the straightest even although they be the newest ways, to the present prescribed purpose. In one word, it must be broad and independent and radical. So that freedom and radicalness in the character of Abraham Lincoln were not separate qualities, but the necessary results of his simplicity and childlikeness and truth.

Here then we have some conception of the man. Out of this character came the life which we admire and the death which we lament to-day. He was called in that character to that life and death. It was just the nature, as you see, which a new nation such as ours ought to produce. All the conditions of his birth, his youth, his manhood, which made him what he was, were not irregular and exceptional, but were the normal conditions of a new and simple country. His pioneer home in Indiana was a type of the pioneer land in which he lived. If ever there was a man who was a part of the time and country he lived in, this was he. The same simple respect for labour won in the school of work and incorporated into blood and muscle; the same unassuming loyalty to the simple virtues of temperance and industry and integrity; the same sagacious judgment which had learned to be quick-eyed and quick-brained in the constant presence of emergency; the same direct and clear thought about things, social, political, and religious, that was in him supremely, was in the people he was sent to rule. Surely, with such a type-man for ruler, there would seem to be but a smooth and even road over which he might lead the people whose character he represented into the new region of national happiness and comfort and usefulness, for which that character had been designed.

But then we come to the beginning of all trouble. Abraham Lincoln was the type-man of the country, but not of the whole country. This character which we have been trying to describe was the character of an American under the discipline of freedom. There was another American character which had been developed under the influence of slavery. There was no one American character embracing the land. There were two characters, with impulses of irrepressible and deadly conflict. This citizen whom we have been honouring and praising represented one. The whole great scheme with which he was ultimately brought in conflict, and which has finally killed him, represented the other. Beside this nature, true and fresh and new, there was another nature, false and effete and old. The one nature found itself in a new world, and set itself to discover the new ways for the new duties that were given it. The other nature, full of the false pride of blood, set itself to reproduce in a new world the institutions and the spirit of the old, to build anew the structure of the feudalism which had been corrupt in its own day, and which had been left far behind by the advancing conscience and needs of the progressing race. The one nature magnified labour, the other nature depreciated and despised it. The one honoured the labourer, and the other scorned him. The one was simple and direct; the other, complex, full of sophistries and self-excuses. The one was free to look all that claimed to be truth in the face, and separate the error from the truth that might be in it; the other did not dare to investigate, because its own established prides and systems were dearer to it than the truth itself, and so even truth went about in it doing the work of error. The one was ready to state broad principles, of the brotherhood of man, the universal fatherhood and justice of God, however imperfectly it might realize them in practice; the other denied even the principles, and so dug deep and laid below its special sins the broad foundation of a consistent, acknowledged sinfulness. In a word, one nature was full of the influences of Freedom, the other nature was full of the influences of Slavery.

In general, these two regions of our national life were separated by a geographical boundary. One was the spirit of the North, the other was the spirit of the South. But the Southern nature was by no means all a Southern thing. There it had an organized, established form, a certain definite, established institution about which it clustered. Here, lacking advantage, it lived in less expressive ways and so lived more weakly. There, there was the horrible sacrament of slavery, the outward and visible sign round which the inward and spiritual temper gathered and kept itself alive. But who doubts that among us the spirit of slavery lived and thrived? Its formal existence had been swept away from one State after another, partly on conscientious, partly on economical grounds, but its spirit was here, in every sympathy that Northern winds carried to the listening ear of the Southern slave-holder, and in every oppression of the weak by the strong, every proud assumption of idleness over labour which echoed the music of Southern life back to us. Here in our midst lived that worse and falser nature, side by side with the true and better nature which God meant should be the nature of Americans, and of which he was shaping out the type and champion in his chosen David of the sheepfold.

Here then we have the two. The history of our country for many years is the history of how these two elements of American life approached collision. They wrought their separate reactions on each other. Men debate and quarrel even now about the rise of Northern Abolitionism, about whether the Northern Abolitionists were right or wrong, whether they did harm or good. How vain the quarrel is! It was inevitable. It was inevitable in the nature of things that two such natures living here together should be set violently against each other. It is inevitable, till man be far more unfeeling and untrue to his convictions than he has always been, that a great wrong asserting itself vehemently should arouse to no less vehement assertion the opposing right. The only wonder is that there was not more of it. The only wonder is that so few were swept away to take by an impulse they could not resist their stand of hatred to the wicked institution. The only wonder is, that only one brave, reckless man came forth to cast himself, almost single-handed, with a hopeless hope, against the proud power that he hated, and trust to the influence of a soul marching on into the history of his countrymen to stir them to a vindication of the truth he loved. At any rate, whether the Abolitionists were wrong or right, there grew up about their violence, as there always will about the extremism of extreme reformers, a great mass of feeling, catching their spirit and asserting it firmly, though in more moderate degrees and methods. About the nucleus of Abolitionism grew up a great American Anti-Slavery determination, which at last gathered strength enough to take its stand to insist upon the checking and limiting the extension of the power of slavery, and to put the type-man, whom God had been preparing for the task before the world, to do the work on which it had resolved. Then came discontent, secession, treason. The two American natures, long advancing to encounter, met at last, and a whole country, yet trembling with the shock, bears witness how terrible the meeting was.

Thus I have tried briefly to trace out the gradual course by which God brought the character which He designed to be the controlling character of this new world into distinct collision with the hostile character which it was to destroy and absorb, and set it in the person of its type-man in the seat of highest power. The character formed under the discipline of Freedom and the character formed under the discipline of Slavery developed all their difference and met in hostile conflict when this war began. Notice, it was not only in what he did and was towards the slave, it was in all he did and was everywhere that we accept Mr Lincoln's character as the true result of our free life and institutions. Nowhere else could have come forth that genuine love of the people, which in him no one could suspect of being either the cheap flattery of the demagogue or the abstract philanthropy of the philosopher, which made our President, while he lived, the centre of a great household land, and when he died so cruelly made every humblest household thrill with a sense of personal bereavement which the death of rulers is not apt to bring. Nowhere else than out of the life of freedom could have come that personal unselfishness and generosity which made so gracious a part of this good man's character. How many soldiers feel yet the pressure of a strong hand that clasped theirs once as they lay sick and weak in the dreary hospital! How many ears will never lose the thrill of some kind word he spoke – he who could speak so kindly to promise a kindness that always matched his word! How often he surprised the land with a clemency which made even those who questioned his policy love him the more for what they called his weakness – seeing how the man in whom God had most embodied the discipline of Freedom not only could not be a slave, but could not be a tyrant! In the heartiness of his mirth and his enjoyment of simple joys; in the directness and shrewdness of perception which constituted his wit; in the untired, undiscouraged faith in human nature which he always kept; and perhaps above all in the plainness and quiet, unostentatious earnestness and independence of his religious life, in his humble love and trust of God – in all, it was a character such as only Freedom knows how to make.

Now it was in this character, rather than in any mere political position, that the fitness of Mr Lincoln to stand forth in the struggle of the two American natures really lay. We are told that he did not come to the Presidential chair pledged to the abolition of Slavery. When will we learn that with all true men it is not what they intend to do, but it is what the qualities of their natures bind them to do, that determines their career! The President came to his power full of the blood, strong in the strength of Freedom. He came there free, and hating slavery. He came there, leaving on record words like these spoken three years before and never contradicted. He had said, 'A house divided against itself cannot stand. I believe this Government cannot endure permanently, half slave and half free. I do not expect the Union to be dissolved; I do not expect the house to fall; but I expect it will cease to be divided. It will become all one thing or all the other.' When the question came, he knew which thing he meant that it should be. His whole nature settled that question for him. Such a man must always live as he used to say he lived (and was blamed for saying it) 'controlled by events, not controlling them'. And with a reverent and clear mind, to be controlled by events means to be controlled by God. For such a man there was no hesitation when God brought him up face to face with Slavery and put the sword into his hand and said, 'Strike it down dead.' He was a willing servant then. If ever the face of a man writing solemn words glowed with a solemn joy, it must have been the face of Abraham Lincoln, as he bent over the page where the Emancipation Proclamation of 1863 was growing into shape, and giving manhood and freedom as he wrote it to hundreds of thousands of his fellow-men. Here was a work in which his whole nature could rejoice. Here was an act that crowned the whole culture of his life. All the past, the free boyhood in the woods, the free youth upon the farm, the free manhood in the honourable citizen's employments – all his freedom gathered and completed itself in this. And as the swarthy multitudes came in, ragged, and tired, and hungry, and ignorant, but free forever from anything but the memorial scars of the fetters and the whip, singing rude songs in which the new triumph of freedom struggled and heaved below the sad melody that had been shaped for bondage; as in their camps and hovels there grew up to their half-superstitious eyes the image of a great Father almost more than man, to whom they owed their freedom – were they not half right? For it was not to one man, driven by stress of policy, or swept off by a whim of pity, that the noble act was due. It was to the American nature, long kept by God in his own intentions till his time should come, at last emerging into sight and power, and bound up and embodied in this best and most American of all Americans, to whom we and those poor frightened slaves at last might look up together and love to call him, with one voice, our Father.

Thus, we have seen something of what the character of Mr Lincoln was, and how it issued in the life he lived. It remains for us to see how it resulted also in the terrible death which has laid his murdered body here in our town among lamenting multitudes to-day. It is not a hard question, though it is sad to answer. We saw the two natures, the nature of Slavery and the nature of Freedom, at last set against each other, come at last to open war. Both fought, fought long, fought bravely; but each, as was perfectly natural, fought with the tools and in the ways which its own character had made familiar to it. The character of Slavery was brutal, barbarous, and treacherous; and so the whole history of the slave power during the war has been full of ways of warfare brutal, barbarous, and treacherous, beyond anything that men bred in freedom could have been driven to by the most hateful passions. It is not to be marvelled at. It is not to be set down as the special sin of the war. It goes back beyond that. It is the sin of the system. It is the barbarism of Slavery. When Slavery went to war to save its life, what wonder if its barbarism grew barbarous a hundred-fold!

One would be attempting a task which once was almost hopeless, but which now is only needless, if one set oneself to convince a Northern congregation that Slavery was a barbarian institution. It would be hardly more necessary to try to prove how its barbarism has shown itself during this war. The same spirit which was blind to the wickedness of breaking sacred ties, of separating man and wife, of beating women till they dropped down dead, of organizing licentiousness and sin into commercial systems, of forbidding knowledge and protecting itself with ignorance, of putting on its arms and riding out to steal a State at the beleaguered ballot-box away from freedom – in one word (for its simplest definition is its worst dishonour), the spirit that gave man the ownership of man in time of peace, has found out yet more terrible barbarisms for the time of war. It has hewed and burned the bodies of the dead. It has starved and mutilated its helpless prisoners. It has dealt by truth, not as men will in a time of excitement lightly and with frequent violations, but with a cool, and deliberate, and systematic contempt. It has sent its agents into Northern towns to fire peaceful hotels where hundreds of peaceful men and women slept. It has undermined the prisons where its victims starved, and made all ready to blow with one blast their wretched life away. It has delighted in the lowest and basest scurrility even on the highest and most honourable lips. It has corrupted the graciousness of women and killed out the truth of men.

I do not count up the terrible catalogue because I like to, nor because I wish to stir your hearts to passion. Even now, you and I have no right to indulge in personal hatred to the men who did these things. But we are not doing right by ourselves, by the President that we have lost, or by God who had a purpose in our losing him, unless we know thoroughly that it was this same spirit which we have seen to be a tyrant in peace and a savage in war, that has crowned itself with the working of this final woe. It was the conflict of the two American natures, the false and the true. It was Slavery and Freedom that met in their two representatives, the assassin and the President; and the victim of the last desperate struggle of the dying Slavery lies dead to-day in Independence Hall.

Solemnly, in the sight of God, I charge this murder where it belongs, on Slavery. I dare not stand here in His sight, and before Him or you speak doubtful and double-meaning words of vague repentance, as if we had killed our President. We have sins enough, but we have not done this sin, save as by weak concessions and timid compromises we have let the spirit of Slavery grow strong and ripe for such a deed. In the barbarism of Slavery the foul act and its foul method had their birth. By all the goodness that there was in him; by all the love we had for him (and who shall tell how great it was); by all the sorrow that has burdened down this desolate and dreadful week – I charge this murder where it belongs, on Slavery. I bid you to remember where the charge belongs, to write it on the door-posts of your mourning houses, to teach it to your wondering children, to give it to the history of these times, that all times to come may hate and dread the sin that killed our noblest President.

If ever anything were clear, this is the clearest. Is there the man alive who thinks that Abraham Lincoln was shot just for himself; that it was that one man for whom the plot was laid? The gentlest, kindest, most indulgent man that ever ruled a State! The man who knew not how to speak a word of harshness or how to make a foe! Was it he for whom the murderer lurked with a mere private hate? It was not he, but what he stood for. It was Law and Liberty, it was Government and Freedom, against which the hate gathered and the treacherous shot was fired. And I know not how the crime of him who shoots at Law and Liberty in the crowded glare of a great theatre differs from theirs who have levelled their aim at the same great beings from behind a thousand ambuscades and on a hundred battle-fields of this long war. Every general in the field, and every false citizen in our midst at home, who has plotted and laboured to destroy the lives of the soldiers of the Republic, is brother to him who did this deed. The American nature, the American truths, of which our President was the anointed and supreme embodiment, have been embodied in multitudes of heroes who marched unknown and fell unnoticed in our ranks. For them, just as for him, character decreed a life and a death. The blood of all of them I charge on the same head. Slavery armed with Treason was their murderer.

Men point out to us the absurdity and folly of this awful crime. Again and again we hear men say, 'It was the worst thing for themselves they could have done. They have shot a representative man, and the cause he represented grows stronger and sterner by his death. Can it be that so wise a devil was so foolish here? Must it not have been the act of one poor madman, born and nursed in his own reckless brain?' My friends, let us understand this matter. It was a foolish act. Its folly was only equalled by its wickedness. It was a foolish act. But when did sin begin to be wise? When did wickedness learn wisdom? When did the fool stop saying in his heart, 'There is no God,' and acting godlessly in the absurdity of his impiety? The cause that Abraham Lincoln died for shall grow stronger by his death, stronger and sterner. Stronger to set its pillars deep into the structure of our nation's life; sterner to execute the justice of the Lord upon his enemies. Stronger to spread its arms and grasp our whole land into freedom; sterner to sweep the last poor ghost of Slavery out of our haunted homes. But while we feel the folly of this act, let not its folly hide its wickedness. It was the wickedness of Slavery putting on a foolishness for which its wickedness and that alone is responsible, that robbed the nation of a President and the people of a father. And remember this, that the folly of the Slave power in striking the representative of Freedom, and thinking that thereby it killed Freedom itself, is only a folly that we shall echo if we dare to think that in punishing the representatives of Slavery who did this deed, we are putting Slavery to death. Dispersing armies and hanging traitors, imperatively as justice and necessity may demand them both, are not killing the spirit out of which they sprang. The traitor must die because he has committed treason. The murderer must die because he has committed murder. Slavery must die, because out of it, and it alone, came forth the treason of the traitor and the murder of the murderer. Do not say that it is dead. It is not, while its essential spirit lives. While one man counts another man as born inferior for the colour of his skin, while both in North and South prejudices and practices, which the law cannot touch, but which God hates, keep alive in our people's hearts the spirit of the old iniquity, it is not dead. The new American nature must supplant the old. We must grow like our President, in his truth, his independence, his religion, and his wide humanity. Then the character by which he died shall be in us, and by it we shall live. Then peace shall come that knows no war, and law that knows no treason; and full of his spirit a grateful land shall gather round his grave, and in the daily psalm of prosperous and righteous living, thank God forever for his life and death.

So let him lie here in our midst to-day, and let our people go and bend with solemn thoughtfulness and look upon his face and read the lessons of his burial. As he paused here on his journey from the Western home and told us what by the help of God he meant to do, so let him pause upon his way back to his Western grave and tell us with a silence more eloquent than words how bravely, how truly, by the strength of God, he did it. God brought him up as he brought David up from the sheepfolds to feed Jacob, his people, and Israel, his inheritance. He came up in earnestness and faith, and he goes back in triumph. As he pauses here to-day, and from his cold lips bids us bear witness how he has met the duty that was laid on him, what can we say out of our full hearts but this – 'He fed them with a faithful and true heart, and ruled them prudently with all his power.' The

Shepherd of the People! that old name that the best rulers ever craved. What ruler ever won it like this dead President of ours? He fed us faithfully and truly. He fed us with counsel when we were in doubt, with inspiration when we sometimes faltered, with caution when we would be rash, with calm, clear, trustful cheerfulness through many an hour when our hearts were dark. He fed hungry souls all over the country with sympathy and consolation. He spread before the whole land feasts of great duty and devotion and patriotism, on which the land grew strong. He fed us with solemn, solid truths. He taught us the sacredness of government, the wickedness of treason. He made our souls glad and vigorous with the love of liberty that was in his. He showed us how to love truth and yet be charitable – how to hate wrong and all oppression, and yet not treasure one personal injury or insult. He fed all his people, from the highest to the lowest, from the most privileged down to the most enslaved. Best of all, he fed us with a reverent and genuine religion. He spread before us the love and fear of God just in that shape in which we need them most, and out of his faithful service of a higher Master who of us has not taken and eaten and grown strong? 'He fed them with a faithful and true heart.' Yes, till the last. For at the last, behold him standing with hand reached out to feed the South with mercy and the North with charity, and the whole land with peace, when the Lord who had sent him called him and his work was done!

He stood once on the battle-field of our own State, and said of the brave men who had saved it words as noble as any country-man of ours ever spoke. Let us stand in the country he has saved, and which is to be his grave and monument, and say of Abraham Lincoln what he said of the soldiers who had died at Gettysburg. He stood there with their graves before him, and these are the words he said:

We cannot dedicate, we cannot consecrate, we cannot hallow this ground. The brave men who struggled here have consecrated it far beyond our power to add or detract. The world will little note nor long remember what we say here, but it can never forget what they did here. It is for us the living rather to be dedicated to the unfinished work which they who fought here have thus far so nobly advanced. It is rather for us to be here dedicated to the great task remaining before us, that from these honoured dead we take increased devotion to that cause for which they gave the last full measure of devotion; that we here highly resolve that these dead shall not have died in vain; and this nation, under God, shall have a new birth of freedom, and that government of the people, by the people, and for the people shall not perish from the earth.

May God make us worthy of the memory of Abraham Lincoln!

Abraham Lincoln's funeral

He is dead, but the God in whom he trusted lives

Dr Phineas D. Gurley, pastor of the New York Avenue Presbyterian Church, which Lincoln had attended while he was President, preached this funeral sermon in the East Room of the White House on 19 April 1865. Dr Gurley had been at Lincoln's bedside when he died on 15 April.

As we stand here today, mourners around this coffin and around the lifeless remains of our beloved chief magistrate, we recognize and we adore the sovereignty of God. His throne is in the heavens, and His kingdom ruleth over all. He hath done, and He hath permitted to be done, whatsoever He pleased. 'Clouds and darkness are round about Him; righteousness and judgment are the habitation of His throne.' His way is in the sea, and His path in the great waters, and His footsteps are not known. 'Canst thou by searching find out God? Canst thou find out the Almighty unto perfection? It is as high as heaven; what canst thou do? Deeper than hell; what canst thou know? The measure thereof is longer than the earth, and broader than the sea. If He cut off, and shut up, or gather together, then who can hinder Him? For He knoweth vain men; he seeth wickedness also; will He not then consider it?' – We bow before His infinite majesty. We bow, we weep, we worship.

Where reason fails, with all her powers,
There faith prevails, and love adores.

It was a cruel, cruel hand, that dark hand of the assassin, which smote our honoured, wise, and noble President, and filled the land with sorrow. But above and beyond that hand there is another which we must see and acknowledge. It is the chastening hand of a wise and a faithful Father. He gives us this bitter cup. And the cup that our Father hath given us, shall we not drink it?

God of the just, Thou gavest us the cup:
We yield to thy behest, and drink it up.

'Whom the Lord loveth He chasteneth.' O how these blessed words have cheered and strengthened and sustained us through all these long and weary years of civil strife, while our friends and brothers on so many ensanguined fields were falling and dying for the cause of Liberty and Union! Let them cheer, and strengthen, and sustain us to-day. True, this new sorrow and chastening has come in such an hour and in such a way as we thought not, and it bears the impress of a rod that is very heavy, and of a mystery that is very deep. That such a life should be sacrificed, at such a time, by such a foul and diabolical agency; that the man at the head of the nation, whom the people had learned to trust with a confiding and a loving confidence, and upon whom more than upon any other were centred, under God, our best hopes for the true and speedy pacification of the country, the restoration of the Union, and the return of harmony and love; that he should be taken from us, and taken just as the prospect of peace was brightly opening upon our torn and bleeding country, and just as he was beginning to be animated and gladdened with the hope of ere long enjoying with the people the blessed fruit and reward of his and their toil, and care, and patience, and self-sacrificing devotion to the interests of Liberty and the Union – O it is a mysterious and a most afflicting visitation! But it is our Father in heaven, the God of our fathers, and our God, who permits us to be so suddenly and sorely smitten; and we know that His judgments are right, and that in faithfulness He has afflicted us. In the midst of our rejoicings we needed this stroke, this dealing, this discipline; and therefore He has sent it. Let us remember, our affliction has not come forth out of the dust, and our trouble has not sprung out of the ground. Through and beyond all second causes let us look, and see the sovereign permissive agency of the great First Cause. It is His prerogative to bring light out of darkness and good out of evil. Surely the wrath of man shall praise Him, and the remainder of wrath He will restrain. In the light of a clearer day we may yet see that the wrath which planned and perpetuated the death of the President, was overruled by Him whose judgements are unsearchable, and His ways are past finding out, for the highest welfare of all those interests which are so dear to the Christian patriot and philanthropist, and for which a loyal people have made such an unexampled sacrifice of treasure and of blood. Let us not be faithless, but believing.

> *Blind unbelief is prone to err,*
> *And scan His work in vain;*
> *God is his own interpreter,*
> *And He will make it plain.*

We will wait for his interpretation, and we will wait in faith, nothing doubting. He who has led us so well, and defended and prospered us so wonderfully during the last four years of toil, and struggle, and sorrow, will not forsake us now. He may chasten, but He will not destroy. He may purify us more and more in the furnace of trial, but He will not consume us. No, no! He has chosen us as He did his people of old in the furnace of affliction, and He has said of us as He said of them, 'This people have I formed for myself; they shall show forth My praise.' Let our principal anxiety now be that this new sorrow may be a sanctified sorrow; that it may lead us to deeper repentance, to a more humbling sense of our dependence upon God, and to the more unreserved consecration of ourselves and all that we have to the cause of truth and justice, of law and order, of liberty and good government, of pure and undefiled religion. Then, though weeping may endure for a night, joy will come in the morning. Blessed be God! despite of this great and sudden and temporary darkness, the morning has begun to dawn – the morning of a bright and glorious day, such as our country has never seen. That day will come and not tarry, and the death of an hundred Presidents and their Cabinets can never, never prevent it. While we are thus hopeful, however, let us also be humble. The occasion calls us to prayerful and tearful humiliation. It demands of us that we lie low, very low, before Him who has smitten us for our sins. O that all our rulers and all our people may bow in the dust to-day beneath the chastening hand of God! and may their voices go up to Him as one voice, and their hearts go up to Him as one heart, pleading with Him for mercy, for grace to sanctify our great and sore bereavement, and for wisdom to guide us in this our time of need. Such a united cry and pleading will not be in vain. It will enter into the ear and heart of Him who sits upon the throne, and He will say to us, as to His ancient Israel, 'In a little wrath I hid my face from thee for a moment: but with everlasting kindness will I have mercy upon thee, saith the Lord, thy Redeemer.'

I have said that the people confided in the late lamented President with a full and a loving confidence. Probably no man since the days of Washington was ever so deeply and firmly embedded and enshrined in the very hearts of the people as Abraham Lincoln. Nor was it a mistaken confidence and love. He deserved it well – deserved it all. He merited it by his character, by his acts, and by the whole tenor, and tone, and spirit of his life. He was simple and sincere, plain and honest, truthful and just, benevolent and kind. His perceptions were quick and clear, his judgments were calm and accurate, and his purposes were good and pure beyond a question. Always and everywhere he aimed and endeavoured to be right and to do right. His integrity was thorough, all-pervading, all-controlling, and incorruptible. It was the same in every place and relation, in the consideration and the control of matters great or small, the same firm and steady principle of power and beauty that shed a clear and crowning lustre upon all his other excellencies of mind and heart, and recommended him to his fellow citizens as the man, who, in a time of unexampled peril, when the very life of the nation was at stake, should be chosen to occupy, in the country and for the country, its highest post of power and responsibility.

How wisely and well, how purely and faithfully, how firmly and steadily, how justly and successfully he did occupy that post and meet its grave demands in circumstances of surpassing trial and difficulty, is known to you all, known to the country and the world. He comprehended from the first the perils to which treason has exposed the freest and best Government on the earth, the vast interests of Liberty and humanity that were to be saved or lost forever in the urgent impending conflict; he rose to the dignity and momentousness of the occasion, saw his duty as the Chief Magistrate of a great and imperilled people, and he determined to do his duty, and his whole duty, seeking the guidance and leaning upon the arm of Him of whom it is written, 'He giveth power to the faint, and to them that have no might He increaseth strength.' Yes, he leaned upon His arm. He recognized and received the truth that the 'kingdom is the Lord's, and He is the governor among the nations.' He remembered that 'God is in history,' and he felt that nowhere had His hand and His mercy been so marvelously conspicuous as in the history of this nation. He hoped and he prayed that that same hand would continue to guide us, and that same mercy continue to abound to us in the time of our greatest need.

I speak what I know, and testify what I have often heard him say, when I affirm that that guidance and mercy were the props on which he humbly and habitually leaned; they were the best hope he had for himself and for his country. Hence, when he was leaving his home in Illinois, and coming to this city to take his seat in the executive chair of a disturbed and troubled nation, he said to the old and tried friends who gathered tearfully around him and bade him farewell, 'I leave you with this request: pray for me.' They did pray for him; and millions of other people prayed for him; nor did they pray in vain. Their prayer was heard, and the answer appears in all his subsequent history; it shines forth with a heavenly radiance in the whole course and tenor of his administration, from its commencement to its close. God raised him up for a great and glorious mission, furnished him for his work, and aided him in its accomplishment. Nor was it merely by strength of mind, and honesty of heart, and purity and pertinacity of purpose, that He furnished him; in addition to these things, He gave him a calm and abiding confidence in the overruling providence of God and in the ultimate triumph of truth and righteousness through the power and the blessing of God. This confidence strengthened him in all his hours of anxiety and toil, and inspired him with calm and cheering hope when others were inclining to despondency and gloom. Never shall I forget the emphasis and the deep emotion with which he said in this very room, to a company of clergymen and others, who called to pay him their respects in the darkest days of our civil conflict: 'Gentlemen, my hope of success in this great and terrible struggle rests on that immutable foundation, the justice and goodness of God. And when events are very threatening, and prospects very dark, I still hope that in some way which man can not see all will be well in the end, because our cause is just, and God is on our side.' Such was his sublime and holy faith, and it was an anchor to his soul, both sure and steadfast. It made him firm and strong. It emboldened him in the pathway of duty, however rugged and perilous it might be. It made him valiant for the right; for the cause of God and humanity, and it held him in a steady, patient, and unswerving adherence to a policy of administration which he thought, and which we all now think, both God and humanity required him to adopt.

We admired and loved him on many accounts – for strong and various reasons: we admired his childlike simplicity, his freedom from guile and deceit, his staunch and sterling integrity, his kind and forgiving temper, his industry and patience, his persistent, self-sacrificing devotion to all the duties of his eminent position, from the least to the greatest; his readiness to hear and consider the cause of the poor and humble, the suffering and the oppressed; his charity toward those who questioned the correctness of his opinions and the wisdom of his policy; his wonderful skill in reconciling differences among the friends of the Union, leading them away from abstractions, and inducing them to work together and harmoniously for the common weal; his true and enlarged philanthropy, that knew no distinction of colour or race, but regarded all men as brethren, and endowed alike by their Creator 'with certain inalienable rights, among which are life, Liberty, and the pursuit of happiness'; his inflexible purpose that what freedom had gained in our terrible civil strife should never be lost, and that the end of the war should be the end of slavery, and, as a consequence, of rebellion; his readiness to spend and be spent for the attainment of such a triumph – a triumph, the blessed fruits of which shall be as wide-spreading as the earth and as enduring as the sun: – all these things commanded and fixed our admiration and the admiration of the world, and stamped upon his character and life the unmistakable impress of greatness. But more sublime than any or all of these, more holy and influential, more beautiful, and strong, and sustaining, was his abiding confidence in God and in the final triumph of truth and righteousness through Him and for His sake. This was his noblest virtue, his grandest principle, the secret alike of his strength, his patience, and his success.

And this, it seems to me, after being near him steadily, and with him often, for more than four years, is the principle by which, more than by any other, 'he, being dead, yet speaketh.' Yes; by his steady enduring confidence in God, and in the complete ultimate success of the cause of God, which is the cause of humanity, more than by any other way, does he now speak to us and to the nation he loved and served so well. By this he speaks to his successor in office, and charges him to 'have faith in God.' By this he speaks to the members of his cabinet, the men with whom he counselled so often and was associated so long, and he charges them to 'have faith in God.' By this he speaks to the officers and men of our noble army and navy, and, as they stand at their posts of duty and peril, he charges them to 'have faith in God.' By this he speaks to all who occupy positions of influence and authority in these sad and troublous times, and he charges them all to 'have faith in God.' By this he speaks to this great people as they sit in sackcloth to-day, and weep for him with a bitter wailing, and refuse to be comforted, and he charges them to 'have faith in God.' And by this he will speak through the ages and to all rulers and peoples in every land, and his message to them will be, 'Cling to Liberty and right; battle for them; bleed for them; die for them, if need be; and have confidence in God.' O that the voice of this testimony may sink down into our hearts today and every day, and into the heart of the nation, and exert its appropriate influence upon our feelings, our faith, our patience, and our devotion to the cause of freedom and humanity – a cause dearer to us now than ever before, because consecrated by the blood of its most conspicuous defender, its wisest and most fondly-trusted friend.

He is dead; but the God in whom he trusted lives, and He can guide and strengthen his successor, as He guided and strengthened him. He is dead; but the memory of his virtues, of his wise and patriotic counsels and labours, of his calm and steady faith in God lives, is precious, and will be a power for good in the country quite down to the end of time. He is dead; but the cause he so ardently loved, so ably, patiently, faithfully represented and defended – not for himself only, not for us only, but for all people in all their coming generations, till time shall be no more – that cause survives his fall, and will survive it. The light of its brightening prospects flashes cheeringly today athwart the gloom occasioned by his death, and the language of God's united providences is telling us that, though the friends of Liberty die, Liberty itself is immortal. There is no assassin strong enough and no weapon deadly enough to quench its inextinguishable life, or arrest its onward march to the conquest and empire of the world. This is our confidence, and this is our consolation, as we weep and mourn today. Though our beloved President is slain, our beloved country is saved. And so we sing of mercy as well as of judgment. Tears of gratitude mingle with those of sorrow. While there is darkness, there is also the dawning of a brighter, happier day upon our stricken and weary land. God be praised that our fallen Chief lived long enough to see the day dawn and the daystar of joy and peace arise upon the nation. He saw it, and he was glad. Alas! alas! He only saw the dawn. When the sun has risen, full-orbed and glorious, and a happy reunited people are rejoicing in its light – alas! alas! it will shine upon his grave. But that grave will be a precious and a consecrated spot. The friends of Liberty and of the Union will repair to it in years and ages to come, to pronounce the memory of its occupant blessed, and, gathering from his very ashes, and from the rehearsal of his deeds and virtues, fresh incentives to patriotism, they will there renew their vows of fidelity to their country and their God.

And now I know not that I can more appropriately conclude this discourse, which is but a sincere and simple utterance of the heart, than by addressing to our departed President, with some slight modification, the language which Tacitus, in his life of Agricola, addresses to his venerable and departed father-in-law:

With you we may now congratulate; you are blessed, not only because your life was a career of glory, but because you were released, when, your country safe, it was happiness to die. We have lost a parent, and, in our distress, it is now an addition to our heartfelt sorrow that we had it not in our power to commune with you on the bed of languishing, and receive your last embrace. Your dying words would have been ever dear to us; your commands we should have treasured up, and graved them on our hearts. This sad comfort we have lost, and the wound for that reason, pierces deeper. From the world of spirits behold your desolate family and people; exalt our minds from fond regret and unavailing grief to contemplation of your virtues. Those we must not lament; it were impiety to sully them with a tear. To cherish their memory, to embalm them with our praises, and, so far as we can, to emulate your bright example, will be the truest mark of our respect, the best tribute we can offer. Your wife will thus preserve the memory of the best of husbands, and thus your children will prove their filial piety. By dwelling constantly on your words and actions, they will have an illustrious character before their eyes, and, not content with the bare image of your mortal frame, they will have what is more valuable – the form and features of your mind. Busts and statues, like their originals, are frail and perishable. The soul is formed of finer elements, and its inward form is not to be expressed by the hand of an artist with unconscious matter – our manners and our morals may in some degree trace the resemblance. All of you that gained our love and raised our admiration still subsists, and will ever subsist, preserved in the minds of men, the register of ages, and the records of fame. Others, who had figured on the stage of life and were the worthies of a former day, will sink, for want of a faithful historian, into the common lot of oblivion, inglorious and unremembered; but you, our lamented friend and head, delineated with truth, and fairly consigned to posterity, will survive yourself, and triumph over the injuries of time.

William Booth

God has had all there was of me

William Booth (1829–1912), English evangelist and social reformer, was the founder of the Salvation Army. The American evangelist, J. Wilbur Chapman, met Booth when he was in his eighties. Chapman asked Booth what the secret of his success was. Below is Booth's reply.

I will tell you the secret. God has had all there was of me. There have been men with greater brains than I, men with greater opportunities; but from the day I got the poor of London on my heart, and a vision of what Jesus Christ could do with the poor of London, I made up my mind that God would have all of William Booth there was. And if there is anything of power in the Salvation Army today, it is because God has all the adoration of my heart, all the power of my will, and all the influence of my life.

William Booth

In Darkest England

Booth's most famous book, *In Darkest England*, described the appalling living conditions endured by many poor people in Victorian England. Below is an extract from the book.

This summer the attention of the civilized world has been arrested by the story which Mr Stanley has told of Darkest Africa and his journeyings across the heart of the Lost Continent. In all that spirited narrative of heroic endeavour, nothing has so much impressed the imagination, as his description of the immense forest, which offered an almost impenetrable barrier to his advance. The intrepid explorer, in his own phrase, 'marched, tore, ploughed, and cut his way for one hundred and sixty days through this inner womb of the true tropical forest.' The mind of man with difficulty endeavours to realize this immensity of wooded wilderness, covering a territory half as large again as the whole of France, where the rays of the sun never penetrate, where in the dark, dank air, filled with the steam of the heated morass, human beings dwarfed into pygmies and brutalized into cannibals lurk and live and die. Mr Stanley vainly endeavours to bring home to us the full horror of that awful gloom. He says:

> *Take a thick Scottish copse dripping with rain; imagine this to be mere undergrowth nourished under the impenetrable shade of ancient trees ranging from 100 to 180 feet high; briars and thorns abundant; lazy creeks meandering through the depths of the jungle, and sometimes a deep affluent of a great river. Imagine this forest and jungle in all stages of decay and growth, rain pattering on you every other day of the year; an impure atmosphere with its dread consequences, fever and dysentery; gloom throughout the day and darkness almost palpable throughout the night; and then if you can imagine such a forest extending the entire distance from Plymouth to Peterhead, you will have a fair idea of some of the inconveniences endured by us in the Congo forest.*

The denizens of this region are filled with a conviction that the forest is endless – interminable. In vain did Mr Stanley and his companions endeavour to convince them that outside the dreary wood were to be found sunlight, pasturage and peaceful meadows. They replied in a manner that seemed to imply that we must be strange creatures to suppose that it would be possible for any world to exist save their illimitable forest. 'No,' they replied, shaking their heads compassionately, and pitying our absurd questions, 'all like this,' and they moved their hand sweepingly to illustrate that the world was all alike, nothing but trees, trees and trees – great trees rising as high as an arrow shot to the sky, lifting their crowns intertwining their branches, pressing and crowding one against the other, until neither the sunbeam nor shaft of light can penetrate it. 'We entered the forest,' says Mr Stanley, 'with confidence; forty pioneers in front with axes and bill hooks to clear a path through the obstructions, praying that God and good fortune would lead us.' But before the conviction of the forest dwellers that the forest was without end, hope faded out of the hearts of the natives of Stanley's company. The men became sodden with despair, preaching was useless to move their brooding sullenness, their morbid gloom.

The little religion they knew was nothing more than legendary lore, and in their memories there dimly floated a story of a land which grew darker and darker as one travelled towards the end of the earth and drew nearer to the place where a great serpent lay supine and coiled round the whole world. Ah! then the ancients must have referred to this, where the light is so ghastly, and the woods are endless, and are so still and solemn and grey; to this oppressive loneliness, amid so much life, which is so chilling to the poor distressed heart; and the horror grew darker with their fancies; the cold of early morning, the comfortless grey of dawn, the dead white mist, the ever-dripping tears of the dew, the deluging rains, the appalling thunder bursts and the echoes, and the wonderful play of the dazzling lightning. And when the night comes with its thick palpable darkness, and they lie huddled in their damp little huts, and they hear the tempest overhead, and the howling of the wild winds, the grinding and groaning of the storm-tost trees, and the dread sounds of the falling giants, and the shock of the trembling earth which sends their hearts with fitful leaps to their throats, and the roaring and a rushing as of a mad overwhelming sea – oh, then the horror is intensified! When the march has begun once again, and the files are slowly moving through the woods, they renew their morbid broodings, and ask themselves: How long is this to last? Is the joy of life to end thus? Must we jog on day after day in this cheerless gloom and this joyless duskiness, until we stagger and fall and rot among the toads? Then they disappear into the woods by twos, and threes, and sixes; and after the caravan has passed they return by the trail, some to reach Yambuya and upset the young officers with their tales of woe and war; some to fall sobbing under a spear-thrust; some to wander and stray in the dark mazes of the woods, hopelessly lost; and some to be carved for the cannibal feast. And those who remain compelled to it by fears of greater danger, mechanically march on, a prey to dread and weakness.

That is the forest. But what of its denizens? They are comparatively few; only some hundreds of thousands living in small tribes from ten to thirty miles apart, scattered over an area on which ten thousand million trees put out the sun from a region four times as wide as Great Britain. Of these pygmies there are two kinds; one a very degraded specimen with ferret like eyes, close-set nose, more nearly approaching the baboon than was supposed to be possible, but very human; the other very handsome, with frank open innocent features, very prepossessing.

They are quick and intelligent, capable of deep affection and gratitude, showing remarkable industry and patience. A pygmy boy of eighteen worked with consuming zeal; time with him was too precious to waste in talk. His mind seemed ever concentrated on work. Mr Stanley said:

> When I once stopped him to ask him his name, his face seemed to say, 'Please don't stop me. I must finish my task.'
>
> All alike, the baboon variety and the handsome innocents, are cannibals. They are possessed with a perfect mania for meat. We were obliged to bury our dead in the river, lest the bodies should be exhumed and eaten, even when they had died from smallpox.

Upon the pygmies and all the dwellers of the forest has descended a devastating visitation in the shape of the ivory raiders of civilization. The race that wrote the *Arabian Nights*, built Baghdad and Granada, and invented Algebra, sends forth men with the hunger for gold in their hearts, and Enfield muskets in their hands, to plunder and to slay. They exploit the domestic affections of the forest dwellers in order to strip them of all they possess in the world. That has been going on for years. It is going on to-day. It has come to be regarded as the natural and normal law of existence. Of the religion of these hunted pygmies Mr Stanley tells us nothing, perhaps because there is nothing to tell. But an earlier traveller, Dr Kraff, says that one of these tribes, by name Doko, had some notion of a Supreme Being, to whom, under the name of Yer, they sometimes addressed prayers in moments of sadness or terror. In these prayers they say; 'Oh Yer, if Thou dost really exist why dost Thou let us be slaves? We ask not for food or clothing, for we live on snakes, ants, and mice. Thou hast made us, wherefore dost Thou let us be trodden down?'

It is a terrible picture, and one that has engraved itself deep on the heart of civilization. But while brooding over the awful presentation of life as it exists in the vast African forest, it seemed to me only too vivid a picture of many parts of our own land. As there is a darkest Africa is there not also a darkest England? Civilization, which can breed its own barbarians, does it not also breed its own pygmies? May we not find a parallel at our own doors, and discover within a stone's throw of our cathedrals and palaces similar horrors to those which Stanley has found existing in the great Equatorial forest?

The more the mind dwells upon the subject, the closer the analogy appears. The ivory raiders who brutally traffic in the unfortunate denizens of the forest glades, what are they but the publicans who flourish on the weakness of our poor? The two tribes of savages, the human baboon and the handsome dwarf, who will not speak lest it impede him in his task, may be accepted as the two varieties who are continually present with us – the vicious, lazy lout, and the toiling slave. They, too, have lost all faith of life being other than it is and has been. As in Africa, it is all trees, trees, trees with no other world conceivable; so is it here – it is all vice and poverty and crime. To many the world is all slum, with the Workhouse as an intermediate purgatory before the grave. And just as Mr Stanley's Zanzibaris lost faith, and could only be induced to plod on in brooding sullenness of dull despair, so the most of our social reformers, no matter how cheerily they may have started off, with forty pioneers swinging blithely their axes as they force their way in to the wood, soon become depressed and despairing. Who can battle against the ten thousand million trees? Who can hope to make headway against the innumerable adverse conditions which doom the dweller in Darkest England to eternal and immutable misery? What wonder is it that many of the warmest hearts and enthusiastic workers feel disposed to repeat the lament of the old English chronicler, who, speaking of the evil days which fell upon our forefathers in the reign of Stephen, said 'It seemed to them as if God and his Saints were dead.'

An analogy is as good as a suggestion; it becomes wearisome when it is pressed too far. But before leaving it, think for a moment how close the parallel is, and how strange it is that so much interest should be excited by a narrative of human squalor and human heroism in a distant continent, while greater squalor and heroism not less magnificent may be observed at our very doors.

The Equatorial Forest traversed by Stanley resembles that Darkest England of which I have to speak, alike in its vast extent – both stretch, in Stanley's phrase, 'as far as from Plymouth to Peterhead'; its monotonous darkness, its malaria and its gloom, its dwarfish dehumanized inhabitants, the slavery to which they are subjected, their privations and their misery. That which sickens the stoutest heart, and causes many of our bravest and best to fold their hands in despair, is the apparent impossibility of doing more than merely to peck at the outside of the endless tangle of monotonous undergrowth; to let light into it, to make a road clear through it, that shall not be immediately choked up by the ooze of the morass and the luxuriant parasitical growth of the forest – who dare hope for that? At present, alas, it would seem as though no one dares even to hope! It is the great Slough of Despond of our time.

And what a slough it is no man can gauge who has not waded therein, as some of us have done, up to the very neck for long years. Talk about Dante's Hell, and all the horrors and cruelties of the torture-chamber of the lost! The man who walks with open eyes and with bleeding heart through the shambles of our civilization needs no such fantastic images of the poet to teach him horror. Often and often, when I have seen the young and the poor and the helpless go down before my eyes into the morass, trampled underfoot by beasts of prey in human shape that haunt these regions, it seemed as if God were no longer in His world, but that in His stead reigned a fiend, merciless as Hell, ruthless as the grave. Hard it is, no doubt, to read in Stanley's pages of the slave-traders coldly arranging for the surprise of a village, the capture of the inhabitants, the massacre of those who resist, and the violation of all the women; but the stony streets of London, if they could but speak, would tell of tragedies as awful, of ruin as complete, of ravishments as horrible, as if we were in Central Africa; only the ghastly devastation is covered, corpse like, with the artificialities and hypocrisies of modern civilization.

The lot of a negress in the Equatorial Forest is not, perhaps, a very happy one, but is it so very much worse than that of many a pretty orphan girl in our Christian capital? We talk about the brutalities of the dark ages, and we profess to shudder as we read in books of the shameful exaction of the rights of feudal superior. And yet here, beneath our very eyes, in our theatres, in our restaurants, and in many other places, unspeakable though it be but to name it, the same hideous abuse flourishes unchecked. A young penniless girl, if she be pretty, is often hunted from pillar to post by her employers, confronted always by the alternative – Starve or Sin. And when once the poor girl has consented to buy the right to earn her living by the sacrifice of her virtue, then she is treated as a slave and an outcast by the very men who have ruined her. Her word becomes unbelievable, her life an ignominy, and she is swept downward, ever downward, into the bottomless perdition of prostitution. But there, even in the lowest depths, excommunicated by Humanity and outcast from God, she is far nearer the pitying heart of the One true Saviour than all the men who forced her down, aye, and than all the

Pharisees and Scribes who stand silently by while these Fiendish wrongs are perpetrated before their very eyes.

The blood boils with impotent rage at the sight of these enormities, callously inflicted, and silently borne by these miserable victims. Nor is it only women who are the victims, although their fate is the most tragic. Those firms which reduce sweating to a fine art, who systematically and deliberately defraud the workman of his pay, who grind the faces of the poor, and who rob the widow and the orphan, and who for a pretence make great professions of public spirit and philanthropy, these men nowadays are sent to Parliament to make laws for the people. The old prophets sent them to Hell – but we have changed all that. They send their victims to Hell, and are rewarded by all that wealth can do to make their lives comfortable. Read the House of Lords' Report on the Sweating System, and ask if any African slave system, making due allowance for the superior civilization, and therefore sensitiveness, of the victims, reveals more misery. Darkest England, like Darkest Africa, reeks with malaria. The foul and fetid breath of our slums is almost as poisonous as that of the African swamp. Fever is almost as chronic there as on the Equator. Every year thousands of children are killed off by what is called defects of our sanitary system. They are in reality starved and poisoned, and all that can be said is that, in many cases, it is better for them that they were taken away from the trouble to come.

Just as in Darkest Africa it is only a part of the evil and misery that comes from the superior race who invade the forest to enslave and massacre its miserable inhabitants, so with us, much of the misery of those whose lot we are considering arises from their own habits. Drunkenness and all manner of uncleanness, moral and physical, abound. Have you ever watched by the bedside of a man in delirium tremens? Multiply the sufferings of that one drunkard by the hundred thousand, and you have some idea of what scenes are being witnessed in all our great cities at this moment. As in Africa streams intersect the forest in every direction, so the gin-shop stands at every corner with its River of the Water of Death flowing seventeen hours out of the twenty-four for the destruction of the people. A population sodden with drink, steeped in vice, eaten up by every social and physical malady, these are the denizens of Darkest England amidst whom my life has been spent, and to whose rescue I would now summon all that is best in the manhood and womanhood of our land.

Hudson Taylor

Spiritual revival

Hudson Taylor (1832–1905) was a missionary to China and the founder of the China Inland Mission. While on furlough in England in 1855, he was preaching one day, when he suddenly stopped and stood speechless for a time with his eyes closed. Then he explained with these words:

I have seen a vision. I saw in this vision a great war that encompasses the world. I saw this war recess and then start again, actually being two wars. After this I saw much unrest and revolts that will affect many nations. I saw in some places spiritual awakenings. In Russia, I saw there will come a general all-encompassing, national spiritual awakening so great that there could never be another like it. From Russia, I saw the awakening spread to many European countries. Then I saw an all-out awakening, followed by the coming of Christ.

C. H. Spurgeon

For by grace are ye saved

C. H. Spurgeon (1834–92) was an English Baptist minister. He preached the following sermon at the Metropolitan Tabernacle in London.

For by grace are ye saved through faith; and that not of yourselves: it is the gift of God.

Ephesians 2:8

There is present salvation

The apostle says, 'Ye are saved.' Not 'ye shall be,' or 'ye may be'; but 'ye are saved.' He says not, 'Ye are partly saved,' nor 'in the way to being saved,' nor 'hopeful of salvation'; but 'by grace are ye saved.' Let us be as clear on this point as he was, and let us never rest till we know that we are saved. At this moment we are either saved or unsaved. That is clear. To which class do we belong? I hope that, by the witness of the Holy Ghost, we may be so assured of our safety as to sing, 'The Lord is my strength and my song; he also is become my salvation.' Upon this I will not linger, but pass on to note the next point.

A present salvation must be through grace

If we can say of any man, or of any set of people, 'Ye are saved,' we shall have to preface it with the words 'by grace.' There is no other present salvation except that which begins and ends with grace. As far as I know, I do not think that anyone in the wide world pretends to preach or to possess a present salvation, except those who believe salvation to be all of grace.

Among those who dwell around us, we find many who are altogether strangers to the doctrine of grace, and these never dream of present salvation. Possibly they trust that they may be saved when they die; they half hope that, after years of watchful holiness, they may, perhaps, be saved at last; but, to be saved now, and to know that they are saved, is quite beyond them, and they think it presumption.

There can be no present salvation unless it be upon this footing: 'By grace are ye saved' ... Salvation must be by grace. If man be lost by sin, how can he be saved except through the grace of God? If he has sinned, he is condemned; and how can he, of himself, reverse that condemnation? Suppose that he should keep the law all the rest of his life, he will then only have done what he was always bound to have done, and he will still be an unprofitable servant. What is to become of the past? How can old sins be blotted out? How can the old ruin be retrieved? According to Scripture, and according to common sense, salvation can only be through the free favour of God...

Paul speaks of this salvation as belonging to the Ephesians, 'By grace are ye saved.' The Ephesians had been given to curious arts and works of divination. They had thus made a covenant with the powers of darkness. Now if such as these were saved, it must be by grace alone. So is it with us also: our original condition and character render it certain that, if saved at all, we must owe it to the free favour of God. I know it is so in my own case; and I believe the same rule holds good in the rest of believers. This is clear enough, and so I advance to the next observation.

Present salvation by grace must be through faith

A present salvation must be through grace, and salvation by grace must be through faith. You cannot get a hold of salvation by grace by any other means than by faith. This live coal from off the altar needs the golden tongs of faith with which to carry it ... Salvation by grace can only be gripped by the hand of faith: the attempt to lay hold upon it by the doing of certain acts of law would cause the grace to evaporate. 'Therefore, it is of faith that it might be by grace.' 'If by grace, then it is no more of works: otherwise grace is no more grace. But if it be of works, then it is no more grace: otherwise work is no more work.'

Some try to lay hold upon salvation by grace through the use of ceremonies; but it will not do. You are christened, confirmed, and caused to receive 'the holy sacrament' from priestly hands, or you are baptized, join the church, sit at the Lord's table: does this bring you salvation? I ask you, 'have you salvation?' You reply, 'I cannot say.' If you did claim salvation of a sort, yet I am sure it would not be in your minds salvation by grace.

Again, you cannot lay hold upon salvation by grace through your feelings. The hand of faith is constructed for the grasping of a present salvation by grace. But feeling is not adapted for that end. If you go about to say, 'I must feel that I am saved. I must feel so much sorrow and so much joy or else I will not admit that I am saved,' you will find that this method will not answer. As well might you hope to see with your ear, or taste with your eye, or hear with your nose, as to believe by feeling: it is the wrong organ. After you have believed, you can enjoy salvation by feeling its heavenly influences; but to dream of getting a grasp of it by your own feelings is as foolish as to attempt to bear away the sunlight in the palm of your hand, or the breath of heaven between the lashes of your eyes. There is an essential absurdity in the whole affair ... Feelings are a set of cloudy, windy phenomena which cannot be trusted in reference to the eternal verities of God. We now go a step further.

Salvation by grace through faith, is not of ourselves. The salvation, and the faith, and the whole gracious work together, are not of ourselves.

First, they are not of our former deservings: they are not the reward of former good endeavours. No unregenerate person has lived so well that God is bound to give him further grace, and to bestow on him eternal life; else it were no longer of grace, but of debt. Salvation is given to us, not earned by us. Our first life is always a wandering away from God, and our new life of return to God is always a work of undeserved mercy, wrought upon those who greatly need, but never deserve it...

Even the will thus to be saved by grace is not of ourselves, but it is the gift of God. There lies the stress of the question. A man ought to believe in Jesus: it is his duty to receive him whom God has set forth to be a propitiation for sins. But man will not believe in Jesus; he prefers anything to faith in his redeemer. Unless the Spirit of God convinces the judgment, and constrains the will, man has no heart to believe in Jesus unto eternal life. I ask any saved man to look back upon his own conversion, and explain how it came about. You turned to Christ, and believed in his name: these were your own acts and deeds. But what caused you thus to turn? What sacred force was that which turned you from sin to righteousness? Do you attribute this singular renewal to the existence of a something better in you than has been yet discovered in your unconverted neighbour? No, you confess that you might have been what he now is if it had not been that there was a potent something which touched the spring of your will, enlightened your understanding, and guided you to the foot of the cross. Gratefully we confess the fact; it must be so. Salvation by grace, through faith, is not of ourselves, and none of us would dream of taking any honour to ourselves from our conversion, or from any gracious effect which has flowed from the first divine cause. Last of all:

**'By grace are ye saved through faith;
and that not of yourselves: it is the gift of God'**

Salvation may be called Theodora, or God's gift: and each saved soul may be surnamed Dorothea, which is another form of the same expression. Multiply your phrases, and expand your expositions; but salvation truly traced to its well-head is all contained in the gift unspeakable, the free, unmeasured benison of love.

Salvation is the gift of God, in opposition to a wage. When a man pays another his wage, he does what is right; and no one dreams of praising him for it. But we praise God for salvation because it is not the payment of debt, but the gift of grace. No man enters eternal life on earth, or in heaven, as his due: it is the gift of God. We say, 'nothing is freer than a gift'. Salvation is so purely, so absolutely a gift of God, that nothing can be more free. God gives it because he chooses to give it, according to that grand text which has made many a man bite his lip in wrath, 'I will have mercy on whom I will have mercy, I will have compassion on whom I will have compassion.' You are all guilty and condemned, and the great King pardons whom he wills from among you. This is his royal prerogative. He saves in infinite sovereignty of grace...

Salvation is the gift of God: that is, it is eternally secure, in opposition to the gifts of men, which soon pass away. 'Not as the world giveth, give I unto you,' says our Lord Jesus. If my Lord Jesus gives you salvation at this moment, you have it, and you have it forever. He will never take it back again; and if he does not take it from you, who can? If he saves you now through faith, you are saved – so saved that you shall never perish, neither shall any pluck you out of his hand. May it be so with every one of us! Amen.

C. H. Spurgeon

Teaching children

Come, my children, listen to me; I will teach you the fear of the LORD.

Psalm 34:11

1. I shall give you one Doctrine.
2. I shall give you two Encouragements.
3. I shall give you three Admonitions.
4. I shall give you four Instructions.
5. I shall give you five Subjects for children.

One doctrine

'Come, my children, listen to me; I will teach you the fear of the LORD.' The doctrine is, that children are capable of being taught the fear of the Lord ... Children are capable of understanding some things in early life, which we hardly understand in later years. Children have a simplicity of faith. Simplicity is analogous to the highest knowledge; indeed, we are not aware that there is little difference between the simplicity of a child and the genius of the profoundest mind. He who receives things simply, as a child, will often have ideas which the man who is prone to use deductive reasoning could never discover. If you wish to know whether children can be taught, I point you to many in our churches, and in godly families – not geniuses, but the more common children – Timothies and Samuels, and little girls too, who have come to know a Saviour's love.

Throughout the churches I have noticed a kind of abhorrence of any thing like early childhood godliness. We are afraid of the idea of a little boy loving Christ; and if we hear of a little girl following the Saviour, we say it is a youthful fancy, and early impression that will die away. My dear friends, I ask you, never to treat the godliness of a young child with suspicion ... Treat it very tenderly. Believe that children can be saved as much as yourselves. When you see the young heart brought to the Saviour, don't stand by and speak harshly, mistrusting everything. It is better sometimes to be deceived than to be the one who causes a young child to be ruined. May God send to his people a more firm belief that little buds of grace are worthy of all of our care.

Two encouragements

Now, secondly, I will give you two encouragements, both of which you will find in the text. The first is that of godly example. David said, 'Come, my children, listen to me; I will teach you the fear of the LORD.' You are not ashamed to walk in the footsteps of David, are you? You won't object to follow the example of one who was first notably holy, and then notably great. Shall the shepherd boy, the giant killer, the psalmist of Israel, and the king, walk in footsteps which you are too proud to follow? Ah! no; you will be happy, I am sure, to be as David was. If you want, however, a higher example, even than that of David, listen to the Son of David while from his lips the sweet words flow, 'Let the little children come to me, and do not hinder them, for the kingdom of heaven belongs to such as these.' I am sure it would encourage you if you always thought of these examples. You teach children – you are not dishonoured by it.

The second encouragement I will give is the encouragement of great success. David said, 'Come, my children, listen to me;' he did not add, 'Perhaps I will teach you the fear of the LORD' but 'I will teach you.' He had success; or if he had not, others have. The success of Sunday Schools! ... Far across the broad ocean in the islands of the south, in lands where those live who bow down before blocks of wood and stone – there are missionaries saved by Sunday Schools, whose thousands, redeemed by their labours, contribute to swell the mighty stream of the tremendous, incalculable, I had almost said infinite success of Sunday School instruction.

Three admonitions

Now, thirdly, I give you three admonitions. The first is, remember who you are teaching. 'Come, my children.' I think we ought always to have respect to our audience, not that we need care that we are preaching to Mr So-an-so, Sir William This, or My Lord That – because in God's sight that is a small matter; but we are to remember that we are preaching to men and women who have souls, so that we should not waste their time with things that are not worth their hearing. But when you teach in Sunday Schools, you are, if it be possible, in a more responsible situation even than a minister.

He preaches to grownup people – men of judgment, who, if they do not like what he preaches, have the option of going somewhere else; you teach children who have no option to go elsewhere. If you teach the child wrongly, he believes you; if you teach him heresies he will receive them; what you teach him now, he will never forget.

The second admonition is, remember that you are teaching for God. 'Come, my children, listen to me; I will teach you the fear of the LORD.' If you, as teachers, were only assembled to teach geography, I am sure I should not interfere if you were to tell the children that the north pole was close to the equator; if you were to say that the extremity of South America lay right next to the coast of Europe; I would smile at your error, and perhaps should even retain it as a joke, if I heard you assure them that England was in the middle of Africa. But you are not teaching geography or astronomy, nor are you teaching for business or for the world; but you are teaching them to the best of your ability for God. You say to them, 'Children, you come here to be taught the Word of God; you come here, if it is possible, that we may be the means of saving your souls' ...

The third admonition is: remember that your children need teaching. The text implies that, when it says, 'Come, my children, listen to me; I will teach you the fear of the Lord.' That makes your work all the more solemn. If children did not need teaching, I would not be so extremely anxious that you should teach them right; for works that are not necessary, men may do as they please. But here the work is necessary. Your child needs teaching! ...

Be careful, then, how you teach, remembering the urgent necessity of the case. This is not a house on fire needing your assistance with a fire hose, nor is it an accident at sea, demanding your oar in the lifeboat, but it is a deathless spirit calling aloud to you, 'Come over and help us.' I beg you, teach 'the fear of the Lord,' and that only; be very anxious to say, and say truly, 'I will teach you the fear of the Lord.'

Four instructions

The first is: 'Get the children to come to your school.' 'Come, my children.' The great complaint with some is that they cannot get children. Go and get them to come. In London we are canvassing the city; that is a good idea, and you ought to canvass every village, and every town, and get every child you can; for David says, 'Come, my children.' My advice then, is, get the children to come, and do any thing to make it happen, but don't bribe them.

Secondly, 'Get the children to love you,' if you can. That also is in the text. 'Come, my children, listen to me.' You know how we used to be taught in our private schools, how we stood up with our hands behind us to repeat our lessons. That was not David's plan. 'Come, my children – come here, and sit upon my knee.' 'Oh!' thinks the child, 'how nice to have such a teacher! A teacher that will let me come near him, a teacher that does not say "go" but "come".' The fault of many teachers is, that they do not let their children near them, but endeavour to foster a kind of awful respect. Before you can teach children you must get the silver key of kindness to unlock their hearts, and get their attention. Say, 'Come, my children.'

The third instruction is, 'Get the children's attention.' That is in the text. 'Come, my children, listen to me.' If they do not listen, you may talk, but you will waste your words. If they do not listen, you go through your labours as an unmeaning drudgery to yourselves and your scholars too. You can do nothing without securing their attention. 'That is just what I cannot do,' says one. Well, that depends upon yourself. If you give them something worth listening to, they will be sure to listen. Give them something worth hearing, and they will certainly listen. This rule may not be universal, but it is very nearly so. Don't forget to give them a few anecdotes. Anecdotes are very much objected to by critics of sermons, who say they ought not to be used in the pulpit. But some of us know better than that; we know what will wake a congregation up; we can speak from experience, that a few anecdotes here and there are first-rate things to get the attention of persons who won't listen to dry doctrine. Try to learn as many short interesting stories, in the week before class, as possible. Wherever you go, if you are really a good teacher, you can always find something to make into a story to tell your children. Make parables, pictures, figures, for them, and you will always get their attention.

The fourth admonition is, 'Care about what you teach the children.' 'Come, my children, listen to me; I will teach you the fear of the LORD.' Not to weary you, however, I only hint at that, and pass on.

Five Sunday-school lessons

Five subjects to teach your children: and these you will find in the verses following the text: 'Come, my children, listen to me; I will teach you the fear of the LORD.'

The first thing to teach is 'morality'. 'Whoever of you loves life and desires to see many good days, keep your tongue from evil and your lips from speaking lies. Turn from evil and do good; seek peace and pursue it.'

The second is 'godliness, and a constant belief in God's oversight'. 'The eyes of the LORD are on the righteous and his ears are attentive to their cry.'

The third thing is 'the evil of sin'. 'The face of the LORD is against those who do evil, to cut off the memory of them from the earth. The righteous cry out, and the LORD hears them; he delivers them from all their troubles.'

The fourth thing is, 'the necessity of a broken heart'. 'The LORD is close to the brokenhearted and saves those who are crushed in spirit.'

The fifth thing is 'the inestimable blessedness of being a child of God'. 'A righteous man may have many troubles, but the LORD delivers him from them all; he protects all his bones, not one of them will be broken. The LORD redeems his servants; no one will be condemned who takes refuge in Him' ...

In conclusion, let me solemnly say, with all the instruction you may give to your children, you must be deeply conscious that you are not capable of doing any thing in the child's salvation, but that it is God Himself who from the first to the last must effect it all. You are a pen; God may write with you, but you can not write yourself. You are a sword; God may with you slay the child's sin, but you cannot slay it yourself. Therefore be always mindful of this, that you must first be taught of God yourself, and then you must ask God to teach, for unless a higher teacher than you instruct the child, that child must perish. It is not all your instruction that saves his soul: it is the blessing of God resting on it. May God bless your labours! He will do it if you are instant in prayer, constant in supplication; for never yet did the earnest preacher or teacher, labour in vain, and never yet has it been found that the bread cast upon the water has been lost.

C. H. Spurgeon

Let the wicked forsake his way

Let the wicked forsake his way, and the unrighteous man his thoughts: and let him return unto the Lord, and he will have mercy upon him; and to our God, for he will abundantly pardon.

Isaiah 55:7

The necessity of conversion

First, let us meditate a while upon the necessity of conversion. If a man is to be saved, he must turn from his sins. 'Right about face!' is the marching order for every sinner. There is no hope of forgiveness for him if he will continue with his face as it now is. He must turn from his sin if he would be saved.

This will be at once evident to you when I ask, How would it be consistent with the holiness of God for him to put aside our past sin, and then to allow us to go on sinning as we did before?

How could he be thought to be just and pure if he should remit the punishment for past transgressions, without seeing in us any determination to abstain from such sin in the future? Christ Jesus came into the world to save sinners, but he never came here to spare their sins. God would never have sent his Son to this earth to be the messenger of sin, yet Christ would be nothing better than the messenger of sin if he had come, and said to men, 'You may continue in your sin, yet I will forgive you. You may live as you like, yet you shall find mercy with the Lord at the last.' It must strike you, in a moment, that such a course as this would be inconsistent with the character of the Judge of all the earth, who must do right. There is no such teaching as that in the whole of the Scriptures; and he who dares to believe it, believes a lie. Nowhere, in the whole compass of revelation, is there a promise of forgiveness to the man who continues in his iniquity. There is a promise of pardon to the sinner who forsakes his wicked way, and turns from his evil thoughts; there are many promises of forgiveness to those who confess their sins in humble penitence, and who seek to live new lives under the power of the Holy Spirit...

It would be a serious injury to the man himself if he could be pardoned, and yet not be changed. For God to forgive us without renewing us, would be a frightful peril to ourselves. A man, finding himself so easily forgiven, and having no change of heart, would plunge into sin worse than ever; and, so far as my observation is concerned, I have come to the conclusion that the very worst form of character is produced in a man who, for some reason or other, thinks himself to be a favourite of heaven, and yet continues to indulge in sin. I recollect the thrill of horror, which passed through me, in my youthful days, when I heard a man, who was accustomed to be drunk, boast that he could say what none of his pot companions could say, namely, that he was one of the elect of God. I felt, child as I was, that he was one of the devil's chosen followers, and I do not doubt that he really was. If a man once gets into his head such a perverted notion of the free grace of God as to imagine that it is compatible with the love of sin, and a life of sin, he is on the high road to being made into the worst conceivable character; and if such a man as that could be delivered from all the consequences of his sin, from all such consequences as might be looked upon as arbitrarily fixed by the punishing hand of God (I know that I am talking of an impossibility), even then he must be miserable. Such a man must go on from bad to worse; and sin, whatever we may think of it, is misery. The worm that never dies is sin; the fire that is never quenched is sin; and hell is sin fully developed. 'Sin, when it is finished, bringeth forth death,' and that second death is hell. O sirs, if you could get rid of the disease, the pain, the headaches, the qualms of conscience which follow upon indulgence in sin, it would be a mischievous riddance for you, for the very pain that is caused by sin is part of God's way of calling to you to come back to him. As long as you are in this world, the consequences that follow after certain forms of sin are really, with all their bitterness – and they are bitter – but a healthful tonic that should make you give up sin, and turn to God.

If you go on sinning, you cannot be saved. If you continue to love sin, and to practise it, you cannot be saved. Think, for a moment, what any other result would involve; if it were possible for a man to live in sin, and yet be forgiven, what would be the value of the work of the Holy Ghost? He has come in order that we may be born again, and have new hearts and right spirits; but if men could be forgiven without having new hearts and right spirits, of what service would the Holy Spirit be? This would be contrary, also, to the whole design of Christ in our salvation. The angel said to Joseph, before our Saviour's birth, 'Thou shalt call his name Jesus: for he shall save his people from their sins'; but if they can be saved in their sins, where is the meaning of his name? When he hung upon the cross, and one of the soldiers with a spear pierced his side, 'forthwith came there out blood and water'; but what is the use of the purifying water if we need not be purified, and can be pardoned without being cleansed? Paul wrote to Titus that Christ 'gave himself for us, that he might redeem us from all iniquity, and purify unto himself a peculiar people, zealous of good works'; but how can that purpose be accomplished if men can be pardoned, and yet continue to live in sin?

Beside that, the very character of heaven prevents such a thing being done; we know that the unholy cannot enter there, nothing that defileth can pass the watchers at the pearly portals; therefore, be ye sure of this – that you can never enter heaven, and you can never have forgiveness, if you continue to cling to your sins. You must forsake them, or mercy cannot be yours.

The nature of conversion

Having spoken thus upon the necessity of conversion, I turn, for a little while, to the second part of our subject, the nature of this conversion. How is it described here?

First, it deals with the life: 'Let the wicked forsake his way.' Observe that it is 'his way' that he is to forsake; that is, his natural way, the way in which he says he was brought up, the way that his natural affections, and propensities, and passions lead him. He must forsake this way, even though it is the way in which he has walked these thirty, forty, fifty, sixty, seventy, or even eighty years; he will have to get out of this way, however much he may delight in it. Possibly, he has now got to love sin so much that he says he could not give it up. There are some sins which men roll under their tongues as dainty morsels; but if you are to be saved, you will have to give them up. If you would have mercy of God, you must give them all up. You must give up your old sins, your sweet sins, your pet sins; the sins of the flesh, with all their pleasure, and the sins of the mind, with all their pride, must be given up; for notice that word 'forsake' ... You must forsake your sin if it is to be forgiven.

'I will tell you what I will do,' says one; 'I will still keep to my old way, but I will not travel quite so rapidly in it; I will not live such a fast life as I have done.' I tell thee, friend, that thou must forsake that old way of thine altogether if thou wouldst be saved. If thou standest still in it, if thou art decent and respectable in it, all that will avail thee nothing. Thou must clear right out of it, for so our text puts it, 'Let the wicked forsake his way' ...

We must forsake our thoughts in the sense of turning from all purposes of evil. That, indeed, is the main meaning of the Hebrew word used here: 'Let the unrighteous man forsake his purposes.' You say that you will do this or that, without any thought of whether God would have it so or not. Possibly it is your purpose, as you express it, 'to have your fling.' You have come up from the country, young man, you are pleased that you have got away from your mother's apron strings, and now you are going to have your own way. Forsake all such thoughts, I implore you; and, if any, whom I am now addressing, have formed any purpose of sin – if you have resolved to indulge in this or that evil, whatever it may be, I charge you, if you desire to have eternal life, to hate all such purposes and thoughts of sin. The garment spotted by the flesh must be flung away from us, and the very thought of evil must be banished from our minds as far as it is possible for us to do so.

Nor is this all, for the text further says, 'and let him return unto the Lord,' so that this conversion deals with the sinner in his relation to God. He who would find mercy must return to

God to obtain it. Do you ask how you are to do so? Well, first, you must begin to think about God. I really believe that some of you do not think half as much about God as you do about the Sultan of Turkey; and with some of you, almost anybody is a greater factor in your life than God is. With some of you, it would not make any difference if there were no God at all, except that you would be rather glad if that could be proved to be the case, for you would feel easier in your mind, and could, in such a case, go on in your sin without any of the compunction that you now feel. Yet, is it not a singular state of mind for a man, who knows that he is a creature made by God, but who really cares so little about him that, if he could be assured that there were no such being, he would be better pleased than he is now? Oh, what a wretched state your heart must be in if it feels like that! It will have to be greatly altered if you are ever to be saved.

So, first, you must begin to think of God; and then, thinking of him, you must yield to him, give up your will to his will; and, doing that, you must pray to him, cry to him for mercy; and then you must trust him. Especially, you must accept his way of salvation by faith in Jesus Christ; and when you do that, then you will be sure to love him. When you get as far as that, you will be a new creature altogether. Then, God will delight in you; then, it will be misery to you to be out of his presence, and it will be the highest joy of your life to have constant communion with him.

The gospel of conversion

Now I finish with the third part of our subject, that is, the gospel of this conversion ... That gracious message, 'Repent ye therefore, and be converted, that your sins may be blotted out,' is the utterance of ... the gospel. I will try briefly to show you the gospel of it. It lies, first, in the fact that God has promised that he will abundantly pardon those who turn from their evil ways:

'Let him return unto the Lord, and he will have mercy upon him; and to our God, for he will abundantly pardon.' To the man who confesses his guilt, the law says, 'Yes, you are guilty, and you must suffer the penalty attached to your crime.' If a person pleads 'guilty' in a court of law, the judge does not say to him, 'If you will promise amendment, you may go free.' No, he pronounces sentence upon him, and God, the righteous Judge, might justly have done the same to us; but, instead of doing so, he says, 'Forsake your wicked way, and your evil thoughts, and turn to me, and I will abundantly pardon you. Only repent of your iniquity, and abandon it, and it shall all be blotted out. All the evil of your past life shall be forgiven and forgotten; and your sins and your transgressions I will not remember against you any more for ever.' Oh, precious gospel message! Who would not turn from his sin when such a gracious promise awaits him in the turning?

Yet there is more even than that, a great deal; for not only does God bid men turn to him, but he enables them to turn to him; so the gospel of this passage is, that God the Holy Ghost is freely given to sinners to turn them, first in their hearts, and then in their lives. What you cannot do of yourself, the Holy Spirit will enable you to do, or will do for you. There is no form of sin which you cannot conquer by the power of the Spirit of God, and that Spirit is freely given to all who sincerely seek his aid. He is here on earth still. On the day of Pentecost, he descended from heaven, and he has never gone back again. 'But,' says someone, 'the Holy Spirit was given to the saints.' Yes, I know he was; but he was also given to sinners like yourself, for Peter said to those who were awakened on the day of Pentecost, 'Repent, and be baptized every one of you in the name of Jesus Christ for the remission of sins, and ye shall receive the gift of the Holy Ghost. For the promise is unto you, and to your children, and to all that are afar off, even as many as the Lord our God shall call.'

I wish that many of you would pray the prayer, 'Turn us, O God, and we shall be turned.' You must be turned, by sovereign grace, if you would really turn unto the Lord; and you must forsake your wicked way, and your evil thoughts, if you are to be saved, and you cannot do this of yourself; but the Holy Spirit has been given on purpose to enable you to do it...

In order that you might be able to believe that God can have mercy on the guilty, and in order that you might be saved, God gave his Son, Jesus Christ, to offer a full and complete atonement for sin. I never weary of preaching that glorious truth to you, but I long that, when I have done so, you may close in with Christ, and that Christ may close in with you, that you may be eternally saved. According to the righteous law of God, sin must be punished. Conscience tells you that it is not possible that guilt should go without its due penalty. Therefore it was that Jesus came, and bore the dread penalty that was due to sin. The lash of the law must fall on someone, so he bared his shoulders to its terrible blows. The sword of divine justice was unsheathed, and it must smite someone; so Jesus gave his heart to that sword's point, and quenched the flaming blade in the crimson fountain of his own blood. Now that this has been done, God can be just, and yet the Justifier of everyone who believes in Jesus; and the effect of that atoning sacrifice upon everyone who truly trusts to it is that he finds himself so changed that he hates the sin he formerly loved, he rushes out of the wicked way in which he once delighted, he abhors the thoughts that once charmed him, and he turns to the Saviour whom once he despised.

Charles Dickens

Many a poor child, sick and neglected
The English novelist Charles Dickens (1812–70) gave the following speech in 1858 at the anniversary festival of the Hospital for Sick Children in London.

Ladies and gentlemen, It is one of my rules in life not to believe a man who may happen to tell me that he feels no interest in children. I hold myself bound to this principle by all kind consideration, because I know, as we all must, that any heart which could really toughen its affections and sympathies against those dear little people must be wanting in so many humanizing experiences of innocence and tenderness, as to be quite an unsafe monstrosity among men ... I wish to speak to you about 'spoilt' children. The spoilt children whom I must show you are the spoilt children of the poor in this great city, the children who are, every year, for ever and ever irrevocably spoilt out of this breathing life of ours by tens of thousands, but who may in vast numbers be preserved if you, assisting and not contravening the ways of Providence, will help to save them. The two grim nurses, Poverty and Sickness, who bring these children before you, preside over their births, rock their wretched cradles, nail down their little coffins, pile up the earth above their graves. Of the annual deaths in this great town, their unnatural deaths form more than one-third. I shall not ask you, according to the custom as to the other class – I shall not ask you on behalf of these children to observe how good they are, how pretty they are, how clever they are, how promising they are, whose beauty they most resemble – I shall only ask you to observe how weak they are, and how like death they are! And I shall ask you, by the remembrance of everything that lies between your own infancy and that so miscalled second childhood when the child's graces are gone and nothing but its helplessness remains; I shall ask you to turn your thoughts to *these* spoilt children in the sacred names of Pity and Compassion.

Some years ago, being in Scotland, I went with one of the most humane members of the humane medical profession, on a morning tour among some of the worst lodged inhabitants of the old town of Edinburgh. In the closes of that picturesque place – I am sorry to remind you what fast friends picturesqueness and typhus often are – we saw more poverty and sickness in an hour than many people would believe in a life. Our way lay from one to another of the most wretched dwellings, reeking with horrible odours; shut out from the sky, shut out from the air, mere pits and dens. In a room in one of these places, where there was an empty porridge-pot on the cold hearth, with a ragged woman and some ragged children crouching on the bare ground near it – where, I remember as I speak, that the very light, refracted from a high damp-stained and time-stained house-wall, came trembling in, as if the fever which had shaken everything else there had shaken even it – there lay, in an old egg-box which the mother had begged from a shop, a little feeble, wasted, wan, sick child. With his little wasted face, and his little hot, worn hands folded over his breast, and his little bright, attentive eyes, I can see him now, as I have seen him for several years, looking steadily at us. There he lay in his little frail box, which was not at all a bad emblem of the little body from which he was slowly parting – there he lay, quite quiet, quite patient, saying never a word.

He seldom cried, the mother said; he seldom complained; 'he lay there, seemin' to woonder what it was a' aboot.' God knows, I thought, as I stood looking at him, he had his reasons for wondering – reasons for wondering how it could possibly come to be that he lay there, left alone, feeble and full of pain, when he ought to have been as bright and as brisk as the birds that never got near him – reasons for wondering how he came to be left there, a little decrepit old man pining to death, quite a thing of course, as if there were no crowds of healthy and happy children playing on the grass under the summer's sun within a stone's throw of him, as if there were no bright, moving sea on the other side of the great hill overhanging the city; as if there were no great clouds rushing over it; as if there were no life, and movement, and vigour anywhere in the world – nothing but stoppage and decay. There he lay looking at us, saying, in his silence, more pathetically than I have ever heard anything said by any orator in my life, 'Will you please to tell me what this means, strange man? and if you can give me any good reason why I should be so soon, so far advanced on my way to Him who said that children were to come into His presence and were not to be forbidden, but who scarcely meant, I think, that they should come by this hard road by which I am travelling; pray give that reason to me, for I seek it very earnestly and wonder about it very much;' and to my mind he has been wondering about it ever since. Many a poor child, sick and neglected, I have seen since that time in this London; many a poor sick child I have seen most affectionately and kindly tended by poor people, in an unwholesome house and under untoward circumstances, wherein its recovery was quite impossible; but at all such times I have seen my poor little drooping friend in his egg-box, and he has always addressed his dumb speech to me, and I have always found him wondering what it meant, and why, in the name of a gracious God, such things should be!

Now, ladies and gentlemen, such things need not be, and will not be, if this company, which is a drop of the life-blood of the great compassionate public heart, will only accept the means of rescue and prevention which it is mine to offer. Within a quarter of a mile of this place where I speak, stands a courtly old house, where once, no doubt, blooming children were born, and grew up to be men and women, and married, and brought their own blooming children back to patter up the old oak staircase which stood but the other day, and to wonder at the old oak carvings on the chimney-pieces. In the airy wards into which the old state drawing-rooms and family bedchambers of that house are now converted are such little patients that the attendant nurses look like reclaimed giantesses, and the kind medical practitioner like an amiable Christian ogre. Grouped about the little low tables in the centre of the rooms are such tiny convalescents that they seem to be playing at having been ill. On the doll's beds are such diminutive creatures that each poor sufferer is supplied with its tray of toys; and, looking round, you may see how the little tired, flushed cheek has toppled over half the brute creation on its way into the ark; or how one little dimpled arm has mowed down (as I saw myself) the whole tin soldiery of Europe. On the walls of these rooms are graceful, pleasant, bright, childish pictures. At the bed's heads, are pictures of the figure which is the universal embodiment of all mercy and compassion, the figure of Him who was once a child himself, and a poor one. Besides these little creatures on the beds, you may learn in that place that the number of small out-patients brought to that house for relief is no fewer than ten thousand in the compass of one single year. In the room in which these are received, you may see against the wall a box, on which it is written, that it has been calculated, that if every grateful mother who brings a child there will drop a penny into it, the Hospital funds may possibly be increased in a year by so large a sum as forty pounds. And you may read in the Hospital Report, with a glow of pleasure, that these poor women are so respondent as to have made, even in a toiling year of difficulty and high prices, this estimated forty, fifty pounds. In the printed papers of this same Hospital, you may read with what a generous earnestness the highest and wisest members of the medical profession testify to the great need of it; to the immense difficulty of treating children in the same hospitals with grown-up people, by reason of their different ailments and requirements, to the vast amount of pain that will be assuaged, and of life that will be saved, through this Hospital; not only among the poor, observe, but among the prosperous too, by reason of the increased knowledge of children's illnesses, which cannot fail to arise from a more systematic mode of studying them.

Lastly, gentlemen, and I am sorry to say, worst of all (for I must present no rose-coloured picture of this place to you – I must not deceive you); lastly, the visitor to this Children's Hospital, reckoning up the number of its beds, will find himself perforce obliged to stop at very little over thirty; and will learn, with sorrow and surprise, that even that small number, so forlornly, so miserably diminutive, compared with this vast London, cannot possibly be maintained, unless the Hospital be made better known; I limit myself to saying better known, because I will not believe that in a Christian community of fathers and mothers, and brothers and sisters, it can fail, being better known, to be well and richly endowed.

Now, ladies and gentlemen, this, without a word of adornment – which I resolved when I got up not to allow myself – this is the simple case. This is the pathetic case which I have to put to you; not only on behalf of the thousands of children who annually die in this great city, but also on behalf of the thousands of children who live half developed, racked with preventible pain, shorn of their natural capacity for health and enjoyment. If these innocent creatures cannot move you for themselves, how can I possibly hope to move you in their name? The most delightful paper, the most charming essay, which the tender imagination of Charles Lamb conceived, represents him as sitting by his fireside on a winter night telling stories to his own dear children, and delighting in their society, until he suddenly comes to his old, solitary, bachelor self, and finds that they were but dream-children who might have been, but never were. 'We are nothing,' they say to him; 'less than nothing, and dreams. We are only what might have been, and we must wait upon the tedious shore of Lethe, millions of ages, before we have existence and a name.' 'And immediately awaking,' he says, 'I found myself in my arm chair.' The dream-children whom I would now raise, if I could, before every one of you, according to your various circumstances, should be the dear child you love, the dearer child you have lost, the child you might have had, the child you certainly have been. Each of these dream-children should hold in its powerful hand one of the little children now lying in the Child's Hospital, or now shut out of it to perish. Each of these dream-children should say to you, 'O, help this little suppliant in my name; O, help it for my sake!' Well! – And immediately awaking, you should find yourselves in the Freemasons' Hall, happily arrived at the end of a rather long speech, drinking 'Prosperity to the Hospital for Sick Children,' and thoroughly resolved that it shall flourish.

Robert Murray M'Cheyne

The cry for revival

Robert Murray M'Cheyne (1813–42) became the pastor of St Peter's Church, Dundee, at the age of 23, and died just six years later. He rarely preached outside Scotland, wrote no books and had frail health. And yet the impact of the ministry of the 'prophet of Dundee', as he was known, was felt throughout Scotland.

Wilt thou not revive us again: that thy people may rejoice in thee?

Psalms 85:6

It is interesting to notice the time when this prayer was offered. It was a time of mercy. 'Lord, thou hast been favourable unto thy land.' It was a time when God had led many to the knowledge of Christ, and covered many sins; 'thou hast forgiven the iniquity of thy people.' It was now they began to feel their need of another visit of mercy – 'Wilt thou not revive us again?'

'Revive us again,' or literally, return and make us live anew. It is the prayer of those who have received some life, but feel their need of more. They had been made alive by the Holy Spirit. They felt the sweetness and excellence of this new, hidden, divine life. They pant for more – 'Wilt thou not revive us again?'

'That thy people may rejoice in thee.' They plead with God to do this for the sake of His people, that their joy may be full; and that it may be in the Lord – in the Lord of their Righteousness – in the Lord their Strength.

In a time of backsliding

When is the prayer needed? In a time of backsliding. There are many times when, like Ephesus, many of God's children lose their first love. Iniquity abounds, and the love of many waxes cold. Believers lose their close and near communion with God. They go out of the holiest, and pray at a distance with a curtain between. They lose their fervency, sweetness, and fullness in secret prayer. They do not pour out their hearts to God.

They have lost their clear discovery of Christ. They see Him but dimly. They have lost the sight of His beauty – the savour of His good ointment – the hold of His garment. They seek him, but find Him not. They cannot stir up the heart to lay hold on Christ.

The Spirit dwells scantily in their soul. The living water seems almost dried up within them. The soul is dry and barren. Corruptions are strong: grace is very weak ... Ah! This is the case, I fear with many. It is a fearfully dangerous time. Nothing but a visit of the Holy Spirit to your soul can persuade you to return. It is not a time this prayer – 'Wilt thou not revive us again?' ...

In a time of concern
'Ask ye of the Lord rain in the time of the latter rain.' When God begins a time of concern in a place – when the dew is beginning to fall – then is the time to pray, 'Lord, stay not thine hand – give us a full shower – leave not one dry.' 'Wilt thou not revive us again?'

Who needs this revival? Ministers need it. Ministers are naturally hard-hearted and unbelieving as other men (Mark 6:14), so that Christ has often to unbraid them. Their faith is all from above. They must receive from God all that they give. In order to speak the truth with power, they need a personal grasp of it. It is impossible to speak with power from mere head knowledge, or even from past experience. If we would speak with energy, it must be from present feeling of the truth as it is in Jesus. We cannot speak of the hidden manna unless we have the taste of it on our mouth. We cannot speak of the living water unless it be springing up within us. Like John the Baptist, we must see Jesus coming, and say, 'Behold the Lamb of God.' We must speak with Christ in our eye, as Stephen did. 'I see Jesus standing on the right hand of God.' We must speak from a present sense of pardon and access to God, or our words will be cold and lifeless. But how can we do this if we are not quickened from above? Ministers are far more exposed to be cast down than other men; they are standard-bearers, and Satan loves [it] when a standard-bearer fainteth. Oh, what need of full supplies out of Christ's fullness! Pray, beloved, that it may be so. 'Wilt thou not revive us again?'

God's children need it

The divine life is all from above. They have no life till they come to Christ. 'Except ye eat the flesh of the Son of Man, and drink his blood, ye have no life in you.' Now this life is maintained by union to Christ, and by getting fresh supplies every moment out of His fullness. 'He that eateth my flesh and drinketh my blood dwelleth in me, and I in Him.' In some believers this life is maintained by a constant inflowing of the Holy Spirit – 'I will water it every moment' – like the constant supply which the branch receives from the vine. These are the happiest and most even Christians. Others have flood-tides of the Spirit carrying them higher and higher. Sometimes they get more in a day than for months before. In the one of these, grace is like a river; in the other, it is like a shower coming down in its season. Still, in both there is need of revival. The natural heart is all prone to wither. Like a garden in summer, it dries up unless watered. The soul grows faint and weary in well-doing. Grace is not natural to the heart. The old heart is always for drying and fading. So the child of God needs to be continually looking out, like Elijah's servant, for the little cloud over the sea. You need to be constantly pressing near the Fountain of living waters; yea, lying down at the well-head of salvation, and drinking the living water. 'Wilt thou not revive us again?'

Those previously awakened need it

A drop fell from heaven upon their hearts. They trembled, wept, prayed. But the showers passed by, and the rocky heart ceased to tremble. The eye again closed in slumber; the lips forgot to pray. Ah, how common and sad is this case! The King of Zion lifted up His voice in this place and cried. Some that were in their graves heard His voice, and began to live. But this passed by, and now they sink back again into the grace of a dead soul. Ah! This is a fearful state! To go back to death, to love death, and wrong your soul. What can save such a one, but another call from Jesus? 'Awake, thou that sleepest, and arise from the dead, and Christ shall give thee light.' For your sake most of all I pray, 'Wilt thou not revive us again?' ...

The children of God should plead with Him. Put your finger on the promise, and plead, 'When the poor and needy seek water, and there is none, I the Lord will hear them' (Isaiah 41:17). Tell Him you are poor and needy. Spread out your wants before Him. Take your emptiness to His Fullness. There is an infinite supply with Him for everything you need, at the very moment you need it...

The effects of a revival

The Lord's children rejoice in Him. They rejoice in Jesus Christ. The purest joy in the world is joy in Christ Jesus. When the Spirit is poured down, His people get very near and clear views of the Lord Jesus. They eat His flesh and drink His blood. They come to a personal cleaving to the Lord. They taste that the Lord is gracious. His blood and righteousness appear infinitely perfect, full, and free to their souls. They sit under His shadow with great delight ... Now, God loves to see His children happy in Himself. He loves to see all our springs in Him. Take and plead that. Oh, you would pray after a different manner if God were to pour water on the thirsty. You would tell Him all, open to Him all sorrows, joys, cares, comforts...

There is an awakening again of those who have gone back. If we have not a time of the outpouring of the Spirit, many who once sought Christ, but have gone back, will perish in a dreadful manner; for they generally turn worse than before. Sometimes they scoff and make a jest of it all. Satan is all the worse, that he once was an angel. So they become all the more wicked who have gone back. They generally go deeper into the mire of sin. But if God graciously pours down His Spirit, the hardened heart will melt. Pray for this.

There is an awakening of fresh sinners. It is a sad state of things when sinners are bold in sin, when multitudes can openly break the Sabbath, and openly frequent the tavern. It is an awful sin when sinners can live in sin, and yet sit unmoved under the preaching of the Word, cast off fear, and restrain prayer before God. But if the Lord were pleased to revive us again, this state of things would change.

I am sure it would be a lovelier sight to see you going in company to the house of prayer, than thronging to the tavern, or the haunts of sin and shame, that will bring down eternal ruin on your poor soul. It would be sweeter to hear the cry of prayer in your closets, than to hear the sounds of oaths and profane jesting, and your hard speeches and reproaches of God's children. Sweeter far to see your hearts panting after Christ, His pardon, His holiness, His glory, than to see them turning after the world and its vain idols.

Oh, lift up your hearts to the Lord for such a time. Plead earnestly the promise, 'I will pour out my Spirit upon all flesh.' Then this wilderness will become a fruitful field, and its name be, Jehovah-Shammah – 'the Lord is there'.

Robert Murray M'Cheyne

Christ, the Way, the Truth and the Life

Jesus saith unto him, 'I am the way, the truth, and the life; no man cometh to the Father but by me.'

John 14:6

Christ is the Way

'I am the way; no man cometh,' etc. The whole Bible bears witness that by nature we have no way to the Father. We are by nature full of sin, and God is by nature infinitely holy – that is, he shrinks away from sin. Just as the sensitive plant, by its very nature, shrinks away from the touch of a human hand, so God, by his very nature, shrinks away from the touch of sin. He is everlastingly separate from sinners; he is of purer eyes than to behold iniquity.

This is impressively taught to Adam and the patriarchs. As long as Adam walked holily, God dwelt in him, and walked in him, and communed with him; but when Adam fell, 'God drove the man out of paradise; and he placed at the east of the garden of Eden, cherubim and a flaming sword, which turned every way to keep the way of the tree of life.' This flaming sword between the cherubim was a magnificent emblem of God – the just and sin-hating God.

But Christ says, 'I am the way.' As he says in the sixteenth Psalm, 'Thou wilt shew me the path of life.' No man could find out this path of life; but Jesus says, 'Thou wilt shew it me; in thy presence is fullness of joy – at thy right hand are pleasures forevermore.' Jesus pitied the poor sons of Adam vainly struggling to find out a way into the paradise of God, and he left the bosom of the Father, just that he might open up a way for us into the bosom of the Father. And how did he do it? Was it by escaping the vigilance of the flaming sword? No; for it turned every way. Was it by exerting his divine authority, and commanding the glittering blade to withdraw? No; for that would have been to dishonour his Father's law, instead of magnifying it. He therefore became a man in our stead – yea, became sin. God caused to meet on him the iniquities of us all. He advanced in our stead to meet that fiery meteor – he fell beneath its piercing blade; for he remembered the word of the Prophet, which is written, 'Awake, O sword! against my shepherd, and against the man that is my fellow, saith the Lord of Hosts.'

And now, since the glittering blade is bathed in the side of the Redeemer, the guiltiest of sinners – whoever you be – whatever you be – may enter in over his bleeding body – may find access to the paradise of God, to eat of the tree of life, and live forever. Come quickly – doubt not; for he says, 'I am the way.'

Christ is the Truth

The whole Bible, and the whole of experience, bear witness that by nature we are ignorant of the truth. No doubt there are many truths which an unconverted man does know. He may know the truths of mathematics and arithmetic – he may know many of the common everyday truths; but still it cannot be said that an unconverted man knows the truth, for Christ is the truth. Christ may be called the key-stone of the arch of truth. Take away the key-stone of an arch, and the whole becomes a heap of rubbish. The very same stones may be there, but they are all fallen, smothered, and confused – without order – without end. Just so – take Christ away, and the whole arch of truth may be there; but they are all fallen – without coherence – without order – without end. Christ may be called the sum of the system of truth. Take away the sun out of our system, and every planet would rush into confusion. The very same planets would be there; but their conflicting forces would draw them hither and thither, orb dashing against orb in endless perplexity. Just so – take Christ away, and the whole system of truth rushes into confusion. The same truths may be in the mind, but all conflicting and jarring in inextricable mazes; for 'the path of the wicked is as darkness; they know not at what they stumble.' But let Christ be revealed to an unconverted soul – let it not be merely a man speaking about Christ unto him – but let the Spirit of God reveal him, and there is revealed, not a truth, but the truth. You put the key-stone into the arch of truth; you restore the sun to the centre of the system. All truth becomes orderly and serviceable in that mind.

Now he knows the truth with regard to himself. Did the Son of God really leave the bosom of the Father to bear wrath in our stead? – then I must be under wrath. Did the Lord Jesus become a servant, that he might obey the will of God instead of sinners? – then I must be without any righteousness, a child of disobedience.

Again, knowing Christ, he knows the truth with regard to God. Did God freely give up his Son to the death for us all? – then, if I believe in Jesus, there is no condemnation to me. God is my Father, and God is love.

My friends, have you seen Christ, who is the truth? Has he been revealed to you, not by flesh and blood, but by the Spirit of our God? Then you know how true it is that in him 'are hid all the treasures of wisdom and knowledge' – that he is the 'Alpha and Omega', the beginning and the ending of all knowledge. But if you have not seen Christ, then you know nothing yet as you ought to know; all your knowledge is like a bridge without a key-stone – like a system without a sun. What good will it do you in hell, that you knew all the sciences in the world – all the events of history, and all the busy politics of your little day? Do you not know that your very knowledge will be turned into an instrument of torture in hell? Oh, how will you wish in that day that you had read your newspaper less and your Bible more – that with all your getting you had got understanding – and that with all your knowledge you had known the Saviour, whom to know is life everlasting.

Christ is the Life

The whole Bible bears witness that by nature we are dead in trespasses and sins – that we are as unable to walk holily in the world as a dead man is unable to rise and walk.

Both Scripture and experience alike testify that we are by nature dead in trespasses and sins; and yet it is not a death in which we are wholly inactive, for in it we are said to walk according to the course of this world – according to the prince of the power of the air.

This truth is taught us impressively in that vision of the prophet Ezekiel, where he was carried out by the Spirit, and set down in the midst of an open valley, full of dry bones; and as he passed by them round about, behold there were very many in the open valley, and lo! they were very dry.

Just such is the view which every child of God gets of the world. The dry bones are very many, and they are very dry; and he asks the same question which God asked of Ezekiel – 'Can these bones live?' Oh yes, my friends; and does not experience teach you the same thing? True, the dead cannot know that they are dead; and yet, if the Lord touch your heart, you will find it out: we prophesy to dry bones; for this is the Lord's way; – while we prophesy the breath enters in. Look back over your life then. See how you have walked according to the course of this world. You have always been like a man swimming with the stream – never like a man swimming against the current. Look into your heart, and see how it has turned against all the commandments; you feel the Sabbath to be a weariness – instead of calling it a delight and honourable. If ever you tried to keep the commandments of God – if ever you tried to keep your eyes from lawful desires, your tongue from words of anger, or gossiping, or bitterness, your heart from malice, and envy, and covetousness – if ever you have tried this, and I fancy most unconverted men have tried it – if ever you have tried this – did you not find it impossible? It was like raising the dead. Did you not find a struggle against yourself? O how plain that you are dead – not born again! Marvel not that we say unto you, ye must be born again. You must be joined to Christ, for Christ is the life. Suppose it were possible for a dead limb to be joined into a living body, so completely that all the veins should receive the purple tide of living blood – suppose bone to join on to bone, and sinew to sinew, and nerve to nerve – do you not see that that limb, however dead before, would become a living limb. Before, it was cold, and stiff, and motionless, and full of corruption; now, it is warm, and pliable, and full of life and motion. It is a living limb, because joined on to that which is its life. Or, suppose it possible for a withered branch to be grafted into a living vine, so completely that all the channels should receive the flow of the generous sap, do you not see that that branch, however dead before, becomes a living branch? Before, it was dry, and fruitless, and withered; now, it is full of sap, of life, and vigour. It is a living branch, for it is joined to the vine, which is its life. Well, then, just in the same way, Christ is the life of every soul that cleaves to him. He that is joined to the Lord is one spirit. Is your soul like a dead limb – cold, stiff, motionless, and full of corruption? Cleave you to Christ – be joined to him by faith, and you shall be one spirit – you shall be made warm, and vigorous, and full of activity, in God's service.

Remember, then, my unbelieving friends, the only way for you to become holy is to become united to Christ. And remember you, my believing friends, that if ever you are relaxing in holiness, the reason is, you are relaxing your hold on Christ. Abide in me, and I in you – so shall ye bear much fruit. Severed from me, ye can do nothing.

David Livingstone

Diffusing the blessings of Christianity

David Livingstone (1813–73), Scottish medical missionary and explorer in Africa, was given the freedom of the City of Edinburgh on 21 September 1857. Below is an extract from the speech which he made on that occasion.

As it would not be much profit to have come home and made myself only a nine days' wonder, I wish to give you a little information, so that your sympathies may be drawn out more effectually to the land from which I have come. I am thankful to see so many assembled and to see the sympathy manifested to me as the representative of that land from which I have come.

In going back to that country my object is to try and get a permanent path into the central region, from which most of the slaves have always been drawn. The native slave-drivers go into the centre of the country and carry our manufactures there and with a few yards of cloth they purchase slaves and then they take them to the sea coast. The people are so anxious to get a little of our manufactures that, in return for them, they part, not with their own children, but with children kidnapped from other tribes. Now, I hope to be able to make a path by the Zambesi into the central country, and then, if we can supply the people with our goods for lawful commerce, I think we have a fair prospect of putting a stop to the slave-trade in a very large tract of country.

From a number of other circumstances I see the probability of the people of the interior cultivating produce for our manufactures, and my great wish is to link the interests of the African with those of the English. I have a two-fold object in view. I believe that commerce is a most important aid in diffusing the blessings of civilization. When one tribe begins to trade with another it feels a sense of dependence; while they are heathens they have no sense of dependence; they like to be independent; they like to depress others; but so soon as they begin to trade with each other they feel a mutual dependence. Now this is a most important aid in diffusing the blessings of Christianity, because one tribe never goes to another without telling the news, and, telling the news, the Gospel comes to be a part of the news.

Again we know that our own country is dependent in a great measure for its supply of cotton upon the United States – that we are dependent for our supplies of this material upon slave labour. Now, I wish to direct the attention of my countrymen to this new field as a means of relieving the slave-owners from feeling it a necessity to have slaves. If we get abundant supplies of raw material from Africa we shall soon find that the slave-holders in America will become rather more enlightened than they are at present. And I have hopes in Africa from the fact that we have in eastern Africa and in western Africa a healthy highland. The form of the continent is a kind of basin. It is not a basin with regard to the level of the sea, but the central part is actually a basin; the rivers run from the sides of it into the centre, showing that the central part is more depressed than the sides. And then, again, there is a slope on both sides down to the sea. Now, this healthy ridge may be regarded as a sanatorium, and both commercial enterprise and missionary enterprise may be carried on from this healthy part to the unhealthy regions beyond. This, I may say, is the great object that I have in view – to open up that part of Africa by means of this path.

I go back to Africa, not expecting to meet with any of this excitement or any of this lionizing, but for the purpose of engaging in hard work; and I hope that your sympathies will continue to go forth to that country, because I see clearly that every year England will become more dependent on that continent for its supply of the raw material for its commerce.

J. C. Ryle

Are you born again?

Jesus Christ says, 'Except a man be born again, he cannot see the kingdom of God' (John 3:3). It is not enough to reply, 'I belong to the church; and I suppose I am.' Thousands of nominal Christians have none of the marks and signs of being born again which the Scripture has given us.

Would you like to know the marks and signs of being born again? Give me your attention, and I will show them to you out of the first epistle of John.

First of all, John says, 'Whosoever is born of God doth not commit sin'; and again, 'Whosoever is born of God sinneth not' (1 John 3:9; 5:18).

A man born again, or regenerate, does not commit sin as a habit. He no longer sins with his heart and will and whole inclination, as an unregenerate man does. There was probably a time when he did not think whether his actions were sinful or not, and never felt grieved after doing evil. There was no quarrel between him and sin; they were friends. Now he hates sin, flees from it, fights against it, counts it his greatest plague, groans under the burden of its presence, mourns when he falls under its influence, and longs to be delivered from it altogether. In one word, sin no longer pleases him, nor is even a matter of indifference; it has become the abominable thing which he hates. He cannot prevent its dwelling within him. If he said he had no sin, there would be no truth in him (1 John 1:8). But he can say that he cordially abhors it, and the great desire of his soul is not to commit sin at all. He cannot prevent bad thoughts arising within him, and short-comings, omissions, and defects appearing, both in his words and actions. He knew, as James says, that 'In many things we offend all' (James 3:2). But he can say truly, and as in the sight of God, that things are a daily grief and sorrow to him, and that his whole nature does not consent unto them.

I place this mark before you. What would the Apostle say about you? Are you born again?

Secondly, John says, 'Whosoever believeth that Jesus is the Christ, is born of God' (1 John 5:1). A man born again, or regenerate, then, believes that Jesus Christ is the only Saviour by whom his soul can be pardoned; that He is the divine person appointed by God the Father for this very purpose, and that beside Him there is no Saviour at all. In himself he sees nothing but unworthiness, but in Christ he sees ground for the fullest confidence, and trusting in Him he believes that his sins are all forgiven. He believes that for the sake of Christ's finished work and death upon the cross, he is reckoned righteous in God's sight, and may look forward to death and judgment without alarm. He may have his fears and doubts. He may sometimes tell you he feels as if he had not faith at all. But ask him whether he will rest his hopes of eternal life on his own goodness, his own amendments, his prayers, his minister, or his church, and see what he will reply. Ask him whether he will give up Christ, and place his confidence in any other way of religion. Depend upon it, he would say that though he does feel weak and bad, he would not give up Christ for all the world. Depend upon it, he would say he found preciousness in Christ, a suitableness to his own soul in Christ, that he found nowhere else, and that he must cling to him.

I place this mark before you. What would the Apostle say about you? Are you born again?

Thirdly, John says, 'Every one that doeth righteousness is born of Him' (1 John 2:29). The man born again, or regenerate, then is, a holy man. He endeavours to live according to God's will, to do the things that please God, to avoid the things that God hates. His aim and desire is to love God with heart and soul and mind and strength, and to love his neighbour as himself. His wish is to be continually looking to Christ as his example as well as his Saviour, and to show himself Christ's friend by doing whatsoever Christ commands. No doubt he is not perfect. None will tell you that sooner than himself. He groans under the burden of indwelling corruption cleaving to him. He finds an evil principle within him constantly warring against Grace, and trying to draw him away from God. But he does not consent to it, though he cannot prevent its presence. In spite of all shortcomings, the average bent and bias of his way is holy – his doings are holy, his tastes holy, and his habits holy. In spite of all this swerving and turning aside, like a ship beating up against a contrary wind, the general course of his life is in one direction – toward God and for God. And though he may sometimes fall so low that he questions whether he is a Christian at all, he will generally be able to say with old John Newton, 'I am not what I ought to be, I am not what I want to be. I am not what I hope to be in another world, but still I am not what I once used to be, and by the Grace of God I am what I am.'

I place this mark also before you. What would the Apostle say about you? Are you born again?

Fourthly, John says, 'We know that we have passed from death unto life, because we love the brethren' (1 John 3:14). A man born again, or regenerate, then, has a special love for all true disciples of Christ. Like his Father in heaven, he loves all men with a great general love, but he has a special love for those who are of one mind with himself. Like his Lord and Saviour, he loves the worst of sinners, and could weep over them; but he has a peculiar love for those who are believers. He is never so much at home as when he is in their company. He is never so happy as when he is among the saints and the excellent of the earth. Others may value learning, or cleverness, or agreeableness, or riches or rank, in the society they choose. The regenerate man values Grace. Those who have most Grace, and are most like Christ, are those he most loves. He feels that they are members of the same family with himself. He feels that they are his fellow-soldiers, warring against the same enemy. He feels that they are his fellow-travellers, journeying along the same road. He understands them, and they understand him. He and they may be very different in many ways – in rank, in station, in wealth. What matter? They are Jesus Christ's people. They are his Father's sons and daughters. Then he cannot help loving them.

I place this mark also before you. What would the Apostle say about you? Are you born again?

Fifthly, John says, 'Whatsoever is born of God overcometh the world' (1 John 5:4). A man born again, or regenerate, does not make the world's opinion his rule of right and wrong. He does not mind going against the stream of the world's way, notions and customs. 'What man will say?' is no longer a turning-point with him. He overcomes the love of the world. He finds no pleasure in things which most around him call happiness. He cannot enjoy their enjoyments: they weary him: they appear to him vain, unprofitable, and unworthy of an immortal being. He overcomes the fear of the world. He is content to do many things which all around him think unnecessary, to say the least. They blame him: it does not move him. They ridicule him: he does not give way. He loves the praise of God more than the praise of men. He fears offending Him more than giving offence to man. He has counted the cost. It is a small thing with him whether he is blamed or praised. He is no longer the servant of fashion and custom. To please the world is quite a secondary consideration with him. His first aim is to please God.

I place this mark also before you. What would the Apostle say about you? Are you born again?

Sixthly, John says, 'He that is begotten of God keepeth himself' (1 John 5:18). A man born again, or regenerate, is very careful of his own soul. He endeavours not only to keep clear of sin, but also to keep clear of everything which may lead to it. He is careful about the company he keeps. He feels that evil communications corrupt the heart, and that evil is for more catching than good, just as disease is more infectious than health. He is careful about the employment of his time: his chief desire about it is to spend it profitably. He is careful about the friendships he forms: it is not enough for him that people are kind and amiable and good-natured; all this is very well; but will they do good to his soul? He is careful over his own daily habits and behaviour: he tries to recollect that his own heart is deceitful, the world full of wickedness, and devil always labouring to do him harm; and, therefore, he would fain be always on his guard. He desires to live like a solider in an enemy's country, to wear his armour continually, and to be prepared for temptation. He finds by experience that his soul is ever among enemies, and he studies to be a watchful, humble, prayerful man.

I place this mark also before you. What would the Apostle say about you? Are you born again?

Such are the six great marks of being born again. Let every one who has gone so far with me, read them over with attention, and lay them to heart.

I know there is a vast difference in the depth and distinctness of these marks in different people. In some they are faint, dim, feeble, and hardly to be discerned. In others they are bold, sharp, clear, plain, and unmistakable, so that any one may read them. Some of these marks are more visible in some, and others are more visible in others. It seldom happens that all are equally manifest in one and the same soul. All this I am quite ready to allow.

But still after every allowance, here we find boldly painted six marks of being born of God. Here is an inspired Apostle writing one of the last general epistles to the Church of Christ, telling us that a man born of God, Does not commit sin, Believes that Jesus is the Christ, Does righteousness, Loves the brethren, Overcomes the world, and Keeps himself. I ask the reader to observe all this.

Now what shall we say to these things? What they can say who hold that regeneration is only an admission to outward church privileges, I am sure I do not know. For myself I say boldly, I can only come to one conclusion. That conclusion is, that only those persons are born again who have these six marks about them; and that all men and women who have not these marks, and not born again. And I firmly believe that this is the conclusion to which the Apostle wished us to come.

Have you these marks? Are you born again?

J. C. Ryle

Holiness

Holiness, without which no man shall see the Lord.
Hebrews 12:14

This text opens up a subject of deep importance. That subject is practical holiness. It suggests a question which demands the attention of all professing Christians – Are we holy? Shall we see the Lord?

That question concerns all ranks and conditions of men. Some are rich and some are poor – some learned and some unlearned – some masters, and some servants; but there is no rank or condition in life in which a man ought not to be holy. Are we?

I ask to be heard today about this question. How stands the account between our souls and God? In this hurrying, bustling world, let us stand still for a few minutes and consider the matter of holiness. I believe I might have chosen a subject more popular and pleasant. I am sure I might have found one more easy to handle. But I feel deeply I could not have chosen one more profitable to our souls. It is a solemn thing to hear the Word of God saying, 'Without holiness no man shall see the Lord' (Hebrews 12:14).

I shall endeavour, by God's help, to examine what true holiness is, and the reason why it is so needful. In conclusion, I shall try to point out the only way in which holiness can be attained.

What true practical holiness is

First, then, let me try to show what true practical holiness is – what sort of persons are those whom God calls holy.

A man may go great lengths, and yet never reach true holiness. It is not knowledge – Balaam had that: nor great profession – Judas Iscariot had that: nor doing many things – Herod had that: nor zeal for certain matters in religion – Jehu had that: nor morality and outward respectability of conduct – the young ruler had that: nor taking pleasure in hearing preachers – the Jews in Ezekiel's time had that: nor keeping company with godly people – Joab and Gehazi and Demas had that. Yet none of these was holy! These things alone are not holiness. A man may have any one of them, and yet never see the Lord.

What then is true practical holiness? ...

(a) Holiness is the habit of being of one mind with God, according as we find His mind described in Scripture. It is the habit of agreeing in God's judgement – hating what He hates – loving what He loves – and measuring everything in this world by the standard of His Word. He who most entirely agrees with God, he is the most holy man.

(b) A holy man will endeavour to shun every known sin, and to keep every known commandment. He will feel what David felt when he said, 'I esteem all Thy precepts concerning all things to be right, and I hate every false way' (Psalm 119:128).

(c) A holy man will strive to be like our Lord Jesus Christ. He will not only live the life of faith in Him, and draw from Him all his daily peace and strength, but he will also labour to have the mind that was in Him, and to be 'conformed to His image' (Romans 8:29).

(d) A holy man will follow after meekness, long-suffering, gentleness, patience, kind tempers, government of his tongue. He will bear much, forbear much, overlook much, and be slow to talk of standing on his rights. We see a bright example of this in the behaviour of David when Shimei cursed him – and of Moses when Aaron and Miriam spake against him (2 Samuel 16:10; Numbers 12:3).

(e) A holy man will follow after temperance and self-denial. He will labour to mortify the desires of his body – to crucify his flesh with his affections and lusts – to curb his passions – to restrain his carnal inclinations, lest at any time they break loose.

(f) A holy man will follow after charity and brotherly kindness. He will endeavour to observe the golden rule of doing as he would have men do to him, and speaking as he would have men speak to him. He will be full of affection towards his brethren – towards their bodies, their property, their characters, their feelings, their souls. 'He that loveth another,' says Paul, 'hath fulfilled the law' (Romans 13:8).

(g) A holy man will follow after a spirit of mercy and benevolence towards others. He will not stand all the day idle. He will not be content with doing no harm – he will try to do good.

(h) A holy man will follow after purity of heart. He will dread all filthiness and uncleanness of spirit, and seek to avoid all things that might draw him into it.

(i) A holy man will follow after the fear of God.

(j) A holy man will follow after humility. He will desire, in lowliness of mind, to esteem all others better than himself. He will see more evil in his own heart than in any other in the world. Holy Bradford, that faithful martyr of Christ, would sometimes finish his letters with these words, 'A most miserable sinner, John Bradford.' Good old Mr Grimshaw's last words, when he lay on his death-bed, were these, 'Here goes an unprofitable servant.'

(k) A holy man will follow after faithfulness in all the duties and relations in life. He will try, not merely to fill his place as well as others who take no thought for their souls, but even better, because he has higher motives, and more help than they. Those words of Paul should never be forgotten, 'Whatever ye do, do it heartily, as unto the Lord' – 'Not slothful in business, fervent in spirit, serving the Lord' (Colossians 3:23; Romans 12:11).

(l) Last, but not least, a holy man will follow after spiritual mindedness. He will endeavour to set his affections entirely on things above, and to hold things on earth with a very loose hand. He will value every thing and place and company, just in proportion as it draws him nearer to God. He will enter into something of David's feeling, when he says, 'My soul followeth hard after Thee.' 'Thou art my portion' (Psalms 63:8; 119:57).

Such is the outline of holiness which I venture to sketch out. Such is the character which those who are called 'holy' follow after. Such are the main features of a holy man.

I do not say for a moment that holiness shuts out the presence of indwelling sin. No: far from it. It is the greatest mystery of a holy man that he carries about with him a 'body of death' – that often when he would do good 'evil is present with him'; that the old man is clogging all his movements, and, as it were, trying to draw him back at every step he takes (Romans 7:21). But it is the excellence of a holy man that he is not at peace with indwelling sin, as others are. He hates it, mourns over it, and longs to be free from its company. The work of sanctification within him is like the wall of Jerusalem – the building goes forward 'even in troublous times' (Daniel 9:25).

Neither do I say that holiness comes to ripeness and perfection all at once, or that these graces I have touched on must be found in full bloom and vigour before you can call a man holy. No: far from it. Sanctification is always a progressive work.

Such are the leading characteristics of practical holiness. Let us examine ourselves and see whether we are acquainted with it. Let us prove our own selves.

Why practical holiness is so important

Let me try, in the next place, to show some reasons why practical holiness is so important.

Can holiness save us? Can holiness put away sin – cover iniquities – make satisfaction for transgressions – pay our debt to God? No: not a whit. God forbid that I should ever say so. Holiness can do none of these things. The brightest saints are all 'unprofitable servants'. Our purest works are no better than filthy rags, when tried by the light of God's holy law. 'By grace are ye saved through faith, and that not of yourselves, it is the gift of God: not of works, lest any man should boast' (Ephesians 2:8–9).

Why then is holiness so important? Why does the Apostle say, 'Without it no man shall see the Lord'? Let me set out in order a few reasons.

(a) For one thing, we must be holy, because the voice of God in Scripture plainly commands it. The Lord Jesus says to His people, 'Except your righteousness shall exceed the righteousness of the scribes and Pharisees, ye shall in no case enter into the kingdom of heaven' (Matthew 5:20). 'Be ye perfect, even as your Father which is in heaven is perfect' (Matthew 5:48). Paul tells the Thessalonians, 'This is the will of God, even your sanctification' (1 Thessalonians 4:3). And Peter says, 'As He which hath called you is holy, so be ye holy in all manner of conversation; because it is written, "Be ye holy, for I am holy"' (1 Peter 1:15–16). 'In this,' says Leighton, 'law and Gospel agree.'

(b) We must be holy, because this is one grand end and purpose for which Christ came into the world. Paul writes to the Corinthians, 'He died for all, that they which live should not henceforth live unto themselves, but unto Him which died for them and rose again' (2 Corinthians 5:15).

(c) We must be holy, because this is the only sound evidence that we have a saving faith in our Lord Jesus Christ. The Twelfth Article of our Church says truly, that 'Although good works cannot put away our sins, and endure the severity of God's judgement, yet are they pleasing and acceptable to God in

Christ, and do spring out necessarily of a true and lively faith; insomuch that by them a lively faith may be as evidently known as a tree discerned by its fruits.' James warns us there is such a thing as a dead faith – a faith which goes no further than the profession of the lips, and has no influence on a man's character (James 2:17).

(d) We must be holy, because this is the only proof that we love the Lord Jesus Christ in sincerity. This is a point on which He has spoken most plainly, in the fourteenth and fifteenth chapters of John. 'If ye love Me, keep my commandments'; 'He that hath my commandments and keepeth them, he it is that loveth Me'; 'If a man love Me he will keep my words'; 'Ye are my friends if ye do whatsoever I command you' (John 14:15, 21, 23; 15:14).

(e) We must be holy, because this is the only sound evidence that we are true children of God. 'Say not,' says Gurnall, 'that thou hast royal blood in thy veins, and art born of God, except thou canst prove thy pedigree by daring to be holy.'

(f) We must be holy, because this is the most likely way to do good to others. We cannot live to ourselves only in this world. Our lives will always be doing either good or harm to those who see them. They are a silent sermon which all can read. Oh, for the sake of others, if for no other reason, let us strive to be holy!

(g) We must be holy, because our present comfort depends much upon it. We cannot be too often reminded of this. We are sadly apt to forget that there is a close connection between sin and sorrow, holiness and happiness, sanctification and consolation. God has so wisely ordered it, that our well-being and our well-doing are linked together. He has mercifully provided that even in this world it shall be in man's interest to be holy. Our justification is not by works – our calling and election are not according to our works – but it is vain for anyone to suppose that he will have a lively sense of his justification, or an assurance of his calling, so long as he neglects good works, or does not strive to live a holy life. 'Hereby we do know that we know Him, if we keep His commandments'; 'Hereby we know that we are of the truth, and shall assure our hearts' (1 John 2:3; 3:19).

(h) Lastly, we must be holy, because without holiness on earth we shall never be prepared to enjoy heaven. Heaven is a holy place. The Lord of heaven is a holy Being. The angels are holy creatures. Holiness is written on everything in heaven. The book of Revelation says expressly, 'There shall in no wise enter into it anything that defileth, neither whatsoever worketh abomination, or maketh a lie' (Revelation 21:27).

And now, before I go any further, let me say a few words by way of application.

(1) Are you holy? Listen, I pray you, to the question I put to you this day. Do you know anything of the holiness of which I have been speaking?

Whatever we may think fit to say, we must be holy, if we would see the Lord. Where is our Christianity if we are not? We must not merely have a Christian name, and Christian knowledge, we must have a Christian character also. We must be saints on earth, if ever we mean to be saints in heaven. God has said it, and He will not go back: 'Without holiness no man shall see the Lord.' 'The Pope's calendar,' says Jenkyn, 'only makes saints of the dead, but Scripture requires sanctity in the living.' 'Let not men deceive themselves,' says Owen; 'sanctification is a qualification indispensably necessary unto those who will be under the conduct of the Lord Christ unto salvation. He leads none to heaven but whom He sanctifies on the earth. This living Head will not admit of dead members.'

Surely we need not wonder that Scripture says 'Ye must be born again' (John 3:7). Surely it is clear as noon-day that many professing Christians need a complete change – new hearts, new natures – if ever they are to be saved. Old things must pass away – they must become new creatures. 'Without holiness no man,' be he who he may, 'shall see the Lord.'

(2) Let me, for another thing, speak a little to believers. I ask you this question, 'Do you think you feel the importance of holiness as much as you should?'

That great divine, John Owen, the Dean of Christ Church, used to say, more than two hundred years ago, that there were people whose whole religion seemed to consist in going about complaining of their own corruptions, and telling everyone that they could do nothing of themselves. I am afraid that after two centuries the same thing might be said with truth of some of Christ's professing people in this day. I know there are texts in Scripture which warrant such complaints. I do not object to them when they come from men who walk in the steps of the Apostle Paul, and fight a good fight, as he did, against sin, the devil, and the world. But I never like such complaints when I see ground for suspecting, as I often do, that they are only a cloak to cover spiritual laziness, and an excuse for spiritual sloth. If we say with Paul, 'O wretched man that I am,' let us also be able to say with him, 'I press toward the mark.' Let us not quote his example in one thing, while we do not follow him in another (Romans 7:24; Philippians 3:14).

A word of advice

Let me, in the last place, offer a word of advice to all who desire to be holy.

Would you be holy? Would you become a new creature? Then you must begin with Christ. You will do just nothing at all, and make no progress till you feel your sin and weakness, and flee to Him. He is the root and beginning of all holiness, and the way to be holy is to come to Him by faith and be joined to Him. Christ is not wisdom and righteousness only to His people, but sanctification also. Men sometimes try to make themselves holy first of all, and sad work they make of it. They toil and labour, and turn over new leaves, and make many changes; and yet, like the woman with the issue of blood, before she came to Christ, they feel 'nothing bettered, but rather worse' (Mark 5:26). 'Without Christ we can do nothing' (John 15:5). It is a strong but true saying of Traill's, 'Wisdom out of Christ is damning folly – righteousness out of Christ is guilt and condemnation – sanctification out of Christ is filth and sin – redemption out of Christ is bondage and slavery.'

Do you want to attain holiness? Do you feel this day a real hearty desire to be holy? Would you be a partaker of the divine nature? Then go to Christ. Wait for nothing. Wait for nobody. Linger not. Think not to make yourself ready. Go and say to Him, in the words of that beautiful hymn:

Nothing in my hand I bring,
Simply to Thy cross I cling;
Naked, flee to Thee for dress;
Helpless, look to Thee for grace.

There is not a brick nor a stone laid in the work of our sanctification till we go to Christ. Holiness is His special gift to His believing people. Holiness is the work He carries on in their hearts, by the Spirit whom He puts within them.

Would you continue holy? Then abide in Christ. He says Himself, 'Abide in Me and I in you – he that abideth in Me and I in him, the same beareth much fruit' (John 15:4–5).

May we all feel the importance of holiness, far more than we have ever done yet! May our years be holy years with our souls, and then they will be happy ones! Whether we live, may we live unto the Lord; or whether we die, may we die unto the Lord; or if He comes for us, may we be found in peace, without spot, and blameless!

Charles Kingsley

Look to the cross this day!

Charles Kingsley (1819–75), English clergyman and social reformer, was also the author of the famous children's book *The Water Babies*. Below is an extract from a sermon which he preached on Good Friday, 1848.

Oh! Sad hears and suffering! Anxious and weary ones! Look to the Cross this day! There hung your King. The King of sorrowing souls, and more the King of Sorrow. Ay, pain and grief, tyranny and desertion, death and hell. He has faced them one and all, and tried their strength, and taught them His, and conquered them right royally! ...

And now, blessed are the poor, if they are poor in heart as well as purse, and theirs is the Kingdom of Heaven. Blessed are the hungry, if they hunger for righteousness as well as food: for Jesus hungered, and they shall be filled. Blessed are those who mourn, if they mourn not only for their afflictions, but for their sins, and the sins of those they see around them: for on this day, Jesus mourned for our sins: on this day He was made sin for us who knew no sin; and they shall be comforted. Blessed are those who are ashamed of themselves and humble themselves before God this day; for on this day Jesus humbled Himself for us, and they shall be exalted. Blessed are the forsaken and despised. Did not all men forsake Jesus this day, in His hour of need? ...

Rejoice and trust on, for after sorrow shall come joy. Trust on; for in man's weakness God's strength shall be made perfect. Trust on, for death is the gate of life. Endure on to the end, and possess your souls in patience for a little while, and that perhaps a very little while. Death comes swiftly, and more swiftly still, perhaps, the day of the Lord. The deeper the sorrow, the nearer the salvation.

The night is darkest before the dawn;
When the pain is sorest, the child is born,
And the day of the Lord is at hand!

Alexander Maclaren

The Cross: the proof of the love of God

Alexander Maclaren (1826–1910) was a British Baptist preacher.

God commendeth His love towards us, in that, whilst we were yet sinners, Christ died for us.

Romans 5:8

'God commendeth His love.' That is true and beautiful, but that is not all that the apostle means. We 'commend' persons and things when we speak of them with praise and confidence. If that were the meaning of my text, it would represent the death of Christ as setting forth, in a manner to win our hearts, the greatness, the excellence, the transcendency, of God's love. But there is more than that in the words. The expression here employed strictly means 'to set two things side by side', and it has two meanings in the New Testament, both derived from that original signification. It sometimes means to set two persons side by side, in the way of introducing and recommending the one to the other. It sometimes means to set two things side by side, in the way of confirming or proving the one by the other. It is used in the latter sense here. God not merely 'commends', but 'proves', His love by Christ's death. It is the one evidence which makes that often-doubted fact certain. Through it alone is it possible to hold the conviction that, in spite of all that seems to contradict the belief, God is Love. And so I wish to take the words in this sermon.

How do we know, in our own happy experiences, that love toward us exists in another heart? Surely, by act. Words are well (and words are acts, of a sort); but we want something more. Paul thinks that – mightier than all demonstrations of a verbal kind, in order to establish the fact of love in the Divine heart to men – there must be some conspicuous and unmistakable act that is the outcome of that love. So mark that, when he wants to enforce this great truth – the shining climax of all the gospel revelation of the love of God, he does not go back to Christ's gentle words, nor to His teaching of God as the Father. Paul does not point to anything that Christ says, but he points to one thing that He did, and he says, 'There! that cross is the demonstration.'

And, since it has a special bearing on my subject, I wish to emphasize that distinction and to beseech you to believe that you have not got within sight of the secret of Jesus, nor come near tapping the sources of His power if you confine yourselves to His words and His teaching, or even to the lower acts of His gentle life. You must go to the cross. It would have been much that Paul would have spoken with certitude and with sweetness else unparalleled of the love of God. But words, however eloquent, however true, are not enough for the soul to rest its weight upon. We must have deeds, and these are all summed up in 'Christ died for us.'

Now, there are but two things that I wish to say about this great proof of the love of God in act.

First, Christ's death proves God's love, because Christ is Divine. How else do you account for that extraordinary shifting of the persons in my text? 'God proves His love because Christ died'? How so? God proved His love because Socrates died? God proved His love because some self-sacrificing doctor went into a hospital and died in curing others? God proved His love because some man sprang into the sea and rescued a drowning woman, at the cost of his own life? Would such talk hold? Then I wish to know how it comes that Paul ventures to say that God proved His love because Jesus Christ died.

Unless we believe that Jesus Christ is the Eternal Son of the Father, whom the Father sent, and who willingly came for us men and for our redemption; unless we believe that, as He Himself said, 'He that hath seen Me hath seen the Father' (John 14:9); unless we believe that His death was the act, the consequence, and the revelation of the love of God, who dwelt in Him as in none other of the sons of men, I, for one, venture to think that Paul is talking nonsense in my text, and that his argument is not worth a straw. You must come to the full-toned belief which, as I think, permeates and binds together every page of the New Testament – God so loved the world, and sent His Son to be the propitiation for sins; that Son who in the beginning was with God, and was God; and then a flood of light is poured on the words of my text, and we can adoringly bow the head and say, 'Amen! God hath, to my understanding, and to my heart, proved and commended His love, in that Christ died for us!'

The second thought about this death that proves the love is, that it does so because it is a death for us. That 'for us' implies two things: one, the voluntary act of God in Christ in giving

Himself up to the death, the other the beneficial effect of that death. It was on our behalf. Therefore, it was the spontaneous outpouring of an infinite love. It was for us in that it brought an infinite benefit. And so it was a token and a manifestation of the love of God such as nothing else could be.

Now, I wish to ask a question very earnestly: In what conceivable way can Christ's death be a real benefit to me? How can it do me any good? A sweet, a tender, an unexampled, beautiful story of innocence and meekness and martyrdom which will shine in the memory of the world, and on the pages of history, as long as the world shall last. It is all that; but what good does it do me? Where does the benefit to me individually come in? There is only one answer, and I urge you to ask yourselves if, in plain, sober, common sense, the death of Jesus Christ means anything at all to anybody, more than other martyrdoms and beautiful deaths, except upon one supposition, that He died for us, because He died instead of us. The two things are not necessarily identical, but, as I believe, and venture to press upon you, in this case they are identical. I do not know where you will find any justification for the rapturous language of the whole New Testament about the death of Christ and its benefits flowing to the whole world, unless you take the Master's own words, 'The Son of Man came to minister, and to give His life a ransom instead of many' (Mark 10:45).

Ah, dear friends, there we touch the bedrock. That is the truth that flashes up the cross into lustre before which the sun's light is but darkness. He who bore it died for the whole world and was the eternal Son of the Father. If we believe that, then we can understand how Paul here blends together the heart of God and the heart of Christ, and sets high above nature and her ambiguous oracles, high above providence and its many perplexities, and in face of all the shrinkings and fears of a reasonably alarmed conscience, the one truth, 'God hath proved His love for us, in that while we were yet sinners, Christ died for us.' Is that your faith, your notion of Christ's death and of its relation to the love of God?

Alexander Whyte

Look to your motives

Alexander Whyte (1836–1921) was a Scottish Presbyterian preacher.

If thine eye be single, thy whole body shall be full of light. But if thine eye be evil, thy whole body shall be full of darkness.
Matthew 6:22–23

Look to your motives! – our Lord says to us over and over again in this chapter. Our Lord's words always go to the bottom of things. They always go to the bottom of our hearts. Our Lord's words are always quick and powerful, and sharper than any two-edged sword, piercing even to the dividing asunder of soul and spirit, and of the joints and marrow: they are discerners also of the thoughts and intents of our hearts. Our Lord's words strip our hearts bare of all affectation and pretence, display and insincerity, ostentation and hypocrisy. 'Thy word, O Lord, is very pure: therefore thy servant loveth it.' 'Search me, O God, and know my heart: try me, and know my thoughts. And see if there be any wicked way in me, and lead me in the way everlasting.'

Our motives are the secret springs of our hearts. Our motives are those hidden things in our hearts that move us to speak and to act. Our lives all issue out from our hearts, like so many streams out of so many deep and hidden springs: and thus it is that we are so often told in the Word of God to 'keep our hearts with all diligence.' And thus it is that our Lord's teaching is so full of all the matters of the heart; and especially of the hidden motives of the heart. Take good heed of your motives, He says three times to us in this single passage. Be simple in your hearts, He says to us. Be sincere in your hearts. Be pure in your hearts. Be not men-pleasers. Be not eye-servants. Be not 'hypocrites'. Seek not to be seen of men. Seek secret places. Seek obscurity. Seek and keep silence. Do nothing for the praise, or for the approval, or for the rewards of men. Let not your left hand know what your right hand doeth. Live all your life in the presence of God. Lay open your heart to His eye alone. Seek to have praise of God. Work for His approval and for His reward, Who seeth in secret. 'The light of the body is the eye: if, therefore, thine eye be single, thy whole body shall be full of light. But if thine eye be evil, thy whole body shall be full of darkness.'

What I am in my motives, that I really am: that, just that, and neither more nor less ... Go down, if need be to your grave, unknown and undiscovered, hated, despised, misjudged, misrepresented, misunderstood: only, keep your heart hidden with Christ in God: and when Christ, who is your life, shall appear, then shall ye also appear with Him in glory!

D. L. Moody

Pentecost isn't over yet!

The American evangelist D. L. Moody (1837–99) toured England and America with the gospel singer Ira Sankey. Below is an extract from one of Moody's sermons on revival.

Revivals are Scriptural. I think you will find that revivals or awakenings are perfectly scriptural. In all ages God has been quickening

His people. I don't know that they had any before the flood; if they had, perhaps there wouldn't have been a flood. But they didn't believe in it, and the flood was the result of their wickedness. But after the flood, in the days of Moses, thee was a mighty awakening when he was sent down into Egypt to bring the children of Israel out of the house of bondage; and from Moses right on down, whenever Israel went back into idolatry, God raised up prophets and men of God to bring the nation back to Him.

Enemies of God's work

Every true work of God has had its bitter enemies, not only outside, but also inside, just as in the days of Nehemiah. There are usually some good people who join with the ungodly, and lift up their voice against the work of God. The best work usually meets the strongest opposition. A man may go into a town and preach for ten years with all the eloquence of Demosthenes, and draw great crowds, and if there are no conversions the papers will applaud him, and there will be a great many fine things said about him. But let there be a few hundred conversions, and the opposition will grow as hot as hell can make it. It always has been, and always will be. The nearer a man lives to Christ, and the more truth he has, the more bitter and vile will be the things that are said against him by the enemies of God.

Denominations and revival

Now, I cannot for the life of me see how any man or woman who knows the Bible can throw his influence against a revival. I am amazed to find, in the history of the church, denomination after denomination setting their faces against what I call the work of God.

I believe when God revives His work, people will go back to His Book. People are tired and sick of this awful controversy.

Sam Jones' motto has been, 'Quit your meanness.' I hope the motto of the ministers of this country will be, 'Quit your fighting and go to work, and preach the simple gospel.' Now the question is, shall we go on discussing our differences? As far as I am concerned, I am terribly tired of it, and I would like before I go hence to see the whole church of God quickened as it was in 1857, and a wave going from Maine to California that shall sweep thousands into the kingdom of God. Why not? Talk about this work not lasting; Pentecost isn't over yet! The revival of 1857 isn't over yet by a good deal. Some of the best men we have in our churches were brought out in 1857.

Why shouldn't we have now at the close of this old century a great shaking up and a mighty wave from heaven? Are you doing anything to hinder it?

PART 8

The Twentieth Century

R. A. Torrey

The Holy Spirit says, Today

The American revivalist R. A. Torrey (1856–1928) was the successor to the mass evangelist D. L. Moody.

The Holy Spirit says, Today.

Hebrews 3:7

The day of golden opportunity is today. Golden opportunities, opportunities of priceless worth, are open to every one of us today. But 'tomorrow' has no sure promise for any one of us. 'The Holy Spirit says, Today,' and Conscience also cries, 'Today,' and the voice of Reason and the voice of History and the voice of Experience unite in one loud chorus and shout, 'Today.' Only the voices of indifference and laziness and folly murmur, 'Tomorrow.' The Holy Spirit is ever calling, 'Today.' Men in their folly are forever saying, 'Tomorrow' ...

A poor wretch came into my office one day. He had been drinking, and drinking had brought misery into his heart and ruin into his life. I asked, 'Will you quit drinking and turn to Jesus Christ?' 'Oh,' he exclaimed, 'there is nothing else that I can do, I will.' 'Will you do it now?' He hung his head, and murmured, 'Not now, tomorrow.' But 'the Holy Spirit says, Today.' Tomorrow is the devil's day and the fool's day. Today is God's day, and the wise man's day.

I wish to give you tonight some conclusive and unanswerable reasons why every man and woman in this auditorium who makes any pretensions to intelligence and common sense should not only accept the Lord Jesus as his Lord and Saviour, but should accept Him here before he leaves this building tonight, if he has not already done it. What I want to get is action, immediate action, intelligent and wise action. And the only action that is intelligent and wise for anyone who has not already accepted Jesus Christ is to accept Him right here tonight. Resolutions to do the right thing and the wise thing at some indefinite time in the future are of no value whatever. God's time is now. 'The Holy Spirit says, Today.'

1. Because the Lord Jesus brings peace to the tormenting conscience

The first reason why every man and woman in this auditorium who has not already accepted Jesus Christ should not only accept Him but accept Him now is because the Lord Jesus brings peace to the tormenting conscience as soon as He is accepted, and the really wise man will not only desire that peace but desire it just as soon as he can get it. Wherever there is sin there will be an accusing conscience. And we 'all have sinned.' If any man has sinned and his conscience does not accuse him and torment him he has sunk very low, very low...

A young man came to me one Sunday morning in Chicago in awful agony. He had sinned grievously and was reaping the harvest. He was contemplating all sorts of sinful actions to escape the inevitable consequences of his sin. I pointed him to the Son of God and the young man accepted Him. Afterward he brought to me his companion in sin. She was fully determined to commit a very wicked and desperate action that was likely to land her in prison or in the cemetery. I pleaded with her and pointed her to the real cure, to the Saviour. When she left me she was still undecided as to what she would do. She afterward decided and decided right. One night a long time afterward, as I was going down the back stairs of the Moody Church to the inquiry room, a young, happy-faced woman stopped me and said, 'I want to thank you for what you did for me, and for my husband and for my child.' I did not recognize her for a moment, and she said, 'I am the young woman who came to you,' and she explained the circumstances. It was the woman who had contemplated the destruction of her child, and her own destruction for time and for eternity. But she had found peace in Jesus Christ. Men and women with tormenting consciences, and with uneasy, restless hearts, there is rest for you in Jesus Christ. If you are wise you will not only find it, but you will find it now. 'The Holy Spirit says, Today.' You need not spend even one more day or one more hour in the agony of your accusing, tormenting conscience.

2. Because Jesus Christ brings inexpressible and glorious joy to those who accept him

The second reason why every man and woman who have not already accepted Jesus Christ should not only accept Him but accept Him now is because Jesus Christ brings inexpressible and glorious joy, a joy to which the joy of this world is as nothing in comparison, to all as soon as they really accept and confess Him. Any really wise man will not only desire this joy but desire it at once. I for one not only wish the best I can get, but I wish it as quickly as I can get it. The joy that is in Jesus Christ is the very best joy one can get...

I know the joy that comes from wealth, I know the joy that comes from the theatre, I know the joy that comes from the dance, from the card table, and the joy that comes from the race track, and the joy that comes from the wine supper, and so on down to the end of the catalogue of this world's joys. I know also the joy that comes from literature and from art, the joy that comes from music, from science, from philosophy and from travel. I know practically every joy that this world has to give, but I say to you that the joy of all these put together is nothing to the inexpressible and glorious joy that comes from a genuine acceptance of Jesus Christ as our Saviour, and a wholehearted surrender to Him as our Lord, and a constant and open confession of Him before the world, and from receiving the Holy Spirit whom He gives to those who do thus accept Him and fully surrender to Him and confess Him. Men and women, if you wish the highest, deepest, purest, and most abounding joy, immeasurably the most satisfying joy that is to be known, not only in the life which is to come, but in the life which now is, not only come to Jesus Christ but come now. 'The Holy Spirit says, Today.'

3. Because Jesus Christ brings deliverance from the power of sin

The third reason why every man and woman in this auditorium who has not already accepted Jesus Christ should not only accept Him but accept Him tonight is because Jesus Christ brings deliverance from the power of sin, and any wise man or woman not only wishes deliverance from the power of sin but wishes it as soon as he or she can get it. There is no other form of slavery known to man so degrading and so wretched as the slavery of sin...

4. Because Jesus Christ brings beauty of character

The fourth reason why every man and woman who has not already accepted Jesus Christ should not only accept Him but accept Him tonight is because Jesus Christ brings beauty of character, and every wise man and woman will not only desire beauty of character, but desire it just as soon as they can get it. I sometimes notice advertisements in the papers that read, 'The Secret of Beauty.' I can tell you the secret of beauty, men and women, the secret of permanent, indestructible beauty. It is Jesus Christ in the heart. He not only beautifies the face, He beautifies the soul. He makes over the soul that trusts in Him into His own glorious likeness. I have seen some of the foulest men and women I ever knew made over into the fairest, and it was Jesus Christ who did it...

Yes, men and women, do you not wish to be good? Not only good in the eyes of man, but good in the eyes of God? You may be. It is Jesus' work to make you so. Let Him begin it at once. Let Him begin it now, 'The Holy Spirit says, Today.' What do you say? 'Tomorrow'? No, not if you have a particle of sense left, and I believe you have. You will say, 'Tonight. Right now.'

5. Because Jesus Christ fills our lives with highest usefulness
The fifth reason why every man and woman who has not already accepted Jesus Christ should not only accept Him but accept Him now is because Jesus Christ fills our lives with highest usefulness; and every wise man and every wise woman desires not only to be useful but desires to begin being useful as soon as possible. The Christian life is the only really useful life. We look at the life of many a one who is not a Christian, and say, 'There is a useful life'; but God looks at it and looks through it, looks at it in all its directions, and writes this verdict on it, 'Useless.' Whether you and I see it or not, the man or woman who is not with Christ is against Him (Matthew 12:30), and the man who is against Jesus Christ is against God and against humanity. His life is useless and worse than useless. But the life that is fully surrendered to Jesus Christ becomes at once a useful life. It may be the mere wreck of a life, but it becomes at once a useful life.

A friend of mine found one of the most hopeless wrecks of womanhood in New York City and brought her to Jesus Christ. I think this poor creature lived less than two years after her conversion and many months of that time were spent on a sick bed. But that woman was used to the eternal salvation of more than a hundred persons while she lay there dying, and the story of the transformed life of 'the Bluebird of Mulberry Bend' has gone around the world and saved thousands.

Come to Christ. Really come to Him. He will make you useful. Come at once, that your usefulness may begin at once. I am glad I came to the Lord Jesus when I did, but oh! if only I had come sooner. How many precious years were wasted! How many golden opportunities were lost, opportunities that will never return! Come, men and women. Come now. 'The Holy Spirit says, Today.'

6. Because the sooner we come to Christ, the fuller and richer will be our eternity

The sixth reason why every man and woman in this auditorium who has not already accepted Jesus Christ should not only accept Him but accept Him tonight is because the sooner we come to Christ, the fuller and richer will be our eternity. The eternity of each one of us will be just what we make it in the life that now is. You are constructing your eternity every day. Every day of true service for Christ makes our reward so much the greater and our eternity so much the fuller and richer. Come to Christ next Sunday and you will be behind for all eternity by as much as you might have accomplished this week. You may cry in coming years, 'Backward, turn backward, O Time, in your flight,' but Time will not turn backward in its flight. Time cannot turn backward. Time is flying by every moment and never returns. Today is hurrying by us at express speed. Tomorrow will soon follow. And as I turn around and peer after Yesterday and Today as they plunge into the unfathomable depths of the Past, I cry, 'Yesterday, where are you?' Out from the fathomless abyss of bygone days comes the answer, 'Gone forever.' And I hear the Holy Spirit crying, 'Today! Today! Today!' 'The Holy Spirit says, Today.'

7. Because if we do not come to Jesus Christ today we may never come at all

I will give you one more reason why every man and woman who has not already accepted Jesus Christ should not only accept Him but accept Him at once, and that is because if we do not come to Jesus Christ today we may never come at all. That is not at all a remote possibility. Thousands and tens of thousands have been as near to an acceptance of Jesus Christ as you are this moment and have said, 'Not tonight,' and now they have passed without Christ into that world in which there is no hope for repentance, no matter how 'diligently with tears' they may seek it, into that world in which there is no opportunity to change their mind or their eternal destiny.

A man came into one of our tents one night in Chicago. It was the first time he had ever been in a meeting of that kind in his life. The words of Mr Schiverea, who spoke that night, made a deep impression on him, and after the meeting was over he lingered with a friend and talked personally with Mr Schiverea. His friend accepted Christ and he was on the very verge of accepting Him. Mr Schiverea said to him, 'Will you accept Jesus Christ right now?' 'No,' the man said, 'this is the first time in my life that I was ever in a meeting of this kind. I cannot decide tonight, but I promise you that I will come back Sunday night and accept Christ.' It was Friday night and there was to be no meeting on Saturday. Mr Schiverea replied that he did not question at all the honesty of the man's intention or the sincerity of his promise to return Sunday night and settle it; but added, 'We have no guarantee whatever that you will live until Sunday night.' 'Oh,' the man said, with a laugh, 'you don't suppose that God is going to cut me off after the first meeting of this kind that I ever attended in my life and not give me another opportunity?' Mr Schiverea replied, 'I do not know. But I do know you are taking a great risk in waiting until Sunday night. I greatly fear that if you do not accept Jesus Christ now you will never accept Him and be lost forever.' 'No,' the man said, 'I give you my word that I will be back here Sunday night and accept Christ.' Mr Schiverea continued to plead with him, but the man would not yield. He went out of the tent with his friend. They got into a carriage and turned toward home. And as they drove up the street they passed a saloon. The man said to his friend, 'Let's stop and have one more drink and then we will both stop drinking permanently.' 'No,' said his friend, 'I have settled it already. I have accepted Christ and I will never take another drink.' 'Well,' said the other, 'I'm going to have one more drink, anyhow. You drive up the street and then come back for me and I will be waiting for you outside.' He entered the saloon. His friend drove up the street, and after a few minutes returned to pick up the man. He was nowhere to be seen. The friend went into the saloon to look for him. He was not there. The friend went into the street again and looked up and down it for the man, but he was nowhere in sight. Passing a high board fence, he heard a groan, and passing swiftly around behind it, he discovered his friend lying behind it stabbed, with an awful gash in his body, unconscious and dying. He was taken to the Presbyterian Hospital and lived until Monday morning, but never regained consciousness and passed into eternity unsaved, lost forever. Why? Because when 'the Holy Spirit said, Today,' the man said, 'Tomorrow.' So he passed unprepared into the presence of God, and so will some of you if you do not listen to the Holy Spirit now as He says, 'Today.'

One night when I was preaching in Bradford, England, a man and his wife sat side by side in the meeting and were deeply moved, but they made no decision. As they walked away from the meeting the wife said to her husband, 'Would it not have been nice if you and I both had accepted Christ?' He answered, 'Yes, it would.' They reached home and retired. About two o'clock the following morning his wife awakened him and said, 'I feel so strange.' In a few minutes from that time she had passed into eternity. After he had laid his wife's body away in the cemetery, he came back to the meeting and told us this story and accepted Christ, but he came alone. Oh, men and women, listen! Do you not hear the Holy Spirit crying, 'Today'?

There are so many things besides death that may make this the last opportunity you will ever have and make a refusal now final and fatal. Loss of opportunity may come. The Holy Spirit is here in power now. It is a great opportunity, the Day of Golden Opportunity. A like opportunity may never come again. It never will come again for some of you. 'The Holy Spirit says, Today.'

A hardened heart may seal your doom. When a human heart is moved on by the Spirit of God, as some of your hearts are, and the heart continues to resist the Holy Spirit, it is likely to become very soon hardened and hopeless...

Men and women, listen! You cannot trifle with God, and you cannot trifle with your own souls, and you cannot trifle with the Holy Spirit. The Holy Spirit is not only saying in our text, but He is saying in your hearts, 'Today! Accept Christ right now.' Will you listen to the mighty, gracious Spirit of God? Will you do as He bids you? Will you listen right now and harden not your heart, but accept Jesus Christ as your Saviour, surrender to Him as your Lord and Master, and begin to confess to Him as such before the world, and be saved, and get right here and now the wonderful blessings that He gives and that He alone can give?

Martyn Lloyd-Jones

Jonathan Edwards and the crucial importance of revival

Martyn Lloyd-Jones (1899–1981), a Welsh Nonconformist doctor and minister, was noted for his expository preaching at London's Westminster Chapel. Below are some extracts from an address which he delivered at the Puritan and Westminster Conference of 1976, subsequently published in *The Puritans: Their Origins and Successors*.

I am to deal with Jonathan Edwards in particular. I take for granted the main facts concerning him. He was born in 1703 and died in 1758 ... He received the education that was available in New England at that time, and went to Yale University. In 1727 he was ordained as assistant pastor to his grandfather, Solomon Stoddard, in the town of Northampton, Massachusetts. Within a year or so the old man died and Jonathan Edwards became the sole pastor. There he remained until 1750 when was literally turned out of his church. That was one of the most amazing things that ever happened, and it should come as a word of encouragement to ministers and preachers. Here was this towering genius, this mighty preacher, this man at the centre of a great revival, yet he was literally voted out of his church by 230 votes against 23 in 1750. Do not be surprised then, brethren, as to what may happen to you in your churches!

Having been driven from his church in Northampton in that way, went to a place that was on the frontier in those days, amongst Indians, called Stockbridge. I believe that in the providence of God he was sent there; because he wrote some of his greatest masterpieces while he was there...

However, the thing that stands out in the life of this man was the remarkable revival that broke out under his ministry in Northampton, beginning at the end of 1734, and in 1735, and then later his participation with others in the so-called Great Awakening in connection with the visit of George Whitefield and others in 1740...

He came upon the scene after a period of considerable lifelessness in the churches. It is very important that we should realize this. It is most comforting for us because we live in a very similar period...

Anyone who knows anything about Jonathan Edwards knows that he was as far removed from being a ranter as it is possible for a man to be. But he did say some very strong and very alarming things which are liable to be misunderstood ... Edwards believed the Bible, which says terrifying things about any man who dies in his sins. That is all Edwards did. It was pure reasoning from the words of Scripture. It was not what Edwards said, it was what the Scriptures said; and he felt it to be his duty to warn the people ... No man was further removed from the violence of a ranting travelling evangelist than Jonathan Edwards. That is the defence which one should make when one hears people referring to him as that terrible man who preached the sermon on 'Sinners in the Hands of an Angry God'...

I am tempted, perhaps foolishly, to compare the Puritans to the Alps, Luther and Calvin to the Himalayas, and Jonathan Edwards to Mount Everest! He has always seemed to me to be the man most like the apostle Paul...

He was a mighty theologian and a great evangelist at the same time ... He was equally expert with adults as with children; and he was a great defender of conversion in children, and paid great attention to children, even allowing them to have meetings on their own. He seems to be everything and to be perfectly balanced. He opposed Hyper-Calvinism and was equally opposed to Arminianism. This element of balance in his teaching, and in his position, is shown in the following statement:

'In efficacious grace we are not merely passive, nor yet does God do some, and we do the rest. But God does all, and we do all. God produces all, and we act all. For that is what he produces, viz. our own acts. God is the only proper author and fountain; we only are the proper actors. We are in different respects, wholly passive and wholly active' (*Works*, Vol. 2, p. 557, para. 64)...

What then was the secret of this man? I have no hesitation in saying this: the spiritual always controlled the intellectual in him. I believe he must have had a great struggle with his towering intellect, and his original thinking. Moreover he was a voracious reader, and it would have been the simplest thing in the world for such a man to have become a pure intellectual such as Oliver Wendell Holmes, Perry Miller and many others wished he had become. But as they put it, theology kept breaking in. But that constitutes the special glory of this man – and this is what explains him – that he always kept his philosophy and his speculations subservient to the Bible and regarded them as mere servants. Whatever he might be tempted to think, the Bible was supreme: everything was subordinate to the Word of God. All his rich and brilliant gifts were not only held to be subservient, but were used as servants. In other words he was God dominated. Someone has said of him that 'he combined passionate devotion and a profoundly integrated mind'...

Jonathan Edwards was pre-eminently the theologian of Revival, the theologian of experience, or as some have put it 'the theologian of the heart'. The most astonishing thing about this phenomenon, this mighty intellect, was that no man knew more about the workings of the human heart, regenerate and unregenerate, than Jonathan Edwards. If you want to know anything about the psychology of religion, conversion, revivals, read Jonathan Edwards...

Edwards wrote these things because in a sense he was compelled to do so, because of criticisms and misunderstandings. He was always fighting on two fronts right through his life. A movement of the Spirit took place in his own church, and spread to other churches in quite an extensive area, and then came the Great Awakening in 1740 associated with his name and also Whitefield and others. All this divided the people and the churches into two groups. There were some who were totally opposed to the revival. They were orthodox men who held the same theology as Edwards. They were Calvinists, but they disliked revival. They disliked the emotional element, they disliked the novelty. They had many objections to what was happening; and Edwards had to defend the revival against these critics. But then there were men at the other extreme, the wild men; and with them the wild fire came in that always tends to come in during a revival. These were the enthusiasts, the men who went to extremes, the men who were guilty of folly. Edwards had to deal with them also; so here he was, fighting on the two fronts. But, of course, his one interest was the glory of God and the benefit of the church. He had no desire to be a controversialist, but he had to write for and defend the truth.

The main works containing these analyses of experiences and these justifications of experiences and revivals are found in works like *A Treatise concerning the Religious Affections*. That is one of his most famous books. It really consisted of a series of sermons on one verse – 1 Peter 1:8: 'Whom having not seen ye love, in whom though now ye see him not, yet believing, ye rejoice with joy unspeakable and full of glory.' What he does in these books is to show the difference between the true and the false in the realm of experience. That is the theme of all these different treatises and it is worked out on the two sides in order to deal with the opponents and the enthusiasts at the same time. Here is the way in which he divides up the subject in the *Treatise concerning the Religious Affections*. He divides it into three parts. Here are his headings: Part One, 'Concerning the nature of the affections and their importance in religion'. He has to establish that they are legitimate. The opponents of revival preached their great doctrinal sermons but they were cold, and any emotion or any fervour was automatically taboo. Edwards therefore has to justify them and to show that there is a place for them. Then he goes on to show that 'True religion lies much in affections', then 'Inferences from this'. Then Part Two, 'Showing that there are no certain signs that religious affections are truly gracious or that they are not'. That is typical Edwards – the negative and the positive. He goes on to show that the fact that affections 'are raised very high is no sign' that they are true; the fact that there are 'great effects on the body is no sign', 'fluency and fervour are no sign', 'that they are not excited by us is no sign', 'that they come with texts of Scripture is no proof that they are real', 'that there is an appearance of love is no sign', 'religious affections of many kinds are no signs', 'joys following in a certain order are no sign', 'much time and zeal in duty', 'many expressions of praise, great confidence, affecting relations are no sign'. None of these are true signs of necessity either that they are or that they are not genuine. Then Part Three shows what are distinguishing signs of truly gracious and holy affections: 'Gracious affections are from Divine influence'; 'Their object is the excellence of Divine things'; 'Christian practice is the chief sign to others and to ourselves' ...

Read Edwards on revival. The term he used always is 'an outpouring of the Spirit'. Today, we are hearing much about what is called 'renewal'. They dislike the term revival; they prefer 'renewal'. What they mean by that is that we have all been baptized with the Spirit at the moment of regeneration, and that all we have to do therefore is to realize what we already have and yield ourselves to it. That is not revival! You can do all they teach and derive many benefits; but you still have not had revival. Revival is an out-pouring of the Spirit. It is something that comes upon us, that happens to us. We are not the agents, we are just aware that something has happened. So Edwards reminds us again of what revival really is...

I close with two special words of application. The first is to preachers. What Edwards said to preachers in his own day is urgently needed by us at this present time:

> *I should think myself in the way of my duty, to raise the affections of my hearers as high as possibly I can, provided that they are affected with nothing but truth, and with affections that are not disagreeable to the nature of the subject. I know it has long been fashionable to despise a very earnest and pathetical way of preaching; and they only have been valued as preachers, who have shown the greatest extent of learning, strength of reason, and correctness of method and language. But I humbly conceive it has been for want of understanding or duly considering human nature, that such preaching has been thought to have the greatest tendency to answer the ends of preaching; and the experience of the present and past ages abundantly confirms the same. Though, as I said before, clearness of distinction, illustration, and strength of reason, and a good method in the doctrinal handling of the truths of religion, is in many ways needful and profitable, and not to be neglected; yet an increase in speculative knowledge in divinity is not what is so much needed by our people as something else. Men may abound in this sort of light and have no heat. How much has there been of this sort of knowledge, in the Christian world, in this age! Was there ever an age, wherein strength and penetration of reason, extent of learning, exactness of distinction,*

correctness of style, and clearness of expression, did so abound? And yet, was there ever an age, wherein there has been so little sense of the evil of sin, so little love to God, heavenly-mindedness, and holiness of life, among the professors of the true religion? Our people do not so much need to have their heads stored, as to have their hearts touched; and they stand in the greatest need of that sort of preaching which has the greatest tendency to do this.

Works, Vol. 1, p. 391

Then a word to church members. Does all I have said make you feel that you are hopeless? Does it make you doubt perhaps whether you are Christian? My advice to you is: Read Jonathan Edwards. Stop going to so many meetings; stop craving for the various forms of entertainment which are so popular in evangelical circles at the present time. Learn to stay at home. Learn to read again, and do not merely read the exciting stories of certain modern people. Go back to something solid and deep and real. Are we losing the art of reading? Revivals have often started as the result of people reading volumes such as these two volumes of Edwards' works. So read this man. Decide to do so. Read his sermons; read his practical treatises, and then go on to the great discourses on theological subjects.

But above all, let all of us, preachers and listeners, having read this man, try to capture and to lay hold upon his greatest emphasis of all – the glory of God. Let us not stop at any benefit we may have had, and not even with the highest experiences we may have enjoyed. Let us seek to know more and more of the glory of God. That is what leads always to a true experience. We need to know the majesty of God, the sovereignty of God, and to feel a sense of awe, and of wonder. Do we know this? Is there in our churches a sense of wonder and of amazement?

This is the impression Jonathan Edwards always conveys and creates. He teaches that these things are possible for the humblest Christian. He was preaching and ministering to most ordinary people, and yet he tells them that these things are possible to all of them. Then, beyond all, and at a time of crisis and uncertainty like the present, I know nothing more wonderful than his emphasis on the 'blessed hope'. Read the sermon which he preached at the funeral of David Brainerd. It is an account of heaven and of the glory that awaits us as God's children. In a collapsing world with everything dissolving before our eyes, is it not time that we lifted up our heads and our eyes, and looked to the glory that is coming. Let the financial position of this country collapse, let everything collapse, God's purposes are sure and certain. Nothing 'can make Him His purpose forego'; and there is a glory awaiting us which baffles description. It has been prepared for us, and there it awaits all who truly look to these things, and 'the blessed appearing of our great God and Saviour'.

So, let us leave Jonathan Edwards by quoting what he himself said of David Brainerd. I cannot think of anything better to say about Edwards himself:

How much is there, in particular, in the things that have been observed of this eminent minister of Christ, to excite us, who are called to the same great work of the gospel-ministry, to earnest care and endeavours, that we may be in like manner faithful in our work; that we may be filled with the same spirit, animated with the like pure and fervent flame of love to God, and the like earnest concern to advance the kingdom and glory of our Lord and Master, and the prosperity of Zion! How amiable did these principles render this servant of Christ in his life, and how blessed in his end! The time will soon come, when we also must leave our earthly tabernacles, and go to our Lord that sent us to labour in his harvest, to render an account of ourselves to him. Oh how does it concern us so to run as not uncertainly; so to fight, not as those that beat the air! And should not what we have heard excite us to depend on God for his help and assistance in our great work, and to be much in seeking the influences of his Spirit, and success in our labours, by fasting and prayer; in which the person spoken of was abundant? This practice he earnestly recommended on his death-bed, from his own experience of its great benefits, to some candidates for the ministry that stood by his bedside. He was often speaking of the great need ministers have of much of the Spirit of Christ in their work, and how little good they are like to do without it; and how, 'when ministers were under the special influences of the Spirit of God, it assisted them to come at the consciences of men, and (as he expressed it) as it were to handle them with hands: whereas, without the Spirit of God, said he, whatever reason and oratory we make use of, we do but make use of stumps, instead of hands.'

Oh that the things that were seen and heard in this extraordinary person, his holiness, heavenliness, labour, and self-denial in his life, his so remarkably devoting himself and his all, in heart and practice to the glory of God, and the wonderful frame of mind manifested in so steadfast a manner, under the expectation of death, and the pains and agonies that brought it on, may excite in us all, both ministers and people, a due sense of the greatness of the work we have to do in the world, the excellency and amiableness of thorough religion in experience and practice, and the blessedness of the end of such a life, and the infinite value of their eternal reward, when absent from the body and present with the Lord; and effectually stir us up to endeavours that, in the way of such a holy life, we may at last come to so blessed an end.

Works, Vol. 2, pp. 35–6

Dietrich Bonhoeffer

This is the end, but also the beginning

Dietrich Bonhoeffer (1906–45), a German Lutheran theologian, was involved in a plot to assassinate Hitler, and was executed by the Nazis on 9 April 1945.

On 8 April at the Flossenburg prison camp, Bonhoeffer preached a sermon to the other prisoners. His text was 'Through his wounds we are healed.' Just after he had finished preaching, the SS arrived. They said, 'Prisoner Bonhoeffer, get ready and come with us.' Bonhoeffer asked a fellow prisoner – an Englishman named Payne Best – to give a message to Bishop Bell of Chichester: 'Tell him that for me this is the end but also the beginning.' These were his last recorded words.

Bonhoeffer was hanged the following day. The prison doctor describes how he died:

Through the half-open door in one room of the huts I saw Pastor Bonhoeffer, before taking off his prison garb, kneeling on the floor praying fervently to his God. I was most deeply moved by the way this lovable man prayed, so devout and so certain that God heard his prayer. At the place of execution, he again said a short prayer and then climbed the steps to the gallows, brave and composed. His death ensued after a few seconds. In almost fifty years that I worked as a doctor, I have hardly ever seen a man die so entirely submissive to the will of God.

Billy Graham

I'm here to represent Jesus Christ

The American evangelist Billy Graham (1918–) has had a powerful preaching ministry in many parts of the world. The following extracts are taken from *Just as I am: The Autobiography of Billy Graham* (1997).

In India, 1956

I am not here to tell you about an American or a Britisher or a European. I am here to tell you about a Man who was born right here in your part of the world, in Asia. He was born at the place where Asia and Africa and Europe meet. He had skin that was darker than mine, and He came to show us that God loves all people. He loves the people of India, and He loves you.

In Manhattan, New York, 1957

We have not come to put on a show or an entertainment. We believe that there are many people here tonight who have hungry hearts. All your life you've been searching for peace and joy, happiness, forgiveness. I want to tell you, before you leave Madison Square Garden this night of May 15, you can find everything you have been searching for, in Christ. He can bring that inward, deepest peace to your soul. He can forgive every sin you've committed ... Forget me as the speaker. Listen only to the message that God would have you to retain from what is to be said tonight.

In Brisbane, Australia, 1959

For what has happened in Australia, I want to give the glory and praise to God ... I hope you will soon forget about us except to pray for us. When you take pictures and applaud, I know it is from your heart, but you're applauding the wrong person, you're taking pictures of the wrong person; I'm here to represent Jesus Christ, the King of kings and the Lord of lords: to Him be the glory and the praise and the honour.

In Zagreb, Yugoslavia, 1967

We are gathered to pray for the Crusade that begins tomorrow ... Nothing ... will unite us ... like praying together. I want to join you in prayer. I cannot understand your language, but we both know the language of Heaven. It is the language that God the Holy Spirit speaks in our hearts ... And so I can join you at the throne of grace.

To John F. Kennedy, when he was President-elect, 1961

I explained what the Bible said about Christ coming the first time, dying on the Cross, raising from the dead, and then promising that He would come back again. 'Only then,' I said, 'are we going to have permanent world peace.'

To President Lyndon B. Johnson

As for my preacher relationship to Johnson, it became very direct at times. At his ranch one evening, he and I sat in his convertible, watching a glorious sunset.

'Mr President, have you ever personally, definitely received Jesus Christ as your Saviour?'

He gazed out across the landscape. 'Well, Billy, I think I have.'

I waited quietly for more.

'I did as a boy at a revival meeting.' He paused. 'I did reading one of the sermons in my great-grandfather's book of evangelistic sermons.' Another pause. 'I guess I've done it *several* times.'

'When someone says that, Mr President,' I said carefully, 'I don't feel too sure of it.'

He looked at me with a puzzled expression.

'It's a once-for-all transaction,' I said. 'You receive Christ and He saves you. His Spirit bears witness with your spirit that you're a child of God.'

At the World Congress on Evangelism, Berlin, 1966

The evangelistic harvest is always urgent. The destiny of men and of nations is always being decided. Every generation is crucial; every generation is strategic. But we are not responsible for the past generation, and we cannot bear full responsibility for the next one. However, we do have *our* generation! God will hold us responsible at the Judgment Seat of Christ for how well we fulfilled our responsibilities and took advantage of our opportunities.

In Durban, South Africa, 1973

Christianity is not a white man's religion, and don't let anybody ever tell you that it's white or black. Christ belongs to *all* people!

At Auschwitz, Poland, 1978

Auschwitz ... stands as a warning for all humanity ... that man is still capable of repeating and even multiplying the barbarism of Aushchwitz. I ... call upon Christians everywhere to work and pray for peace ... The issues we face are not only political; they are also moral.

At the International Conference for Itinerant Evangelists, Amsterdam, 1983

These itinerant evangelists are the most important ambassadors and messengers on earth. They are a mighty army of proclaimers, energized by the power of the Holy Spirit, spreading out across the world with a renewed vision to reach their own people for Christ.

John Stott

Make friends with unbelievers

John Stott (1921–) is Rector Emeritus of All Souls Church, Langham Place, London.

It is often said that you can tell what a person is like by the company he keeps. Look at his friends, and from them you can deduce what his character is like. There is some truth in it. Birds of a feather, as we often say in the well-known proverb, flock together. But you know it's not the whole truth by any means for the simple reason that you have to consider the motives of people for the company they keep. Why do they choose particular people to fraternize with? It is possible to seek people's company not because you like what they are and acquiesce in what they are, but because you hope to have some influence in changing them.

Teachers, for example, spend their lives in the company of children not because they prefer the company of children to the company of adults, but because they regard it a great privilege to have some share in developing the potential of children to become adults. Again, social workers spend their time with problem families not because they prefer families with problems to families without problems, but because they hope to be able to help to solve the problems in the families they serve. Now that's elementary, isn't it? But it was a failure to discern, to recognize, this and to inquire into the motive of Jesus in fraternizing with publicans and sinners that led the Pharisees to make a false judgment about him.

Jesus was the friend of publicans and sinners, so they assumed he preferred their company to the company of the righteous. In fact, they assumed that he approved of their sinful conduct. It doesn't seem to have occurred to these Pharisees that Jesus might have kept bad company for a good reason. But he did, you know. So should we. The problem we're going to face is that most of us don't have any bad company, as we ought to have if we are followers of Jesus.

It's going to be very challenging for us this morning to consider whether we are more like the Lord Jesus in the company he kept or more like the Pharisees, who avoided that company. There is a great deal of Christian Pharisaism in the church today. So, you see, what we're going to consider from the passage set for us this morning has something to do with mission.

It is also very relevant to the coming of the Holy Spirit on the first day of Pentecost, because the Holy Spirit is a missionary spirit. If Jesus kept bad company, so does the Holy Spirit. He's reaching out to people – to people we often neglect and avoid. He loves them more than we do. That's the theme.

Would you be good enough to take your Bible and turn to Mark's gospel, chapter 2, and I read from verse 13:

> *Jesus went out again beside the sea [that's the Lake of Galilee]; and all the crowd gathered about him, and he taught them. And as he passed on, he saw Levi the son of Alpheus [you know from the other gospel that his name was Matthew; he's the same person] sitting at the tax office, and he said to him, 'Follow me.' And he rose and followed him. And as he [Jesus] sat at the table in his [Levi's] house, many tax collectors and sinners were sitting with Jesus and his disciples; for there were many who followed him. The scribes and Pharisees, when they saw that he was eating with sinners and tax collectors, said to his disciples, 'Why does he eat with tax collectors and sinners?' When Jesus heard it, he said to them, 'Those who are well have no need of a physician, but those who are sick; I came not to call the righteous, but sinners.'*

This well-known story of Levi Matthew is usually taken as a model of conversion because Jesus called him and he rose up and followed him. But it seems that it is incorporated by the three synoptic evangelists in their gospels much more because it was a model of mission than that it was a model of conversion. What is most important in the story is not the response that Matthew Levi gave to the call of Jesus but its sequel, namely, the dinner party. That was the real essence of this story.

It's an exquisite little drama which Matthew, Mark, and Luke record in their gospels. In this little drama are three actors, and the attitudes of these three actors to sinners or to outsiders are contrasted with one another. That's the whole point. First, there is Levi Matthew, who, after responding to the call of Jesus, throws a party for his colleagues in order to introduce them to Jesus. Second, the Pharisees, who criticize Jesus for accepting the invitation to the party and attending it. Thirdly, there is Jesus himself, who defended his behaviour by likening himself to a doctor.

We've got to ask ourselves where we fit in the drama. Are we like Matthew Levi, or are we like the Pharisees, or are we like Jesus? Their attitudes are contrasted. Every one of us belongs somewhere, so don't switch off. This is for you and me.

We begin with Levi Matthew. Verse 40: 'And Jesus saw him sitting at the tax collector's office.' Well, tax collectors were regarded as unclean by the Jewish rabbis on three counts: politically, because they were in the employment of the hated Roman occupation of Palestine; ceremonially, because their job brought them into constant contact with Gentiles; and morally, because they were almost always dishonest. That is, they were guilty of extortion and they exploited their clients by demanding more tax than they had any right to demand. So politically, ceremonially, and morally they were despised and even hated by the common people, and the Pharisees, the scribes, and the Jewish rabbis condemned them. That's why they are bracketed with sinners: publicans, that is tax collectors, and sinners. But Jesus did not regard them as being beyond the pale. On the contrary, here was one – Levi Matthew – sitting at the tax collector's booth, and Jesus called him to himself.

Jesus Christ has room in his kingdom community for disreputable people like Levi Matthew and disreputable people like us. Christianity is not a religion for the respectable. It is a religion for the disreputable. Jesus had room for people like that. He called Levi Matthew.

Moreover, Levi Matthew responded wholeheartedly. It's Luke actually who says he left everything. Luke has a particular interest in money matters – the poor, the rich. There's more in Luke than in the other gospels about these. Levi Matthew left everything and followed Jesus. And the first thing he did as a follower of Jesus was to arrange a party in his own home to which he invited his erstwhile colleagues and Jesus, because he wanted Jesus to meet them and he wanted them to meet Jesus. He wanted to bring them together, and what better way to bring them together than a dinner party in his own home?

I learned two elementary mission lessons from this sequence of events. Could we learn them together?

Levi Matthew couldn't invite his friends to meet Jesus until he'd met him himself. Is it too elementary to say that? It's the first lesson we have to learn in Christian evangelism. The first and major and indispensable prerequisite for evangelism is our own personal conversion. *We* have to know Christ before we can make him known. It had been the same with Andrew, who when he met Jesus went to fetch Simon. It was the same with Philip, who met Jesus and then went to fetch Nathanael. And now it is the same with Levi Matthew, who finds Jesus, or is found by him, and goes out to win his colleagues.

Many years ago I used to lead a thing at St Peter's called 'The Children's Church'. There was a little girl who was a member many years ago. Jillie was 10 at the time. We'd been studying Matthew's gospel, and in those days at the end of the year we set these poor kids an examination – a written examination. Having asked them 30-odd academic questions, I permitted myself a final personal one. This is what I said, because we'd been studying the Gospel of John, chapter 1: 'Andrew brought Simon to Jesus. Philip brought Nathanael to Jesus. Whom have you brought to Jesus?'

Do you know what Jillie answered? 'I have brought myself to Jesus.' She was quite right. Have you? You can't bring anybody else till you've brought yourself.

If I may turn from a child of 10 to an Archbishop of Canterbury, here is a lovely quotation that some of you know from William Temple: 'It's quite futile saying to people, "Go to the cross." We've got to be able to say "Come to the cross." There are only two voices that can issue that invitation. One is the voice of the sinless Redeemer, with which we cannot speak, and the other is the voice of the forgiven sinner who knows himself forgiven. And that is our part.'

So the first lesson is, we've got to know Jesus ourselves before we make him known. The second is that once Levi Matthew had met Jesus himself, it was the most natural thing in the world that he should want to introduce his friends to him. New converts ought to be discouraged from dreaming about exotic and distant places to evangelize. The first thing Jesus says to them is, 'Go home to your friends and tell them what great things the Lord has done for you.' Our friends and our family, our colleagues at work, and our neighbours where we live – these are the people who have the first call on our evangelistic witness, and our home is the best place in which to introduce them to

Jesus. There are many people today uncomfortable about accepting your invitation to come to church tonight to the invitation service, but they accept your invitation to come to your home. That's where they can relax. In the home among friends and neighbours we can talk freely of Jesus. Well, that's the first thing Levi Matthew did. Let's copy him.

Now secondly, let's go to the Pharisees. You know, don't you, that the word Pharisee means more or less 'separatist'. And that is what they were, unlike the Sadducees. To oversimplify the difference between them, the Sadducees compromised with Roman culture. The Pharisees held themselves aloof from it altogether. We can applaud the motive of the Pharisees. They wanted to live a holy life. They wanted to live a righteous life. They wanted to live a life that was pleasing to God, which is fine. Their mistake was that they interpreted holiness in terms of insulation. They thought the best way to be righteous is to avoid contact with the unrighteous, so they were shocked to see the company Jesus kept. Why, he even went into the home of a tax collector and a sinner! He even made friends with disreputable people like that! In their view, Jesus was contaminated by that company. But they had a false view of holiness. The Pharisees didn't understand the meaning of holiness.

True holiness is quite different from Pharisaic holiness. True holiness is not a matter of our external contacts. True holiness is a matter of the heart. It's the pure in heart, Jesus said, who see God. It's the heart that is at the heart of holiness in the Sermon on the Mount. The Pharisees didn't understand the meaning of holiness.

Well, the tragedy is that ever since those days, there have been in the Christian church many Christian Pharisees and many Sadducees. The Christian Sadducees are so determined to live in the real world and not isolate themselves from it that they adopted its standards and surrendered the standards of Jesus Christ. The Christian Pharisees are so determined to live a holy life and not surrender the standards of Jesus that they withdraw from the world altogether. The Sadducees were conformists, and the Pharisees were separatists. Both got it wrong. Jesus was neither.

So we turn, thirdly, to Jesus himself. You will remember in verse 16 the Pharisees complained to the disciples of Jesus: 'Why does your master eat with tax collectors and sinners?' Jesus overheard the complaint. He didn't apparently give the disciples an opportunity to reply. He replied to the Pharisees' question himself. He said – his actual phrase you'll see in verse 17 – 'Those who are well do not need a doctor, but those who are ill; I came not to call the righteous, but sinners.' As a doctor spends his time with the sick not because he likes sickness nor because he approves of being sick (still less because he wants to perpetuate disease in the world), but because he is dedicated to healing, just so, Jesus mixed with tax collectors and sinners – and still does – not because he likes their ways or approves of them (still less because he wants to encourage and promote sin in the world), but because he came into the world to save them. He is the physician of our souls.

Christianity, Jesus taught here, is a rescue religion. The doctor has no relevance for those who are well. You don't go to the doctor if you are well. You only go to the doctor if you're sick. So Jesus Christ has no relevance to the righteous, but only to those who are sinners. Now please listen carefully to this; don't misunderstand this point. Not that there are any righteous people who don't need Jesus, but rather there are self-righteous people who think they don't need Jesus. He didn't come for them, the self-righteous. The people Jesus came for are those who humble themselves to acknowledge the fact of their sin and guilt and their need of his forgiveness. But for those who are self-righteous, he has no message except that it's time they humbled themselves.

Now this reaching out to people in need, this outreach to sinners that we call mission, is of the very essence of the being of God. It tells us what kind of God he is.

Christ came into the world to save sinners, and his entry into the world in order to reach us was not a superficial entry. He didn't just touch down upon the earth as the Apollo astronauts touched down on the moon and then withdrew again. They never identified with the moon. They would have been dead in a moment if they'd tried to. The Apollo mission – it's interesting that it's given the same name – is quite different from the mission of Jesus. Jesus identified with the earth. He identified by incarnation. He entered into our world by assuming a human nature. He exposed himself to our temptations. He experienced something of our loneliness and of our pain. And on the cross he even bore our sin and died our death. It was total identification. He entered right into the world where we are in order to reach us for God.

So the way of Jesus was poles apart from the Pharisees'. The Pharisees' philosophy was withdrawal. Jesus' philosophy was involvement. The Pharisees' philosophy was insulation from the world. Jesus' philosophy was identification with the world. And the Holy Spirit, whose wonderful coming we celebrate today, has the very same nature. He is God. Father, Son, and Holy Spirit have the same nature, and it is a nature that is given to outreach. In other words, love. Reaching out in love. God is love. The Father is love. The Son is love. The Spirit is love. Reaching out in love to those who need to be loved and to be rescued.

There is, as some writers have said, something centrifugal about the being of God. He flings himself out into the world. So the Father sent the Son, and the Son sent the Spirit and sent the church into the world. That's mission. That's why Jesus said that any believer who is filled with the Holy Spirit – you know what happens – out of his innermost being there flow rivers of living water. He cannot keep the Spirit to himself.

William Temple, in his Readings in John's Gospel, says, 'Nobody can be indwelt by the Spirit of God and keep that Spirit to himself. Where the Spirit is, he flows forth. And where there is no flowing forth, he is not there.' That's striking isn't it? You cannot keep the Holy Spirit yourself. If he fills the Christian, the believer, he overflows. We drink sips of water, as it were, when we receive the Spirit, and the sips are transmuted into rivers that flow out into the world of drought and need.

So, Pentecost was just as much a missionary event as the Incarnation. There's an interesting book called *Pentecost and Missions* written by a Dutch-American called Harry Boer, who worked for many years in West Africa. His whole theme is that the great motivation for mission in the Book of Acts was not the Great Commission, which isn't mentioned once, but the Holy Spirit. Let me just quote: 'One hardly knows where in Acts to look for a distinction between church and mission. Restlessly the Spirit drives the church to witness, and continually churches rise out of the witness. The church is a missionary church, because the Spirit is a missionary spirit. This is the very essence of God himself.'

So you see, the mistake the Pharisees made was worse than being a mistake about the meaning of holiness. It was actually a mistake about the very being of God. They misunderstood the nature of God. They thought he avoided sinners, whereas God doesn't avoid sinners. God loves sinners. He comes after them. He went after them to the desolate agony of the Cross. He has come after them in the Holy Spirit. He is pursuing them himself today.

A way even more dramatic than the imagery of the doctor is that of the shepherd who goes out after the lost sheep to seek and to save. It is the unique thing in the Christian religion. Bishop Steve O'Neil used often to say that it is at this point Christianity is different from every other religion. Even in Judaism, if a sinner came back to God, God would accept the sinner. But Judaism never taught that God went out into the wilderness like a shepherd to seek and to save the lost. Neither does any other religion. Only Christianity: God in Christ, God through the Holy Spirit reaching out to people in need.

Well, we've looked at the three actors of the drama. We've seen that Matthew Levi by throwing a party for his former colleagues understood more of the heart and the mind of Christ than the Pharisees, who avoided contact with people like that and criticized Jesus for his contact.

What about us? Where do we fit in the picture? Do we care for outsiders like Matthew, who understood the mind of Christ, or do we avoid them like the Pharisees?

Two things in conclusion. One is, this is a personal question – for me and for everybody else. Do we have any non-Christian friends? Could we be described as Jesus was: the friend of publicans and sinners? Are all our friends Christians? If so, we are more like the Pharisees than we are like Jesus. We need to be the friends of publicans and sinners.

Yes, we shall be criticized for it. Matthew was. Jesus was. The fact that we're not criticized for it shows the measure of our departure from the example of Christ. It's a personal thing. I found in university missions again and again that the mission succeeds in a university when the Christian students are infiltrating the non-Christian segments of university life. But when the Christian Union is a little holy hospital, and all they have among their friends is themselves and one another, and they don't have any friends that are non-Christians, and they're not in the rugby 15 or football 11, or they don't play at the games, they don't get into the student union, and they avoid contact – no mission will ever succeed where Christian students are not in contact with non-Christians. It's a personal question.

Second, it is a church question. It's a question as to whether our church is penetrating the secular world around it for Christ. I know our director of evangelism is very concerned about this. We thank God for our Clubhouse, which is a Christian community centre in the parish that has a constant outreach. We thank God for the visitors who came two by two, house to house in visitation with the message of Jesus. We thank God for our invitation services like tonight.

But if we made a careful survey of the parish – the BBC next door, St George's Hotel on the other side, the Polytechnic of Central London, the business houses, the professional institutions – I think we would still find that there are whole secular segments of our local society that have never even begun to be penetrated by the followers of Jesus Christ. So let us determine not to be like the Pharisees. Let us repent of Pharisaic Christianity or evangelical Pharisaism, and let us determine to follow Jesus like his apostle Matthew, to make friends with unbelievers, to love them, and to seek to introduce them to Christ.

Preached at All Souls Church, Langham Place, 18 May 1986

Martin Luther King

I have a dream

Martin Luther King (1929–68), Baptist minister and black civil rights campaigner, delivered the following speech on the steps of the Lincoln

Memorial in Washington DC on 28 August 1963. London's *Guardian* newspaper voted it the greatest speech of the twentieth century.

Five score years ago, a great American, in whose symbolic shadow we stand, signed the Emancipation Proclamation. This momentous decree came as a great beacon light of hope to millions of Negro slaves who had been seared in the flames of withering injustice. It came as a joyous daybreak to end the long night of captivity.

But one hundred years later, we must face the tragic fact that the Negro is still not free. One hundred years later, the life of the Negro is still sadly crippled by the manacles of segregation and the chains of discrimination. One hundred years later, the Negro lives on a lonely island of poverty in the midst of a vast ocean of material prosperity. One hundred years later, the Negro is still languished in the corners of American society and finds himself an exile in his own land. So we have come here today to dramatize an appalling condition.

In a sense we have come to our nation's capital to cash a check. When the architects of our republic wrote the magnificent words of the Constitution and the Declaration of Independence, they were signing a promissory note to which every American was to fall heir. This note was a promise that all men would be guaranteed the unalienable rights of life, liberty, and the pursuit of happiness.

It is obvious today that America has defaulted on this promissory note insofar as her citizens of Color are concerned. Instead of honoring this sacred obligation, America has given the Negro people a bad check; a check which has come back marked 'insufficient funds'. But we refuse to believe that the bank of justice is bankrupt. We refuse to believe that there are insufficient funds in the great vaults of opportunity of this nation. So we have come to cash this check – a check that will give us upon demand the riches of freedom and the security of justice. We have also come to this hallowed spot to remind America of the fierce urgency of *now*. This is no time to engage in the luxury of cooling off or to take the tranquilizing drug of gradualism.

Now is the time to make real the promises of Democracy.

Now is the time to rise from the dark and desolate valley of segregation to the sunlit path of racial justice.

Now is the time to open the doors of opportunity to all of God's children.

Now is the time to lift our nation from the quicksands of racial injustice to the solid rock of brotherhood.

It would be fatal for our nation to overlook the urgency of the moment and to underestimate the determination of the Negro. This sweltering summer of the Negro's legitimate discontent will not pass until there is an invigorating autumn of freedom and equality. Nineteen sixty-three is not an end, but a beginning. Those who hope that the Negro needed to blow off steam and will now be content will have a rude awakening if the nation returns to business as usual. There will be neither rest nor tranquility in America until the Negro is granted his citizenship rights. The whirlwinds of revolt will continue to shake the foundations of our nation until the bright day of justice emerges.

But there is something that I must say to my people who stand on the warm threshold which leads into the palace of justice. In the process of gaining our rightful place we must not be guilty of wrongful deeds. Let us not seek to satisfy our thirst for freedom by drinking from the cup of bitterness and hatred. We must forever conduct our struggle on the high place of dignity and discipline. We must not allow our creative protest to degenerate into physical violence. Again and again we must rise to the majestic heights of meeting physical force with soul force.

The marvellous new militancy which has engulfed the Negro community must not lead us to a distrust of all white people, for many of our white brothers, as evidenced by their presence here today, have come to realize that their destiny is tied up with our destiny and their freedom is inextricably bound to our freedom. We cannot walk alone.

And as we walk, we must make the pledge that we shall march ahead. We cannot turn back. There are those who are asking the devotees of civil rights, 'When will you be satisfied?' We can never be satisfied as long as the Negro is the victim of the unspeakable horrors of police brutality. We can never be satisfied as long as our bodies, heavy with the fatigue of travel, cannot gain lodging in the motels of the highways and the hotels of the cities. We cannot be satisfied as long as the Negro's basic mobility is from a smaller ghetto to a larger one. We can never be satisfied as long as a Negro in Mississippi cannot vote and a Negro in New York believes he has nothing for which to vote. No, no, we are not satisfied, and we will not be satisfied until justice rolls down like waters and righteousness like a mighty stream.

I am not unmindful that some of you have come here out of great trails and tribulations. Some of you have come fresh from narrow jail cells. Some of you have come from areas where your quest for freedom left you battered by the storms of persecution and staggered by the winds of police brutality. You have been the veterans of creative suffering. Continue to work with the faith that unearned suffering is redemptive.

Go back to Mississippi, go back to Alabama, go back to South Carolina, go back to Georgia, go back to Louisiana, go back to the slums and ghettos of our northern cities, knowing that somehow this situation can and will be changed. Let us not wallow in the valley of despair.

I say to you today, my friends, that in spite of the difficulties and frustrations of the moment I still have a dream. It is a dream deeply rooted in the American dream.

I have a dream that one day this nation will rise up and live out the true meaning of its creed: 'We hold these truths to be self-evident; that all men are created equal.'

I have a dream that one day on the red hills of Georgia the sons of former slaves and the sons of former slave owners will be able to sit down together at the table of brotherhood.

I have a dream that one day even the state of Mississippi, a desert state sweltering with the heat of injustice and oppression, will be transformed into an oasis of freedom and justice.

I have a dream that my four little children will one day live in a nation where they will not be judged by the Color of their skin but by the content of their character.

I have a dream today.

I have a dream that one day the state of Alabama, whose governor's lips are presently dripping with the words of interposition and nullification, will be transformed into a situation where little black boys and black girls will be able to join hands with little white boys and white girls and walk together as sisters and brothers.

I have a dream today.

I have a dream that one day every valley shall be exalted, every hill and mountain shall be made low, the rough places will be made plains, and the crooked places will be made straight, and the glory of the Lord will be revealed, and all flesh shall see it together.

This is our hope. This is the faith with which I return to the South. With this faith we will be able to hew out of the mountain of despair a stone of hope. With this faith we will be able to transform the jangling discords of our nation into a beautiful symphony of brotherhood. With this faith we will be able to work together, to pray together, to struggle together, to go to jail together, to stand up for freedom together, knowing that we will be free one day.

This will be the day when all of God's children will be able to sing with new meaning

> *My country, 'tis of thee,*
> *Sweet land of liberty,*
>   *Of thee I sing:*
> *Land where my fathers died,*
> *Land of the pilgrims' pride,*
> *From every mountainside*
>   *Let freedom ring.*

And if America is to be a great nation this must become true. So let freedom ring from the prodigious hilltops of New Hampshire. Let freedom ring from the mighty mountains of New York. Let freedom ring from the heightening Alleghenies of Pennsylvania!

Let freedom ring from the snowcapped Rockies of Colorado!

Let freedom right from the curvacious peaks of California!

But not only that; let freedom ring from Stone Mountain of Georgia!

Let freedom ring from Lookout Mountain of Tenessee!

Let freedom ring from every hill and molehill of Mississippi. From every mountainside, let freedom ring.

When we let freedom ring, when we let it ring from every village and every hamlet, from every state and every city, we will be able to speed up that day when all God's children, black men and white men, Jews and Gentiles, Protestants and Catholics, will be able to join hands and sing in the words of the old Negro spiritual, 'Free at last! free at last! thank God almighty, we are free at last!'